S0-EOH-502

THE ROMANESQUE LYRIC

THE
ROMANESQUE LYRIC

*STUDIES IN ITS BACKGROUND AND DEVELOPMENT
FROM PETRONIUS TO THE CAMBRIDGE SONGS
50-1050*

By PHILIP SCHUYLER ALLEN

WITH RENDERINGS INTO ENGLISH VERSE
By HOWARD MUMFORD JONES

BARNES & NOBLE, Inc.
NEW YORK
PUBLISHERS & BOOKSELLERS SINCE 1873

Copyright, 1928, by
The University of North Carolina Press
Reprinted 1969, by
Barnes & Noble, Inc.

SBN 389 01172 X

Printed in the United States of America

TO
HORACE S. OAKLEY

CONTENTS

CHAPTER		PAGE
	Introduction	xi
I.	The Province of Gaul	1
II.	The Gallo-Roman World	17
III.	Merovingian Gaul	37
IV.	The Continuity of Themes	51
V.	The Approach to Romanesque Poetry	66
VI.	Main Trends of Early Romanesque Poetry	84
VII.	Romanesque Outlook on Nature	115
VIII.	Fortunatus and the Platonic Tradition	136
IX.	Irish Culture in the Sixth Century	152
X.	Irish Lyrics and Ballads	174
XI.	Romanesque and the Near East	189
XII.	The Carolingian Lyric	214
XIII.	Romanesque Mimes, Monks, and Minstrels	244
XIV.	The Cambridge Songs	271
	Notes to Chapters	293
	Latin Texts of the Translations	319
	Index of First Lines	367
	Index	370

INTRODUCTION

While many recent scholars agree with Osborn in believing that the creative sources of French and Spanish character lie far back in prehistoric times, it is sufficient for the purposes of this book that when the investigator arrives at the threshold of literary and artistic history in Northern Europe, he finds in Gaul the relatively firm ground of a splendid civilization that synchronizes with the flourishing of Greece and early Rome. It is with the study of the possible factors in this civilization that the volume opens; that is to say, two of the earliest chapters are devoted to the portrayal of Gallic and Gallo-Romanic culture previous to the seventh century of our era. It may seem to the reader that the presentation of Romanesque lyric poetry in its unfolding is unnecessarily postponed; if he feels this to be the case I beg him to remember certain matters of the gravest historical importance. Whatever may have been the organization and expansion of Teutonic society from Clovis, say, to the reappearance of the antique empire under Charles the Great, and however we may picture the exact nature of the barbarian "invasions," all available evidence witnesses to the enormous cultural superiority of the Celts over the Germans down to, and including, the days of Merovingian occupation of Gaul; and witnesses no less to the fact that the victorious German tribes respected and assimilated this superior Gallo-Roman culture as they did the equally transcendent Roman civilization in Italy.

Moreover, criticism is agreed that there is a constant element in Latin poetry which is not Roman and not Greek but something else; an element to which (as Garrod contends) Latin verse owes what it has of fire, sensibility, and romance. The ethnic presence of a magic which cannot be defined and cannot be neglected at any moment during the whole sombre progression of that poetry may perhaps be called the primitive Italian contribution. It is not my province to discuss this contribution in my book. But we must have another, wider, and more technical name for this, the real soul of Latin poetry—this demon that lurks deep beneath its changing mask and is animate of its psychic qualities, its sensitive response to external stimuli. All the long way from the hymns of the Dancing Men and of the Arval Brotherhood to that English Canterbury which housed the eleventh-century anthology of "Cambridge Songs," we feel in Latin poetry an inventiveness, a quick sensibility, a swift mental response, a sort of nervous texture which preserves it at its best from being mere rhetoric and at its worst from being mere prose. No phrase more exact than *Celtic temper* exists as a descriptive term for the fire and romance of Latin and Romanesque poetry. When fuller revelation comes, some more profoundly significant phrase may gloss processes so important to its development; but against the dawning of a prophetic day when the inward nature of Latin verse finds utterance, *Celtic* must suffice. Hence, the perhaps undue attention which I have given to Gaul.

There is yet another reason why the chapters on the backgrounds of Latin poetry are so long and so replete with obvious facts. In them I wished to drive home with a hammer a point which is quite generally forgotten: namely, that from the beginning of recorded history in Gaul this province was shot through with oriental influences that had a determinant effect on the development of Latin poetry—neo-Platonism, Asiatic rhetoric, Gallic exuberance, the melodic structure of hymnody, the figurative imagery of mysticism, gaudiness of color, personalization of human feeling—which broke classical modes and molds, widened the range of western sensibility, and led to that profound change in its imaginative processes which we call romanticism or Romanesque. These are but a few of the most evident obligations of Gallo-Roman poetry to the Near East and by no means exhaust the account. It is true that many acknowledgments of debts owed by provincial western Latin poetry to the Levant have been separately listed, but they have never been summed up, and their total applied in an inventory of Gallo-Roman verse. This task I am attempting. How else can I indicate my belief in the deep and continuing debt which Latin poetry owes to the Orient? By dismissing most of my materials with mere reference to some convenient handbook? I prefer to summon all my troops—horse, foot, and dragoons—and deploy them in mass formation.

For the current and conventional view is too widely diffused to be easily broken down. The facts of the conventional view are notoriously familiar. Greek, so the argument runs, was the only form of literature the Romans knew. The ancient poetry of India and Babylon and Persia, the Egyptian *Book of the Dead*, were all unsuspected. By the middle of the first century B. C. rumors permeated through Philo of a people whose writings described the creation of the world by a tribal god not even dignified by a statue, but until Longinus pointed out that the legislator of the Jews could write sublimely, the Hebrew Scriptures were quite outside the Roman horizon. As late as the Augustans literature was identified with Greece. The Carthaginians, the former rivals of Roman, were no less illiterate than such contemporaries as the Parthians and the Moors, as Germans and Gauls and Spaniards, tribes whose highest poetic flight was a war-song, rude and unpolished, like the Saturnian verse which the Romans had rejected in disgust. But such a picture of Latin poetry, particularly in the early ages of Romanesque, is to my mind too stark in its outlines, too black-on-white, too unshaded and uncolored to be in any true sense a living likeness of it. Hence it is that my early chapters seem to deal but remotely with my theme.

I acknowledge gratefully the help which Mr. E. K. Rand, and my colleagues, Mr. C. H. Beeson, Mr. J. W. Thompson, Mr. C. N. Gould, and Mr. Archer Taylor have given my writing.

PHILIP SCHUYLER ALLEN.

THE UNIVERSITY OF CHICAGO
September, 1927

The policy on which the various poems in this volume have been translated is not susceptible of any simple formulation. I have in each case tried to cut my cloth to fit the need of the text and of the poem. Where the original meter seemed to me to be an integral part of the poem, I have tried to keep it in English verse, or at least to keep an equivalent effect, for meters, no more than words, are capable of exact transfusion from one language to another. Examples of such handling may be found in the cases of *Poetry and Time* by Phocas, where, I am afraid, I have singularly failed at English sapphics; of the *Planctus de obitu Karoli;* of the *Ply the Oar* attributed to Columban, where the very swing of the boat is found in the Latin meter; and of a number of the *Cambridge Songs*. Oftener, I have tried to find an English meter which would, without effect of strangeness (that curse of exact metrical adaptation), reproduce the particular effect of the original poem. Thus I have remade the gorgeous artificiality of Ausonius's poem *Of Roses* into the meter of the *Rubaiyat*, which in spirit the original resembles. Thus the substance and structure of the *Lydia* poem from the *Appendix Vergiliana* come so near to being a brace of sonnets that I have thought little damage would be done were I to rearrange certain lines of the poem and turn it into Petrarchan form. For the Roman elegiac measure I have sometimes used English blank verse and sometimes the heroic couplet; when the couplet is employed, it is, quite frankly, a mannered couplet, and I have chosen the manner from whatever period of English verse seemed to me most suitable to the task in hand. An excellent instance in Ausonius's poem to his dead wife, which I have attempted to rework with a dignity and with a certain slight stiffness characteristic of seventeenth-century heroic couplet.

Elsewhere I have departed utterly from the Latin meter. For example, the *Nealce* poem of Petronius came out well in the measure of Byron's "When we two parted." The mood fits that measure; why should I seek a closer approximation to elegiac verse? The rattling inconsequence of the correspondence of the Bishops, which I have satirically entitled *Episcopal Courtesies*, is, I think, best reproduced in the manner of Barham when he wrote *The Ingoldsby Legends*, and if the result is frankly periphrastic rather than literal, I must plead in excuse the bad state of the text and the fun I had in writing the translation. In at least two or three

INTRODUCTION

cases my translation must affect the scholar as positively bizarre: one is the *Kaiser Otto* poem, which, in my version, reads like *Frankie and Johnny* or *Jesse James*. What can I say, except that when I turned the Latin into English prose, the thing under my hand was so close to the manner of contemporary illiterate folk-ballad as to cry out for that treatment; and I stoutly maintain that such a version comes closer to the probable origin of the piece than a dignified scholarly version would do. In sum, I have tried to work flexibly.

The matter of tenses and of diction is equally troublesome with that of meters. Before the scholar complains that I have misread my originals, let him consider that it was my task to re-create in English the effect which the author had created in Latin; let him sit down, not merely to translate, but to recreate the effect of what he has read in a tongue that seems to us absurdly stiff and stately; if then he can not justify changes that I have made, keeping in mind the problems of syntax, diction, meter, and rhyme (that *bête noir* of good translating), he may make what comment he pleases.

Perhaps a single illustration of method will help to convince the sceptical. Let us select a passage from Claudian's idyl on the marriage of Honorius and Maria, and let it be the garden of Venus passage:

> Mons latus Ionium Cypri praeruptus obumbrat,
> Invius humano gressu, Phariumque cubile
> Proteos et septem despectat cornua Nili.
> Hunc neque canentes audent vestire pruinae
> Nec venti pulsare, timent hunc laedere nimbi;
> Luxuriae Venerique vacat. Pars acrior anni
> Exulat; aeterni patet indulgentia veris.
> In campum se fundit apex; hunc aurea saepes
> Circuit et fulvo defendit prata metallo.
> Mulciber, ut perhibent, his oscula conjugis emit
> Moenibus et talis uxorius obtulit arces.
> Intus rura micant, manibus quae subdita nullis
> Perpetuum florent, Zephyro contenta colono,
> Umbrosumque nemus, quo non admittitur ales,
> Ni probet ante suos diva sub judice cantus:
> Quae placuit, fruitur ramis; quae victa, recedit.
> Vivunt in Venerem frondes omnisque vicissim

> Felix arbor amat; nutant ad mutua palmae
> Foedera, populeo suspirat populus ictu
> Et platani platanis alnoque adsibilat alnus.

This is artificial, it is voluptuous, it is full of luscious pictures. Observe the heavy alliteration and the swooning effect which the alteration of vowels with liquids and nasals produces. Into what English measure shall we cast a translation? The difficulty of hexameters puts them out of the question. Blank verse will not do because we can not get it jeweled enough; moreover, the difficulty of articulating the lines so that they will not fall apart of their own weight under all this imagery is excessive. We are forced to some form of rhyme, for I assume that the reader will agree that free verse in so long a passage will not do. What shall our rhyme form be? We want one in which we can make a sensuous music, one in which we can make pictures, and one in which we can be a little archaic, as the spirit of the Latin is. If we choose quatrains or ottava rima, we shall lose in richness what we shall gain in ease. I therefore believe that the stanza of Spenser is worth a trial. Let us face, however, the difficulties of the task. These are the intricate rhyme scheme, which is bound to throw literalness askew, the troublesome feat of getting smoothly over from the first four lines of the stanza into the last five without break, and the concluding alexandrine. But the alexandrine is only symptomatic of the greatest difficulty of all: how shall we fill all our stately stanza without obvious padding? We must give up literality for effect; we shall have to expand the Latin here and there; but if we can secure atmosphere and picture and melody, we shall perhaps have approximated this purple passage in Claudian. Thus, at any rate, we reason; and here is the translation:

> Amid the Ionian sea doth Cyprus lie
> O'ershadowed by a hanging mountain wall,
> Where never living man hath climbed so high
> As from that top to see old Nilus fall
> By seven horns into the ocean's brawl,
> And islands that to Proteus are dear;
> White frost upon that land doth never fall,

And never ruinous rains have they to fear,
Or blowing winds, who live in that Saturnian year.

For all the joys of love men there have leisure,
Since every ruder month is banishèd,
And never-ending spring with all its pleasure
Forever smiles upon that isle instead;
The mountain rises from a meadow bed,
And round its side there runs a precious hedge,
A tawny wall that, mixing gold with red,
Protects the lowlands with its shining ledge
Between the highland and the blue sea's creamy edge.

Men say that Mulciber, to win him kisses,
Did for a bridal gift this wall prepare,
Love-smitten, building it to keep his blisses
Where only Zephyrus with pleasant air
May enter, for those shining fields to care
That with perpetual vernal flowers blow.
They have no need for human gardeners there;
And in the shadowy woods no birds may go
Save Venus first approve the sylvan songs they know.

And every leaf lives but for Venus' sake—
What she mislikes, the selfsame falls and dies;
The very trees that all day softly shake
Live in her looks and flourish in her eyes:
Each bush, entangled with its fellow, lies—
Meek palms bend down their leaves to palm trees meek,
The murmuring poplar for its fellow sighs,
The plane trees murmur to the mates they seek,
And alders all day long an amorous whisper speak.

Well, our translation has led us into certain serious difficulties. Claudian says nothing about "blue sea's creamy edge"; our islands that to Proteus are dear are only implicit in the Latin; and the mountain is now defended by both a "precious hedge" and a "tawny wall"—clearly a weakness. But on the other hand, our last stanza, though expanded, keeps the antitheses of the concluding lines in the original; we have not done badly by Zephyrus; and perhaps we have the general swoon and glamor of the original. The worst of our translation is that it is diffuse and inexact; the best of it is that it is pictorial, artificial, and melodious. We have had to choose. The art of translation is the art of sacrifice. Such will be each problem that confronts us; to gain an essential quality we shall have to give up other qualities; and the problem of choices is the essential one, the one which makes translation at once so baffling and so delightful.

HOWARD MUMFORD JONES.

THE UNIVERSITY OF NORTH CAROLINA
September, 1927

NOTE

The Latin originals of the translated pieces will be found, numbered consecutively by chapters, in the appendix. The same number appears under the translation in the text as over the original in the appendix. No originals are given for pieces from the Greek, Arabic, and Gaelic.

THE ROMANESQUE LYRIC

Chapter I

THE PROVINCE OF GAUL

So far as we know at present, or may ever know, Gaul fostered, and could foster, nothing that we call embodied literature prior to the outthrown bulwark of the *pax et lex Romana*. Let us therefore examine the nature of this civilizing cincture which Italian statecraft gave to the eighty races living in Gaul. Let us study the causes which lent the Roman government in this territory so genitive a power at any period after 10 B. C., when the centralizing altars of Rome-and-Augustus were installed at Lyons.

Properly my story of the civilization of Gaul, like Haverfield's narrative of the Roman occupation of Britain, should begin with an outline of the military conquest of the new colony, should estimate the size and character of its Roman garrison, the number and distribution of its forts, the extent and massiveness of its frontier lines. For, as that author asserts, it was the peculiar glory of the Roman army that it saved, not a single nation, but civilization itself, that behind its encircling shelter the culture of the old world took firm root in western Europe, and that the final triumph of the barbarian involved a corresponding triumph of civilization over the worst evils of barbarism. But, none the less, the real interest attaches to the end and not to the means, to the civilization that was protected and not to the sheltering army. That civilization is the thing that counts in the history of poetry as of mankind, and so it must be our main concern here.[1]

The general peace of Gaul was safeguarded by a thorough system of frontier defense. A new civil service was begun in all the settled areas, one largely based on home rule. The coveted prize of Roman citizenship was granted freely to representative provincials. The governors of Gaul were made to feel a direct, personal responsibility to the emperor and, if unjust, were haled before him for trial. Fixed salaries were paid to Gaulish office holders.[2] Taxation and its method of levy were organized in a spirit of fairness. And as a result of these things, even before the days of Nero and St. Paul, there was one fully Romanized province, with its capital at Narbonne and with towns like Arles and Nîmes, in which a Roman might live and feel himself as well off as in Italy.[3] The growth of clean traditions of conduct among Narbonnese subjects in the administration of their affairs was such that it reacted upon the lowered standard of honesty that had come to be expected of Roman senators.

The province first established was a region over the coast of which the culture of Greece had managed to stray, centuries before, through the accident of a Greek colony founded at Marseilles.[4] But beyond it lay the Gaul of trousered, long-haired, and mustachioed Celts—no easy soil to be won for a new civilization. Tucker describes them as prone to give adherence only to clans or tribes, uniting no further than impulse dictated, forming no towns larger than a village, living in huts scattered through forests, hills, marshes, and pasture land, content to sleep on straw if only they could wear a fine plaid and boast of a gold ornament. Such in the days of Cæsar were the Ambiani (whence Amiens), the Remi (whence Rheims), the Parisii and Treveri (whence Paris and Treves). But by the time of Nero this country had wide corn lands and was rich in minerals and cattle, from which the hides came regularly down the Rhone to be carried to Mediterranean markets. The proverbial passion of the Gaul (except for drunkenness and the making of war) was for the art of speaking. The Gaulish provinces united at a point on the Rhone, near which necessarily arose the largest city of that part of the world, Lugdunum or Lyons, which speedily became the seat of a noted school of eloquence. And before we proceed far in our later survey of Latin poetry, we shall find the immature and tremulous cadences of the Celtic spirit embedded there.

Greatly improved means of communication between Gaul and other parts of the empire were due to lavish expenditure for road building and for a splendid imperial postal service—news from Rome reaching far across Gaul regularly and quickly.[5] The personal example set by the emperor in the remedy of distress from famine and epidemic, his development of great works of public utility, his redress of honest grievances—these bound Gaul ever more closely to its master. Emperors and important members of their households frequently traveled through Gaul, fostering and subsidizing municipal institutions.

Now these are by no means all the causes that contributed to a rapid improvement in the condition of the province, but they are amply sufficient to prove that the only political and religious unity Gaul ever possessed was bestowed upon it by Rome. Before it was accorded its place in the sunlight of western civilization, Gaul has been but an empty name for the habitat of eighty different races: fair long-headed foresters from the Nordic plan, who flooded the fertile lowlands from Belgium to Bordeaux; dark long-headed fruit growers from the Mediterranean coast, who occupied the summer-drought portion of the productive Rhone valley; Alpine round heads, who were isolated in regions unattractive enough, perhaps, but yet hard to reach and therefore easily defensible. Previous to the coming of Rome, each of the races in Gaul had been living on a hostile footing with most of its near neighbors, but soon thereafter there grew up a greater unanimity of purpose, a more sustained consciousness of racial integrity around the *ara Romæ et Augusti* at Lyons and Narbonne than there had ever been around the altars of a native Vercingetorix. General constitutional assemblies such as the empire created in the temples of Gaulish cities had not been known in any heyday of national independence. The commonalty of endeavor, the community of viewpoint established by these gatherings, remained during every subsequent invasion and revolt the sole solid guarantee of ultimate Gaulish unity.

The official measures which I have listed above doubtless encouraged the quick growth of Roman civilization in Gaul, but they do not quite explain it.[6] In the main it seems to have been, as Haverfield suggests, a voluntary movement—perhaps the best instance in all history of the influence of a higher culture on lower races fitted to assimilate it.[7] It represented on a gigantic scale the change that can be seen proceeding today in any country district where the peasantry desert their native and picturesque costumes for the stamped calicoes of town fashions. Like enough, it was the entire absence of any coercion that contributed most powerfully to the destruction of the old national sentiment—a sentiment which recurs obstinately only whenever attempts are made to eject it with a pitchfork.

If there will never be a ready-made and mechanical explanation of Rome's quick engorging of Gaulish culture, we can at least admire the sure mastery with which she carried off her high adventure of gaining control of every strategic dominant of the provincial terrain. By the land route Rome's first push—Turin and Tarragona—brought her north to Vienne on the Rhone and west to Toulouse. This area, long known as Gallia Narbonensis, roughly speaking, comprised the later Provence and Languedoc east and west of the Rhone. In each case Rome gained control of a climatic divide with its supplementary products on opposite sides, thus winning a position that made naturally for a commercial and political center; a proof of which is that when Gaul for a brief time included in its dominion both Britain and Spain, Vienne remained the capital of this vast region. It used to be said of the old Gallo-Roman city that her wealth was so great the streets were paved with mosaic.

We see the Romans threading the Durance valley until they reach Avignon and there weave a filament that is significantly renewed by the popes of the trecento. Rounding the Pyrenees, the resistless conquerors come to Narbo Martius on the Latin side of the Aude. In their advance from each focus they smother important posts of liaison inside the best discoverable river-front: Valence, between the Rhone and the Isere, Carcassonne in the wide bend of the Aude. The earliest colony is established at Narbonne—because at first the Spanish connection was more important to Rome than the Italian one—and here the tireless army of crusaders for western civilization gains a fine commanding site protected by lagoon and sea and river on every hand except the west. And this place is made the capital city of Mediterranean Gaul, with high roads to Toulouse and Avignon.[8]

Human hearts are the same as centuries roll by and religions alter. A modern French grave near La Rochelle contains in the cross above it a glass case with a doll's dinner service enclosed, a favorite toy of the mite buried there. Ancient Roman graves are found to hold collections of infants' playthings: ivory dolls, a rattle, bells, an earthenware bank, a terra-cotta horse dappled with yellow spots. So the museum in the Hôtel de Ville at Narbonne (like those at Arles and Avignon) preserves for us the last gifts of distracted parents who could not endure the seeing of darling toys about the home, and consigned them to the last resting place of departed children: bronze Gaulish sun-wheels of four and eight spokes, cocks and hens of clay, pigs and horses such as might be bought for a sou at the fair. Very rude, these tokens, but infinitely touching and a reminder as good as any of the unalterable march westward since Phœnician days of a world whose every shining facet is like unto our own.[9]

Gallia Lugdunensis was made to pivot on Lyons even though it comprised the whole stretch of land between the Seine and the Loire and held two other garrisons at Autun and Sens. Its river-girt peninsula in the midst of the great trade route in the Saone-Rhone depression furnished perfect connection with Italy by the upper Rhone and commanded the best short trail into the Loire valley just northwest of St. Etienne. Between rivers that drain to the Atlantic and the Mediterranean, the post of Autun held the Gold Coast gap and occupied a river-encircled hill on a tributary of the Loire. Through this gap streamed a traffic that was unresting—incomputable.

So much of a picture I have stopped to give of a panorama of conquest that remains a wonder of history and has helped create us as we are. The more minute our examination of Rome's unwearying campaign in Gaul, the greater our inclination to reverent awe. If we study the *carte de l'etat-major* (with its scale a half-inch to the mile) we never find the Roman napping or in a single instance failing to grasp even the slightest advantage of topography. And yet it must be emphasized that in his most important choices of settlement, the Roman invariably found himself anticipated by ancient Gaulish selection: for example, Vienne was the old center of the Allobroges, Sens of the Senones, Tours of the Rurones, Paris of the Parisii, Rheims of the Remi, and so on and on. When confronted by this recurrent fact, I begin frankly to doubt whether there had not developed in pre-Roman Gaul a civilization which in its essential attitudes was closer to the purposes of the new invaders from the south than is ordinarily granted. For I can understand best the quick surrender of paganism to Roman ideas by agreeing with Cumont that the two opposed creeds moved in the same intellectual and moral sphere, and that the Gaul could therefore pass without notable shock from one to the other.

Roman invasion not only found itself anticipated in choice of settlement by flourishing native capitals selected with conscious emphasis on strategic points and with unconscious response to climatic control, but when Rome began to apply to Gaul the customary policy of consolidating her new conquests by a network of roads and fortresses, she discovered she had again been preceded by a skill as uncanny as her own. At the time of Cæsar's appearance within her borders Gaul was well supplied with roads and navigable water-courses, and the presumption that Roman highways followed the old lines of connection is nearly always right—even if the difference between new road and traditional forest trail was greatly to the advantage of the former.

The oldest road into Gaul followed the coast from Genoa to the Forum Julii, where it turned inland and ran due west to Aix, Marseilles, and Arles—here it crossed the Rhone and continued by Nîmes to Narbo. At this town it forked, on the one hand holding straight ahead to the Pyrenees, and on the other continuing to Toulouse on the upper Garonne and to Bordeaux near its mouth. It was by this causeway that the early traffic between Italy and the tin district of southwestern Britain was carried on.[10]

A second notable linking of Italy and Gaul was the road that crossed the Alps by the pass of Mont Genevre a hundred miles farther north—it was reached from Turin on the upper Po by a road that followed a tributary westward to Susa. This is a low and easy pass communicating southwest with Arles, and northwest with Vienne and Lyons.

Augustus also opened the St. Bernard passes, after he had wiped out the greedy natives whose extortions had practically closed them to travelers—passes that were reached from Milan, the chief road-center of cisalpine Gaul, by way of Ivrea and Aosta. The little St. Bernard led westward down the Isere to Vienne, the great St. Bernard into the upper Rhone above the lake of Geneva, and ran thence through Swiss valleys to the Rhine.

The road system of central and northern Gaul had its center at Lyons. One important highway ran west through Aquitaine to Saintes at the mouth of the Garonne; another descended the valley of the Loire to Bourges and Tours, with branches to Orleans and Poitiers; another followed the Saone to Chalons, where it forked, the eastern branch trailing the river Doubs to the Rhine, the western arm proceeding via Autun to the port of Lillebonne at the mouth of the Seine, and to Boulogne, where passengers embarked for Britain. The road from Chalons to Boulogne skirted the basin of the Seine and its tributaries on the east, passing by Troyes, Rheims, Soissons, and Amiens. At Rheims a branch turned east to reach the Moselle at Trier, ultimately joining the main Rhine valley road a little below Mainz—thence it followed the river frontier by Cologne to Leyden near its mouth.

From the time of the proper policing of these highways there was an enormous increase in both travel and trade—probably for the first time the commercial industries came into their own, and the evidence of general prosperity in Gaul admits of no denial. Gaul, like Germany, must have had a considerable transit-trade, importing Baltic amber, slaves, furs, and other foreign goods, which were paid for partly in wine, partly in coin, cloth, cutlery, hardware, weapons. Markets were established along the frontier for traffic between the Gauls and the Germans or other barbarians, and there is reason to believe that some of these trading posts lasted into the late Middle Ages. The minerals of Gaul were insignificant in comparison with those of Spain —some silver and copper was mined in Aquitaine, some iron near Berri and at Périgord. But there were important textile industries: woolens were made at Arras and Saintes, linens especially at Cahors. Pottery was manufactured at Aveyron and Auvergne, and there was much founding of bronze and other hardwares, and of glass. The vine, which was largely cultivated in southern Gaul in spite of restrictions imposed in the interest of Italian growers, gradually spread northwards until in the fourth century there were vineyards along the Seine and the Moselle. Arles took the place of Marseilles as the chief port on the south coast— an important route led from Narbo to Bordeaux—the tin trade with Britain passed, as we have seen, through Lillebonne and Boulogne.[11]

Gaul then, as France now, was endowed with several requisites for a great economic development: a very fertile soil; a population dense for early times, and one that was wide-awake and intelligent; a climate which, though somewhat cold and foggy, was well suited to sustained activity; and (supreme advantage in ancient civilization) Gaul was everywhere intersected by navigable rivers, as by a network of canals. In older days water was always the economic route of commerce; civilization often successfully entered the interior of new countries only by way of the rivers, the railroads of antiquity.

The new and stable jurisdiction of the landed proprietary was responsible for another result, in that it promoted the cultivation of cereals and textile plants. Rome soon came to buy her grain not only in Egypt but in Gaul—in fact, the latter colony seems to have been the sole area of Europe fertile enough to export its wheat and flax. The growing of flax (to the ancient world what cotton is to us) progressed so rapidly in Gaul that it was early able to rival Egypt in this product. All Gaul makes sails, said Pliny, and their linen is more beautiful to the eyes than are their women.

Gaul was a new country like the Argentine Republic or the United States of yesterday, in which the soil had still almost its natural pristine fecundity, bringing forth easily a marvelous abundance of the plants that clothe and feed mankind.[12] In Gaul under the empire immense fortunes in land were realized, proof of which, if such were needed, is furnished by the ruins of the splendid Gallo-Roman villas which are far more sumptuous and extensive than their

Italian counterparts. But Gaul was not restricted to the better cultivation of its productive soil—alone among the countries of the western world it became an industrial nation, manufacturing not only for home consumption but for export. Ferrero tells how the more frequent contact with Oriental races acquainted the Gauls with the beautiful objects made by the artisans of Laodicea, Tyre, and Sidon, and how this incited them so to improve their industries and widen their markets that they soon were outselling the world in Italy, in Spain, beyond the Rhine, and in the Danube provinces.

The Gauls had mastered weaving and invented vegetable dyes to compete with the animal colors of the Orient. From various passages in Juvenal and Martial we know that the woolen clothing worn by the populace of Rome in the second century was woven in Gaul in the districts known today as Arras, Langres, Saintonge. Pliny attributes to the Gauls the invention of an incombustible wool used to make mattresses. Glass making was another art carried from the East across the Mediterranean into Gaul; jewelry making flourished side by side with silver-plating and tinning—we might almost say (remarks Ferrero) that Gallic industry did to its older colleagues in the ancient world what German wares have done not long since, compared with the older, more aristocratic products of England and France—popularized objects of luxury for the many and the merely well-to-do. Lastly, Dechelette has shown that in the first century of the empire many manufactories of ceramics flourished in Gaul, especially in the valley of the Allier; further, that a host of such products found among the ruins of Pompeii were made in Gaul—discoveries most noteworthy, for in connection with extracts from Pliny which are confirmed by inscriptions and archæological discoveries, they uncover that real Roman Gaul whose amazing relics but half tell the tale of its wealth.

Here, then, is Gaul with her roads open to the world, and the stream of travel on her highways and water routes surely included every movable type of humanity afoot, awheel, or afloat in the western world. Let us study the passing show a short while.

Humble inns abounded on the main roads. The smaller taverns and those who kept them had a bad name. Then as now, landlords were generally accused of cheating, overcharging, and watering the wine. Their beds were often said to be stuffed with rushes instead of feathers—guests were so apt to suffer in wayside inns from smoke, dirt, heat, smells, noise, the insolence of hostlers, and the activities of the *cimex lectularius*, that travelers of rank and substance preferred to sleep in one of their own villas, accept the hospitality of a convenient friend, spend the night in their coaches (built for that purpose), or camp out in a tent. There was better accommodation in the towns, of course, and really good hotels were to be found (for a price!) in large commercial centers and watering-places. So far this picture is an intensely modern one.

Private enterprise, Bosanquet tells us, provided for the transport of casual travelers; officials, judges on circuit, and soldiers could claim public hospitality and be billeted in private houses by the local magistrates. In towns there were liverymen who kept horses and mules for hire, with vehicles requisite for any occasion. A driver might be engaged for a single stage of the journey or for a succession of them; humbler travelers rode, sometimes attended by a servant on foot—it was a mark of poverty to venture forth afoot and unattended.

Traveling carriages were large and heavy, planned for comfort rather than speed, so that it was possible to write or read in them; they were drawn by teams of mules or Gaulish ponies. There were servants of state who journeyed in the course of their duty—among them many a courier or postman driving at express speed; officers and civil functionaries, each with his retinue, proceeding by easy stages to a new post, separated, it may be, by the whole length of empire from the last place of service; recruits for the legions and auxiliary troops marching to the frontier; embassies on their way to Rome; deputations bringing compliments or petitions to the emperor; burgesses going to urge some suit at court; and many others whose business was litigation or commerce.

According to modern ideas, the rapidity with which every development in Gaulish life influenced Rome is proof of the intimate and vital connection between the two imperial parts. Intercommunication was fostered to the utmost, and Ramsay thinks it proper to say that under the empire traveling between France and Italy was more highly developed, that the dividing power of distance was weaker than at any time before or since, until we come to the transportation facilities of the steam railroad. Who does not recall the vogue of Antioch, Athens, and Alexandria for western students; the Phrygian merchant who made seventy-two journeys to Rome; and the man of Cadiz who traveled all the way to Rome and back merely to set his eyes on the historian Livy?[13]

As the facilities for travel increased, as speech, coinage, and law became more homogeneous, professional men of all sorts migrated from place to place more freely than they do even today. Doctors, teachers of philosophy and rhetoric, painters and sculptors, actors, musicians, athletes, and all kinds of craftsmen sought a new market for their skill far from their native cities. Then as nowadays persons of means and leisure traveled extensively, some for their health to baths or healing sanctuaries, others from a desire to see the world or from sheer *tædium vitæ*. Greeks, Syrians, and Jews were everywhere. The result was a singularly uniform and cosmopolitan civilization throughout the western Roman world—one from which the local and provincial spirit was strikingly absent and through which ideas passed with exceptional ease.

This is no primitive world. It is the yesterday of our own. In the Gaul that intervenes between St. Paul and St. Augustine, I fear we shall look long to find any of the inherited types of poetry which our romantic notions lead criticism to assign to it. I have no desire to hurry other minds to a conclusion and am more than glad to await my reader's decision after he has finished later chapters of this book. But in my own estimation, whatever song rang along the highways of Gaul in the salad years of new conversion was due to one of two sources: (a) such poets as Ovid and Horace and Vergil and Catullus and Juvenal and all their innumerable smaller kind; or (b) the music-hall skits, the barrack-room ballads, and the fescennine snatches of brothel, mimic stage, and *circenses*.[14] The tradition of the first of these sources was kept alive, as we shall soon see, by Claudian and Ausonius and Rutilius and Sidonius and Tiberianus, not to mention whole groups of lesser scribblers who companioned them. The second kind of verse which sang itself on Gaulish roads was of the stamp called popular, because its origin is not known to be in learned manuscript writing, because it is without conscious pride of authorship and individualizing technic, because it leads its life and earns its daily bread outside the walls of school, church, or library.

Now it may be true that from the earliest Latin times such folk-song had led a submerged existence among unlettered strata of the Roman people, who were largely untrammeled by the changing literary fashions of the town and court. It may likewise be that a few types of ancient folk-song lived precariously on in connection with the celebration of festal occasions (of which the Latin had as many as the modern Spaniard) or the recurrence of set activities such as seasonal popular rites, games, and play. It may be the fact that primitive Latin possessed at least six distinguishable sorts of traditional folk-song that were rhythmical (accentual) in verse structure, at least to the extent that word accent and line stress were identical: chanteys, marching jingles, erotic odes, fescennine verses, beggar stanzas, and rustic dance measures.

But just because here and there in Gaul we are to come across the traces of an accentual verse, popular in type, which clothes a sailor's song, a soldier's doggerel, a hymn for a festival of Venus, a smutty gag, a topical hit, or a reaping couplet, we cannot assume that these are inherited survivals of a primitive Latin poetry sung in the saturnian meter and transmitted bodily from Italy to Gaul within historic times. We have no philological testimony to validate such a thesis. In fact, the very texts on which Niebuhr based his ballad theory and his belief in the existence of a national Roman epos behind the histories of the regal period, are thought by recent criticism to prove only the practice in the early republican age of singing (at meals and funerals) the praises of famous men to the accompaniment of the *tibia*. And we do not know what these songs were really like, for their words and their music have utterly vanished. This disappearance is perhaps mainly due to the influence of Ennius, a foreigner who came on the crest of the wave of Greek tendency at a time of momentous change in the modes of thought and habits of the Romans, a writer whose genius simply overwhelmed the earliest Italian poetry and gave them something better to think about.[15]

So the native art of accentual Latin verse, doubtless a good one, sank into oblivion, and its place in the realm of conscious literature was taken by poetry of a deliberately learned origin like the hexameters and elegiacs chanted by tragedians and epic reciters. For a century after Ennius, Rome produced no great poet. When at last Roman poetry suddenly became great, it was because men of real genius had so thoroughly absorbed all the Greeks had to teach them that they were now free to assert their own poetic individuality, to express their own national traditions in their own way. But this does not mean that vaudeville artists and circus clowns, harlequins, mimes, and minstrels along the routes of travel did not constantly renew the pulse and beat of accentual verse wherever their voices were upraised in song. We need not permit the vexing question of accent versus quantity—rhythm versus meter—to be a bone of contention.[16] We can leave undisturbed the quaint belief that it took several Christian centuries to effect the miracle of accentual utterance in Latin poetry of the definitely artful and artificial sort. It is enough for us to know that while Vergil (who was perhaps a Celt) was toiling with never a misplaced quantity at the funeral pyre of distracted Dido, that while for Catullus (who was perhaps a Celt) the sole uncertain quantity in all his elegies was Lesbia—nightingales were singing in the woods of the Côte d'Or, and near at hand gipsying artists harked to their rhythm.

There are in Gallo-Roman literature no distinct survivals of Latin chanteys, at least in popular accentual form, although it is likely Columban once wrote a metrical exercise based upon an extant *celeuma*, or boating song. Familiar to our ears, however, are the thudding measures of soldiers who were tramping the highways of Gaul:

> Ecce Cæsar nunc triumphat qui subegit Gallias

(hrrrrrm! hrrrrrm! hrrrrrm! hrrrrrm!), or

> Tantum vini nemo habet quantum fudit sanguinis

and the heavy beat of these *ictus* often meets our ears again in the mocking songs of the Merovingian and Carolingian age. We should not expect either sailor or soldier songs as a separate genus to outlast the conditions of the world that bore them and to reappear centuries later unchanged— nor do they. When we meet them again in the twelfth century they have been entirely refitted to an altered environment; our last look at the original type is presumably in the seventh century during the rule of Clothair II, if the *Life of St. Faro* tells us true:

> De Chlothario est canere rege Francorum
> Qui ivit pugnare in gentem Saxonum. . . .

The third type of archaizing popular Latin accentuals (the festival ode to Venus) likewise seems to have had no direct line of continuance after the *Vigils of Venus*, unless we may view the late medieval maying-songs as its posterity, and (possibly here and there) a learned revival, such as the tenth-century

> O admirabile Veneris idolum.

But the smashing fifteen-syllabled trochaic line of the *pervigilium*

> Cras amet qui numquam (am)avit, quiqu(e) amavit cras amet

and of Tiberianus's

> Amnis ibat inter arva valle fusus frigida

which was the undoubted marching rhythm of many such festival odes sounds in Fulbert's wonderful panegyric of the nightingale

> Implet silvas atque cuncta modulis arbustula,
> Gloriosa valde facta veris præ lætitia;
> Volitando scandit alta arborum cacumina,
> Ac festiva satis gliscit sibilare carmina

and not less surely in William of Poitou's

> Qu'una domna s'es clamada de sos gardadors a mei.[17]

The fescennine verses that pagan Latin knew appear throughout all the early centuries in Gaul—at least they are marked down for strict censure by churchmen everywhere. Grossly obscene they were (like thousands of modern limericks that never get into books), so that none may deny the proud claim of their singers: *non es poeta, Priape, fascinosior nostro.* Caustic rhymes[18] these pot-house offerings were, apart from the calm decency of narrative poetry as the sting of a bee is from the song of a lark—but so clutching in their ribald wit that all the fulmination of clerk and chancel availed as nothing against them.

We may be sure, too, that the rustic dance measures had prolific littering in the province, for their very spirit lay in a scurrilous wit that changeth not save in the choice of an object: in truth, the one immutable element in the age-long history of any popular literature is the rank verbiage of tormenting, coarse-fibred satire. Its descendants are the fabliaux, *facetiæ, jeux partis,* sequence parodies, hymnal blasphemies, *schwänke, schnurren, schnaderhüpfel, gestanzeln*—identical in their attacks on the frailty of humankind, unvarying in their grotesque gallows-humor and caricature. *Schimpflied* never failed in a time dedicated to simple hate, boasting, and revenge. *Schlumperlied* flourished in days pervaded by drunkenness, rapine, and slavery. *Spottlied* multiplied in an age when deformity and disease were scourges from heaven, and when impulse was father to the deed, with no intervening obstacle. *Gestanzeln* galore accompanied the most amazing ritual that filled the time between *polterabend* and *brautbett.*

And the mendicant songs. Gipsy and outlaw, mime and minstrel, bear-leader and itinerant peddler, clerk and quack and monk—each was on his own pilgrimage bent. Every age has its freemasonry of wayfarers; and every time that has given us living record of such has left behind it whining stanzas to elicit pity and alms. In our days in Gaul when the sky was often the only roof for the wanderer, long before the adoration of the Virgin had furnished models for *pota-*

toria, the evangels for *lusoria,* and verses from Ovid and Horace the mold for *amatoria*—the welkin rang with vagabond lyric. This we must not doubt unless we wish to deny the solace of communal singing to an age that needed it sorely in the open and at the chimney-breast, merely because most of the tones that have reached us in the conscious literature of the educated classes of that age are those of harp and organ.

Chapter II

THE GALLO-ROMAN WORLD

And what a freemasonry of travel it was that thronged the Gaulish highways in the time of Nero, when the whole character of the Roman empire was changing! Large elements of the provincial population were foreigners. Africans, Greeks, Jews, Syrians, and Egyptians were perhaps the most commonly to be seen, but particularly prominent were the Greeks and the Jews. The former were recognized, above all, as the clever men, the artists, the social entertainers, and the literary guides. The latter were not yet the princes of high finance. They were chiefly the hucksters and petty traders, notorious for their strange habits and for the fanaticism of their religion, which made many proselytes even in high places, especially among the women —Poppæa herself is confidently asserted to have been such a convert.

Depopulated Italy needed more and more foreign hands to carry on its work of war and colonization, not only in the great cities of the west, where the scum of an alien world was already rising to the top, but in the Gaulish countrysides as well. The importation of slaves rapidly increased, Syria furnishing a large quota of this forced levy of cultivators, laborers on the public works, legionaries for Gaulish garrisons, sailors, truckmen, litter bearers, porters, and clerks. From the beginning of our era the Syrian merchants had undertaken a veritable colonization of Gaul. We can trace the history of these establishments down to the seventh century, but only in recent years has scholarship begun to estimate at its true worth their social and economic importance.

The Italian ports that harbored a considerable share of the Mediterranean tonnage (Pozzuoli, Ostia, later Naples) drew them like flies to the honey pot. But these dwellers from both sides of the Euphrates did not long confine themselves to the coastal towns—they penetrated the interior of the new countries to the northwest wherever they sensed profitable trade. We follow them as they pad the commercial highways of Gaul and travel its big rivers. By way of the Rhone they reach Lyons, spreading over the valley and soon thereafter over Gaul. For in this new country just opened to world commerce, fortunes can be made quickly.

Now as they swarm northward with their chattels and their gods (Baals of various sorts and the *dea Syria*), they find themselves in competition with other oriental immigrants in Gaul who have already become part of its body politic—notably the Egyptians and the Greeks. For with the beginning of the empire, merchants and sailors from Egypt, slaves, artisans, men of letters, even the discharged soldiers of the legions cantoned in the valley of the Nile, found diffusion in the great emporium of Aquileja and throughout the north of Italy. Gaul was scarcely won before they invaded it peacefully in search of wealth and adventure, and a full list of the inscriptions and monuments which mark the presence of Egyptians in the various cities of Gaul is little less than staggering to the uninitiate. Intimate relations existed from early days between Arles and Alexandria, and we know that a colony of Egyptian Greeks established at Nîmes by Augustus took the gods of their native country thither.

Cumont rightly insists that archæology alone can hope to fill the enormous blanks left in the written tradition in Gaul, for, although the question of the artistic and industrial influence exercised by the Orient on this province during the Roman period has often been broached, it has never been seriously studied in its entirety. By working out the arrangements of the temples and the religious furniture that adorned them, by critical interpretation of statuary relics, we can hope to reconstruct with some approach to correctness many sacred legends that found their final embodiment in profane medieval art in Gaul. And thus we can gain a better idea of how the invasion of oriental ideas not only helped to transform society and the nationalizing doctrines of the young province, but actually foreshadowed and prepared the final victory in Gaul of Christianity. An illustration or two of the service archæology has been able to render in supplementing other records must suffice:

Twenty years ago Michaelis showed the vital influence of Greek art on early Gaul and the domination of Marseilles by the towns of Hellenic Asia, by pointing out the great difference between the works of sculpture unearthed along the upper Rhine, which had been civilized by Italian legions, and those discovered on the other side of the Vosges. He believes the contrast in culture thus exposed is due to the activities of Marseilles traders traveling the ancient tin road towards Brittany and the amber road towards Germany.

Quite recently Mâle has convincingly indicated how the oriental rugs and silk hangings that were used on the floors, walls, and porches of sacred buildings in Gaul gave the pattern, as well as the colors and the subjects, of carvings of animals, mosaics, and stained windows in twelfth-century French cathedrals. The great church at Sens still preserves some of the very textiles that were brought to Gaul in Merovingian days—and if it were not on such tissues from China, Persia, and Syria that Gaulish artists had learned their natural history, the most interesting part of the medieval menagerie would be absent from ecclesiastical architecture and fenestration: lions confronting the opposite sides of a tree, two-headed eagles, symmetrical birds with entwined necks, two-bodied monsters with a single head, to say nothing of sphinxes, griffins, sirens, fauns, and evil spirits masquerading as gargoyles.

We see by the use of this key that her Levantine citizens not only taught imperial Gaul the artistic solution of architectonic problems like the erection of a cupola on a rectangular or octagonal edifice, and paved the way for Romanesque art in the early Middle Ages; they taught Gaul to accept oriental taste, they saturated her with their genius, their love of luxuriant decoration and of violent polychromy. Syrian painters vied with Alexandrian goldsmiths to enrich the villas of Gaulish noblemen in the days of the Antonines—the great manufacturing centers of the East gradually transformed the material civilization from which the great landed estates of Gaul derived their revenues. It is now no shock to us to learn of the discovery on the Lebanon range of a rescript addressed to sailors from Arles, but it still seems strange that we know the very name of a decurio in Syria who in the third century owned two factories in the Rhone basin, where he handled goods from Aquitaine. Colonies of orientals, like the strong establishment of Syrians in Treves, introduced into Gaul exotic patterns and processes which changed the old native industry and gave its products a perfection hitherto unknown. Not even the barbarian invasions of the fifth century stopped eastern immigration into all parts of Gaul, for, prompted by the lust of gain, they defied every danger except that of missing the chance of turning a dishonest penny.

In this barbarian society the part played by the civilized and city-bred element from the Levant was more considerable than ever. Under the Merovingian kings (about the year 591) the Syrians had sufficient influence at Paris to gain possession of many subordinate ecclesiastical posts, and one of their number was elevated to the episcopal throne. Gregory of Tours tells how King Gontrand on entering Orleans in 585 was received by a crowd acclaiming him in Latin, Hebrew, and Syriac.[1] The merchant colonies existed until Saracen corsairs destroyed commerce on the Mediterranean.

Those establishments, Cumont tells us, were a dominant factor in the economic and material life of Gaul. As bankers the Syrians concentrated a large share of the exchange business in their hands and monopolized the importing of valuable Levantine commodities as well as of the articles of luxury. They sold wines, spices, glassware, silks and purple fabrics, and objects wrought by goldsmiths to be used as patterns by the native artisans. Their moral and religious influence was not less considerable; for instance, it has been shown that they furthered the development of the monastic life in Gaul during the Christian period—that the devotion to the crucifix was introduced by them. Up to the Merovingian days Christians had felt an unconquerable repugnance to the representation of the Saviour nailed to an instrument of punishment more infamous than the guillotine of a later age.

It is perhaps not an overstatement when Strzygowski asserts that, in all artistic matters, fourth-century Gaul was only a province of the oriental church. For surely no better single proof of this fact can be demanded than that in Ireland, where the original forms of occidental Christianity were preserved (after their disappearance in Gaul and in Britain), the messengers of Gregory the Great discovered what had been long lost elsewhere in the western world: the knowledge of Greek. The only visible explanation of this phenomenon lies in the isolation of the old Irish Christianity, which had managed to maintain, after great masses of cultured Gauls had fled to it to escape the barbarian onset, the classical knowledge characteristic of former conditions, together with the speech in which much of it was cast. Accessory to the fact of this continuance of Greek in Ireland are of course the Irish connections with oriental cloisters, kept alive by the coming to Erin of a steady, if thin, stream of monks from Egypt, Syria, and Asia Minor. Except for their influence it would be hard to understand how Greek could be so cherished for three centuries that, when the Irishmen were received into the bosom of the Roman church, they could go as educating forces to the Orient, and set up as teachers of Greek in the realm of Charles the Bald.[2]

In any case I cannot regard my attempt to show how wide-thrown the doors of early Gaul were to the eastern world as finished, even in outline, until I have dealt with the open gateway which the West found in the Danube valley. The ancient city of Aquileja, situated at the northern tip of the Adriatic, was an emporium of the first rank from the first centuries of our era. Even in pre-Roman days this port had played an important role in uniting West and East, for it was the tidewater terminal of an old Celtic road which led to the north. Since its repaving by Augustus, this highroad had remained a most important link between the Italian peninsula and the Near East, because it led by way of Julium Carnutum to the river Drave (thence to the Danube) and followed the Danube road to Byzantium, the gateway of the Orient.

We have the record, but not the name, of a man who followed this road in his overland route from Bordeaux to Jerusalem in the year 333, and who gives the name of every stopping place on his way, with occasional summaries of the distance in miles—in leagues for the stretch from Bordeaux to Toulouse. The points where he adds up his miles are Arles, Milan, Aquileja, Mitrowitza, Sophia, and so to Constantinople, where he reckons that he has already traveled 2,221 miles with only 112 halts.

This metaled road, however, was but one of many military and commercial arteries radiating from Aquileja. That city was connected via Tridentum and Pons Æni by an imperial route with Augsburg; and by more than one road with Virunum, whence the way extended straight northward to Salzburg. These two systems knit Italy closely with the German provinces south of the upper reaches of the Danube. Here marched the legions on their way to the border; here traveled chapmen, hucksters, costermongers, peddlers, all the billow and bilge of camp life—and as odd a commingling of aristocrats, slaves, and cutthroats as ever set forth on a mission or scuttled a ship. Nor were the ladies lacking.

Pilgrimage to the Holy Land, or to the shrine of a god who was stranger to Christ, grew to be a great fad with the women of the West long before the fourth century. Females of every class of life undertook the long trip to Jerusalem and Bethlehem, if from no higher motive, because it offered movement, change of scene, escape from the dullness of household routine, from stagnation. Pilgrimage involved adventure with a capital A, danger real or fancied, masculine society—if only that of military guards and Egyptian monks—the ability to secure exotic talismans, amulets, and relics, and something to talk about all the rest of one's life. Paula writes from Palestine to St. Jerome: "The chief men of Gaul come hither, the Briton forsakes the setting sun and seeks the spot he knows by fame. Chrysostom says the whole world is coming to the manger, many traveling from the ends of the earth to see Job's dunghill in Arabia." Many women, like Silvia of Aquitaine, probably went unattended to Jerusalem as their modern sisters go to Paris, for no better reason than that they had been so picturesquely and alluringly warned against the trip. Gregory of Nyassa told women in no uncertain terms that every known species of impurity was dared in Jerusalem, that flagitious actions and adulteries and thefts and idolatries and witchcrafts and envyings and murders throve like swarming flies on carrion. Jerome described the sites of the Cross and the Resurrection as a city where are a curia, a garrison, harlots, actors, jesters, and other urban conveniences.[3]

In the post-houses along these routes slept civil and military authorities, hurrying to the frontier or returning on furlough. Over these roads passed colonials from Asturia in northwestern Spain, sons of the Nile Valley, Moors from Mauretania, recruits from Cyprus and distant Commagene —for these and a score of other provincial regiments derived from the empire anywhere between Britain and the Euphrates or the Sahara, were employed to police against the disturber that farflung district made up of Styria, Carinthia, Austria, and part of Carniola, which the Romans knew as Noricum.

These troops in the garrisoned armies of occupation carried with them their titular divinities, priests, and rituals, and, just as surely, their language with its colorful poetry and tales. There were thus transported to the Roman forts in Noricum, to be later carried into Gaul, the worship of Aphrodite of Paphos, the cult of Jupiter Dolichenus of Asia Minor, and the mysteries of Isis and of Serapis. Nor was this all, for the Great Mother of the Syrians had devotees along the upper Danube; the Persian Mithras confessed his followers in these outlying billets; and the influence that underlay his pretensions was so real that there is some warrant for Renan's view that it was an even wager whether the current of life as it flowed away into the Dark Ages should assume a Mithraic or a Christian tinge. For in the third century the old national religion of Rome lay stark in death and the only quickening cults were those of the Orient. The barbarian gods had taken the place of defunct immortals in the devotion of western pagans—they alone had empire over the occidental soul.

Let us suppose, says Cumont,[4] that in modern Europe the faithful had deserted the Christian churches to worship Allah or Brahma, to follow the precepts of Buddha or Confucius, or to adopt the maxims of the Shinto. Let us imagine a great confusion of all the races of the world in which Arabian mullahs, Chinese scholars, Japanese bonzes, Tibetan lamas, and Hindu pundits would be preaching fatalism and predestination, ancestor worship and devotion to a deified sovereign, pessimism and deliverance through annihilation—a confusion in which all those priests would erect temples of exotic architecture in our cities and celebrate their disparate rites therein. Such a dream would offer a fair picture of the religious chaos in which the ancient world was struggling before the reign of Constantine.

But why is it so important for the purpose of this book to emphasize the diffusion of these religious doctrines among the Gauls? Because the oriental reaction that we perceive so strongly at work in this province from the beginning of our era expressed itself, not alone in the religious sphere, but often with incomparably greater power in the domain of art, literature, and philosophy. In a certain way of truth, history is only the resultant of economic and social forces; and a preponderance in Gaul of oriental religions would indicate a growing industrial and cultural importance there of peoples from the Levant. It was not grain alone that Gaul bought in Egypt—she purchased men as well. She brought slaves from Phrygia, Cappadocia, Syria, and Alexandria to perform her menial and domestic tasks. Who may say what influence handmaidens from Antioch and Memphis came to exert over the minds of their mistresses? Conscripts who came to the army posts of Gaul from far eastern districts introduced their gods indeed, but also their folkways, customs, their codes of conduct.

At first blush the modern mind believes such a road to the East as the Danube post route to be the best possible means Rome could have devised to further the material side of her civilization. But we know this chain with the East was viewed with horror by the conservative party, which was devoted to the retention of old Roman thought and manners, the party whose ideas were stubbornly opposed to imperial rule although they were powerless to check it. Without being told, these conservatives realized that the ancient national character of Italy was being changed, that traditional beliefs were being destroyed by the influx of provincial ideals of life and manners. Verily in their eyes was the Orontes pouring its waters into the Tiber—Syrian and Greek "vices" were incontrovertibly coming to hold the place of Roman "virtues." And so far as these conservatives could see, their judgment was sound. For, due to the penetration of the West by oriental culture, they were witnessing the first strong lifting tide of a renaissance beside which the vaunted Risorgimento of fifteen hundred years later, with its rediscovery of classical culture, was to prove a comparatively slight affair. This first renaissance, which followed hard on the heels of Augustan orientalism and was partly the effect of it, is often only dimly sensed because it did not somehow leave in its wake a complete overturn of the human spirit—as if this spirit were an omelet! Nor was this renaissance either thorough or final, since its colporteurs were like as not the barbarian, the slave, and the humble foreigner or mercenary; since, too, of the four or five civilizations of the unknown East which it might have assimilated, only one typically oriental culture, the Hebraic, and particularly in its garbled Christian form, was actually absorbed by Rome during all the days of the empire. With the Levantine and southeastern treasures on the near horizon of her experience, Rome miserably failed consciously either to plumb or to plunder them, and as a result went to meet the Middle Ages with her moral life centering about a collection of Palestinian writings.

But although Rome and her colonies stood only in the vestibule, although the vast storehouses of Asiatic nurture were scarcely opened to them, enough in the way of oriental influence had occurred to cause profound changes in their ideas regarding the world and life, to disturb their opinions of the very nature of essential realities, to widen the range of their imagination, and to double the keyboard of their emotional sensibilities. Let us study the result of this in the culture that Goths brought west to Gaul.

Strzygowski believes there are two distinct currents in the development of early Christian art in Gaul—an older Hellenic influence that is revived with the entrance of the Visigoths into Gaul, and a Roman influence which begins with the Christianizing of the Franks.[5] Characteristic of the first current is the plenitude of vaulted architectural forms still visible in the main structure of certain Gaulish and Spanish churches, surviving most clearly in San Pedro de Nave. The second stream, the Roman(esque) art of construction, is perhaps merely a grafting on the first, for it makes definite, though not necessarily dominant, use of the Visigothic system of vaulted arching.

In connection with Gothic influence during the Franco-Roman period that begins in the late fifth century, too little attention is apt to be paid to a circumstance which helps explain the validity of the later use of the term Gothic in architecture. In the days of Gothic rule in Italy under Theodoric, the monuments of Rome get their first adequate protection, and an efflorescence of all the arts sets in at Ravenna.[6] Now all this can scarcely be accredited to the influence of a single man, even if that man be a very great king—nor should it be carelessly ascribed to Theodoric's sojourn in Byzantium, nor to the suggestions of Greek and Roman officials at his court. It is more likely that we see in this burgeoning of the arts as definite a result of the upward march of Gothic culture during the "period of captivity" by the Black Sea, as ever we do in the Bible of Ulfilas.

It is certain that the Visigoths in southern Gaul and Spain were at least the continuators of a special manner of quarrying and cutting stone (modern ashlar or squared stone), and that they continued this craft through the Merovingian days into the tenth century, as passages from Venantius, Gregory of Tours, and the *Life of St. Audeonius* prove. This technic of cutting and of cupola building is curiously reminiscent of Armenian practice—it cannot be indigenous to Gaul, for the natives were addicted to rubblestone and straight lines in bearing surfaces. It will doubtless long remain a moot question whether the Goths learned their peculiar style of construction with monumental material in Gaul from Greek architects, or brought their art from the East, where they had got it from Armenians or other folk in Asia Minor. But there is one alien form—the horseshoe arch—which appears in pre-Islamic days in Spain and during the Carolingian rule in Switzerland and on the Loire, that can best be explained as an Armenian (or Asia Minor) contribution to Gaulish art introduced by the Goths.

Perhaps it would be better to divide the Hellenistic influence on the plastic arts in Gaul before the time of Frankish domination into two currents: the first of which embraces the southern impulses from Alexandria and Antioch; the second of which appears in the train of the Goths and originates in Armenia and Asia Minor. The clearest survivals of both influences do not occur until Carolingian times—the cathedrals at Aix and St. Vitale being evident copies of the lost Octagon of Constantine the Great in Antioch—and Germigny-des-Pres being a most typical representative of the Armenian style of Bagaran, and therefore a shining example of the northern form with which the Goths came in contact on their long land-journey over to Gaul.[7]

A most interesting spot, this Aquileja and the Friuli region north of it, where Gothic hordes hesitated before taking up the last lap of their interminable progress towards the western stars. Far from separating the German north and the Romanic south with its Alpine wall, this borderland facilitated their acquaintanceship and opened wide an avenue by which the philosophy and the literature of the East might invade the Occident. Here in the fifth century shortly after the death of Attila, came on his way to Vienne that holiest servant of God, St. Severinus, bringing from Egypt the orthodoxy preached by St. Anthony and Athanasius—whereas there had dwelt there for two generations before his arrival Gothic missionaries spreading the Arian faith of their great master Ulfilas. What the Aquilejans said about the Christ that is *homoousian* and the Other that is *homoiousian*, we shall never know, but it was just such missionaries that introduced into the Merovingian realm the parchment manuscripts containing illuminated chapter-initials in the shapes of birds and fish, which began a fashion that was continued for centuries with equal zeal by Gauls, Armenians, and Copts.

The one greatest lesson that we learn from a study of trade routes such as those which converged in Aquileja is that we often do not need to consider Rome and Italy as intermediaries between eastern culture and the western provinces. Now it is true, of course, that not all of the carriers of Asiatic and African influences swept northward (as to Augsburg and Carnutum) by way of Aquileja—for a great many of them wandered up the Danube valley from the Euxine. They followed the Danube path as it had been trodden towards the setting sun long centuries before the coming of Christ—for the Romans had developed and patrolled a system of frontier posts and fortifications from the head of navigation on this river down to Tomi in Mœsia (where Ovid once penned his *Tristia ex Ponto* and said harsh things about the Goths). This *via Danubii* was an unflagging highway of commerce; along it there plodded the Syrian trader and the Jewish merchant, and a host of dark-skinned Asiatics from Armenia, Persia, and the lands that bordered the Black Sea—with goods and ideas for sale. The valley of the Lower Danube must have been a veritable melting pot of civilizing forces at least as late as the tenth century of our era. For one invasion and migration follows hard on the heels of another—and whether the tribe involved were German, Slav, Hun, Avar, Bulgar, or Magyar, it at least had vivid contact with Byzantium on the one side, and Rome and Carolingian France on the other. For example, our old friends the Goths had touch with the Latins, the Greeks, the Slavs, and the Huns; they became Christians. They were so influential at the court of Theodosius that they became the arbiters of fashion in sophisticated Byzantium. Their language left its imprint on certain Slavic dialects. Their missionaries converted many tribes to Arianism. When they were overcome by the Huns, they still dominated their physical masters by their superior culture. They migrated to western Europe to avoid annihilation—and as a consequence Italy and Spain became Gothic peninsulas. Their influence, either reaching out from Italy or up from the mouth of the Danube, made itself deeply felt in Bavaria and Salzburg.

Now as the Goths were moving westward, their place along the Lower Danube was filled by Slavs, Avars, and Bulgars. These peoples in turn harrassed the Byzantine empire, besieged Constantinople and Saloniki, clashed with the Persians in Asia Minor, invaded the coasts of the Ægean, and fought with the Greeks and the Franks. And as their intimacy with Byzantium grew—especially that of the Slavs and the Bulgars—Hellenistic ideas filtered into their land and swayed their literature, religion, court etiquette, and commercial methods. After the rout of the Avars by Charles the Great, the Bulgars became neighbors of the Carolingian empire on the west, while in the east their rule prevailed to the walls of Constantinople. Throughout the ninth century, intercourse, both hostile and otherwise, between Bulgars and Franks was so constant that it is difficult to doubt their mutual cultural exchanges in the century that followed the death of Charles. By the middle of the tenth century the country of the Bulgars had become a hotbed of religious activity, and King Boris was between the devil and the deep sea—for he did not know whether to turn to Byzantium and adopt the orthodox faith for his people and himself, or to enter the fold of the Bishop of Rome and thereby attach himself definitely to the western empire. For a while Boris decided in favor of the Greek church, but he soon severed this connection and admitted bishops that were sent to his land by Pope Nicholas I. At the time when the king was attempting to find a satisfactory solution for his religious scruples, his country was invaded by Mohammedan missionaries—Passau and Salzburg had sent preachers into Pannonia and Moravia; and doubtless there were everywhere in Bulgaria representatives of the western church. Jews were active there, as well as Monophysites from Armenia, and Paulikians from Asia Minor; and naturally the bishops of the Greek church were not idle. Just as in the fourth century Mœsia had been the intermediary of oriental and occidental Christianity, so now in the ninth century East and West again meet in the Danube valley, in order to win the Bulgars for Christ or Allah, for pope or patriarch, for Jahweh or for what later developed into the creed of the Bogomils.

Geographical perspectives and historical occasion again combine in the ninth century, as they did five hundred years and more before, to make of the region occupied by the Bulgars an economic and social clearing-house between Gaul and Germany on the one hand, on the other the realm of Byzantium. Eastern artistic influences were as strongly at work as ever at the doors of western Europe—only this time it was the Franks, and not the Goths, who were chiefly responsible for the transmission of manner and idea, tales and legends which we shall find they carried back through and from the Bulgars to Austrian and Bavarian cloisters—and it seems also to be they who not only revived the Platonic ideal of friendship in strictly literary form but who made the greatest individual contribution to medieval poetry (not even excepting the Arthur stories) by the introduction of the courtly and chivalric ideal of love.

Any further discussion of the matters mentioned in this last paragraph, however, would not be pertinent to the growth of my argument at this point—for they belong to the superstructure of medieval literature and not to its bases. I reserve them therefore for a later survey. In fact, I have been led to carry my history of the ancient Mœsian district as far as I have done, and thus somewhat anticipate my later presentation, because, until the end of the tale of Asiatic and Gaulish (German) mergings has been brought in this Danube region to its definite end, there are few who could believe the deep and full import that this Mongolian-Slav state of the Balkan Peninsula came to have for western poetry and art. For in this realm one of the rarest and most difficult mergers in history became an accomplished fact: the union of white and yellow races. After two hundred years of living side by side with their Slavic subjects, the Bulgars gave up their language and customs and intermarried freely with the conquered race, soon thereafter becoming indistinguishable from them. The Bulgar state, though Asiatic in origin and institutions, thus became essentially a Slav realm. From about the middle of the ninth century therefore we must dismiss thinking of their Mongolian descent and regard the Bulgars as a Slav people with a not unimportant Asiatic strain. Exactly what the social and intellectual significance of the Mongolian contribution to Bulgar nationality was, there is of course no means of telling, but so far as literary history is concerned I feel warranted in saying that I believe this contribution was not only a broad but a vital one in western development.

If this prophetic remark prove but half as true as I think it will, in the light of investigation already well under way among ethnologists and students of the origins of plastic art, then we shall finally come to a far better understanding of what is called a tribal migration or an invasion. Then we shall no longer group together as agencies of destruction and disaster two very different things: (1) the permanent new settlements of hostile foreign tribes in a conquered country, and (2) merely passing storms of conquest which disrupt and uproot. Thus a differentiation will be established between (1) infiltrations such as those of the Slavs in the Balkans or of the Germans in Gaul, and (2) the invasions of Attila or the series of forays by Asiatic nomads of the yellow race that followed in the Hun's wake. The conquests of Attila, which had grown like a snowball, melted away like one—and the Huns themselves, the scourge and terror of their age, vanished from history as mysteriously as they had entered it; whereas the Slavs and the Germans became a permanent element in the racial evolution of the Balkans and of Gaul. Of both peoples it may summarily be said that, sound of limb and mind, though backward in artistic experience, they served in their respective areas as forces of destruction, only with the slow passing of the years to become significant and invaluable instruments of social and artistic rebirth.

When all is said and done, the tribal migrations (like the Crusades) remain a perpetually astonishing act in the great drama of life. In the words of Barker, they touched the summits of daring and devotion, if they also sank into the abysms of shame. In all of them lurked motives of self-interest—worldly desire for the achievement of riches and the acquisition of lands at a little price. Yet it would be treason to the majesty of man's incessant struggle towards an ideal goal, if we were to deny that in the migrations men strove to extend the kingdom of their ideas upon the earth. Humanity is not only richer for the memory of those millions of wandering men forever treading western roads; but we should never call those ages dark which brought the early medieval world into living contact with new faiths and institutions.[8]

Nor should we feel that a time was unillumined when, as in Gaul even in the earliest days of our era, there was so thorough a system of education in process that, despite the very large importation of all sorts of immigrants into her borders, the total number of Gaulish illiterates cannot have been excessive. We do not have much actual information about elementary education in Gaul except that it was by no means neglected. We know more, however, about the higher schools or universities that flourished in Lyons and Treves, Marseilles and Autun from the days of Augustus on. The institutions of the last two cities held the front rank. Although its prime was long past, Marseilles remained the greatest focus of Greek learning in the western world, and here sons of the famous Roman families, as well as the scions of influential Gauls, could obtain the same instruction as in Athens, with the added advantage of cheapness, nearness to home altars, and an atmosphere decidedly less immoral.

The cleverest writer in extant Greek literature (unless he find a peer in Aristophanes), Lucian of Samosata in Commagene, spent some years between 145 and 155 A.D. in Marseilles. Lucian was a Syrian with a love for sculpture, which he laid aside to become one of the best art critics of antiquity. His family was bitterly poor and so, to make a living, he studied Greek and launched himself as a rhetorician. This study made a Greek of me, he says, went with me from town to town in Hellas and Ionia, sailed the sea with me even as far as Gaul, never failing to scatter plenty in my path. For I was one of those professors who could command high fees, and I made a good living in Gaul.

Let us examine at close range this university lecturer, for, although one cannot assume he was companioned on Gaulish rostra by colleagues of like genius, yet we know he differed from his fellow rhetors only in degree and not in kind. We find him reviving an old type of teaching in his classroom talks as well as establishing a new type of literature in his dialogues. His characters talk, Glover tells us, as men may talk of their affairs when they are not conscious of being overheard—with a naive frankness not always very wise, but with a freedom and common sense and sometimes with a folly that together reveal the speaker. The dialogue is slight and easy and flickers about from one idea to another, but it conveys the strong impression of reality. Lucian's skill is amazing. He will take an episode from Homer and change no single detail; and yet as we listen to the offhand chatter of the gods we are startled by its effect—irony is everywhere and nowhere; surprises are irresistible; the frankness of the gentlemen of heaven compels us; they become astonishingly human, bourgeois even. We may safely count upon Lucian's popularity as a professor at the university of Marseilles, so far as the student body is concerned.

Nor was this school famous alone for its humanistic branches. Bloch recalls that its scientific tradition was one of its chief glories; although it no longer produced astronomers and geographers as in the days of Pytheas, it still graduated physicians who were illustrious and accumulated great wealth. One of them in the days of Nero was rich enough to pay for restoring the city walls that had been leveled in a siege not long before.

The picture I am drawing of teaching in Gaul comports badly with that offered from a later age by Julian, Lavisse, and Roger. In order to give my seeming opponents their place I present the summary of this matter as stated by the last-named of the trio in his history of the teaching of classical literature from Ausonius to Alcuin. Roger says: "We have been present at the decadence of Roman teaching; we have seen Sidonius appear after Ausonius, have seen Gregory of Tours follow Sidonius. This march of ignorance first caused some regrets, but then came resignation, and finally forgetfulness. After having sheltered the remains of culture and furnished the last learned men in Gaul from its ranks, the church allowed its interest to be drawn away from the teaching of the classics. Laying aside their fears for the outcome, the Church Fathers, it is true, had declared the study of liberal arts indispensable to the understanding of sacred writ; but events had rendered vain their efforts in this regard. Two centuries of invasion and tumult had brought about the result sighed for by the first monks of the West. They dreaded the reading of pagan authors—the pagan poets were forsaken and the world almost forgot their existence. Ignorance grew rapidly to be a greater ignorance; the mass of humanity showed itself empty of all desire for knowledge. Night fell. After one or two centuries of darkness, the teaching of ancient literature reappeared in Gaul. What center of studies had survived? What Gallo-Roman families had preserved from father to son the discipline of the Roman schools, as if by miracle, in the midst of continual tempest? Not one of them. But at least, you will guess, it was some Roman clerk or other, some distant disciple of Cassiodorus sprung from a monastery where the precious trust of antique tradition had been guarded? Again, the answer is no. The teachers who with the authority of Charles the Great toiled to reinstate literature in Gaul came from Ireland and Britain. Irishmen who had never known Rome, Anglo-Saxons resting on the ruins of an imperial province—these it was who brought back the Roman university."

However the details of the latter half of the story of teaching in Gaul may differ in my version of it and in that of Roger, the narratives reach the same happy conclusion in the Carolingian age. And I think it more germane to the evidence I have been thus far gathering from the several realms of culture in the "dark" centuries in western Europe not to draw down upon its schools the final curtain of disillusionment and oblivion in a phrase: *la nuit se fait.* And after all, the difference between Roger's way and mine is not so wide as the arc of the sky—I but leave a little more in the seventh century on which the (Roger's!) Irish monks may build.

So we end our chapter with the portals of the Gaulish schools gaping wide in welcome to youthful westerners and present a last bouquet of evidence. In the second century Rheims is more than once glossed as another Athens, and Treves, particularly when it was the thriving capital of the Cæsars, had aspirations to achieve intellectual supremacy. Lyons entertained a successful college of the liberal arts that was famous abroad, and not without reason. But it was after all Autun which the Gauls appear most to have esteemed as a great national university, the Oxford or the Harvard of its day. A happy chance informs us that its classrooms were crowded as early as 21 A.D., and while we hear no more as to its fortunes until the second half of the third century, when its beautiful buildings fell a prey to flames kindled by civil war, yet we know that it recovered its prestige somewhat at least, since at the end of the third century an emperor appoints one of his secretaries, the rhetorician Eumenius, to be its president with a salary of thirty thousand dollars a year. Unfortunately for Eumenius a debased coinage reduced the value of his income to about a tenth of its nominal figure.

It is, however, in Aquitaine that one finds the most advantageous region for classical learning and study. For, says Bloch, the sounds of war that rang across Belgium and the Lyons territory echo but feebly here. Its profound peace, its uninterrupted leisure, the inviolate riches of its fields and cities marked it out as the last refuge in the West for ancient learning. The happy genius of its people did the rest, and the reputation of its rhetoricians became so great that it supplied them to Italy and the East. St. Jerome assigns them a place in his chronicle, and Symmachus, the most illustrious representative of Latin eloquence at the end of the fourth century, tells us in glowing words how deep was the debt he owed to their lessons.

To understand the antagonism that existed during the last centuries of paganism between the new religion and the old education, we must recall that most men believed the old education and culture were inseparable from the ancient form of devotion and ceremonial. In the minds of Christians and pagans alike, the fall of the one tradition meant the fall of the other. All the literary material which formed the basis of study in the parent universities of the East and their successors in the West was drawn from ancient life and history—all the associations of literature and art were connected with ancient religion and worship. So to the reasonable sophist Christ might seem to be one who in an evil hour burst in upon us like a drunken reveler.

Upon the accession of Julian the Apostate altars took again their wonted blood, smoke rolled heavenward the savor of the sacrifice, gods were honored with festivals, divination recovered its license, Roman men took heart, the barbarians were hurled back or threatened with defeat, and—Rhetoric regained the respect of humanity. Immediately on the death of Julian (363) the study of rhetoric began rapidly to decline, at least in its accustomed seats.[9]

We are to see in a subsequent chapter the direct importance that the study ôf rhetoric had for the development of Romanesque poetry and at this point are little concerned with the question of its maintenance or its desuetude as a specifically university discipline either in the East or the West. But it was just at this time, when the study of rhetoric was falling into academic disfavor and was becoming more and more a matter of technical detail, that the schools again prepared an offering that was to be of vast import to the development of Romanesque poetry, one that furnishes us with a master-key to much in this body of verse that would otherwise be unintelligible. I mean of course neo-Platonism.

This system, which pretended to be simply a development of the ideas contained in the writings of Plato, was, as a matter of fact, composed of elements of Platonism and oriental beliefs, and in its later stages was influenced by Gnosticism and Christianity.[10] The doctrine was started in Alexandria but established in the last half of the third century at Rome. In the fourth and fifth centuries neo-Platonism gathered within itself most of the philosophy of the age, and came to be a religion as well; for, as we might expect, all those who were opposed to Christianity and were attached to the old culture and education and traditions arrayed themselves on the side of this faith.

Chapter III

MEROVINGIAN GAUL

I suppose Haskins is right when he asserts that unity of life and ideas came to an end in the West with the Germanic invasions, and in the region of the Mediterranean with the Saracen conquests.[1] For it is certain that from then forward, localism is written large across the Europe of the early Middle Ages; also that ideas and information spread but slowly and against great resistance from one district to another. Happily, Haskins proceeds to state that the spread of ideas in these ages is only in part a history of slow diffusing through the resisting medium of local habit and custom. It is chiefly concerned with the relations of scattered centers of another sort, stations of high tension communicating with other stations of the same type with comparatively little reference to distance or the nature of the intervening space. Such centers, representing different social strata, Haskins finds to have consisted chiefly of monasteries and cathedrals, courts, towns, and universities.

Because, however, the last century of the western empire forms the turning point in the story of Gallo-Roman poetry and art, no effort we may reasonably put forth to synthesize its bases of culture should be regarded as spendthrift toil. For if Latin poetry on Gaulish soil survive the reputed rough handling of Gothic and Frankish invasion, then it will indeed endure to be the cornerstone in the building of Carolingian renascence. Otherwise we shall be forced to view the latter either as an importation from outside the theater of its activity (which is a little absurd), or a sheer creation of the clarifying barbarian intelligence in Gaul (which is somehow unsatisfactory).

Let us see, therefore, in how far we may assume the German conquerors to have been strangers to that Roman civilization which seemingly they caused to totter and almost upset. Let us discover in what degree they were really hostile or unreceptive to the ideas which had long prevailed in Gaul. It will consume no great space to give in outline a picture of that occupation of provincial western empire by German peoples which is the salient feature of European history in the fifth century. And unless we go back of this period somewhat and study the origins and earlier history of the German nations presumptively involved in the Gaulish debâcle, we can hardly hope to attain the perspective needful for an estimate of their share in the dissolution of Roman art and culture.

It is believed that the Germans included in the movement ordinarily called tribal migrations, had originally lived in the Scandinavian peninsula but had passed during the first millennium before Christ to their home on the Baltic coast in the plain between the Elbe and Vistula. Little was known by the Romans of these East Germanic peoples—Goths, Vandals, Burgundians, Lombards—prior to the second century B. C., when they first came into conflict with the empire.

By this time it was no doubt a long-established custom for the Goths to undertake that Dnieper journey southward to the Black Sea and Bosporus, which Constantine Porphyrogenitus (A.D. 950) describes in his chapter on the Swedes who come in their boats from Russia to Constantinople. I conjecture the trip from Novgorod onwards was no new thing for Goths and their related tribes in the second century for three reasons.

First, it is no unknown objective that lures confederated nations permanently away from settled homesteads. Enormous and well-devised preparations must be made, based upon the most specific knowledge of natural obstacles to be overcome. For instance, the Dnieper forms for a distance of about fifty miles from a little below the modern town of Yekaterinoslav a long series of rapids—and, as Thomsen[2] tells us, it is not alone their natural conformation that makes the passage of these seven *porogi* dangerous, but their neighborhood was always infested by tribes of plundering nomads, ready to take advantage of the least carelessness on the part of the traveler. When whole nations journey one or two thousand miles away from their original base of supplies, through hostile tribes where every unexpected turn presents new danger, they must plan carefully on communication and subsistence.

Second, a reason that argues long preknowledge of the South on the part of the Goths and their allies is that we find in Finnish dialects east of the Baltic Sea and its gulfs remains of a Gothic idiom older in form than that of fourth-century Ulfilas. Now when we know that the people speaking this idiom in the third century of our era were successfully beginning to drive a Balkan wedge of Gothia between the eastern and western Latin empire, it looks as if they must have known their business well for a long previous period.

Third, prehistoric survivals of various sorts evidence an unexpectedly early connection (during the Stone and Bronze ages) between west Baltic and Russian art-culture, which continued of course down into the succeeding Iron Age. Under the conditions, it is unthinkable that the original impulse of this culture should be otherwise than in the west Baltic region.

The purpose of this inquiry into the background of early experience of East German peoples is evident, for unless we accept the evidence given us through an investigation of their social past previous to their meeting with Greece and Rome, we are forced to look at invading nations through the jaundiced eyes and the biased testimonies of their opponents—which is largely a futile thing to do. We know infinitely more about the prehistory of the Goths than did the early medieval chroniclers before Cassiodorus and Jordanes, for archæology and philology have taught us much, and these, our older-fashioned informants, have had nothing to teach us except rumor and fable. And it is important to know, before we make up our minds regarding the peoples who are in the most direct sense our spiritual ancestors, what manner of human beings they were. Barbarians they were, of course, in many or most of the superficial manifestations of life when contrasted with Roman incandescence. But were they blind to, inept for, the deeper issues of thought and feeling that make for regeneration? It seems to me the answer is clear enough.

When the Goths and their confederates first clashed with the South and East, an ancient civilization (in the words of Ferrero) had for ten centuries been untiringly at work to create a state that would be perfect and wise, human and generous, free and just. This consummate institution had been the supreme ambition of both Greece and Rome. For a myriad years soldiers, statesmen, and orators had given their best powers to this egregious task—philosophers, poets, and artists had collaborated in this creative work. And how in the third century did this sustained effort of genius culminate? In anarchy brought about by the corrupt despotism of brute force despoiled of moral authority. In the violent destruction of a most refined life. In the obligation of kneeling before an Asiatic sovereign as before a living god. In Mithra.

In the face of so ignominious a bondage, so utter a despair—who knew how to cope with this catastrophe, annihilate the whole conception of ancient life; how to rescue what treasures remained to be saved; how to prepare the ground for the most audacious, the most original spiritual revolution the earth has ever seen? There is but one answer: it was the German barbarian after he had been warmed and lightened by Christianity. Whatever the modern mind may think of the kind of instrument chosen to accomplish the task of revival, this making of Baltic Goth and Salian Frank the western fishers of Galilee—they were none the less the historical means of it.[3]

We have already seen how influential were Visigoths in fourth and fifth-century Gaul as carriers there of eastern art, and later we shall meet many further instances of their intellectual transcendence in medieval western life. During migration times the Bosporian kingdom of the Goths acted as a vent through which spiritual and practical goods of every sort came to the western world of Gaul and Germany. In great wavelike movements a stream of cultural influence flows from southeastern Europe towards the northwest, and this very Gothic current is only one in a long succession of such irrigations. The most seductive thing about this theory of the source and progress of early Gaulish and Germanic culture is that practically every field of investigation (archæology, history of art, runology, science of religion, literary history, linguistics) leads us to an acknowledgment of the dominant role played by the Goths, and of the existence of a head source in their realm.

We have known for a long time that the *Song of Hildebrand* and its type of dramatic ballad were no folk-song. This is no writing derived from roughly hewn minstrelsy of the communal brand. It is artistic poetry of an upper caste, the product of an advanced culture which finds its chief expression in heroic balladry and is the derivative of a society which would fain live and judge by the sword.[4] The *Song of Hildebrand* is a bit of court literature of a soldier race whose horizon has been measurably opened by contact with foreign peoples and novel associations. In the oldest historic Germanic period Roman influence, proceeding from the provinces on the Danube and the Rhine, was in many ways of lasting importance: the building of houses, care of gardens, cultivation of the soil. But apparently in matters of the spirit this influence was of small effect. During the later migration time the Roman influence is side-tracked by the Gothic transmission of civilization which seems to have possessed a much deeper psychological result. After the Goths disappear, the Franks become the real enunciators of this Gothic influence—and so Gaul grows to be the originating source of this culture, as once the Pontine region was. And Gaul continues this task until Gothic tradition dies out entirely among the West Germans through the hegemony of Romance notions and ideals.

In the light of our present knowledge it is not possible longer to regard the period from Tacitus to Charles the Great as a unified one in the story of the development of the human mind. To protect such a view one is forced to make uncritical use of random testimonies (whether from first or eighth century) and move them rather arbitrarily about on the chessboard. It was during the latter half of this age of migration that a new type of poetry grew up among the Bosporian Goths, together with a caste of poets and minstrels of which Tacitus had no cognizance. We should no longer cherish fond illusions regarding the older Germanic age; but the epoch during and following the migration period we must consider one of efflorescence, as Wilhelm Scherer was keen enough to suspect fifty years ago. The heroic balladry of this stirred Gothic civilization, in its characters and its themes, envisions the vast theater of migration from the lush meadows of the Dnieper to the red cliffs of the Rhine.

Naumann asserts that even the Nordic sphere of poetry merely presents to us in a thousand different variants the older south-Germanic center of diffusion. Any individual value this northern balladry may possess dwindles before the fact that it is both echo and mirror of what was achieved centuries earlier by southern clans. The best of the Eddic balladry is no indigenous growth of Icelandic or peninsular Scandinavian singing—it is but a copy, a translation, at best an adaptation, of originals created among the Goths and Franks. These ballads were conceived, born, and nourished in the southland,[5] and there they remained until new fashions came, until they were first crowded aside, and then forgotten of men. But the northland, to which they had slowly mounted, managed to retain them long enough to insure their preservation for all time to come.

It required more than fifteen centuries for runic script to outlive the period of its usefulness, from the time of its first slow march northward to that moment, almost in our own day, when it was finally driven from its last Scandinavian stronghold. Sometimes a development has reached its full maturity in the North alone, as did animal ornamentation when it attained the so-called third type, as did Germanic poetry in skaldic technique. The South, which of course included both these developments in its art, never managed to bring them to full utterance because it was Romanicized. In the realm of religion, too, the sublimated picture of the Asen and of world destruction appears but the final evolution in the northern territory of what the South, which was familiar with all the seeds of the doctrine, could no longer bring to fruition. To us, therefore, the value of Old Norse is a double one: it is a preserver, and besides this, a preserver in which the processes of things it has retained develop further according to their own inherent laws.

Now a main reason why critics have not earlier apprehended the importance of Gothic contributions to culture is doubtless because this Bosporian nation, in common with other Eastern Germans who founded kingdoms on imperial soil, left no permanent state behind them. It is a remarkable fact that not one of the East German political fabrics was permanent. Vandals, Visigoths, Ostrogoths, Gepids, all passed away and were clean forgotten—"oblivion," says Sir Thomas Browne aptly, "is a kind of annihilation; and for things to be as though they had not been is like unto never being." We recall Burgundians and Lombards only because of minor geographical names. Bury reminds us that the only Germans who on Roman territory created states destined to endure were the Saxons in England and the Franks in Gaul and Germany. And these tribes both belonged to the west-Germanic group.[6]

The dismemberment of Gaul, Bury continues, would have been a far more violent process except for a gradual change wrought in the third and fourth centuries by the infiltration of Germanic elements into that province. It must be remembered that the western fringe of Germany had already been more than halfway won to the cause of civilization, while other parts could no longer be as savage and unrepentant as the picturesque phrase of Velleius would indicate: *in summa feritate versutissimi natusque mendacio genus*. Rome had already applied its patient and irresistible energy to the districts along the Rhine; and from as early as the second decade of the Christian Era two frontier Roman Germanies on this river were incorporated with Belgic Gaul and administered from Treves and Rheims—Cologne, Mainz, and Treves were German towns.

Besides this, many Germans had been colonized as farmers in the unsettled wastes of Gaul even before the days of Marcus Aurelius; and in the reign of this emperor much vaster masses of German landholders had been admitted into the province, where broad acres were turned over to them in return for stipulated terms of service. If from our memory of Cæsar's experience in Germany we are surprised to confront the German in the rôle of farmer, we must be reminded that a change had come over the spirit of his dreams. Because of the scarcity of laborers of the soil in Gaul and elsewhere in the empire, as early as the second century agriculture had begun to fall into disuse. Now while this was going forward in Gaul, and broad ranges sparsely settled by herders of flocks were there replacing cornfields and vineyards, in the western part of Germany one piece of waste land after another was cleared and placed under cultivation. Of course it was the work of centuries to win finally for the yielding of profitable crops all the swamps and rock-strewn valleys which, because of their primitive methods of tilling, had at first appeared unfit for farming purposes. But wherever the soil did not offer too stout a resistance to simple tools, the Germans soon learned to devote every acre not needed for pasturage to the plow.

Seeck recalls to us that Julius Cæsar had been forced to end his campaigns against the Swabians because he could not get adequate forage for his legions from the lean crops of their fields; but it was not later than the second century that the hostile terrain of Germany offered plentiful grain supplies for the Romans across both Rhine and Danube. Even in the days of Augustus, the only tribute that could successfully be collected from the Frisians was cowhides and sheepskins; but when towards the close of the second century, Commodus granted peace to the Marcomanni he demanded and got from them the payment of an annual tax in corn. It was not long thereafter that Germans were beginning to abandon their poverty-stricken huts and building extensive country houses after the plans of Gallo-Roman architects.[7]

It is not Seeck's belief, however, that this astonishing advance in welfare made by the German peoples was due to their overcoming of that ingrained indolence in the pursuit of the arts of peace which Tacitus stresses. They were able to achieve so notable a progress in culture in so short a space of time only because they set to work in the fields the immense hordes of slaves they captured as booty in their raids. As the Romans kept on walling up the Germans within ever narrowing limits, more intensive work than usual was required to gain sustenance from the soil. Thus the Germans began to think less of cattle as a mainstay of plunder in foray and neighborhood feud, and paid more attention to human flesh. They no longer murdered prisoners won in the course of war, but set them to work creating food supplies.

In many of the frontier districts of Gaul, the population became chiefly German—as was to be expected since the army along the borderlands was more and more recruited from this race—but the cities everywhere in the interior of the province came (much sooner than one might think possible) to hold large colonies of German inhabitants: Batavians in Arras, Franks in Rennes, Swabians in Coutances, Mans, Bayeux, and Auvergne—Sarmatians in Paris, Poitiers, and Amiens. Everywhere these intruders seem to have been accepted on an equal footing as more or less friendly neighbors.

In the second century German influence in Gaul is not especially visible, but all during the following hundred years we find the German element insidiously seeping in from every hand like water through the opening seams of a leaky vessel —in fact, at no moment after Marcus Aurelius emancipated the captive barbarian warriors on Roman soil was there the least doubt as to the outcome of this peaceful economic invasion on the part of the German. From the time of Constantine this alien ingredient in Gaul began to rise to the top, and we can tell how high the barbarian star is in the ascendant by the adoption in the legions of German customs. We find in this period a Gaul flooded by Germans, not only in the army, plowing and sowing for Gallo-Roman masters, and maintaining their huge colonies of tradespeople in the towns, but servants in every wealthy household, acting as stewards, butlers, bakers, and personal attendants. Marriages of any sort by even the most menial barbarians were looked upon with favor and rendered easy by the provincial government, in case they promised progeny: farmer fodder and soldier fodder; men at any reasonable cost—but at least men. Such an attitude on the part of the state made for the quick denationalization of Germans in Gaul; two generations at most made (in the third as in the twentieth century) a German in Gaul a Gallo-Roman half ashamed, or half-forgetful, of his birthright.

Many of the German officers and politicians were (as we know) men of great talents and polished address. As the old-time exclusiveness disappeared towards the end of the empire, consulships and even the imperial purple were bestowed again and again on men of the humblest German origin. Long before its distant outworks were stormed, says Dill, Germans had stolen their way into the very citadel of the empire. One of the most amusing, as well as the most trenchant, signs of the great social influence of Germans at the close of the fourth century is the edict of Honorius (in 397) forbidding the wearing of trousers, long hair, and fur coats of barbarian cut within the precincts of Rome.[8] The thought that Germans were setting the fashion in toilet and dress for the gay world of Italy and Gaul before as well as after the Goths and Vandals and other tribes swept the province—this is a fact to ponder. An edict in 416 by the same Honorius in the same tone as the one twenty years before, shows that the first prohibition regarding dress had been disregarded. A Gallo-Roman, even after the scenes of 410, would have smiled at the thought that the empire was in serious danger from the Germans. If this statement appear curious to my adult and thoughtful reader, let him compare his own thoughts along similar lines previous to a very day in the year 1914 with those of some arithmetical ancestor of his fifteen hundred years before.

Dalton has drawn for us from the letters of Apollinaris Sidonius a picture of the life on a Gaulish estate during this period. Here it is: The nobleman has his town house and his country villa, the latter with its large establishment of slaves, its elaborate baths, and all the amenities of country existence as understood by Gallo-Roman civilization. In his well-stocked library your gentleman reads his favorite authors, writes himself down in verse and prose, or maintains a continual correspondence with friends of equal wealth and leisure. For diversion, he hunts and fishes, or rides abroad to visit his neighbors. If interested in the development of his land, he goes around the estate, watches the work in progress, and is present at harvest or vintage. In other words, the man of birth and culture in the fifth century—despite German invasion and conquest—leads in

Gaul the life of a landed proprietor in a country at profound peace, where soldiers appear to be neither seen nor thought of, and where the only sense of insecurity arises from the presence of native bandits and highwaymen on the lonelier roads. But for the seeming predominance of literary over sporting interests, says Dalton, we might be reading of the life in English shires during the reign of the Georges, when the carriages of nobles were stopped by highwaymen on Bagshot Heath. And such was the state of affairs, according to the best of testimonies, after the Visigoths had been established half a century in Aquitaine, after the Burgundians were settled along the Rhone, after the Franks had long been pressing on such territory in northern Gaul as still retained even the shadow of imperial authority.[9]

But if the change from Gallo-Roman to Visigothic or Frankish citizenship implied for the noblemen at best a comparative loss of acreage and income, how was it that the possibility of such a change of masters seemed to have had no terrors for the majority of the population? This is reasonably explained by the fact that, as Dalton asserts, the small landowners and townsmen had suffered to such an extent from maladministration in the past, that they regarded the future with indifference—and so far as the lower classes generally might judge from the fate of their fellows who had already passed under German sway, a change in government held out for them the possibility of actual gain. It was the good fortune of central and southern Gaul that the two peoples who fell heir to the Roman legacy were the best type of conquering German. The Visigoths, as we have seen (and shall see again), were a nation that had been for centuries in contact with imperial civilization and had adopted much from it in the way of custom, law, and the practice of social and creative arts, whereas the Burgundians seem to have been the most genial and goodnatured of all the Germans. These two peoples ordinarily shine in history as more humane than the pagan Frank, but it must not be forgotten that the perfidiousness and the murderous brutality of the last have been embalmed for posterity in the amber of Gregory's remarkable history, while the untrustworthiness and the homicidal mania characteristic of the family relations in both Visigothic and Burgundian royal houses enjoy a comparative oblivion. Even Salvianus of Marseilles, who holds a brief for German integrity against Roman corruption, does not close his eyes to their faults.

And yet, according to Dill, the country districts of Gaul suffered more from native brigands than they did from German bands on the warpath or from German spies. The student of Sidonius will find the notices of violence and widespread calamity faint and infrequent—there was nothing in the fortunes of Gaul in his days to match the social chaos and suffering of Noricum. There is a wide interval between the first wild cries of terror which rose as the Sueves and Vandals swept over Gaul, and the more or less willing acquiescence in the rule of the Burgundians and the Visigoths.

It may be felt that in the two chapters just ending, this book has striven to emulate the writing of that English professor of modern history who refused to be bound by restrictions of date; who treated as modern and natural every occurrence since the call of Abraham; whose most sympathetic interest centered in fifth-century Gaul and Germany whenever it was not focused upon the Norman conquest of England; and who could bring himself to regard as obsolete and nefarious only two historic phenomena: the rule of the Turk in Europe and the conservatism of Bishop Stubbs.[10] If such an impeachment be brought, I am not minded to deny it, for I feel no apology is due my reader anent the "modern" attitude towards the early society of Gaul and Germany thus far manifested by this book, since this attitude is a proper one historically, is derived from a study of actual sources, and rests upon them. None the less, I believe a few words of explanation may prove helpful.

Until Freeman and Dill published their lustrous articles on the Goth and the Frank in Gallo-Roman society,[11] it was generally understood that on the eve of its collapse before the barbarian the whole inner life of western Europe was corrupt beyond naming and effete beyond recovery. This judgment, endlessly reproduced by successive generations of historians, was founded on the censure of contemporary morals contained in the *Governance of God*, written by the ascetic Salvianus of Marseilles some time between the cap-

GAUL IN MEROVINGIAN TIMES 49

ture of Carthage by the Vandals in 439 and the invasion of Gaul by the Huns in 451. This book is a wholesale indictment of the most vehement and pitiless sort, and is filled with the gloomy presage of the approaching end of all things: the constitution, the civilization, and the learning of Rome. Other satirists before Salvianus had passed adverse judgments on the society at the close of the fourth century: notably St. Jerome in his letters and sermons, and Ammianus Marcellinus in his *Histories*. The writings of all three of these men are characterized by a sort of ferocious energy and tireless iteration when condemning the frantic excess, the drunken debauchery, the turpitude, rapacity, cruelty, greed, faithlessness, and prostitution of their day.

Now Dill did not believe, nor did Freeman, because of the diatribes of two evangelistic preachers (one a buffoon for God, another the logical precursor of Bernard of Morlaix) and an old soldier whose liver was as unsettled as an Indian veteran's, that for a hundred years or more in western Europe all men were monsters of depravity, hardened and venal. And he felt the truth of this the less since, in the other literary remains of that age, there were materials for forming an estimate independent of either Christian or pagan censors, an estimate in almost every way diametrically opposed to theirs. Luckily for posterity, we possess invaluable storehouses of information as to the tone and habits of Gallo-Roman society in the years when shadowy emperors were puppets of a German soldier, when Visigothic government brooded over Aquitaine. These great testimonies to a past in Gaul which the modern mind can envision are the letters of Symmachus, the poems of Ausonius, the *Saturnalia* of Macrobius, and the voluminous correspondence of Sidonius.

The question, then, as to the character of Gallo-Roman society on the verge of debâcle is this: Two priests and a soldier come before the court to prosecute their fellow-men, accusing them of every crime on the Roman calendar. What have the defendants to offer in rebuttal of these sensational charges? Nothing. They do not even enter an appearance. Because of this default a verdict of guilt established is about to be awarded to the plaintiffs, when an interested taxpayer (Dill) appears and, being duly sworn, puts in evidence the depositions of certain character-witnesses—four poets and publicists. These run to the effect that their authors have known the defendants long and intimately and, except for their sharing the futility and asininity common to humankind in all ages, the affiants know nothing to the discredit of the accused. And there the case rests.

Now in these circumstances it is a fair method of procedure for him who would inquire into the backgrounds of the Gallo-Roman lyric, to go behind the unsavory denunciations of provincial society brought by disaffected descendants of Juvenal, to gather all testimonies pertinent to the subject, and to illumine them with the cool analyses of such scholars as have studied at first hand the situation of Gaulish institutional life from the viewpoint of ethnology, economics, and industry, as well as from that of literature and plastic art. When this has been done, it is equitable to admit to the record whatever is said about Gaulish folkways in contemporary poems and letters, as well as in atrabilious satires. If the result seems to speak for a modernity of attitude on the part of Gaulish citizens, I do not see that we can avoid the issue.

Chapter IV

THE CONTINUITY OF THEMES

Even if the readers of this book be few in number, more than one of them has by now become oppressed, I imagine, by my leisurely progress along the road from Rome to Canterbury and by my expansive consideration of materials that seem not only irrelevant to a study of the Romanesque Lyric but positively sundered from it. And the impatient reader may have given my argument quite over long before this.

I have no thought of censure for such restless minds—they frequently further research and adorn scholarship in their fields of endeavor by their very commitment to only the definite, ascertainable facts in a case, by their quick and passionate dismissal of what lies over the edge of the far hill. And yet if honest minds are brought to but a pipeful of reflection, well they wot that any structure they erect on the long pilgrimage road of Latin poetry will prove ere long untenable, unless its base strikes down to rest on some stout substratum of historical growth, unless it be, both as to fashion and materials, a type of building consonant with the scene where it appears. It must be in character.

Twenty years ago I printed in *Modern Philology* several essays which assemble an array of facts pertinent to the Romanesque Lyric, though never for a moment have I felt that this series of articles merited the diuturnity of book form. But, try as I would to win it, a composite picture—a character portrait—of the weaving and inter-relationship of early medieval lyrics escaped me. Be it understood, I was searching for bedrock, for the bottom facts, the basic secrets underlying the genesis of vernacular medieval poetry as a distinctive literary type. And my essays seemed to achieve little more than the routine juxtaposition of insoluble ingredients. Of the cooking of this poetry I came to learn much; of its chemistry, exactly nothing. My words regarding

Latin poetry wore the insouciant air of a refined scholasticism, but they meant little that I could determine.

So I did the one thing left me to do: I delved deeper. Nor had I dug far before I realized that my beginning the study of western European poetry with the decline of Roman civilization and the barbarian invasions was both misleading and harmful. For it did not take sufficiently into account the probability that prior to Cæsar's campaigns there existed in Gaul a highly developed and flourishing social expression in the descriptive as well as the industrial arts. So prone had I been to assign the prodigal growth of Romanesque poetry to a single group of roots, to assume the remarkable development of Gaulish art as an immediate result of Latin culture, that I was no little put out of countenance by the flustering appearance in Halstatt and La Tene periods of a many-faceted emotional outlook. Confronted by this, I could no longer be perforce content to believe that in the fifth Christian century a Nazarene-Barbarian culture had come to replace that Alexandrian-Roman revival of what had once been Greek indeed, but also of what had lived in Egypt, Judæa, and Phœnicia.

What has the early medieval genius to do with Egypt, Judæa, and Phœnicia? I asked. Antecedents of it they may well have been, but was it worth while to cast even a passing glance at the archaic body of ideas summed up by these three forgotten civilizations? What influence could they have exercised upon a matter so foreign to their thought and activity as post-Augustan poetry?

There are worlds of the past, the vestiges of which we never tire in disinterring, which in the light of our present knowledge have no direct connection with modern generations of men. In recondite and unexpected places such ancient cultures arise from beneath the excavator's shovel—Siberia, Central America, Africa of the Desert. Thus ruined cities bear mute but infallible witness to epochs of splendor when a remote terrain had advanced far in the creation of the arts of life. But from these communities we feel ourselves apart as we do from the dim stars in the night sky. In a sense they belong to our cosmos, but still they seem to possess for us no affinity either of essence or intention.

THE CONTINUITY OF THEMES 53

Mystery shrouds the manner of their rise and the reason for their fall. They are pitifully isolated from us who are eager to learn our present life the better by studying the lessons of its past.

There survive, however, traces of other civilizations whose sources are equally lost in the thin azure of antiquity but which touch very closely subsequent western society and its symbols. If in our search for these we do not wander far from the borders of the Mediterranean basin, we come upon the story of one great human enlightenment after another, which has come, contributed its unfailing quota to the medieval spirit, and vanished.

When on a chronological chart we study the duration of the various polities which have made important social and economic contributions to western art and ideas, we are first struck with the extraordinary longevity of Egyptian groups, some of which were of fabulous age by the time of Herodotus. Little as we yet know of the Cretans, the Hittites, the Phrygians, and other early peoples of Asia Minor, thanks to a warm dry climate, the records of Egypt from the fifth millenium before Christ have been so well preserved that we can rightly determine their proper stage in the evolution of our western ages. The historic beginnings of Phœnicia's greatness, and of Judæa's as well, much transcend the first millenium prior to our era; and two imposing world powers in which early medieval civilization takes its roots—Carthage and Greece—swing a century or two thereafter.

Now these communities do not command our interest or respect merely because they stretch away from us far into the romantic past, but because, by a meticulous study of their problems and opportunities, we gain a beacon light to pour its steady radiance upon the similar experiences of later ages. An instance:

Ancient Greece had its Middle Ages two thousand years or so before western Europe. This period was idealized into an epic age by its own descendants as well as by the conquerors from the north who had mingled with them in blood and speech. Mackail tells how the new Greek generation inherited its rich tradition of song and story from the medieval life out of which it had risen:

To the colonists on the Asiatic coast, where the fusion of the races was most complete, came the appeal of a half legendary Homeric or Mycenæan past, with an overlordship of Argos and great deeds of a confederacy of princes. It came home to them all, as that of Arthur the Briton, the kingdom of Logres and the feats of the Round Table, came home to English, Normans, and French, no less than to Britons on both sides of the English Channel.[1]

Again, ancient communities compel our study because by carefully examining the image reflected by the external world on their imagination—their poetic description of nature, their landscape painting, their cultivation of the physiognomy of nature—we may be made more quick to the philosophy and poetry of the Romanesque age. By knowing the principal momenta among the ancients which have influenced their physical intellection of the universe, and by grouping these main causes of the extension of their idea of the cosmos as a whole, we can arrive at a suitable background for that period after Christ which was heir to all the early gems of natural knowledge garnered by Greece and Rome.

This idea is infinitely less subtle than it sounds when put in awkward scientific terminology. Let me, therefore, express it more simply: By studying the *religio laici* of men who lived long ago we gain the best angle from which to adjudge the poetic attitude of men in the nearer present. It is more than a winged phrase of Santayana's, that religion and poetry are identical in essence, differing only in the way in which they are attached to practical affairs. For when it intervenes in life, poetry really is religion; but when it only supervenes upon life, religion is seen to be nothing but poetry. As a case much in point, how could Santayana possibly have prepared us better to grasp the poetry of barbarism than by writing the sentence which advertises his conversance with both classic and Christian systems of religious endeavor? Each was a system of ideas, an attempt to seize the eternal morphology of reality and describe its unchanging constitution.

In this venturesome endeavor, poetry is as definite a unifying force in western civilization as either science or philosophy, for like them the commonwealth of its ideas is embedded in the past. Modern poetry derives primarily from the unity of Romanesque Christendom, where it profited by the high advantage of a monopolizing language of learning.[2] Through this Latin, modern poetry, like science and philosophy, derives from the Græco-Roman world and ultimately from Hellenic Greece,[3] and Greece in turn was conscious of its artistic debt to the great Eastern cultures and their poetry. Thus, we are forced to envision a continuity of almost identical poetic systematization reaching back at least six thousand years, lost to sight only at the faraway rim of recorded culture.[4] The thread of poetic continuity has often been near to rupture, but some strand or other of it has always managed to hold. And so it is in this world of continuing poetical ideas, as in that of science and philosophy, that we acquire our main evidence of such progress as human history contains.

Scarcely conscious though the modern amateur of Romanesque poetry may be of its indebtedness to the Bronze Age of physical religions underlying it, the somewhat concise indications of Humboldt regarding the tight seams which unite this poetry with older Mediterranean struggles toward enlightenment will aid in convincing him that one cannot know Romanesque development without them.[5]

Civilization in the Nile alone makes possible the advancement of the Phœnicians. Their efforts in the tin and amber trade lead us to the geographical myth of the Elysion. The expeditions of Hiram and Solomon open Ophir to the world's enchanted vision. If we neglect to assay the gloomy bent of mind of the Etruscan, we shall fail fully to apprehend the nature of Rome's ancient political institutions, likewise their secondary effect when they came permanently to be stamped upon the mental attitudes of mankind. If we omit to take into consideration the gayer Ionic mobility of mind, and likewise the stimulus it gave to an eager spirit of inquiry in the West, then we shall miss sight of that objective bent in Romanesque modes of thought which, adorned with a sensuous luxuriance of fancy in poetry and art, remained a beneficent germ of progress wherever these selfsame Ionians had scattered their seed in western colonies.

I can have no especial objection, therefore, to regarding Count William IX of Poitou as the creator of a school that includes every modern lyric poet. Nor may my spirit be ruffled by the statement that everything commonly called poetry in the modern tongues in one way or another traces its pedigree back to the *Farai chansoneta nova*. Further, I should agree that the thrill of rhymes like William's is the reawakening of the modern world for that long progress of literature in which the Renaissance and other momentous changes are only incidental things, compared with the miracle of their new beginning. And I could nod my head in unqualified assent to the dogma that our poetry of recent days is related by blood to Provençal verse of the year 1120, as it is not in bond to anything in the earlier Middle Age. In fact, nothing would lead me to consider the contentions thus far other than amazingly well-taken and propounded with much gentle lucidity. For they flow from the pen of the lamented W. P. Ker.

But when this critic prefaces his statement with the remark that the beginning of modern literature came with hardly a warning—then, forsooth, I am rudely startled from my mood of complaisance and minded to voice a strenuous denial. For from its earliest recorded utterance, the whole history of lyric poetry is instinct with warning that a body of rhythmic utterance impends which is to be the common property of all minds that understand Goethe, Hugo, and Tennyson; or for that matter, Heine, Villon, and Burns.

This remark I do not base upon hazardous speculation regarding poetic affinities but upon historical evidence. First, in witness, permit me to summon Archilochus, who flourished in Paros well before the end of the eighth pre-Christian century. Like Walt Whitman, this Parian sings of himself in a voice at once personal, poignant, and revolutionary. He has nothing to learn from modern Parnassians, as one may realize from the miserable scanty fragments of his astonishing talk. "Damn Paros, and these figs, and a life at sea!" "One thing I know—and that's to pay back in bitter kind the man who wrongs me." "This island sticks up like an ass's backbone wreathed in wild woods." "The plagues of all Greece have rushed in a body to Thasos."

indeed. In fact it has already done so, as I shall now attempt to prove.

We are forever trying to compare our achievements and attitudes with those of men long gone to their reward. It is only by measuring the expression of human forces from some point arbitrarily fixed in the past that we can determine the character and amount of motion involved in our own development, as well as the relative stage of progress attained by those who have preceded us.

Now when Henry Adams sought to establish two points of relation between which he might project his lines of dynamic energy forward and backward indefinitely, psychology seemed to furnish him as the far-limit of his measuring scale a unit in that place in history when man held himself in highest esteem as an integer in a united universe. That other end of the rule (from which he proposed to fix his own position amidst twentieth-century multiplicity) Adams conceived to lie in the years immediately following 1150 A. D., because of Amiens cathedral and the writings of Thomas Aquinas. From that period as a point of departure Adams felt he might ascertain the acceleration in the flow of motion toward his own time, without assuming as true or untrue anything except relation.

But although Adams wished to study this human current chiefly in terms of philosophy and mechanics, it lends itself equally well to observation in terms of poetry and criticism, because the last half of the twelfth century is notable as a self-conscious and renascent period of Latin and vernacular verse of a type high and (in terms of the age) universal. By then, the exultant strains of troubadour, trouvère, minnesinger, and goliard were making the whole earth vocal, in answer to the call of that new life we understand so well: chivalry and the cloth of gold, love of sensuous beauty and of every luxury that spiced and embellished it. Not one of these bodies of song had grown by insensible gradations from precedent traditional forms. One single social change of a subversive sort had added a new vitalizing unit to poetry — a single mutation had occurred. And in a flash medieval love-lyrics of a novel species had been born to vernacular and dog-Latin idioms.

children's yarns of Charles Perrault and the Brothers Grimm. Far more than this, we find positive convertibility of moral attitude and metaphysical idea—similar beliefs in the personality of a vivified universe related in essentially a coincident imaginative manner. How do these sagas and stories come to resemble one another so closely in all parts of the world? Were they invented once for all and transmitted clear around the habitable globe from some center? What was that endemic focus, and what was the period and the process of poetic permeation?[6]

At the present stage of the science of folk-lore we can of course do no more than confess ignorance as to the last two questions. But as to the first of the three, the blending of the universal elements of imaginative narration, we can affirm that a story's power of flight was given it by the exchanges and contacts of semi-civilized communities. No tale can be a fortuitous congeries of story-atoms and diamond dust, but rather—as we are finely informed by Lang—it wanders wherever merchants wander, wherever slaves are sold, wherever the custom of exogamy commands the choice of alien wives. The story flits wherever human communication is possible—and the space of time during which the courses of the sea and the paths of the land have been open to story is dateless. Here the story may dwindle to a fireside tale; there it may become an epic in the mouth of Homer or a novel in the hands of Miss Thackeray. It has drunk the waters of immortality.

From the above it will be evident that if, in order to envision the exact situation of Romanesque poetry with regard to life, we are forced to cross-section the early Middle Ages at the point where we wish to establish a test-rating—none the less, it is futile for us to attempt to evaluate whatever rating we thereby secure without referring it to its approximate and ascertainable kin as far back in Mediterranean genealogy as we can ascend toward a source. And this fact is an explanation of my first chapters, which, to the casual glance, may seem leisurely and at times irrelevant to the point at issue, but which as a composite picture of the weaving in and out of the ethnic and social backgrounds of Latin poetry are, I presume, succinct enough. At least, it is not their breadth that gives me concern—my only fear has to do with their possible lack of depth.

Suppose I had omitted so painstaking a sketch of the multiple possibilities of the development of Romanesque poetry as occupies these initial chapters. Then I should have had to confront Latin literature through the Silver Age and beyond, as but an otiose replica of Greek models. I should have found, with Saintsbury, that the Romans invented no new type of elevated expression, that even when they pilfered Greek civilization for their themes, symbols, figurative imagery, conventional epithets, meters, and meanings, the Romans did not refashion or make their own these borrowed garments. I should have dismissed Roman tragedy as but the death-mask of the Greek and have said that, despite a spurious local spirit imparted to Roman comedy by the sprightliness of Plautus and Terence, this too was only a plaster cast of the later Athens mode. Roman mimus would be sprung straight from the loins of Ægean *pægnion*, Roman oratory would move in the channels marked out for it first by Hellenic rhetor. I should insist that Roman epic was slavishly imitative and say that Vergil walked forever unwavering in the footprints of Homer and Apollonius. Roman historians would seem to write with the dread of missing Greek perfection if by but a particle. And I should have sworn that Latin poets of lyric verse—whether pastoral, elegy, or ode—dared invent no fresh scheme prior to the hymns of St. Ambrose.

And, except for what is laid bare in the opening chapters of this book, the above characterization would have been a speaking likeness of the state of affairs in Latin literature and might well have been considered an adequate portrait—especially as we should be confirmed in this attitude by our reading of the testimonies brought forward by the three sister arts of painting, music, and the dance. We should thus never have come to establish the genre of Romanesque poetry as a separate form either during the first century of the Christian Era or ever thereafter. And the birthplace of modern romantic poetry—erotic, pathetic, fanciful—would have remained unknown to us. Would this have created an unhappy situation for modern criticism to confront? Yes, nations than that which gave it birth. Through its psalms, hymns, canticles, and ecstatic prose, Hebrew literature had a fructifying influence, not alone upon Romanesque sacred poetry, but upon secular verse as well. As the holy land of western reverence and enthusiasm Palestine played an outstanding rôle in the spectacle of the occidental Middle Ages. The burning racial integrity of the children of Israel has perpetuated itself in a score of cultural foci down to our present day. How then can we obliterate from our historical record a statement of the special features of the ancient land in which the Jews were nurtured? How should we fail to regard the minute conditions of that period at which they attained their highest prosperity? For any really critical knowledge of Romanesque poetry demands, as an indispensable preliminary on the part of its possessor, a study of Semitic and Greek culture, because these things have inestimable power to form the minds of sculptors, architects, painters, and poets, and condition the very flight of their originality. Similarly, if they wish to understand and transcend the poetry of today, the modern critic and the historian must study, not alone the conceptions of that world and that life which shaped the temperaments of their medieval ancestors; they must lean equally upon what Greek philosophy, religion, and poetry saved for us out of the debris of older Asiatic and African civilization.

But this is only half the story of our ineluctable obligation to the remote past. Let us lay aside all reference to the utterances of enlightened man and for the nonce deal only with primitive, half-savage, and rustic poetry; with household tales, popular romances, anonymous narratives peering from the prehistory of backward and partly-visioned races; with fables, folk-ballads, epics, supernatural sagas, fairy lore, and myths. What do we find when we study these illiterate products of submerged suburban art?

We find similarity and often identity of stuff: theme, fabric, phenomena, characters, plot, incident—whether we are examining the survivals of Hindustan, Phœnicia, and Judæa; or reckoning with Bushmen, Kaffirs, Swahilis, Mincopies, Gypsies, Huarochiri, Finns, Japanese, Arabs, Mongols, Samoyeds, Zulus, and Blackfeet; or dealing with the

The founding of Greek cities in Asia and the passage of sea-roving adventures beyond the Pillars of Hercules opened to mankind a vast sphere of new concepts. The campaigns of Alexander first made known the natural products of the new countries to which Macedon penetrated; first gave occasion on a grand scale for a comparison of African races dominant in Egypt with Aryan tribes beyond the Tigris and with Indian aborigines who were dark colored but not woolly haired. Here we have apparently the beginning of that ethnological attitude toward strictly national religions and customs—myth, ritual, poetry, and art—which, with the staunch aid of Aristotle and his school, finally won universal sway over the area of Roman dominion.

The first three Ptolemies, whose combined reigns endured a century, founded institutions for the promotion of scientific culture and worked unremittingly for an extension of trade. Their efforts brought about an increase of knowledge previously unattainable, and by way of Greek settlers in Egypt this was passed on to the Romans. The caravan routes were as important as medieval pilgrimage roads for disseminating literary themes and types among contemporary and subsequent generations. And the great university of Alexandrian schools—the precursor of Paris, fifteen hundred years later—not only inclined to accumulate the results of past wisdom but devoted its energy to observing new and immediate particularities of science. This great temple of learning so submitted its results to classification, comparison, and elaboration that never again were they forgotten for a considerable period. Finally, the Alexandrian museum and the libraries at Bruchium and Rhakotis stored the intellectual treasures of antiquity for us.

Which of these tight seams that unite antiquity with Romanesque endeavors can be omitted by the student of its poetry, even if he have no further wish than to gauge its significance for more modern expressions of art? Nor should the student forget that other philosophical movements than Hellenism—Hebraism, as only one example—have been important factors in the upbuilding of western poetry. As the precursor of Christianity, Judaism had much to do with shaping the esoteric and æsthetic ideas of later

"Let us hide the bitter gifts of the Lord Poseidon." "Thirty there were that died—we overtook them with our feet—a thousand were we who slew." "I saw Neobule playing with a branch of myrtle, in the shadow of her falling hair."

I pass by Anacreon and Simonides, Ibycus and Sappho, and the poets of the Greek Anthology, since they are too well-known to need citation as harbingers of the impending change that shall make poetry modern. But another intensely "modern" poet is Callimachus, who lived B. C. 260 at Alexandria. Walter Headlam[7] rightly finds that the qualities which characterize this poet's manner are a packed concentration of phrase and a peculiarly dry and pungent flavor; a sad bitterness drawn from the irony of worldly disillusionment. Callimachus gets this effect as Wordsworth often does by the simple figure of antithesis:

> She lived unknown, and few could know
>   When Lucy ceased to be;
> But she is in her grave, and oh,
>   The difference to me!

Browning in "I wish that when you died last May," and Heine in "Ein Jüngling liebt ein Mädchen" achieve the very same end by identical means. Another stylistic peculiarity Callimachus shares with Heine and Browning (also with Catullus: "Cæli, Lesbia nostra, Lesbia illa") is the use of flat words from everyday speech to indicate moments of terrific emotional stress.

Such illustrations as the above prove clearly that, no matter how convenient Ker's and Adams's foot-rule may be in the measurement of short distances along a well surveyed terrain such as intervenes between William of Poitou and Keats, a much longer chain is required to reduce to scale the coincidences and the contrasts that mark the greater stretch between two more widely separated horizons. For in the realest sort of way modern poetry derives from the unity of medieval Christendom, where it profited by the high advantage of a single language of learning: Latin. And through this medieval Christian Latin, modern poetry (like science and philosophy) harks back to the pagan Græco-Roman world and ultimately to Hellenic Greece. And Hellenic Greece was never for a moment unconscious of the debt it owed to the accentual rhythms of the Nile and the Euphrates. Suppose, for instance, we are hunting the world through for the perfect analogy to a certain cloying rapture explicit in many an Alexandrian epigram. We should most likely turn to the modern odes of Keats and Shelley; but the identical note we are seeking might be found equally well in ancient Egyptian and Semitic wedding songs, particularly in the ante-nuptial soliloquies of the bride:

> Gladly I sit in his shadow,
> And his fruit is sweet to my taste.
> To the house of wine let him bring me
> And let his banner above me be love.
> Stay me with cakes of raisins,
> With apples revive my strength;
> For I am sick because of love.
>
> My beloved spoke and said to me,
> Rise up, my fair one, and come away.
> For see, the winter is past,
> The rain is over and gone,
> The flowers appear on the earth,
> The time of singing is here,
> And the voice of the turtle dove is heard;
> The fig tree ripens her figs,
> And the vines give forth their fragrance.
> Open to me, my sister,
> For my head is filled with dew,
> My locks with the drops of the night.

In this snatch of old Hebrew court poetry with its modern note of personal passion and simplicity, we have the very mold of later erotic verse anywhere along the line of descent from Catullus's *Marriage Song for Mallius and Vinia* to the *Vigils of Venus*, as well as anywhere along the line from Tiberianus to the *Eve of St. Agnes*.

Suppose, again, that we were seeking the counterpart of those feminine complaints of male infidelity to love which look out so oddly from medieval vernacular verse. Our first impulse would surely be to consult modern poetesses of passion who have justified their sex so simply, but we could find a closer complement in an Alexandrian erotic fragment of the first century of our era:

We were two who loved and chose each other,
Loved, and Cypris only was our bondsman.—
Now when I remember how he kissed me,
Meaning all that kissing time to leave me,
Madness overcomes me at his treason.
Now thy passion, Eros, has me wholly,
Overwhelming all my soul, and never
Wilt thou leave me strength to make denial
How I hold him in my bosom always.

    Stars of love, and thou, O Night, my lady,
Thou who shared'st him, bring me to my lover.
Love that seized so mightily upon me,
Love and Aphrodite, they together
Lead me like a slave—ah, bring me to him.
And the torch to light me on my pathway
Is the inward fire that burns my bosom.
Ah the sorrow! Ah the desolation!
He that so denied the sway of Cypris,
He that was so arrogant aforetime—
O the traitor—he it is that wronged me!

    Ai, I shall go mad, for I am jealous—
Nay, I am on fire, for I am lonely.
Me deserting, this at least I ask you:
Throw me down your garlands, let me have them,
Hug them to my breasts and lie upon them.—
My belovèd, do not drive me from you—
Take me, do not shut your doors upon me—
Let me be your slave, for I am jealous.

    Love is torment, and if one love wildly,
Jealousy and silent pain and sorrow
Follow him; and therefore let no maiden
Yield her heart unto one person only.
They're insane that love a single lover;
Give your heart, and madness comes upon you!

    Then beware lest I should come to hate you
And my heart be adamant against you.—
Nay, I am beside myself. The harlot!—
O that you should run to her and leave me,
Me to lie alone deserted!
                             Come then,
Let's give over storming at each other,
Let's be quickly friends and no more quarrels.
Which of us is wrong, and which offended?
That's a point we'll leave our friends to settle.

But let us not longer insist upon the continuity of almost identical poetic attitude and technique which reaches back into the twilight of six thousand years ago and which furnishes us with the main evidence of such progress as human history affords. We have said enough for the better guidance of those who are inclined to believe that the modern world of poetry began with hardly a warning in that proximate yesterday of the year 1120. Let us proceed to discover what we may find in the way of very definite warnings of modernity in the Romanesque verse of the generation which followed immediately upon the age of Augustus.

Chapter V

THE APPROACH TO ROMANESQUE POETRY

In my preceding narrative I have several times used the phrase Romanesque poetry to describe a certain manner of early European metrical writing.

As so applied, my choice of the word Romanesque is determined by the current application of the same attributive term to transitional types in the history of the fine and decorative arts. When thus employed Romanesque of course specifies "belonging to or designating the early medieval style of art and ornament derived from those of the Roman empire." As hitherto used in the domain of art Romanesque describes mainly that modification of the classical Roman form which was introduced between the reigns of Constantine and Justinian and which was an avowed attempt to adapt classical forms to Christian purposes.

Now I want to have a single word with which to refer to whatever poetry in western Europe since the Augustan Age derives its main elements of plan and construction, its purpose, theme, and imagery from Roman verse. I need one term like Romanesque to specify a distinct departure from Roman writing and yet a sideline descendant of it—a term, in short, which will run like a stout golden thread through the Silver Age, through the revival of letters under Hadrian, the African schools of Fronto and Tertullian, the fourth-century renaissance, and those two centuries after the troubadour Fortunatus, which seem so sterile of creative literary production but are so fruitful and significant with regard to polyphonic music. It is the lack of animating ideation of six centuries of Latin writing, caused by the failure to achieve one all-embracing phrase for their activity, which has led critics to speak of decay, debasement, preciosity, and final extinction when characterizing the natural and ordered stages that poetry had to undergo on its long pilgrimage from Rome to Canterbury. Whatever else may be said of such a phrase as Romanesque poetry, it will be agreed that its use may help to explain every historical departure of Latin writing from the classic idealism or formalism of Augustan Rome. No phrase is so satisfactory, so little vague as Romanesque poetry to indicate that the matter of verse has come to predominate over its form. Romanesque presumes in art the quality of the personal, ephemeral, emotional, or sensual, as opposed to that of the ideal or ethos. It notes that less attention is paid to objective methods of composition than to the expression of subjective feeling—hence it always suggests *romantic* as opposed to *classical.*

It will still be rashly contended by some people that Romanesque poetry is but a corrupted imitation of Roman writing, and yet this is never true, for it is a new thing in the world, the slowly matured product of a long period and of many influences. Let me say most emphatically that even where Romanesque poetry is but a short remove from debased Roman art, if it is yet definitely removed and contains at least one new element or unit which is entirely absent from Roman—no matter how slight that element (as of personal appeal or pathos or fancy) may seem to be—then the style of art and ornament in poetry is no longer Roman, it is Romanesque; whether in whole or in part, it is an entity as separate from Roman as a Romance language is separate from the Latin tongue.

There are two well worn paths between which the modern student of Romanesque poetry ordinarily chooses when he approaches the merging of Latin tradition with Gothic and Frankish culture in the Gaul of the fifth and sixth centuries. Because I propose to follow neither of these clearly marked trails, I feel it incumbent upon me to state promptly the reasons for my nonconformance to custom in this regard.

The first of these hallowed routist routes from decadent classical poetry to that which we term Romanesque *starts* with Horace and Catullus and with such moments of Vergil as carry the idyllic manner to a higher tension. A beginning is made with this trio because most modern critics not unreasonably consider them to be the finest exemplars of Latin lyric verse. This first path *ends* with Martianus Capella,

Cassiodorus, Boethius, Colum Cille, Columban, Gregory of Tours, and Venantius Fortunatus, and—except for a vivid revival in the rococo measures of fourth-century lyric art—is felt to run all the way downhill to the tawdry Romanesque rhetoric that marks its inglorious close. The critic who pads the hoof along this route and approaches the study of Romanesque poetry from this direction finds, laudably enough, that the successors of the Augustan Age are less and less able to sustain the splendor of Horatian diction, and to him poor sixth-century poets inevitably assume the rôle of mendicants at the end of a trail that swoops sharply down from the summits to the sunset.

Now I gain neither healing nor help in my poetic pilgrimage by proceeding from the assumption that Romanesque poetry is only a barbarous corruption of classical molds. Such an assumption feeds me indeed with Rome but robs me of Whitechapel and Strawberry Hill. It causes my historic sense to atrophy, for it fosters a biased scholastic connoisseurship at the expense of all power fully to enjoy poetry written during the parlous centuries of Gothic Night. Such preconception as to the nature of Romanesque verse takes no account of that changed character of people in western Europe and of that consequent shifting in expression to embody new social conditions to which I have devoted much space in my opening chapters. Such prejudgment demands of me æsthetic snobbery, in that I am supposed to prefer meticulous copyings of poetic masterpieces to the confusing experiments and innovations of rebellious racy art. It blinds me to all values that lie outside the pale of conventional classic complacency. Such a recapture of the romantic spirit in verse as mirrors, no matter if dully, new efforts put forth by men in the first century of Christ, finds no sympathetic response in him who willfully ascribes each deviation from Augustan norm to a perversion of taste. This amateur of decadent Græco-Roman verse extols the ancient priests of poetry but decries its newer prophets. He is so content to exalt the stagnant art of the pagan past that he belittles the advance in poetic endeavor during six centuries—their incessant, restless experiment; their tireless speculation about æsthetics; their unwearying effort to apply them to the actual production of poetry and to exert the conscious human will upon art as it had not been exerted before.

So much, then, in the way of reaction against the first of the paths by which the modern student of Romanesque is unfortunately wont to approach the merging of Roman pagan tradition with Gothic and Frankish ideals of taste. Let us now turn to the second path, the one that starts with the world of medieval poetry, of which, by consensus of opinion, the ecclesiastical and vagabond Latin verse of the twelfth and thirteenth centuries furnishes him with many noblest examples. From this point of audition the modernist critic harks back to thin earliest notes of Latin Romanesque as these loose themselves waveringly from the full-stopped diapason of classical sound. Such a critic's ears still tingle reminiscently with the mad catachresis of canonical Latin poured forth by Gerbert and Fulbert and Wipo, by Serlo and Gerald and Baudri, by Alan and Adam and Hildebert and Nigel, Bernard and Walter, and Philip le Breton, by him of Salisbury and Vinesauf and Vendôme and Rennes and Morlaix and Grevia, by Peter of Blois and Reginald of Canterbury and Henry of Huntingdon and Hildebert of Lavardin and Hugo of Orleans and Godefrid of Rheims, by Hilary and Abelard and Odo of Orleans, Golias, Archipoeta, Mapes and Primas, and all who belong to the graceless Order of Goliards, whose names do not linger in the knowledge of men but who wrote imperishable MSS of modern song, like Cambridge and St. Omer and Queen Christine and Benedictbeurn. And to the ears of such a critic the Latin poems of fourth and sixth-century Gaul—Gothic, baroque, and rococo—give out a satisfying tone; their singers no longer seem to seek our alms but rather stand prophetic and erect at the beginning of that polyphonic path which strikes sharply upward from a dawn-filled horizon to the table-land of medieval Latin lyric utterance.

I cannot truthfully say that I treasure the result gained from following this second pathway chosen by the modernist more highly than the attitude gained through following the first one, the way invariably affected by the classicist. For neither classicist nor modernist regards his journeying in Romanesque poetry as an end in itself. To either critic the road offers no place of sojourn, but only a causeway between two points. It has to them no high reason for individual existence in and of itself—both types of critic see it only in direct relation to what has preceded it or to what follows after. They do not apply their historical sense to the study of Romanesque poetry. They do not apply to it certain psychological tests that are now familiar to every modern man of culture, in an attempt to discover if Romanesque verse (like sculpture, architecture, mosaic, carving) is a characteristic art, or, on the other hand, if it expresses the racial and social temper of the time which produces it. Critics seek no real values in Romanesque poetry as such, and, therefore, find none. Critics censure the rebellious quality in Romanesque, forgetful that it is just the mark of high artistry so to exercise its individual will as to die fighting a world that will not change. Better far is such rebellion than the harmony of dull and complacent monotones that ruled the Græco-Roman decadence; particularly after new ages and novel societies had come to the front of the western stage.

In our critical analysis of poetry, any judgment at which we may arrive depends upon the viewpoint from which the subject is approached. It is maintained by some that an atom has energy when studied in *vacuo animæ*, irrespective of the mood of the scientific observer. But certainly a Romanesque poem—or sculpture or cathedral or carving or mosaic—has neither charm nor meaning unless it be in the mind of its beholder. "Reared as I had been among people who despised Gothic architecture," said Goethe, "I fed fat my distaste for those overloaded and complex ornaments which by their grotesquerie appeared to preach the gospel of gloom. And then all at once I saw the new revelation—the very thing that had seemed to me so contemptible now engaged my spirit, and conversely. A sudden perception of beauty in all its forms thereupon flooded my soul."

It is as hard for us to realize there was a time when Goethe turned his back upon the Strasbourg minster, as it was for his contemporaries to learn he could regard this edifice with a favoring eye. But that is not the point. The point is that Gothic notions such as dwell in a church wall, the doggerel of folk-song, the broadsides of Lutheran prose, the art of Shakespeare and even of Pindar were not conceptually or conceivably beautiful to Goethe until the moment when through Herder's teaching he felt them so to be. And thereafter they had for him necessitous, inherent beauty.

When with a mind single to the beauty of classical Roman poetry the student pursues a path which leads from Horace to the provinces, he finds the long flourishing of Romanesque a dreary time indeed. And in a Gallo-Roman society subservient to its military element, where barbarian slaves who gained ascendancy over a brutal soldiery might spawn on the throne of the Cæsars, he cannot hope to see the profession of poetry in a flourishing condition. Then it seems to him inevitable that the cult represented by Horace and the elegiac poets should become esoteric, and its enjoyment be confined to a rapidly diminishing class, whose sole source of inspiration and whose only audience is of the academy. Then he sighs at the divorce of tradition from contemporary thought, at the very moment when the opposite is true. He grieves over the increasing divergence of written and spoken Latin, and makes an ill face as an *elocutio novella*, the idiom of common life, rises ever more sensibly to the surface. And finally, when a poet's meaning can no longer be deciphered by reference to the pages of Forcellini's *totius latinitatis lexicon*—what wicked irony sparkles in this title!—when a poet's contemporaries exalt him if he but spell correctly and his phrases parse, then does the amateur of Augustan poetry exclaim with unction, Rome is dead! And he refuses to sanction the Hisperic speech of a sixth century which has basely denied its birthright.

But when with a mind full of the beauty of resurgent thirteenth-century Latin lyric verse the modern student impatiently seeks the first indications of breaking in the stiff, implacable ritual of classical meters, then there is a freshness as of dawn in the new style that makes itself felt in the latter years of the principate of Augustus: the straining after romantic effect, the love of startling color and gorgeous imagery, the surfeit of brilliant epigram, the sense of masquerade and elaborate felicity of expression. Such a student holds high the Silver Age for the unexpected service it was to render that period of the Middle Ages when Greek was a hidden mystery to the western world—it was then that Lucan and Statius, Juvenal and Persius, and even the humble author of the *Ilias Latina* did their part in keeping the lamp alive and illumining the darkness before the budding morrow of the Renaissance. He finds vastly engaging many a half-forgotten line of Ausonius, Sidonius, and Venantius. For he sees a new nation coming into existence among the ruins of classical civilization in Gaul, and knows that a new idiom with firefly gleams of *lai* and *chanson* is being evolved. And his spirit chafes for the bright morning that is to come when Rome shall at last give up her reluctant ghost—a suicide, like Werther's, too long delayed! And the moment this modern student's eye surely catches the first gray foreshadowings of Carolingian renaissance, he longs to cry out, Rome is not dead but risen! And for him there exists meaning in every poetic excrescence of this old life that is real, not alone in the happier births of literary genius, but in the lucubrations of Vergil the Grammarian, and in the *Hisperica famina*, the *Lorica*, the *Rubisca*, the *Adelphus adelpha*, the *Vita Columbani*, and the *Antiphonary of Bangor*.

Perhaps I shall make myself clearest in distinguishing the attitude of classicist and modernist (romanticist) towards Romanesque poetry by taking refuge in concrete illustration.

A classicist who would derive his criteria for judging all Romanesque poetry by Horace's standard of performance finds little to admire in the verses of Petronius. For Horace, in the words of Garrod, is not profound, not ecstatic. He has discovered what we might have thought did not exist: the poetry of good sense. It is in virtue of this that he appeals to nearly all the moods of the average man and satisfies most needs, save the very highest. Horace is wise without pedantry, noble without cant, at all points humane and genuine. He has a hard, cool mind. For him life streams by like the passage of some peaceful Saturnalia. The scene has its dark patches, but Horace moves serenely amid its shifting phases; solidly content with life, the kindly uncle of the whole human race. By habit he speaks in lofty tones to Time and the world; his sonorous verse is pitched to the greatness of the empire it reflects; he has a high, moral seriousness and a supreme instinct for measure and proportion.

Whereas, if he speak of them at all, the classicist refers to the epigrams of lyric Petronius with bare tolerance, citing them for want of better as stock examples of a Latin that has already become Silver, on its foredoomed way to being of baser metal yet: bronze, iron, pewter, lead, tin, and scrap. For by the day of Petronius the great movement of the Latin-speaking provinces had begun. While still in a sense subordinate to Italy, these provinces had grown to be organic parts of the empire instead of subject countries. The municipal institutions and civic energy of Rome were multiplied in a thousand centers of local life in Italy and Gaul, Spain and Africa. Like the empire itself, Latin poetry had taken a broader basis. The exquisite austerity of the old verse was gone, and its diction, formed by a purer taste amid a grave and exclusive public, was eclipsed by new and striking styles. As the political extinction of Rome proper approached and the one overwhelming interest of the City ceased to absorb individual passion and emotion, the tension on poetry and art became relaxed. Feeling grew more humane and personal, social and family life reassumed their real importance; and gradually there grew up a thing new to literature, the Romanesque, the romantic spirit. With its passionate sense of beauty in nature, idyllic poetry reacted on the sense of beauty in simple human life; the elegy and the epigram are full of a new freshness of feeling, and the personal lyric is born, with its premonitions of a simple pathos which is as alien to the older Roman spirit as it is close to the feeling of medieval romance.

Now no one has brought the phantom of freshness into the Latin poetry of love and nature more definitely than Petronius. In fact, if we except a very few of the best poems of Propertius, Latin elegiacs have nothing to show that combines such perfection of form with such sensuous charm.

Therefore, your modernist finds (with a start of surprise) in the lyric Petronius the words and the tone of today:

ENCOURAGEMENT TO EXILE*

Leave thine own home, O youth, seek distant shores!
For thee a larger order somewhere shines—
Fear not thy fate! For thee through unknown pines
Under the cold north-wind the Danube pours;
For thee in Egypt the untroubled lands
Wait, and strange men behold the setting sun
Fall down and rise. Greatly be thou as one
Who disembarks, fearless, on alien sands. (1)

THE MALADY OF LOVE IS NERVES

Night's first sweet silence fell, and on my bed
Scarcely I closed defeated eyes in sleep
When fierce Love seized me by the hair, and said,
(Night's bitter vigil he had bade me keep),
"Thou slave," he said, "a thousand amorous girls
Hast thou not loved? And canst thou lie alone?
O hard of heart!" I leaped, and he was gone,
And with my garment in disordered swirls,
And with bare feet I sought his path where none
There was by which to go. And now I run,
Being weary, and to move brings me no peace;
And turning back is bitter, and to stay
Most shames me in the midmost of my way—
And all men's voices slowly sink and cease;
The singing birds, my dogs that, faithful, keep
My house, the roaring streets, to me are still.
Alone of men, I dread my couch, my sleep—
I follow after Love, lord of my will. (2)

NOBLESSE OBLIGE

Pride of birth or degree proves no man to be upright—
Noble alone is he whose hands have never known fear.
(3)

ILLUSION

Our eyes deceive us, and our sense
Weighs down our reason with pretense,
And in false ways goes wandering:
The tower that stands wellnigh four-square
Loses sharp corners in blue air

*The Latin originals of poems given in the text will be found in the appendix.

And softens to a rounded thing;
The liquor of Hyblæan bees,
My hunger sated, fails to please;
I hate the smell of cinnamon!
For this thing or for that, why weep
Or smile, except our senses keep
A doubtful battle never won.   (4)

WE ARE SUCH STUFF AS DREAMS...

Dreams that delude with flying shade men's minds
No airy phantoms are, nor sent by gods
From any shrine of theirs, but each man only
Weaves for himself his dream. And when in sleep,
Conquered, his limbs repose, and quiet comes,
Then the imponderable mind pursues
In darkness the slow circuit of the day.—
If towns have shook before him and sad cities
Under the weight of flames have been down-razed,
Javelins and fleeing armies he beholds,
The funerals of kings and plains wide-watered
With rivers of shed blood. If he's an orator,
Statutes and courts appear before his eyes;
He looks with terror on tribunals thronged
With multitudes. The miser hides his riches
And digs up buried treasure, and the huntsman
Drives through the shaken woods his yelling dogs.
The sailor dreams of shipwreck; from the waves,
Gasping, he takes his vessel, or in death
Seizes on it and sinks. And the adultress
Dreams, and so yields herself. The woman writes
In dreams unto her lover: why, the dog,
Sleeping, believes he follows on the hare!—
So all night long endured, the wounds of day
Doubly are sorrow to the miserable.   (5)

NEALCE

Nealce, forever
    That night shall be dear
Asleep in my bosom
    That first saw you here;
And dear be the spirit,
    The lamp and the bed
When softly you came to
    A joy that is fled.
And now we are older
    We still must endure

>   The pitiful trouble
>   Of age that is sure;
>   And since the brief years
>   We shall lose with delay,
>   Let us kiss as of old,
>   Let us love as we may.
>   Ours once was a passion
>   Too sudden to spend—
>   Ah, now let us guard it
>   Lest quickly it end!   (6)

REMEMBERED SHORES

O sweeter to me than life may be is the sea and the sand where I
May come once more, a remembered shore that I love changelessly;
And day is fair in that region where I swam as the naiad swims,
The cold sea-maid with whom I played a wager of hands and limbs.
And the fountain's pool all day is cool, and the seaweed washes in,
And O the sand, and the quiet land where love knows never a sin!
I have lived my life. And not the strife of fortune can take from me
What time has given—a quiet haven, the past, and the shore, and
    the sea.   (7)

Now Petronius, as my reader will recall, lived in the days of Nero and would be famous as a lyric poet but for two things: first, his verse is overshadowed by his most remarkable novel, the *Satyricon*; second, classicist critics are prone to abuse him, in common with his great contemporaries Seneca, Martial, Juvenal, Lucan, Phædrus, and Statius, because he did not follow in all things linguistic and literary the mold of an age long dead—as if the future should abuse our poets for doing aught but ape Dryden and Pope. Be that as it may, there is but one first-century lyric with which we may reasonably compare the above-given odes of Petronius, and that one is Statius's well-known *Apostrophe to Sleep*. From the classicist point of view, it is a far more deserving ode than any of Petronius (because it adheres more tightly in form and manner to traditional verse). But I doubt if the modernist will agree with this verdict, although the translation has been designedly cast into a form best suited to display to English readers the virtues of its original: a verse-scheme after Sir Philip Sidney's hexameter sonnet.

APOSTROPHE TO SLEEP

What have I done, O Sleep, gentlest of heaven's sons,
  That, miserable, I only forfeit the boons you spill?
The flocks are silent each one, and beast and bird are still,
The truculent streams lie quiet, the sea-wave no more runs,
Curved tree-tops droop in slumber like men (and weary ones)—
  The seventh moon my staring eyeballs now doth fill,
And morning and evening stars, seven dawns with dewy chill
Have sprinkled me in pity. Where shall I speak my orisons?

Sleep, is there any, lying in a fair girl's arms all night
  Who sighs and sends you from him? Hither let him send!
    Shed not your wing-feathers upon my sleepless eyes—
    Let happier souls pray so. Mine be the lesser prize:
  Go by with airy stride, touching with your wand's end—
No more than that—my face, even though the touch be light. (8)

But, however classicist and modernist may feel as to the difference between the art of Petronius and Statius, one important fact is manifest. A crack of division has occurred—call it a flaw, if you insist—which marks off two sorts of lyric verse in the first century. One sort is the Statius ode which clings to traditional Roman ideas and forms, as ivy clings to an old oak; it represents the past. The other sort is the Petronius epigram which varies, if slightly, yet always definitely, from Roman ideas and forms of the past. It foreshadows the end of ancient poetry; it contains germinally the inner spirit of romantic revolt; the amateur of modern verse turns to it without shock of sudden transition. It is not Roman except in the modeling of its verses. It is Romanesque.

For the first time in Latin verse we have in the epigrams of Petronius the most genuine and pathetic expression of a man's weariness. The best of them speak of quiet country and seaside, of love deeper than desire and founded on the durable grace of mind as well as the loveliness of the flesh,[1] of simplicity and escape from court. They speak of these things in a new way and with unmatched sincerity—they give us a poetic naturalism as unexpected as it is real. Therefore, as I am more concerned to describe the actualities of poetry than to characterize it according to the passing notions of any one day, I conceive it my duty not to give Petronius a bad name and then proceed to depreciate him—

nor a good name and then rush forward in his praise—but rather to assign him his presumptive place in the scheme of things.

There is no more convenient place to which to assign the beginning of the history of the Romanesque lyric than the considerable number of epigrams, attributed with more or less certainty to Petronius,[2] which are preserved in the fragments of the *Latin Anthology*, seven of which have been quoted in translation above. It is with these epigrams of the age of Nero that the crack of division appears in Latin poetry which never thereafter heals, no matter how powerfully one abortive attempt after another is put forth during the following centuries to bridge the widening gap between western European verse and its pagan predecessors.

We must pause here to be quite sure of our ground. First, we must acknowledge readily that long before Petronius there veined Latin poetry elements that are curiously not Greek and not Roman, that breathe somehow of modernity of mood; of a tenderness and a sensibility that belong to romantic rather than to classic worlds. No one, it seems to me, not even Mackail, has written so well of this elusive Italian quality in Roman poetry as has H. W. Garrod, this quality that robs it of the danger of passing at its best for rhetoric, and at its worst for prose. This *ingenium molle*, we are told, whether in passion as with Propertius[3] or as with Vergil in reflection, is that deep and tender sensibility which is the least Roman thing in the world and which in its subtlest manifestations is perhaps the peculiar possession of the Celt.[4] The unelaborate magic of Catullus is that of the Celtic temperament—the fourth *Æneid* is the triumph of an unconscious Celticism over the whole moral plan of Vergil's epic. Even before the Augustan Age Latin poetry is *facetus*—it glows and dances; has *lepor*—is clean and sprightly; has *venustas*—is possessed of a melting charm. Often enough, too, in the poetry of personal invective—in the *Epodes* and some of the *Odes* of Horace, in Catullus, and in the Vergilian *Catalepton*—we have that *Italum acetum*, that vinegar of coarse and biting wit from the countryside which has its origin in the casual ribaldry of the *vindemiatores*, in the rudely improvised dramatic contests of the harvest-home; pert and ready and unscrupulous in assigning its object inalienably to the pit. And the quickened force of this wit is like to seem to a modern man as up-to-date and recent as any songs irrepressible Heine borrowed from a similar source: the south-German reaping-couplets, *schnaderhüpfeln*.

If these things be true, then why not begin our history of the Romanesque lyric with Catullus, say, whose poetry is much less actually classic than that of Vergil and Horace, wherein are exhibited in a greater degree the qualities of grandeur, harmony, and stability? The passion of the senses so lifts more than one elegy of Catullus into regions where the moral judgment stands abashed, that nothing in the world seems significant save the personal trouble of a soul on fire. Why not begin with him?

Because, as Garrod is prompt to explain, although the quickening force in the best Augustan poetry is the Italian blood, yet not without reason do we speak of this poetry as Roman. For it was made by Italians who were already Romanized; the Italian spirit worked always under the spell of Rome and not under any merely external compulsion. And the spell of Rome was still over the whole of Roman poetry. The Italians were only a nation through Rome—it had behind it a great life and expressed a great people, their conscious deeds and their national ideals. Until the Christian Era has begun and we possess in the date of the birth of Christ a greatest symbolic indication of the ending of an ancient world of Roman life and poetry, it is vastly convenient for us to regard that world as a classical entity and to disregard the patent fact that side by side with it— ever since the influx into Italian art of Alexandrian models, at least—there had been a new world of poetry growing up which had with that classical entity so little in common that it is only confusing to take the former into account. In the way of literary analysis it is worth while to hunt out even in Ennius (B. C. 239-169) an Italian vividness and a colored phraseology that is neither Greek nor Roman—a swiftness, wild agitated tones, and a prophetic fury wrought in fire that are mayhap half Calabrian, half Celtic. But we must not forget that the Italian and the Roman elements of Latin poetry are never really so separate and disparate as in literary analysis they would seem to be. And thus for many reasons it is best to treat as of one composite but integrating mold the poetry written in Latin to the closing days of the Augustan Age—for the sound of it all is the sound of a great nation.[5]

That there is more than the convenience of criticism in such a position is evident when we recall with Mackail that it is only in the growth and life of the new (Christian) world that the decay and death of the old can be viewed with equanimity, or in a certain sense can be historically justified. For it is the law of poetry that life comes only by death—she replenishes one thing out of another and does not suffer anything to be forgotten before she has been recruited by the death of something else: *materies opus est ut crescant postera saecla.* Poetry works out Roman classical forms towards a definite goal of perfection: the expression of one great national life and spirit. For such forms we have one name that fits like a tight cap: Roman. When great new forces begin to destroy the beauty of Roman forms of verse, forces that are strangers to them, and flaw them beyond their ability to recover, then poetry with passionless action breaks up perishable Roman materials and begins anew. Here, late in the afternoon of the Augustan Age, comes this new melting down of the primitive matter of Roman forms, to prepare it for alien civilizations. This moment in the gradual evolution of the purpose of history begins the period of Romanesque.

Other lyric poets of early Romanesque besides Petronius are but names to us: Gætulicus, consul in 26 A.D., whose mistress, Cæsennia, was herself a poetess; Cæsius Bassus, Vagellius, Sosianus, Montanus, Lucilius junior, Sulpicia, and some of Pliny's poet friends. Luckily, however, there has survived to us from these days the pastoral writing of an unknown author, from the first twenty-four lines of whose *Lydia* the following brace of sonnets have been most honestly derived:

LYDIA

I

Fair fields and meadows, how I envy you
    That are more fair since in you, silent-wise,
        Love's fairest damsel plays or stands and sighs.
You have my Lydia's voice, you have her view,
Her eyes to smile before. Doth she pursue
        Some song of mine her voice hath learned to prize?
    She sings—my ears have heard her in that guise.
Teach her to love. Ye fields, I envy you.

O there is no place made so fortunate,
    And there's no earth knows such beatitude
        As that wherein she sets her snowy feet;
Or where with rosy hand the vine-branch rude
    She plucks somewhile before the grape is sweet
        And ripens to its Dionysian state.

II

Among the many colors of the flowers
    She'll lay her limbs that breathe the breath of spring,
        And to the sweet crushed grasses whispering,
Shyly retell the story of love's hours.
Then shall rejoice the fields and forest-bowers,
    The water-brooks shall then run loitering,
        The fountains freeze, and bright birds cease to sing
What time my dear makes lament for love's powers.

I envy you, ye fields. You have my joy,
    And she is yours my bliss is fashioned of.
        My dying members waste away with sorrow,
My heat of life the cold of death doth borrow—
    She is not here, my lady and my love!
        I envy you, ye fields. You have my joy. (9)

The appearance so early in the history of Romanesque idyl of the Petrarchistic manner is of vital interest. Judged by Vergil's standard of performance, the *Lydia* is deemed not only too slight and ineffectual to be included with his works but too negligible even to be the famous poem of like name written by Valerius Cato.[6] Says Frank, our verse abounds with conceits that a neurotic and sentimental pupil of Propertius—not too well practiced in verse writing

—would be likely to cull from his master. We have here the situation of Goethe and the Strasbourg minster over again, in the case of Frank and *Lydia;* but of Goethe before the moment of conversion to that "grotesquerie" which is a glory of the Elizabethan lyrics.

This grotesquerie is the final triumph of the romantic over the classical attitude. Whether more implicitly real, as in our pieces from Petronius, or definitely mannered, as in the *Lydia,* we have come with it from an age of reason to an age of feeling.

Romanticism is a literature dominated by the lyrical element. Lyricism is individualism; it expresses ideas and emotions that are ours. Emotions, in turn, are of two sorts: sentiments of love and hate, hope and despair, enthusiasm and melancholy. Some of these emotions are concerned with the universe, the materials with which we construct the image of the exterior world—sensations. Others of these emotions are muscular—odors and taste. This second set romanticists leave to the realists; their own lyricism is sentimental and picturesque.

Under romanticism the emotions of others interest us only as they are men like us; hence the poet becomes the representative of humanity. Lyricism transports us into the realm of the universal—the sadness and desire of the individual become the problem of life and death, emotionally considered. Ours not to seek the reason behind the *moi* that is sad or desirous; ours to lay aside the exercise of intelligence and reflection, to leave behind psychology, science, exact method, steps in logic, the art of thinking and rationalizing. Lyric poetry, picturesque literature, living history—these are the things that count in an age of Romanesque. Against the rules are the definition of genres, the interior laws of each form, all precepts of taste.

To the modern reader who—whether consciously or not —studies classical Roman poetry with a bias that favors the personal element in art, the most serious defect of Augustan writing lies in ·the weakness of its lyrical impulse. In the words of Sikes, whether we understand lyric in its original sense as a poem sung by a single voice or a chorus, to the lyre, or extend the definition to any short poem which gives perfect expression to a mood of the highest imaginative intensity, we must admit that Roman poetry does not often satisfy the definition.[7] Quintilian's remark that "Horace is about the only lyric poet of Rome" indicates that the Romans themselves realized this weakness and knew their poets rarely *sing*.[8] They speak, says Sikes, they recite or even chant; but they do not commonly break out into that ecstasy of emotion which seems to demand music as its medium. Though he never lacks the perfect expression, Horace seldom rises to imaginative intensity: no burning moments, no absorbing passion, no thrill of rapture for gratified desire, no spasm of torture in frustrate hope; his equal muse is strange alike to the highest joys and the deepest despair.

The most that we may expect from such a situation is the social lyric suited exactly to the whims and tastes of a leisured caste. In so far as Catullus in the intimate lyric and Vergil in the more personal type of idyl had anticipated Romanesque elements of poetry, they were destined to be without discoverable posterity. The individual lyric of Catullus had been made of no account by Horace.

Chapter VI

MAIN TRENDS OF EARLY ROMANESQUE POETRY

It seems odd indeed that criticism did not long ago arrive at the phrase Romanesque poetry to signify a definite new manner of Roman verse arising toward the close of the Augustan Age or very soon thereafter. When dealing with Greek poetry and its derivatives we possess the convenience of a treble division: Classical, Alexandrian, Byzantine—when dealing with Latin poetry of the same period, of like aptitude and bent, of similar form and inclination, we are permitted only a single locution: Roman. Thus, when by reason of its very nature, and in response to the clutch of unalterable circumstance, the Roman poetry of the Christian Era departs from the fashions in vogue during the late Republic and the early Empire, we are forced to regard this shift as a debasement and not as a wholesome change. In the absence of some specific name with which to indicate the emergence of a new type, we exhaust ourselves in the coining of phrases wherewith to consign what we conceive to be a perversion of good poetry (but what actually is a separate literary genre), to Avernus. No pot is black just because it is not a kettle. No lyric is *fons et origo malorum*, just because it is not an Augustan idyl or elegy. If objurgation is to pass muster as criticism, then for all post-Augustan poetry from Petronius to Alcuin no other class-name than Roman is needed. Otherwise, that we may know the truth when we see it, let us add Romanesque.

Perhaps it does not at once occur to the mind how convenient the rubric Romanesque proves to be at times when the phrase Roman poetry fits loosely or fails to fit at all. For instance, although frequently used in older histories of literature, the term Christian Roman poetry is now felt to be a solecism, because it implies that Latin verse created through Christian agencies is in the line of descent from

Roman prosodical forms and from the figurative imagery and temper of Roman paganism, whereas the direct opposite is quite apt to be true. On the other hand, the substitute phrase "Christian Latin poetry" fails of its purpose, because it designedly avoids the opportunity of relating with traditional Roman poetry—either through identity of source, parallelism of experience, or reaction to literary influence— a body of intensely interesting and often beautiful verse. No umbilical connection with pagan poetry is asserted by the periphrasis Christian Latin poetry—it designates a form whose origin is unknown, whose development is dark, and whose grave is some potter's field of the sixth century. How different a tale there is to tell the moment we borrow from the domain of art the term Romanesque as signifying mainly that mutation of the classical Roman form which resulted from the avowed attempt to adapt classical forms to Christian purposes. Then we have one substance, two forms, and (like Tertullian) can illuminate our discussion with *distinctio, non divisio; conjunctio, non confusio; discreti, non separati*. Then we can avoid that direct comparison with pagan poetry which Christian verse cannot bear. Then, although it produced no epic poet of great breadth of vision, no dramatic poet, not even a fabulist; although a few passably happy lyrics and a few beautiful hymns form its only productions that will live, we can (to use the phrase of de Labriolle) guard against the rigid type of humanism which judges Christian writing from the viewpoint of the classical ideal.[1]

Thus far in our argument we have of course not achieved a formula which defines just what sort of literary genre the Romanesque lyric is. We have distinguished it roughly from the Roman elegy, idyl, and personal lyric by according it certain romantic factors which are either absent from classical poetry or distinctly subordinate to its dominant aim. By this we have established its right to existence as a transitional type and have finally separated it from the classical Roman lyric and from every intentional imitation of the latter. In other words, although we have not yet said exactly what the Romanesque lyric is, we already definitely know what it is not and can not be. We are going on to show how the Romanesque lyric lived side by side with the Roman lyric for five centuries after the death ₊of Vergil, in fact until the close of classicizing Roman poetry of Claudian and Rutilius. From this point forward the actual Roman lyric exists only as a dormant part of the classical heritage, forgotten in monastic libraries. But there is no cessation of the Romanesque lyric in the fifth century. It proceeds to its climacteric in the works of the Carolingian poets and does not for a moment yield the field to other forms until in the *Cambridge Songs* of the early eleventh century beneath the Latin superficies, we feel the beat and thud of irresistible vernaculars.

Let us now take up our story of early Romanesque lyricality where we left it in our last chapter—with Petronius and Statius. We have seen the latter poet trembling on the verge of breaking with a tradition of Latin verse purely classical in form and sentiment, but hesitant to take the decisive step that marks the effort of Petronian epigrams. The *Silvæ* of Statius deal largely with subjects of a familiar nature and contain here and there passages of strictly romantic fancy and genuine personal feeling, but in his lyric measures as in his epic Statius was too much the child of the conventional taste of his age to strike out a new manner in ancient poetry. The same may be said of the only other lyric poet of the century after Horace whose work has descended to us: Martial the epigrammatist. While in much of his work—some twelve hundred pieces—he appeals strongly to all that is worst in Roman taste—its heavyhandedness, its admiration of verbal cleverness, its tendency towards brutality; still one would not willingly forget in little Erotion's epitaph the turn Martial gives to the conventional "Earth be light" of the tombstones, nor the dove that as harbinger of her exiled brother's imminent return refuses dislodgment from Aratulla's bosom. Other touches like the closing prayer of a bridal ode: "and when age comes may she no less adore, he deem her wrinkled face young as of yore"—like Nigrina's finding the long journey from Asia Minor all too short, in her reluctance to part with her husband's ashes she is bringing home for burial—what are these but renewed indications of an impending pathos, a romantic irony to which a stilted world of poetry has not learned quite to yield? The epigrams of Seneca are often graceful lyrics from which an occasional line of power shines out in astonishing splendor: "Where the cold constellation of the heaven gleams ever with unsetting stars." At times the feeling in Seneca's lyrics rings true, and the never-absent rhetoric is transmuted to a more precious substance with some resemblance to modern lyrical passion—but perhaps the most romantic attribute in Seneca's, as in Lucan's, lyrically transfused moments resides in a certain Titanic quality which strikes a familiar note concordant with that of thirteenth and nineteenth-century Romanticism. Thus far, however, in all the measures of the Silver Age we have found Petronius the one sure enunciator of Romanesque lyric art.

The second and third centuries of the Christian Era are ordinarily accounted a Dark Age[2] dividing the silver twilight of the hundred years succeeding the age of Horace from the brief but brilliant renaissance of the fourth century. This is the panoramic picture of poetic development as viewed by the professed classicist. But to the vision of the student of Romanesque the second and third centuries of our era contain in embryo all that the future has in store for Latin medieval verse.

The emperor Hadrian died in the year 138. He once lived in Athens for three years together, adding the imperial patronage to the munificent expenditures already undertaken in that city for the embellishment of art and letters. By his repeated visits to Athens Hadrian added force to the other causes (already mentioned) which made Greek take fresh growth and become for a time a dominant language in the Empire.[3] This partial renaissance in art and letters which occurred in the long, peaceful reign of Hadrian spells of course to the classical Latinist the morn of Judgment Day, because it was on the whole a Greek rather than even a Græco-Roman movement. Poor Rome! sighs the classicist—forever exposed in its literature, because of conditions surrounding its birth and growth, on the one hand to a tendency towards artificiality, on the other to inadequacy of thought. Wonderful as had been the fruit produced by the graft of Hellenism, it contained the seeds of over-ripeness and decay—for Rome owed too little to early Greek epic and to the golden literature of Athens, too much to the later age when rhetoric had become a knack, when the love of letters overdone had swamped the sacred poets with themselves.[4] What Greece gave with the right hand to classical Roman poetry, she took away with the left all too soon thereafter. The moment the fresh Italian blood failed to win conciliation of its Roman and its Celtic elements with Alexandrianism, that moment Roman poetry fell away from its own greatness and ceased to be a quickening force. For the first time it reproduced the East without transmuting it.[5] In the place of an easy-flowing style whose phrases adorn, without obscuring, the sense, there appears in Roman poetry, now that its great luminaries are extinguished, a blight. We face a body of verse void of moral enthusiasm, close observation, and genuine insight. These have been replaced by a straining after effect, a love of startling color, produced by too meticulous and over-gorgeous an imagery or by a surfeit of obvious epigram—good sense is in abeyance, all due proportion is lost, an imitative preciosity is sure to masquerade as originality.[6] The controls are down; no longer can it be said of Roman poetry: *urbem fecit quod prius orbis erat*. She uses outlying genius without absorbing it.[7]

So far, the case of the classical Latinist. And he is right to grieve over the final destruction of so much that was formally and often enough spiritually perfect. But the Rome of the Civil Wars had to pass in the changing order of things, whatever the private woes of him who would hold eternal the fairness of an ephemeral instant in a progress that was not to stop short of Romania and Romanesque, Gothia and Gothic, and papal Rome, *caput mundi* of Middle Ages renascent and reformatory. And who would be the stay-at-home from such a journey?

So, conscious of whither the march of Latin verse is tending, let us look with undismayed eyes at the efforts of Fronto and Apuleius to create an *elocutio novella*. When Fronto came from Africa to Rome he found a Latin permanently weakened and restricted in its power to develop;

a literary language so divorced from the spoken idiom that no new Lucan, Tacitus, or Juvenal might be hoped for; a poetry that bade fair to become an unimportant genre of the Hellenistic world of literature. Fronto was sprung from a region which the influence of Silver Latin had hardly penetrated, which still spoke the popular dialect of the veterans of Sittius, where the ante-classical writings were still loved and taught. He conceived the idea of restoring strength to the Roman literary idiom by shaking off the authority of Seneca, and by returning to the simpler models of the Republic.

This is no place to assemble for the hundredth time the evident faults in Fronto's antiquarian revival which, like other innovations, was partly sound and partly mistaken. It is imperative only for us (with Bouchier) to note Fronto's plan for repelling the assaults of Greek on Italy and the western provinces, and in restoring to Latin something of its old place in literature. Nor should, says Bouchier, the issue be regarded merely as a struggle for mastery between Latin and Greek. In no case could the rough-spoken Hellenistic Greek have been generally adopted at this period in the West. But Latin might perhaps have sunk to the condition of a patois which would have offered no better resistance to Visigoths, Lombards, and Franks than it did to their kinsmen in Britain. The *elocutio novella*, of which Fronto and Apuleius are joint founders, was succeeded by the great patristic literature of the Africans, Tertullian, Cyprian, and Lactantius—and these again by the rhetorical schools of Bordeaux, Autun, and other Gallic towns. The inrush of barbarism produced far less effect on Romanesque poetry than would otherwise have been the case, because church, school, and populace were thus united in the use of Latin.[8]

The failure of Fronto and his contemporaries to create a new language may in a way be truly said to open the age of the base metals. But even if the collapse of the imperial system after Marcus Aurelius be not more striking or more complete than the collapse of classical Roman literature after Fronto, yet for the literature of Romanesque a great thing has been brought about: viz., the instilling into Latin rhythmic prose and poetry of that distinctively romantic or medieval note which, except in so far as it had been anticipated by the genius of Vergil and Petronius, appears now in literature almost for the first time.[9]

Like Fronto, Apuleius was of African origin, belonging to a civilization which was not purely European. Together with the Græco-Syrian Lucian, this Romano-African represents the last extension taken by ancient culture before it finally faded away or became absorbed in new forms. By profession both were traveling lecturers—the nearest approach which the ancient world made to what we now call the higher class of journalist. The diction of Apuleius evinces the greatest art, carefully concealed so as to present the appearance of perfect spontaneity. He is the first to introduce the oriental warmth of coloring into Latin, the minute description which invests with a new charm the poetical prose which is now superseding regular verse.[10]

This poetical prose of Apuleius, notably in his more elaborate passages, identifies itself absolutely with a type of assonant or rhyming poetry. Such verse forms, viewed not as prose but poetry, occur frequently enough in the ancient Latin Apuleius knew so well; besides, it is quite clear that both rhyme and assonance continue as deliberate devices in folk-poetry and its sophisticated imitations throughout the period of classical Roman literature. Even Vergil is known to have experimented in combining these twin figures of repetition with rhythms. Now this joining together of cadence and rhyme (or heavy assonance) by the *neoterici* under Hadrian into a prose-form was doomed to failure from the start—the result was too strained and pedantic, too artificially heavy with fanciful ornament, too inchoate for endurance. It lent an air of fatal unreality to description and to dialogue, which defeated the very purpose of prose narrative. But none the less it was an immortal contribution to the treasury of world literature that was made by Fronto and Gellius and Apuleius and the African school of *novelli poetæ*, who were striving to regenerate a threadbare Latin. For their effort, where it failed to revive a worn out prose, created a departure in Romanesque poetry that established a new type. There seems to be little doubt that by this means, and at this time, accentual Romantic poetry was born.

I shall not call to witness for this contention the *Pervigilium Veneris*, because it seems to me that such evidence as exists for its date pleads for the authorship of Tiberianus. But certainly, whether this remarkable poem was written in the second century or the fourth, it could not have been achieved in whole or in any part of it prior to that reversion to the trochaic meters which were the natural cadence of sung and spoken Latin signalizing the work of Fronto and his school. This is the first definite following up of the half instinctive initiative of Petronius, a century before. Modern as Petronius is in spirit, there is no sign that it occurred to him to engage in fresh experimentation with hitherto untried meters, to revive former trochaic movements from pre-Alexandrian models, to go in heavily for assonance and rhyme so as to establish a break with classical forms, to make his treatment of measures answer to an accentual beat rather than to quantitative scansion—but just these things were done by the poets under Hadrian and by nobody whom we know before them. The beginning of the history of Romanesque lyric we have found in the epigrams of Petronius which breathe so distinctly modern a mood— the first full springtide which brought this lyric into just those forms that were to hold captive a thousand years of poetic endeavor, came to the world in the second century of our era.

It is not, however, until the middle of the third century that Commodian's *Carmen apologeticum* furnishes us with a document showing clearly the manner in which Romanesque developed from Roman poetry. It is a poem of more than a thousand hexameters, half-quantitative and half-accentual, indicating a peculiar but a deliberate prosody. Nothing better illustrates the fresh strength gained in the third century by the accentual or rhythmical tendencies of Latin than such semi-popular hexameters of the early Christian poets; the general form and accent of classical Roman verse are kept, and yet the rules of quantity have been so relaxed as at times to be entirely negligible.[11] Side by side with this definitely new assertion of popular measures, we find even in the works which continue the classical models of Roman verse a fresh language that is changing to meet the necessity of scriptural content.[12] Thus in the *Phœnix*, ascribed to Lactantius (about 300), we have the earthly paradise east of the sun described in imagery which mingles touches of the Vergilian elysium and the apocalyptic New Jerusalem—the sun is a bridegroom coming out of his chamber—night and day utter knowledge in a speech not of words. And likewise in the four eclogues of the Carthaginian poet Nemesianus (about 260), although we have a close imitation of Vergil and a fairly correct style, the mythological legends are treated with a romantic naturalism unlike anything in classical verse.

It is in the century before Constantine that the growth of a wholly new thought and art finds itself mirrored in a new type of poetry, a new series of symbols, conventionalized epithets and figurative images—in short, a new style of Latin. With Mackail, to call the directness and the racy simplicity of this fresh Romanesque idiom "the second childhood of Latin literature" is exactly wrong. I should rather term it: A sign of the coming up like thunder of the provincial West. For Gaul in the third century was the rival of Africa in this fluent and ornate rhythmic speech that brimmed like irrepressible milk from the full udders of a young and vigorous civilization. Nursed by its rhetoric, a new Gallic school of Christian poets flourished in the the fourth century, notably in Hilarius of Poitiers, the first known author of Latin hymns, the precursor of Prudentius, and not less in Ambrose, born, and doubtless educated, at Treves.[13] A morning hymn of each will show how near they are in reality and turn of thought to the speech of modern times:

MORNING HYMN OF HILARIUS

Thou splendid giver of our light,
   O luminous serenity,
By whom beyond the lapse of night
   The day pours backward, and we see!

Thou morning star of verity,
   Another orb is messenger

Of fainter morn—Thou art not he,
 That dim and little Lucifer.

But clearer than the cloudless sun,
 Thyself being day and light, Thou art
That radiance whose bright beams run
 To view the chambers of the heart.

Draw near us, Thou who madest space,
 Light whom the Father glorified,
Before the presence of Thy grace
 The body's doorways open wide,

And with Thy spirit nourish us,
 Fulfilling us with God till we
From fraud, and from the covetous,
 And from the sins of greed are free.

This is that hope our spirits know,
 And this the prayer we offer thee:
O bid Thy morning with us go
 Into the night's captivity!   (1)

AMBROSE'S ÆTERNE RERUM CONDITOR

Eternal author of the world,[14]
Thou governor of night and day,
O bringer in of times and hours,
Joy upon our rugged way!

Now the herald of the morning,
Watchman of the deep midnight,
Sounds, dividing day and day,
Promising the traveler light.

When at dawning Lucifer
Leads the night-mist from the sky,
From the road at cock-crow driven
Troops of wicked robbers fly.

And the voice which wrung from Peter
Tears upon that sinful day
Now gives courage to the seaman
While the tempest dies away.

Up then, and begin your task—
Let us not be too long lying;
The bird who wakes us brings to shame
Hearts that still will be denying.

At his calling hope returns,
Health returneth to the ailing;
Then the coward hides his sword,
Faith comes in where strength was failing.

Jesus, guard us when we fall,
Aid us with Thy sight in sin;
If we fail Thou seest it,
Seest when our griefs begin.

To our senses Thou art light;
Break the bond of sleep and hear
How our morning psalm is Thine,
How our singing seeks Thy ear.   (2)

And so at last, except for some half-hearted revival now and then, except for the belated appearance of some inglorious classicist fallen, like Claudian and Rutilius, on evil days—the ancient world of poetry is dead, a new generation of authors throngs the stage. First Tiberianus, count of Africa, vicar of Spain, pretorian prefect of Gaul, with a descriptive passage consisting of twenty lines of finely written trochaics rich in language, delicately simple in style:

A WOODLAND SCENE

In the valley coolly flowing o'er the pebbles laughing light,
Through the fields the brooklet going is with herbs and flowers
    bright.
Smooth among the budded myrtles and the verdant laurel trees
Whispering with the voice of turtles, scarcely moving, walks the
    breeze.
And beneath, the seeds in flower burst as silently as snow,
Reddening, whitening all the bower, crocuses and lilies grow.
Where the woodland smells of sweetness with the violets in bloom
There, amid the Spring's completeness, gifts and graces and
    perfume,
Shines the rose, the star of morning, Aphrodite's special care,
Radiant in her pride and scorning lesser glories gathered there.
Moss and myrtle all the passes conquer with their verdant feet,
And amidst the dew-sweet grasses stands the orchard dewy sweet.
Here and there the streamlets wander, murmuring with frequent
    falls,
Flow and tinkle and meander, dropping down with liquid calls.
Birds among the shadows singing lyrics lovelier than you dream
Emulate the spring with ringing changes on a dulcet theme.

And the brooklet too rejoices, in the branches stirred to song
While the zephyr's liquid voices move in melody along.
Wherefore, going through the meadow and the music and the scents,
Bird and brook and light and shadow give me happiness intense.

(3)

Now to the same poet do we accord the *Pervigilium Veneris* whose lines make their creator the herald of a first medieval renaissance of Latin poetry:

THE NIGHT-WATCH OF VENUS

He that loved not shall love on the morrow, he that has loved shall love again,
For spring is new in the world once more, young spring, and the singing of birds in spring;
Spring when the young loves come together, spring when the birds find mates—ah! then
The woodland looses her maiden tresses under the marriage showers of spring.
(He that loved not shall love on the morrow, he that has loved shall love again.)

For ah, the morrow's a marriage-maker (her loves shall be where the tree-shadows fall)
Weaving her mansions of green in the forests, building her houses of myrtle spray,
Ay, through woodland, through singing woodland, leading her chorus in festival—
Tomorrow the throned Dione shall rule us, tomorrow her own high laws have sway!
(He that loved not shall love on the morrow, he that has loved shall love again.)

Tomorrow—Tomorrow wed once with Æther, in the old world that now is dead—
Out of the dew o'erhead thereafter, out of the orbèd foam—ah me!—
Sprung from the emerald host of the waters there where the sea-horse has his bed,
Came from that marriage sea-born Dione, sprung from the marriage of shower and sea.
(He that loved not shall love on the morrow, he that has loved shall love again.)

'Tis she that colors the crimsoning seasons bright with the jewels that men call flowers,

She that under the wind's warm breathing to wind-warm clusters
    brings the bud,
She that sprinkles the glittering dew left by the breath of the deep
    night's hours,
Rosy-hearted, glistening dew drops, dripping and wet, on the
    flowers for food.
(He that loved not shall love on the morrow, he that has loved
    shall love again.)

Tremble of tears that sparkle and fall, heavily fall with their
    sleepy weight,
Beads of the dew, O tiniest globes that cling together and fall,
    and they—
Why, stars drip down on cloudless nights their humors, but ah,
    when dawn's at the gate
Out of their wet sheaths push the buds, virginal paps laid bare
    to day!
(He that loved not shall love on the morrow, he that has loved
    shall love again.)

And lo! the petals, blushing and crimson, stand forth naked from
    wet green nests,
And a flame of roses, a fire of roses, burns through the clusters
    all for her sake;
The goddess herself has bidden the roses loose the garments from
    off their breasts—
Now they are virgins naked for bridal, fresh sweet brides in the
    bright day-break.
(He that loved not shall love on the morrow, he that has loved
    shall love again.)

The blood of Venus, the kiss of Love, jewel and flame and the flush
    of the sun,
Tomorrow she that is made of these, tomorrow the bride that is all
    one rose,
Unashamed, will put off her vestment as, with its dewy knot un-
    done,
The fire in the sheaf of the rose concealed, unfolds, and the flame
    of the rosebud shows.
(He that loved not shall love on the morrow, he that has loved
    shall love again.) (4)

Surely the Romanesque poets of fourth-century Gaul deserve a broad niche in the chambered labyrinth of Latin progression, since, to find a parallel to their brilliance and enthusiasm, we must go back to the school of poets which grew up around Valerius Cato in Transpadane Gaul in the first century before Christ. Surely the Romanesque poets of the fifth and sixth centuries have their assignable station quite as definitely as the Roman poets of Republic, Empire, and Western Decline. It is as essential to know Tiberianus as to know Vergil—Ausonius, as Horace—Symmachus, as Catullus—Sidonius, as Ovid. For, as a clearer realization comes to us of the immensely important function the later poets exercised in transmitting and transmuting the classical heritage of poetry for the Middle Ages, then we shall no longer consider it so heavenwide an arc from the days when Vergil was reviving the early poetry of Greece and creating the early romance of Italy, over to the sunny medieval times when the Celtic spirit came again to quicken the poetry of western Europe, and aided it to strike off the bondage of outworn inherited forms and the burden of ritualistic theology.

Far a cry as it first seems, from sixth-century poet to Augustan—from Colum Cille, say, to Vergil—sufficient signs prove that each is deeply conscious in his own day of subversive social and spiritual changes in the world of ideas, that each anticipates the advent of a new era towards which national forms are rapidly drifting. Despite their adherence to classical traditions and molds, to Vergil as to Colum Cille a new romantic prospect opened, a rich vein of modern sentiment lay bare. It has been well said of the Augustan that he anticipated papal Rome; that he conceived in Æneas a type adumbrating some mild spiritual ruler of medieval Rome rather than suggestive of some Homeric hero or a consul or emperor who commanded pagan armies and administered the city-state. In Vergil, too, there dwelt that romantic longing for lonely communion with nature in its wilder and more desolate aspects which we associate with Gaelic saint rather than with classical poet. Vergil's poems thus seem no more remarkable for their piety to ancient traditions than for their forerunning hints of a wider humanity that the Christian Era is to inaugurate and the ecclesiastic ages to foster—which description fits Columba's every writing to a nicety.

There are deeper identities still between sixth-century poet and Augustan: In the creations of both, divinity descends to earth to interfere with the affairs of men and shape their ends. Only latterly the gods and titans are become the saints, and it is no Olympian who intervenes in favor of human distress, but Peter and Paul. St. This and St. That lead forlorn causes, in substitution for heathen demiurge—one holy spirit of medieval Christendom vying with another for the palm of victory, often enough playing malicious tricks upon his fellow angel. And a sixth-century poem places the loss or gain of a chosen fight in the performance by its protagonist of an act of worship, or in the omission of the act; which is for all the world just what happens in narratives of Græco-Roman contrivance. Nay, Croce contends that this medieval scaffolding of motive is not alone analogous to the antique, but in a real sense its continuation. Haply, credulity and ignorance, myth, magic, and miracle, fable and superstition of an unaltered recipe invade the fabric of Christian humanism as they do that of pagan enlightenment.[15]

And yet right here is the point to underscore: No matter how striking the coalescence in motive and theme-presentment of sixth-century poem and its antique counterpart may be, we shall never discover real identity between them. For myth and miracle have been intensified by a religious element before unknown; they are no longer a base alloy of humanistic attitudes, or secondarily derivative—they are now harmonized to novel supernatural ideas, have become at once deeper and more wide. Myth and miracle are now not mere poetic device—they are Reality itself. They are not drawn from a classical past whose back is to the west, but from the environment of a changeful romantic present. They are not Roman but Romanesque.

Fourth-century verse shows us distinctly how close poetry has remained to what Croce calls the ideal categories of the pagan past, and yet how very far away it is. When at the end of the century and the very beginning of the fifth we come upon the verse of Claudian and Rutilius, it seems almost untouched by romantic influences, or represents, it may be, a reaction against them. The standards of this poetry are essentially those of Domitian—its fervid and sumptuous rhetoric still speaks of the age of Seneca,

Lucan, and Persius. Yet again and again (as Garrod says), the reader stops to ask himself whether all this grandeur is more than a dying masquerade of the Roman empire:

THE OLD MAN OF VERONA WHO NEVER LEFT HIS HOME

Happy is he who on his own estate
Lives his whole life, and that same roof beholds
In age which childhood saw; who with his stick
Totters across those fields where as a babe
He crept, and numbers out his lengthening years
In one ancestral home. Him fortune vexed
With no wild tumults; as a wanderer
He drank no draught from alien wells; he feared
No seas as merchant and no wars as soldier,
And him the noisy lawcourts never lured
From his own home. Unskilled in men's affairs
And unfamiliar with the neighboring town,
A freer sight of heaven he has to enjoy,
Who by the seasons marks his calendar
And not by consulates. His autumn is
By apples, and his spring by blossoms, known;
His farm beholds the sun arise and set,
And by its light he tells laborious hours.
The oak which as an acorn once he knew
He yet remembers, and his eyes have seen
The mighty grove grow old along with him.
He thinks Verona is as far away
As sun-scorched India—and Benacus seems
The Arabian Sea. But he keeps unimpaired
His health and strength till a third generation
Reveres in him their stout and robust sire.
Let others wander to Iberian shores;
They have a varied, he a truer, life.   (5)

THE LONELY ISLE

Deep in a distant bay, and deeply hidden,
There is an island far away from me
Which lulls the tumbling waves to dreamy quiet;
And there steep cliffs against the water's riot
Stand up, and to their shelter ships are bidden,
Where those curved arms shut in a tranquil sea.

(6)

EPITAPH

Fate to beauty still must give
Shortened life and fugitive;
All that's noble, all that's fair
Suddenly to death repair.
Here a lovely woman lies,
Venus in her hair and eyes;
Since with these she must divide
Heaven's envy, here she died.   (7)

FAREWELL TO ROME

Hear me, fair queen of the wide universe,
Victorious Rome, ruler from sky to sky,
Mother of men, of deities the nurse,
O hear! Within thy temples we are nigh
To heav'n, and thee we sing eternally,
And while the fates permit us we shall sing.
No man unhurt shall put thy memory by;
And ere thy glory from our hearts takes wing,
Let dark forgetfulness the sun to ruin bring!

Unto all corners of the world which ocean
With circumfluent wave bounds in, thou art
An equal benefactor; and the motion
Wherewith Apollo's steeds take in each part
Measures the road whereon thy coursers start.
The south her flame-struck sands in vain defends,
Nor the armed north with cold dismays thy heart;
Under whatever skies the world extends,
So far thy power goes unto the world's great ends.

Thou art one race, where many nations were,
One land, where there were many. By thy worth
The wicked man is taken prisoner,
But prisoners know thy justice hath not dearth.
Thou art a city which was once the earth;
We know that Mars and Venus founded thee
From whom Æneas, Romulus, had birth—
O thou who mixest war with clemency
As though the gods had made their dwelling place in thee.

Thy goodness conquers those thou mak'st afraid,
The conquered love the mercy that is thine;
For thou rever'st the olive-giving maid
And him that was the planter of the vine,

And him that ploughed thy furrows first. A sign
Thou holdest dear Apollo's healing skill
And Hercules, by greatness grown divine,
Thine altars are; thy lawful triumphs fill
A world where states and cities flourish by thy will.

And Romans, come from everywhere to thee,
Shall praise thee, O thou goddess, for they bear
Lightly thy peaceful yoke of Liberty.
And in the eternal circles that they wear
The armies of the stars see naught so fair
As thine imperial splendor. Thou alone
Couldst send thy far-flung host of soldiery where
Assyria is, and to the boundary stone
Of Persia has thy conquest spread its mighty zone.

Ay, thou hast beaten powerful Parthian kings
And tyrants ruling Macedonia,
Changing their various laws to certain things;
Nor didst thou need more hands or hearts, for they
But brought thee deeper counsel, fairer play
Of wisdom. O thou hast thy noblest state
Not in proud peace, nor war's most just array!
Splendid thou art, thy merit's yet more great,
And by thy mighty acts thou dost surpass thy fate!
(8)

Masquerade, too, is the Platonic hymn to the Nameless God, another noble monument of the dying paganism of the fourth century carved by the chisel of Tiberianus. Masquerade likewise is much of the writing of Ausonius: *vide* his lines to his dead wife, and to Cupid crucified:

TO HIS DEAD WIFE

A wound I cannot close, long pain and sorrow,
A wife whom death did most untimely borrow—
These I remember and, remembering, tell.
Your birth was noble, and your rank as well,
But though a senator's wife Sabina bore,
Your life good actions did ennoble more;
A youth, I wept you, lost in tender years,
And nine Olympiads have not stopped my tears.
Old age will not permit my pangs to cease
For, since they're ever fresh, so they increase.
And though time brings to others balm for grief,
In length of days my hurt finds no relief—

My widowed state mocks the gray locks I tear,
The more I live, the greater woe I bear.
My house, the unwarmed bed, the good or ill
I share with none: these make my wound bleed still;
At good men's wives I grieve and, if they're bad,
You are the pattern others should have had.

From either part for you my pain doth strike;
If bad, she is not you; if good, she's like.
I mourn no useless wealth, no empty joy
But the young wife snatched from me when a boy.
For beauty and for birth alike renowned,
Bright, modest, quiet, you Ausonius crowned,
And yet you were his grief, since ere were sped
Some eight and twenty winters o'er your head,
Deserting them, you did yourself remove
From two young children, pledges of our love.
By heaven's grace, in virtue of your prayers
They flourish, and all worldly goods are theirs.
Fortune to them, I pray, shall freely give—
And more: that your dust from my own receive
The tidings I am dead and that they live.   (9)

CUPID CRUCIFIED

In fields of shadow (such the Maronian muse
Remembers) where dark myrtles gloom above
The souls of lovers grown insensible,
Heroic women, to mysterious rites
Assembling, once went forth. And as they died,
So they bore with them emblems of their doom,
Wandering the mighty forest and the beds
Of heavy-headed poppies and long reeds
Under a doubtful light beside dead lakes
Without a motion, streams unmurmuring.
In cloudy twilight by these margined waters
Are flowers with the names of lads and princes
By anguish written on their petaled leaves:
Crocus the golden-haired and Hyacinth
Child of Œbalus and Narcissus, he
That saw his own sweet face, and purple-hued
Adonis, Salaminian Ajax there
Depicted in his sorrowful last cry.
And these remembrances of love and sorrow
And doom and lamentation bring to mind
Remembered woes that were oblivious else
In death, until these mournful heroines
Relive again their own forgotten past. . . .   (10)

Masquerade is the ode to Poetry and Time, which Phocas (about 500) prefixed to his *Life of Vergil:*

POETRY AND TIME

Thou ancient guardian over time's treasures,
Bringer back of royal kings! O thou that also
Rememberest our flying, momentary pleasures,
    Aureate Clio!

All noble acts thou preservest; men's glories
Death cannot hide since great deeds enfold thee,
Who in thy volumes sealest up the stories
    Past years have told thee.

Thou only knowest not to dye thy pages,
Thou from whom truth proceeds, bold, never wearied,
Singing one story through unchanging ages
    Clear and unvaried.

Great names grow dim. Thou, bringing flowers,
Blooms of immortal youth, ever renewest them.
Virtue thy soldier is. Life's evil powers
    Fail if thou viewest them.

Tumult and rumor—thou to escape them
Fleest to mold sweet song at thy pleasure,
Halting the words of none, though thou dost shape them
    To even measure.

Bless thou my lines revealing Vergil's story,
Seer and Etruscan, to the Romans bringing
Timeless honor through the eternal glory
    Of sacred singing.   (11)

I have been at pains to heap up examples of learned revival of ancient meters and mannerisms which occur in the fourth and fifth centuries, and to label them masquerades—i. e., costume-pieces illustrative of bygone dress and usage—because I do not wish to have them interfere with our story of the progress of Roman literature, as if they were in any real sense an integral part of it. Such costume-pieces fill the sixth century and for that matter every later century (including our own) when poets either as a stated task of school routine or an act of elegant leisure have indited whimsical counterfoils of Horace and Vergil. Because it is easier for Walter Headlam to write Greek than English, we do not group him in the story of Hellenistic verse along with Theocritus, Meleager, and Musæus—because of Postgate's rarefied resummonings of Latin hexameters and elegiacs, we do not hold open the account of lyric begun in the Augustan Age until we establish him as antipodal to Propertius and Tibullus. It is to my mind futile to protract the tale of classical Roman poetry beyond the first century of the Christian Era simply because after that date there were so many *rifacimenti* of classical meters and conventions. Such copyings are forgeries, stereotyped retracings, continuation of gallery favorites and museum pieces—they betoken only that sublimation of *sitzfleisch* which is the opposite of genius. Who, after Alexander Pope, may not aspire to write better than Pope, if he forget not a single Popian touch and come to be measured by the standard of Pope alone—*absit omen?* It is not the redoings and overworkings of Republican and Augustan models which constitute the contribution of the Silver Age to Latin literature. It is the invention by Martial and Juvenal of the pointed epigram and invective satire, by Petronius of the romantic novel and epigram, by the younger Pliny of the rhetorical epistle—all of them new Latin genres. Lucan attains sustained beauty of narrative through simple pathos, as in the climactic moment of farewell after Cornelia's speech when Pompey and his wife are parting—here Lucan gains an effect unequaled again in the poetry of southern Europe till Dante tells the story of Francesca and Paolo. Quintilian's breadth of outlook and critical acumen command respect from the severest critics of Rome's literary ideals. Seneca and Tacitus are admittedly two of the greatest names in Roman literature. Had all else that Statius wrote been merely mediocre, Statius's one short invocation to Sleep would give him a claim on the grateful memory of posterity. There is no immeasurable distance between the *Argonautica* of Flaccus and much of *The Idylls of the King.* Persius speaks straight from the heart, is one of the few writers of Rome whose personality awakens affection. His tribute to Cornutus reveals in an age of corruption a moral ardor and an unclouded nobility of thought. Many centuries were to elapse on the continent of Europe ere, within the compass of one hundred years, there would be again produced a body of poetry and poetic prose comparable in diversity, originality, and sterling excellence with work created by Romans in the Silver Age of their literature.

So think critics like Summers and Butler, who view the period from Seneca to Juvenal, not as a classical continuance, but as a romantic revolt. And so I would view my fourth century, not as a time which marks the dusk of any possible reversion to the touted splendors of antique measures (although in efforts as abortive as those of Julian the Apostate our poets strive to reforge cold classical glories)—I would view this century as the dawn of a romantic humanism when for the first time in any modern sense Byzantium, Carthage, and Rome, Spain, Gaul, and Britain might mingle and find in free verse realistic expression. For this century is the age of Athanasius, Ambrose, and Gregory Nazianzen; of Augustine, Jerome, and Ulfilas; of Ausonius, Tiberianus, and that Prudentius whom Erasmus calls *unum inter Christianos vere facundum poetam*. It fills betimes the leathern bottles of an older poetry, but with wine of a new spirit. The Plutarch of this age is the *Vitæ patrum sive eremitarum;* its Herodotus is Eusebius of Cæsarea and the Church Fathers. Its epics do not sing the warring of Greek and barbarian, but the conflict of the faithful with unbelievers. Sole capital of this new realm of ideas and letters is not now Constantinople, not now Rome—but heaven alone knows what incontiguous outpost of a changing order: Mœsia or Bethlehem, Carthage or Saragossa, Spolato or Bordeaux, Aix-la-Chapelle or York.

It is only when I regard the start or close of a spiritual medium like poetry as an absolute beginning or a definitive end that I fail to discover Roman culture and ideas in the fourth century as I am describing it. It is only by conceiving this epoch as mechanistically limiting itself to classical models that I find it a repellant pole of the Augustan Age.

No. Life is stupendous energy. Sometimes it seems to falter, its pulse grows weak or intermittent in stroke. But every moment of life that achieves dynamic expression in poetry adheres ideally to both what precedes and what follows it. Each such symbolizing moment of poetry as it lives out its flash makes its response to the eternal symbols of humanity, and is, therefore, worthy of our interest and belief. But because it is impossible for us to chronicle all such moments, we are forced to choose for our notation only a few of the many valuable currents of poetic utterance— and in our periodizing and contrasting of these we are sure to pay toll to the fashion of that time when we write our criticism. We come thus to view with contempt (like the classicist) the story of poetry envisioned from any philosophical angle except our own. When we see, for example, Ausonius using his words in a French, and not a Latin, sense, we stamp him a very paradox of human perversity— so prone are we to forget (unless Croce recall us to a proper Hegelianism) that the story of dead poetry is not its real story, but rather the tale of how, from our angle of convenience, we care to regard it. The poetic history of the fourth century is not something for our studies blindly to pursue, but only a phantom that our studies more or less blindly create. Ausonius is then not the spiritual father of my present moment, but its child.[16]

In the light of this reasoning, let me formulate the backgrounds of poetry in sixth-century Gaul. It is here that most historians have said a perfunctory goodnight to culture and civilization—as understood in Augustan Rome. They call the start of this century a plunge downward, its middle a ditch, its consummation a bottomless pit. And yet, just this age fills the scene with figures of restless demoniac energy who are to set in motion poetic impulses destined not to halt in their career until the full meaning of twelfth-century humanism is achieved: Gregory the Great and Columban; Gregory of Tours and Fortunatus; Cassiodorus and Boethius.

The first of these giants placed the Middle Ages beneath the real rule of Rome—incidentally he gave us the Gregorian hymn and the *Dialogues*.[17] The second brought back to Gaul the intellectual forms of antiquity, fruit for the disciples that gathered around him all the stationed road from Annegray to Bobbio. With no touch of the dogmatic, dread-inspired egotism characteristic of the bishop of Hippo, this Irishman found sure channels for his creative whims in an elegant Latin and (reputedly) a fluent Greek.

Cassiodorus of Verona lends his documents a living force that engages the modern reader as much as it did Theodoric. His encyclopedic compendia more than maintain the wonted level of patriarchal usage of the older sophists; they avoid metaphysic and fustian; they reduce irritating traditional formulæ to something like common sense, thus dispensing scientific knowledge in a way monks could adopt—and even we can understand. Boethius likewise summed up with prim neatness the culture of antiquity, creating the last known original work of classical philosophy, which had unheard-of vogue throughout the Middle Ages. His translations of Greek philosophers and his commentaries on them united the schoolrooms of monasteries with the intellectual past as by cables of steel—and we may owe our present attitudes toward Aristotle's logic and a major portion of Hellenic thought more to Boethius than to Arab mediation. In the province of *belles lettres* Boethius was quite the virtuoso of meters, not only furnishing us with striking examples of their use, but surcharging them as well with ideas that watermark the experience and the longing of his day.

If I were not hesitant further to bury the continuity of my arguments regarding Romanesque poetry beneath the accumulation of evidences for the greatness of the sixth century, I should pause at this point to cite the added testimony of other names: Ennodius, for instance, and Benedict of Nursia, and Isidore of Seville. But at least I must not permit my reader to forget it was in this period that the famous *Latin Anthology* was compiled in Carthage.[18] Scholarship is still wary of putting many of the poems in this splendid collection to proper use and analysis, because suspicion is rife that the anthology still harbors a long list of pseudo-antique pieces, which are, in reality, products of the fifteenth century. It is none the less a remarkable phenomenon of philological irony—particularly in the light of the spendthrift effort which has been devoted to the *Greek Anthology*—that there is yet no thoroughfare for the amateur of the earliest Middle Age through the gateway of one of its most allusive collections.

Why is our Carthage compilation an "allusive" collection? Because it offers us a few occasional verses which indicate sufficiently how unfair it is to view the sixth century as a time when the lyric muse groped in twilight. Our earliest Latin anthology proves as conclusively as do its congeners of ninth and tenth-century Romanesque poetry, how futile it is for us to assume that the golden thread of continuity wore thin to the snapping point at any dark moment of steady (if sluggish) Latin lyrical progression, just because that dimly sensed moment fails to flash into our eyes manifest examples of personalized cadence. It is well worth pausing but for a short breath while we record a few outstanding instances of such graceful Romanesque singing:

PAINTED PASSION

Paint a whitelimbed girl for me
Such as love himself might fashion;
So that nothing hidden be,
Paint her with a lover's passion.
Through her silken garments show
All her body's rosy wonder—
Love will set your sense aglow,
Longing tear your heart asunder.
Call it, when your work you scan,
"Portrait of a wretched man." (12)

PRAYER TO VENUS

Tell me, Venus, what's to do?
   Loving does not win a lover.
Youth declines and beauty passes;
Violets die in dewy grasses;
Roses lose their fragrance, too;
Lilies, when the spring is over,
Their lost whiteness ne'er recover!
O let these examples be
Arguments for clemency!
   Grant me aid,
And in loving be repaid. (13)

REPLIQUE

She that finds in sin a pleasure,
  She is not among true lovers;
    She hath lost her virgin flower—
      Only what's denied is sweet.
Such a maiden keeps no measure
  In her love and ne'er recovers
    The delight of one white hour—
      For my love she's all unmeet. (14)

THE EUNUCH'S DELIGHT

Still let me love though I may not possess;
Though others taste enjoyment, I'll not die;
Their raptures do not bring me bitterness;
Myself for them I shall not crucify.
Venus makes lovers fit for amorous blisses;
We're made desirous and deny desire.
Well, let the others pluck their crimson kisses,
Nipping with tender bites red lips of fire.
Let white teeth in their kissing meet on white,
And let them smell the apples of her mouth,
The perfume of her cheeks; and on the bright
Twin diamonds of her eyeballs slake their drouth.
When her soft body on the soft, silk bed
They clasp in Venus' melting close embraces,
May hot desire, by which a woman's led,
Flame in her flesh and wanton in her graces.
Amid the murmurings of her love-sick voice,
Feed on her paps until your limbs shall harden
. . . .

. . . .
These things they do whom Venus doth not spite;
But when we love we are content with less;
And if my leaping is a maimed delight,
Still let me love though I may not possess. (15)

Luckily, however, we have another witness from the sixth century than the *Latin Anthology* to convince us of the actual presence in this age of most unusual poetic power, in the elegies of Maximian, the favored pupil of Boethius. In her recent essay on the wandering scholars Miss Waddell describes this writing not unjustly as one of the strangest documents of the human mind: Ecclesiastes without its austere reconciliation; the *ossa arida* of the Valley of Dead

asures, but no breath from the four winds will blow upon
se slain. It is possible of course that Maximian's work
ιn autobiography (as he suggests), one written with a
·ible sincerity but redeemed from over-intimacy by the
umanity of its art: a consummate egotism aware of every
ing of its power, every circumstance and squalor of its
line, mocking even the impulse that drugs the presence
h its garrulous resurrection of the past. But, in spite of
 appealing idyl of schoolboy passion, in spite of the dream-
e for Candida, in spite of the Greek girl at the end, I
uld prefer to regard the *Elegies* as a saturnine charac-
·zation of human pride and sensuality, done with the
ꓯ blood of a Swift and the bludgeoning thoroughness of
)efoe. How oddly the following lines contrast with the
.tle platonism of Venantius:

OLD AGE

Old age is jealous and delays my end,
I know not why, nor why in this tired flesh
Life, lingering, stays when I implore release
From the poor prison of my sorry body.
Go find out Death, Old Age! Mere living is
A weary weight—I am not what I was,
My better parts being dead, and what remains
Is horror and debility, when light,
The loveliest of lovely things to man,
Becomes a burden in my desolation.
O worst of ills to be a living corpse!
. . . .
For me, alas, whose frame these many years
Hath been defunct, to walk the ways of hell
Yet living, is appointed. Lessened hearing,
A lessened taste, and lessened eyes—by touch
Scarce able to pick out the shape of things—
No perfume sweet, no pleasure grateful to me—
How can I be more expert than my senses?
Lethean darkness overcomes my mind;
Confusedly, I scarcely know myself.
No tasks to finish—I am weak in body,
And my intentions smothered in my ills.
I sing no song, for song's supremest joy
Flies when the beauty of the voice is fled;
I speak before no court; I feign no poems,
(I gain hard wages in a fiercer trial!)

And bodily beauty, once my dear delight,
Beauty itself forsakes me, and I seem
Cadaverous in my very frame. That red
Which o'erlaid my lips, crimson no more,
Turns pale, a leprous white, a bloodless color;
My skin dries up, my every nerve is stiff;
With crooked hands I scrape my scabrous sides;
And rheumy eyes, where laughter once looked out,
Weep, a perpetual fountain, day and night,
My punishment. Eyebrows, of old in beauty
Meeting above and shadowing them, are now
A shaggy thicket-tangle, fallen down
Where under, hidden in a sunless cave,
Eyes peer our wildly like a madman's eyes.
Fearful it is to look upon the old!
You can not think them human, can not think
That they have reason, even as you and I!

. . . .
Such the first fruits of death, such the degrees
By which age flows away or bores within
By sluggish, slow gradation. Neither health
Nor color nor one's step in going out,
Nor even one's face stays as it was before.
From his shrunk arms and his diminished body
The clothes fall, slipping down, and what was brief
Of old is lengthy now, and we contract
And lessen in a most admired disorder.
You'd think the very bones had shrunk!
                              To heaven
You can't look up; the old man, bending down,
Beholds the earth, to which, being born of it,
He shall return, making a three-legged thing
And then a four, and like a puling infant
Creeping in weakness on the dirty ground.
For all things seek their origins, all return
To her who bore them; what was naught before
Once more reverts to nothingness. Whence it is
The old man, leaning on his stick beats, beats
With feeble stroke assiduously the earth
Which is so dilatory. With short steps
And frequent motion he from wrinkled mouth
Utters such prayer as this: "O earth my mother,
Take back what is so wretched in its labors,
And let me lay once more upon your lap
My worn-out limbs. The boys make sport of me—
I can not be what I have been. Ah, why,
Why have you given birth to such abortions?
To me nothing remains. I have spent my life.

Receive once more, I pray, a dying man
Into his native element. Who can guard
From life's strange ills those that are miserable?
A mother's heart not thus, not thus is shown!"

And having said, he takes his tremulous joints
And lays them on his bed of unkept straw,
Where after that he stays, not differing greatly
From a dead pauper, for you see the bones
Stick through his skin.
. . . .
We are conquered by the weakness of the flesh,
And where we would not, thither are we dragged.
Our bowels dissolve. O that a work so splendid
Should come to such an end! Yet an old man,
Bent down and burdened by infirmities,
Must school himself to yield beneath the load.
Who now can wish to drag out so long life,
While bit by bit the soul slips into dying?
Better be with the dead than be yet living
Among the dead and, being sensible,
Yet bury one's own members in the tomb!
. . . .
           (16)

LYCORIS

Lovely Lycoris that was my delight,
(We two were one, we two had but one soul!)
After the many years we've lived together,
Now she, even she, like one who's stupefied,
Repudiates my embraces; now she seeks
(Alas that it is so!) for other lovers
And younger loves and calls me impotent,
A senile, weak old man, nor will remember
The sweets that have gone by nor that she gladly
Gave herself to me, being old. And now,
Perfidious and lacking gratitude,
She trumps up accusations, she will have me
A scorner of her in my viciousness!
Just now she passed me by; when me she saw,
She spat and with her garments covered up
Her face and spoke: "Did ever I delight
In him? Or know in his embraces love?
Did I once give him ('tis unthinkable!)
Soft, frequent kisses?" Then like one who rids
Old bitterness by vomit, she turned sick,
And hurled a thousand curses at my head.

Alas, what will the long day next bring forth?
There's none but finds it shameful to surrender
The dear delights he had! Were it not better
At such a time for me to die, who am
For this just shame despised? Yes, it were better,
When all the beauty of a man is dead,
Than to live on amid deserved disgrace
Like one extinct. Nothing remains of all
We two have lived and known. Time, going by,
Takes all things with him, takes our deepest hours.

Yet while white hairs surround my temples, while
The crimson of the lips fades into purple,
Lycoris still lives on and to herself
Was never lovelier, and all her years,
Victorious, she scorns. I do confess
She keeps the beauty of her youthful body,
And in my ashes an old flame survives.

I see the years still spare your loveliness;
Not all the charms you had have perished wholly,
And new loves pasture where the old loves fed.
Because you are the you you were before,
You please me still. The fresh limbs of your youth
Stand up before me, to a lost luxury
Tempting. But since the function of my members
Deserts me wholly, there's no embracing left,
Not even in delay. O when all's gone,
Bitter complaint alone is left to the unhappy!
The many joys I had, they're now so many
Afflictions to be wept!

                    And yet the nymph
Not always loves, and at all times the wife
Is not desirous. A submissive woman
Conquers her conqueror. Why should not we
Be like the herd to whom the day avails?
Nothing of all that past which you remember
Shall be. The brutes dislike and flee new fields;
The quick flocks seek the pasture they have known;
Under accustomed shade the bull is used
To find delight in quiet; and the sheep
Hunt their old fields, and the sweet nightingale
Makes music in all solitary thickets,
Singing wild beats to jocund marriage beds.
These, the familiar and the known, you leave
To find an unknown, strange abiding place.
Is it not wiser and more sweet to trust

In certain things? The unknown always has
A dubious event, and though I am
A grandfather, your hair is not less gray.
Our equal ages should make equal souls.
And if I am not what I was, remember
That I am charmed because you charmed of old.
Unto the ancient husbandman some reverence
Is due when he is ill and past his prime;
And what the veteran had, the soldier loves.
The rustic weeps because his youthful skill
Hath ceased, and knights pay honor to their horses
When they (like them) grow old. Age hath not spoiled me
Of pristine flowers yet. Do you not see
How I make verse and sing what I have made?
Let gravity, let age itself bring reverence
In you, and let it be that since you know
How we have lived, we shall live longer so.
Who in another's crime damns his own life,
Or who drags out a journey that is ended?
Call me a brother, if you will, or if you scorn
The name, then call me father. Either holds
Some portion of affection. Then shall honor
Succeed to lust, and piety to love,
And reason, stronger than blind strength, will come,
And we together in our tears shall weep
The lengthening years as much as they deserve,
And know 'tis hard long to remember pain. (17)

Chapter VII

ROMANESQUE OUTLOOK ON NATURE

Ever since I first began to discuss Romanesque as a type separate from Roman poetry, it has irked me not to companion my indications regarding this mutation in the purely lyric Latin genres—erotic ode, personal idyl, elegy, and epigram—with evidences of a similarly decisive shift garnered from epic, narrative, and dramatic forms. My distress over not fulfilling this attractive task is doubled, because, in the epic and narrative forms particularly, traces of subversive change from the classical Latin to the romantic Latin style are visible on every hand. And by thus enriching my argument with examples of epic and narrative mutation I might gain a background against which would stand forth in high relief the process of lyric change from the manner of Roman to the whim of Romanesque, from urbane to rustic, from metropolitan to provincial, from conventional to realistic, from metrical to rhythmical, from melodic to polyphonic, from restrained to pathetic, from artificial to popular and colloquial. In short, if I could only show in related genres of Latin poetry the development from one sort of Romanic fiber to another, then my contention that the purely lyric genres underwent an identical alteration would be more than half won from the start.

Unhappily, however, before it is possible to synopsize the results to be gained from a study of these other poetic genres, with a view to comparing them with the facts derived from lyric progress, it will be necessary to establish much more clearly than has yet been done the metes and bounds which separate one from another—for from the Augustan Age onward the divisions between epic, narrative, and dramatic types break down altogether. By this I mean that in linguistic dress, technique, method of presentation, purpose, and appeal these three forms so merge their initially separate identities that it is not yet the convenience of scholarship to study them as containing genres of precedent entities. I shall not baldly state that epic, narrative, and dramatic forms do not somehow span the chasm of a thousand years which yawns devouringly between the Græco-Roman prototypes and Latin reappearances in the late Middle Ages and the early Renaissance. I do not contend that the essential oils of classical epic, narrative, and drama were not mysteriously preserved in the "slave-dungeons" of a darkened world, so that they later appeared to nourish and renew unexpected medieval Latin descendants. I say merely that scholarship has not yet investigated and formulated sufficiently their aberrant forms to make it possible for one to reason from their known idiosyncrasies, in order by analogy the better to understand transitional fashions and whimsies in Latin lyrical descent. None regrets this fact more than I. None believes more firmly that it does not mark a permanently inarticulate state of critical invalidism.

It will be recalled that in our last chapter we presented in English translation certain revivals or masquerades of classical Roman manner and form by Claudian, Rutilius, Ausonius, and Phocas, thereby showing how closely during the fourth and fifth centuries Latin lyrical poetry might adhere to the ideal categories of the pagan past. It is now much in point to contrast with these museum pieces of poetic petrefaction some examples of Romanesque which—like the *Woodland Scene* and the *Night-Watch of Venus* of Tiberianus—show how far away from accepted classical categories the same period had got. And first let me choose poems like the Ausonian *Of Roses* and the burnished description of a dinner-dance by Sidonius, each of which may be honestly said so to oscillate between the objective manner of the ancients and the subjective mood of the moderns that it is amazingly difficult to draw a dividing line which shall separate one from another because of this external characteristic or that inner device. Strands in the same silken weaving are, on the one hand, classical style and meter, the old-fashioned motives, and archaizing machinery of Roman supernaturalism; on the other hand, the neologisms of a new school of taste and rhetoric, novelties of pretty word-painting and provincial atmosphere. Coleridge discovered such duplicity of presentment in Claudian; nor can it escape our notice in Tiberian's apostrophe to Gold—*Aurum quod nigri manes*—and the epigram on Too Adventurous Wings—*Ales dum madidis*. In the rose-poem we have the Roman imagery and scaffolding, but we also have the Romanesque viewpoint of a poet who has often been called one of the first of modern men, that Ausonius who is walking by fourfold paths in an Italian garden and describing his chosen flower in words curiously blended of passionate interest and cold, keen observation:

OF ROSES

Spring, and the faint first dawn to skies less cold
Returning, grew with breathing into gold,
    And going just before the harnessed steeds
The velvet breeze a sultry day foretold,

When, wandering a watered garden through
By fourfold paths, my vigor to renew
    Ere the full heat, I saw the bended grass
And fragrant flowers starred with frozen dew;

Saw the bright drops on leaf and stem descend
Till with the weight of heavenly dew they bend,.
    While to the Pæstan rosebeds burning there
The orient skies a rosier glory lend.

The rare gems bend the bushes with their weight
And perish as the radiant day grows late;
    I wonder if the dawn from roses steals,.
Or gives, being born, that splendor roseate.

One rose, one dawn, one color feel thy powers,
Venus—thou lady of the stars and flowers!
    It may be that same odor through the sky
Breathes, that here perfumes more immediate hours.

O Paphian! Deity of flower and star,
Thou teachest that thy purple garments are
    One; that the moment came when separate buds
Took form and grew till now these roses are.

One, covered close and capped with green,
One, whose bright red peeps from a verdant sheen;

One, a steep-sloping pyramid of flame,
Spires to a spear-point of purpureal sheen;

One, thrusting off the veils that hid her hair,
Numbers her petals to herself, aware,
    Laughing, how she displays her glorious cup
Veined dense with gold and naked to the air.

But one, who burned with that consuming flame,
Now droops her leaves and is grown pale for blame;
    I wonder that the rape of swift-flying time
Brings, even with its birth, the rose to shame.

For even as I speak, the Punic hair
Of the red rose falls, strewn earthwise everywhere;
    Birth after birth, kind after kind renewed,
One day sprung forth, the next day fade to air.

Weep that the time of flowers is so slight,
By nature shown, then stolen from our sight;
    Long as the day, so long the rose may live,
And on the heels of youth age comes like night.

That flower just born which morning doth behold,
Pale evening, coming at its hour, finds old;
    And well it is if, after some days dying,
Herself in later buds she sees unfold. . . .

Pluck roses, girl, while youth and roses flower.
Think! Age prepares for you its fatal hour! (1)

INVITATION TO THE DANCE

Spread the board with linen snow,
Bid ivy and the laurel grow
Over it, and with them twine
The green branches of the vine.
Bring great baskets that shall hold
Cytisus and the marigold,
Cassia and starwort bring
And crocuses, till everything,
Couch and sideboard, all shall be
A garland of perfumery.
Then with balsam-perfumed hand
Smooth disheveled locks; and stand
Frankincense about, to rise—
An Arabian sacrifice—
Smoking to the lofty roof.

>   Next, let darkness be a proof
>   That our lamps with day may vie,
>   Glittering from the chamber's sky.
>   Only in their bowls be spilled
>   Oil nor grease, but have them filled
>   With such odorous balm as came
>   From the east to give them flame.
>   Then bid loaded servants bring
>   Viands that shall please a king,
>   Bowing underneath the weight
>   Of chased silver rich and great.
>   Last, in bowl and patera
>   And in cauldron mingle a
>   Portion of Falernian wine
>   With due nard, while roses shine
>   Wreathed about the cup and round
>   The cup's tripod. We'll confound—
>   Where the garlands sway in grace
>   From vase to alabaster vase—
>   All the measures of the dance;
>   And our languid limbs shall glance
>   In a mazy, Mænad play.—
>   Step and voice shall Bacchus sway,
>   And in garment let each man
>   Be a Dionysian!   (2)

The most remarkable novelty suggested by the lines of Sidonius, however, lies neither in their theme nor form, but in their mention of private dancing, for the older Roman world knew only professional ballet.[1] A thousand years after Homer represents on the shield of Achilles a social dance that Paris considered strikingly similar to the medieval French caroles, we know that the Hellenic world had not lost the tradition of this courtly pastime, for Origen says that in the dance the devil makes war on man by the show of woman's form, by her voice and her touch—one sees the tripping woman the more for the dress she wears, one hears her singing, her laughter and chatter—hands come in contact. With such means at his disposal the Fiend is sure of his victory. But from the Roman world no document shows a trace of dancing for the simple enjoyment of it by young people of free birth. The mention of social dancing by Tibullus is in a passage describing the fabled paradise of Love and is doubtless imitated from a Greek source:

> But I, that have been easily moved to love,
> With Venus through Elysian fields shall move.
> There song and dancing flourish. Birds fly there
> With their small throats to sound a tender air.
> The unlabored fields bear cassia, and there grows
> In all that kindly earth the scented rose.
> And there with tender girls the young men play
> And love forever leads them to the fray.   (3)

Soon enough after the crumbling of Roman civilization in Gaul we see the custom of private dancing attested everywhere. Because of lack of reference to it in Latin texts, we may assume that it can hardly be a Roman fashion, nor does western dancing probably hark back to Gaulish tradition prior to the Roman conquest. The art is either an importation from Germany or, because of the weight of oriental influences indicated in previous chapters of this book, perhaps more likely a borrowing by Gaul from the Near East.

It is not because of such songs as the above, however, that I should make of either Ausonius or Sidonius a modern poet—nor should I call them, by the same token, harbingers of coming medieval dawn. Perhaps not even the famous lines in which Ausonius describes the singing of folksongs on the banks of the Moselle, nor yet his tribute to the love of Darby and Joan would impel me to insist that we have at last come across the threshold into the modern world:

SINGING ON THE MOSELLE

A folk rejoicing in labor, husbandmen busy and nimble
Move and work on the heights and along the slopes of the valley,
Singing their country ditties. To some the traveler journeying
Under the bank responds; and some from his vessel the sailor
Mocks in answering song because they are late to the vineyards.
Echoes ring from the rocks and the shore and the trembling forests.
                                                            (4)

DARBY AND JOAN

> Live out, my wife, the life that we have had,
>   Guarding love's name
> As when unto our bride-bed love first came;
>   And with no day be sad

> That we are growing old, for you shall ever be
> > The girl you were to me,
> > And I the lad you knew.
> > And had I Nestor's age—if you
> > Should overcount the Sibyl's years or be
> > > The rival of Deiphobe—
> > We should not say, we two, that we've grown old;
> > To know the best of age (O this is true!)
> > The number of past years need not be told. (5)

And yet I should be thoroughly justified in considering such evidence as these pieces afford sufficient to establish a new type of poetry, did I but care to base my claims for the existence of this new species upon their testimony alone. Any new species is to a dominant fractional extent like some other type from which it is in large part derived—let us examine this fact at once—but at the same time different from that other type because of the presence of some small percentage of absolute novelty.

Fifteen hundred years after Ausonius, another Gallic poet, Victor Hugo, felt impelled to free dramatic verse from those classical rules which he considered a fatal impediment to genius. The innovations effected by *Hernani* therefore consist first of all in violating the rules of the alexandrine. The play begins with a run-over line of the sort no classicist could tolerate. Again, many lines discard the set division of the alexandrine into two equal halves and employ an irregular division into three frequently unequal periods. Now these innovations are not as deep as a well nor as broad as a church door; in fact, they seem amazingly slight to cause a riot from February 25, 1830, until far into the following March. And yet these two features of enjambement and free cesura, under the leadership of Hugo, Dumas the elder, Musset, Gautier, and Vigny, made the romantic drama of France an accomplished fact and inalienably distinguish from classicism a poetic form, although even *the romanticists cleave to classic regularity in ninety per cent of their verse*. It is true that *Hernani* also offended the classical purists by calling a spade a spade on occasion and by "moody" dialogue, by sometimes violating the unities, or by indulging in elaborate stage-directions, or by paying sporadic attention to concrete action. But first as last it is the two slight irregularities in tonic utterance which remain the determinant factors of the Romantic School in French poetry.

Likewise, although nine-tenths of the time—or even more if you wish—Ausonius, because of the purity of his Vergilian rhythm, the classic beauty of his diction, and the lettered ease of his images, certainly reminds one of the Augustan days in Rome, yet when he comes to be compared in his *Mosella* with the great contemporary Claudian in his *Rape of Proserpine*, we realize that what seems to be but an occasional difference between the two poets is a cataclysmic one. Claudian turns out to be a continuator of obsolete classical Roman form, Ausonius the first of French poets. So absolutely may slight turns of phrase determine a new type.

I feel that a dividing line between Roman and Romanesque poetry in the fourth century may be established by their difference in the treatment of external nature. Other criteria exist as aids to differentiation at this and later periods, but none, by half, so obvious and so important. This statement does not mean that I tend to find living significance and deep spiritual meaning in every tag of threadbare nature formalism used by Ausonius and Prudentius, the while I denominate description of nature in the Roman elegiac poets a careless thing, a chance embellishment, a flourish, a gesture, a *cliché*. I merely mean there is a classical way of referring to nature, in poetry, and a romantic way.[2]

Critics often argue that the mere presence of nature, in Roman verse denotes a love for nature on the part of the versifier—an inconsequential deduction which vitiates the writings in this respect of Biese, Friedlander, Geikie, de Laprade, Motz, Secretan, and Woermann. I cannot afford to get caught in the trap which besets the unwary feet of investigators, and therefore hasten to say that there is a clear, hard manner of treating nature, which Mackail characterizes as elaborately ornate, executed without a trace of vibrant sensitiveness, reminding one of the sculptured friezes of Greek art, severe in outline, immensely adroit, but a little chilly and colorless. This is the classical manner all the way from Lucretius' picture of a countryside after the spring rains (*De rerum natura*, 1, 250-261) to Claudian's description of flowery spring meadows where Proserpine and her companions gather blossoms for garlands. Side by side with this there is a romantic manner which assigns to nature an independent importance, sentimentalizes its every delicate shading, pretends to uncover in it a latent sympathy for every possible human emotion, vivifies and personalizes landscape. This romantic picture may not bespeak a real attitude on the part of its enunciator. It may be only the continuation of such descriptions of scenery as formed a stock item in the routine of rhetoric courses, only the regular patter of Graveyard and Twilight and Melancholy themes —but it is decidedly different from the classical manner of treating nature. It does not matter for the sheer adjudgment of type whether the picture be a school device, a calculated rhetorical explosion—or the honest expression of a poet's vision; the result is romantic and not classical,[3] Romanesque and not Roman.

In the sudden burgeoning of landscape in Prudentius' *Hymn for All Hours* and *Hymn for Christmas Day* we have sensuous images of nature that are ordinarily considered distinctive of the work of Adam of St. Victor, more than seven hundred years later:

HYMN AGAINST THE LAST JUDGMENT

But while God with golden glory filled the hoary caves of night,
And by candid daylight frightened shadows brightened, passed in
 light,
Lo! in sorrowing skies the paling starlight failing, hid from sight.

For the sun turned back and, hiding in abiding woe its light,
Left his path and left his burning, never turning dark to bright,
Round a world in panic flinging chaos, bringing endless night.

Then be glad my tongue rejoices! Soul, your voice is full and
 bright—
Sing, O sing, His passion glorious, the victorious cross's might,
Sing his emblem on man's forehead in that horrid hour of night!

(6)

HYMN FOR CHRISTMAS DAY

The crying Babe is prophecy
Of universal spring to bless
The new born earth as it puts by
Its lethargy and sordidness.

I think the world is spread with flowers
In every meadow for His feet,
And sands of Syrtis shall be bowers
Where nectar and where nard smell sweet.

Waste places, barbarous lands have felt,
Dear Child, thy birth must come to pass;
The very mountains yield and melt,
And clothe their flinty sides with grass.

And from their boulders honey flows,
And from the leafless oak distills
Strange perfume, and the tamarisk knows
A balsam dewy as the hills.   (7)

We shall later on frequently find such nature parallelism of the directest kind in Carolingian sequences like the Easter poem of Notker, and in secular verse of St. Gall and Reichenau like the songs of welcome Walahfrid, Ratpert, and Notker addressed to visiting sovereigns.

It is in the poetic renascence of the fourth century that the modern treatment of romantic, sympathizing nature has broken silence. Forest solitudes, bubbling springs, and wild flowers now dawn on our sight and are vested with a mysterious life and grace. They are nature's own children (to quote Arnold) and utter her secret in a way that makes them something quite different from the woods, waters, and plants of Roman poetry. A prime cause for this changed attitude to nature is the spirit manifest in Christian hymnody.[4] Let us examine (with what precision we may) the manner of this change.

We have seen that the classical outlook on nature was bounded by certain well-marked lines beyond which the eye of the Roman poet rarely traveled. Sikes believes that, consciously or instinctively, the poet chose those aspects of nature that best harmonized with his philosophy of life.

Even three of the four greatest poetic names have small claim to be considered poets of nature by modern men, if we interpret nature in a wide sense as existing by itself and independent of human interest. It would be absurd to suppose Horace insensible to the pure impressions of nature, but ordinarily his choice of natural beauty depends on its utility.[5] Lucretius and Catullus enlarge somewhat the scope of this narrow classical vision by glimpses of a scene whose beauty is not conditioned by practical concerns. But Lucretius deals by preference with the universe and not the earth, finding his satisfaction in the majesty of the heaven and not on the surface of the world. And Catullus is too wrapped up in the life of a Roman aristocrat, too wholly busied with the society of men, to do more than turn aside now and then to respond to the beauty of a flower or a sunlit sea.[6] Alone of the four greater Roman poets, Vergil may claim to be a connecting link between the strict classicism of the Greek and modern romanticism,[7] although of course he is far closer to the former than is sometimes carelessly imagined. He knows the pure æsthetic pleasure of color and sound, he shows us natural beauty that is independent of material purpose, he even joins together in a moment of close union his scene and his people—as when the grove weeps for beloved Umbro.[8] But always it is the man and not his circumstances that matters; the place itself never serves as an excuse for landscape painting; the environment is never thrust to the front. Vergil does not allow the scenery to divert his attention from his actors—a passing reference marks the spot and thereafter all his art concentrates upon the people.[9]

But beginning with the age of Petronius and rising to the brim of poetry in the art of the fourth century, a new symbolism of nature comes to set our spirit dreaming. A new magic moves in it. Not merely the beauty of nature, says Arnold, that the Greeks and Latins had; not merely an honest smack of the soil, a faithful realism—but the intimate life of nature, her weird power, and her fairy charm.[10] In the faithful way of handling nature the eye is on the object, and that is all you can say; in the Greek and Latin way the eye is on the object, but lightness and brightness are added; in the magical way the eye is on the object, but charm and magic are added. In this last we reach a radical difference between classical and Romanesque art. The classical poet deals sparingly, if at all, in this sort of magic, and seems disinclined to see nature with the enchanted eyes of the fourth-century African, Spanish, and Gallo-Roman provincials who record a most romantic passion for it. Nothing can sweep away this true—if fine—distinction between classic and Romanesque attitude towards nature, which is first fully manifest in fourth-century Latin poetry. These poems express more personal or intimate relation to nature than was ever shown by the Augustans—with them we have begun the sentimental journey that leads to Keats's "magic casements opening on the foam of perilous seas in faery lands forlorn," to Shakespeare's "On such a night stood Dido with a willow in her hand upon the wild sea-banks and waved her love to come again to Carthage."[11]

Now I do believe that Christianity paved the way for this radical change in the function of nature in poetry simply because it had led thoughtful men to insist upon the recognition of the soul as a desirable element in all formal art. But such recognition was by no means an inalienable element in formal poetry, for as late as the fifth and sixth centuries cultivated Christians like Sidonius or Paulinus or Fortunatus retained very generally a purely classical outlook on nature, while more ascetic poets had no sense of natural beauty whatever, and were prone to love Christ so singly as to feel all phenomenal nature repugnant.

In the very nature of the case, we know that a new energy must enter the arts of poetry and music when enlisted in the ministry of the religion of Christ, because a new motive, one unknown to the classical world, had then taken hold of the religious consciousness. But this religious consciousness does not necessarily develop the creative sense—making melody in the heart does not inevitably result in codified song. Popular verse and musical strophes do not spring up full grown in response to the novel demands of a fresh philosophy of life, particularly when the emotion that is yearning to realize itself in a new poetic philosophy is of a separatist type. The old forms will no longer suffice, since they are emptied of meaning; there must be time allotted for the mastery of new materials and forms, and such mastery is of tedious growth. It was long indeed before Christian poetry and music developed an exclusively vocal art, parted company with pagan instrumentation and rhythm, broke loose from the restrictions of antique meters that had for centuries forced melody to keep step with strict prosodic measure.[12]

The history of Christian poetry and music in the East ends with the separation of the eastern and western churches. It was only among the western nations which reared new civilizations on the base of Rome, that social conditions were created which gave free scope to motives adequate to inspire a progressive Christian art. But even here the hieratic principle soon entered.[13] Although the singing of psalms and hymns by the body of worshipers was undoubtedly the custom in primitive churches, the steady growth of ritualism inevitably deprived the people of initiative in the worship, including song, and placed this exclusively in the hands of the clergy. This change was complete by the middle of the fourth century. The ideal of the church style of poetry and music thus soon became distinct from the secular style. It voiced the universal mood of prayer rather than the passionate emotion with which the profane lyric and song deal. It expressed that rapt tone of exaltation which makes no attempt at detailed painting of objects or events or superficial mental states.

For these reasons I should be slow to contend that religion invested poetry with a romantic interest. I should rather say that from the fourth century on, various Christian poets, notably Prudentius, possessed qualities which made them, in spite of their classical training, forerunners of medievalism. They try to invest religion with a romantic interest consecrated by the sufferings of the believers of old, and attested by the witness of an external nature which is invited to adorn with flowers the cradle of Christ. A half-grotesque realism was the immediate result of this new manner of presenting a scene utterly subservient to human emotion—a manner that, for two fairly evident reasons, achieved a vogue outlasting the Middle Ages. First, whatever may be said of the tedious style and the ghastly detail of the poems in which Prudentius flays heretics and exalts the cult of martyrs, some of his hymns—even the doctrinal ones—display a grace and feeling for environment that engage the modern mind as definitely as they appealed to the medieval one. Second, and this is infinitely more important, Prudentius for the first time in the history of art achieves a picture of a sharply personalized Nature in a state of unconscious ecstasy, reaching union with the Divine.

Here we have in lyric poetry at last the residuum of the doctrinal teaching of Philo regarding the direct or mystic vision of God. Prudentius shows nature in its original state, liberated from its material body, a stringed instrument vibrating to the touch of the spirit. It is small wonder that, through the compelling analogy of this picture to human life as it may be led by the isolated individual, Prudentius beckoned the ready minds of later poets to seek in nature a fellowship with the divine essence until they shone, full alchemized and free of space. Verily he had builded better than he knew, for (as Ker rightly says) no literary work of the Dark Ages can compare in the extent and far-reaching results of its influence with the development of popular Latin verse. Hymns, like those of Prudentius, affected a larger number of people than anything else in their literature. They gave a much needed impulse to fresh experiment. Those who had no desire to sit down and compose an epithalamium in hexameters or a birthday epistle in elegiacs might still write poetry in the Romanesque manner—in a language not dull, not ungentle, but capable of melody in verse and impressiveness in diction. The mold was made for ready imitation, the fashion was set; to follow it in all its imagistic particulars was pleasing.

Perhaps without knowing it, Prudentius stood at the parting of the roads in poetry, for his verses, like those of Ambrose, were often not intended for reading; they were meant to be sung; they were part of an innovation in Church music according to the use of the East.[14] Authors less poetical than he, could and did neglect both accent and quantity, for they found practically there was no need to be careful about either, since the hymn-tune could make the syllables anything it pleased, even if the hymn had no original rhythm of its own. So from now on we are beginning to deal with a large amount of Romanesque verse which is really not verse at all in either of the two great classes used by Bede. Such verse is neither metrical nor rhythmical, but simply a provision of syllables to fit a tune, leaving it to the tune to impose its own quantity and accent.

And there are tunes running in the heads of Romanesque versifiers other than those of church and festival: first, the stress of unliterary barbarian dialects and provincial Latin utterances; second, and this is all-important, the pointed style of the rhetorical schools where, ever since early in the Silver Age, prose had so encroached upon the domain of poetry that it could often be distinguished from the latter only by its greater cadence and more determined rhetoric.

Oratory was an obsession in the older days of Greece and Rome. This fixed idea of eloquence as a highest goal towards which ambitious youth might strive had its origin in ancient democratic states, where men like Pericles or Gaius Gracchus swayed the decisions of popular assemblies and determined the policies of their time by the sheer weight of their public addresses.[15] But when the republican age had passed and there was no longer an opportunity for the individual to create for himself a great career by directing his oratorical talents at bodies that originated legislation and statecraft, no inheritance was guarded with such unquestioning piety as this laudation of rhetoric and *bel esprit*. True, it was no longer a great force in the world, but it had become an art. And not a profitless art, either, since if one ardently wished to attract the envy and attention of his contemporaries, this ambition could in no way be more easily attained than through the practice of eloquence.

When, towards the beginning of the first century before Christ, the Greek conception of oratory as an art had been established in Rome, it was debated whether Latin rhetorical prose should follow the sententious point and the florid declamation of the Asiatic fashion or should strive for the unadorned plainness and lucidity of the stricter Attic mode.

On his return from Rhodes in 77 B. C., Cicero lent the weight of his authority to the adoption of that blending of the best traits of both manners which has been neatly called Rhodian eclecticism. This greatest master of prose style practiced what he preached, for in his speeches one finds as Asiatic characteristics a wealth of words leading on like a winding river; smoothness due to a studied avoidance of hiatus; musical beauty of phrasing; amplitude in antithetic and redundant expression; meticulous care for the rhythm of final clauses in each period. But the Attic qualities of his argument are no less striking, since in all his work it would be hard to find a purple patch: there is a relative absence of passion (except of invective), a sparing use of ornament for its own sake, the ability to draw from a well-spring of eloquence a plain and noble diction, to continue a persuasive naturalness without descending into commonplace.

Cicero's example and precepts, however, were powerless to stem the tidal wave of interest in bombastic expression, for by the opening years of the Christian Era there had developed, from the abuse of the habit of rhetorical declamation, the *auditoria*, and no properly equipped college of rhetoric or oratory was without such a hall, in which the most amateurish and halting genius might find a stage for his speech-making talents. Gaius Petronius protests in vain against the swollen language due to the practice of declamation. I believe the colleges make complete fools of our young men, he says, because they see and hear nothing of ordinary life there. It is all pirates standing in chains on the beach, tyrants, pen in hand, ordering sons to cut off their fathers' heads, oracles in time of pestilence demanding the blood of three virgins or more—honey balls of speech, every word and act besprinkled with poppy seed and sesame. Students who are fed on this diet can no more be sensible than people who live in the kitchen can be savory; you teachers have been the ruin of true eloquence. Your tripping, hollow tones, continues the accuser, stimulate to life certain absurd effects, with the result that the substance of your speech languishes and dies. In the age when Sophocles and Euripides found the inevitable word for their verse, young men were not yet being confined to set speeches. When Pindar and the nine lyric poets were too modest to use Homer's lines, no cloistered pedant had yet ruined young men's brains—I do not find that Plato or Demosthenes took any course of training of this sort. Great style is also modest style and is never blotchy or bloated. It rises supreme by reason of its natural beauty. Your flatulent and formless flow of words is a modern immigrant from Asia to Rome. Its breath fell upon the mind of ambitious youth like the influence of a baleful planet, and when the old tradition was once broken, eloquence halted and grew dumb—for who after this time has come to equal the splendor of Thucydides? Even poetry does not glow with the color of health, but the whole of art that was nourished on one universal diet lacks the vigor to reach the gray hairs of old age.

What is this modern immigrant from Asia to Rome? What is this flatulent and formless flow of words which is like the breath of a baleful planet? The answer is: The one thing which aids us in making graphic the development of all syllabizing rhythmic poetry (whether ecclesiastic or secular); *rhetoricus sermo,* in the phrase of Sedulius; *rhythmic polyphonic prose; free rhythms,* curiously like Heine's and Walt Whitman's; *vers libre,* in modern parlance; *kunstprosa* in Norden's title; *Gallican eloquence,* as Fortunatus terms it; *Gaulish pomposity and gaudiness of style,* as St. Jerome would have it; *elocutionary address,* in the words of Irish Vergil; *dithyrambic rhapsody,* after the manner of Isaiah; *rosc,* as the Gaels knew it.

One of the above terms will do as well as another, for they are all names for the identical phenomenon. One and all they characterize the style of the Gaulish rhetors of the fifth century which is well known to us. Now this *rhetoricus sermo* (as we shall call it) is a rhythmical prose divided into sections or periods which are linked together by parallelism and the set recurrence of a rhythmical cadence at the end of each section. It shows a complete transfusion of the style of prose and poetry. Its most prominent criteria are:

An artificial order of words;
A fondness for antithesis;
An abundance of odd words (archaisms, neologisms);
A use of Greek, Hebrew, Arabic words;

A reliance on sound tricks such as alliteration, assonance, echo, repetition, rhyme.

Nowhere did this new style find so fertile a soil, nowhere was it handled with such brilliance and skill as in Gaul, where the Romanized Celts carried their preciosity of speech —*argute loqui*—into Latin. We can trace it in the Christian sermons from the third century onward: Cyprian, Augustine, Faustus of Riez, Cæsarius of Arles. It was taught by Gaulish rhetors throughout the empire and by eminent professors at Bordeaux and other universities.

The speech heard in many parts of Ireland after the arrival there of hordes of Gaulish fugitives was not bookish Latin, but a living idiom—and the oratory practiced by the men from Gaul in their declamations, recitations, debates, and speeches was a living literature in the making. Now, prior to the rush from the continent in the fifth century, the Irish had had their native schools of oratory and poetry, in which their *brehons* and *filid* were trained. But just as we see that in the seventh century these Irish bards introduced into their native poetry the metrical system of Latin hymns they heard in church, with its regularly recurring number of syllables—so we may also assert that at an earlier period (fifth century) the technique of the *rhetoricus sermo* exercised a great influence upon the art of the vernacular bards.

We know this tremendously important fact from a study of the ancient Irish saga-forms. For while in the older period of Irish literature the form for narrative was not poetry but prose, later on there grew up a narrative verse-form, although this was never able to drive out prose stories—in fact, what actually happened is that the versified stories were, often enough, afterwards resolved into prose. Still, passages in poetic form (or at least in *rhetoricus sermo*) remained scattered all through the older prosaic versions. These wordballets were much beloved, continued undisturbed down into the twelfth-century sagas, and were called *retoric*.

True to form, this species of dithyramb consists of quite short sentences and clauses bound together by alliteration, and containing extremely flowery speech, so curiously ordered, so filled with cryptic and irrelevant vocables, so careless of syntax as to be noteworthy. Frequently there is a deliberate parallelism striven for—one is thereby forcefully reminded of church sequences. As the title *retoric* indicates, the language of these insertions in the saga breviary is derived from the highly treasured, hifalutin idiom of vulgar Latin that had previously become rampant in western Gaul. A good example of how Irish Latinists handled this sort of thing is the introduction to the *Hisperica famina*:[16]

Ampla pectoralem   suscitat vernia cavernam
   mestum   extrico pulmone tonstrum.
Sed gaudifluam pectoreis   arto procellam arthereis.
Cum insignes   sophie speculator arcatores.
Qui egregiam   urbani tenoris propinant faucibus
   linpham.
Vipereos   que litterature plasmant syllogismos.

Nonsensical as this quotation may appear to modern eyes, it is in spirit scarcely less so than the exordium of a Christmas sermon written and preached by St. Augustine:

Ipse apud patrum præcedit cuncta spatia sæculorum,
Ipse de matre in hac die cursibus se ingessit annorum.
    Homo factus   hominum factor,
    Ut sugeret ubera   regens sidera,
    Ut esuriret panis,
    Ut sitiret fons,
    Dormiret lux,
Ab itinere via fatigaretur,
Falsis testibus veritas accusaretur,
Judex vivorum et mortuorum a judice mortali judicaretur.
Ab injustis justitia damnaretur,
Flagellis disciplina cæderetur,
Spinis botrus coronaretur,
In ligno fundamentum suspenderetur,
Virtus infirmaretur,
Salus vulneraretur,
Vita moreretur.

This was the style with which the Irish became familiar after the influx of Gaulish scholars and preachers in the fifth century. Although not indigenous to Ireland, it existed there in many forms from the sixth century onward, until it was in part superseded by syllabizing rhymed poetry that follows the metrical system of church hymns. And this metrical system of church hymns (like that of all syllabizing rhythmic secular poetry) was a development of just such Gaulish *rhetoricus sermo* as we see lavishly used in Ireland from the sixth century onward. For there is only one unit to add to *rhetoricus sermo* in order to secure any conceivable number of metrical variants—and this one new unit is *syllable counting*.

Syllable equality of adjacent lines within a given stanza grows up naturally—necessarily—on the basis of a speech-stress that inheres in all vernacular language, and in all music and poetry which follows, however unconsciously, such speech-stress. Just the moment that an artificial prosody and stilted molds of enunciation are swept aside, the moment that the cleft is healed between written literature and naive expression of commonplace thought—that moment modern poetry is born. Now, as under the circumstances we should expect, the first models to feel the impact of what we may call the sway and thud of vernacular emotion in literature were the sermons and the hymns. As to the first of these, I cannot imagine any other mold so ever-present to the monk, cultured lay-brother, artist, or minstrel as the intonation and chanting of præludium and exordium of the church homily. For this was the place where elaborate imaginative pictures were tried out in cadenced prose, where sanction of a literary and religious sort was accorded honest, middle-class euphuism. Small wonder if oratory, now become an anointed branch of human homiletics, went its unimpeded way until, drunk with the exuberance of its own fancy, it waxed orgiastic.

And that the hymn in the hands of a devout layman of Cæsaraugusta should first crystallize vernacular emotion in a modern way is not unfitting when we recall that during his lifetime the western empire was crumbling into a dozen independent kingdoms, and that thenceforward one speaks of the poetry of Africa, Gaul, Spain, and Britain more aptly than of Roman verse, whether it be written in provincial Romanesque or in the Latin handed down from the empire and artificially preserved by the Church. For (as Mackail says) the Catholic church now became the center of European cohesion, giving continuity and common life to the scattered remains of the ancient civilization. Already in the fifth century Pope Leo the Great is a more important figure than his pale contemporary, Valentinian the Second.

Chapter VIII

FORTUNATUS AND THE PLATONIC TRADITION

In the ninth century of our era we know that the poets of Bagdad had cast the myth of immaculate love into a mold as precise as the one which three hundred years later in western Europe was to express the conventional attitudinizings of Mariolatry, worship of liege lady, and mysticism. This Arabic theory of love, however, and its formulæ could not have been a new thing in the world, for we come upon the same ideal of platonic love as an apotheosis of sexual relationship in the Romanesque poets Fortunatus, Alcuin, and Walahfrid. But until new revelation appears we must believe it was an oriental (Arabic?) continuance of Platonistic canon which carries to the West not later than the sixth century a codified ideal of tenderness in human love, refined to the last degree, and in sharp contrast to other prevalent eastern examples of violent sensuality alternating with cruelty when dealing with woman.

In connection with the *Book of the Planet Venus* by Ibn Dawoud (868-918) we gain the poetic autobiography of its author's love, which reveals his whole character and lays bare the sentimental hostility that actuated his attacks on heretic Al Hallaj. This *ars amandi* has all the spontaneity of youth and is yet couched in a supple and vibrant rhyming prose which in the purity of its style equals classical Arabian rhetoric of the third century after the hegira.[1] On the confines of the Yemen in the desert to the south of Arabia there lived a chosen people preëminently chaste, the Banou 'Odhrah[2]—among whom one would die when he loved —where it was thought that to die of love was a gentle and noble death. And there more radiantly than Majnoun, mad with love for Laylah, or than the loving couple of Kothayir and of 'Azzah, shone the pure glory of the perfect 'Odhrite lover, Jamil, who died without having laid his hand for evil on his beloved Buthaina:

Buthaina, if the flower of youth could raise its head anew,
The hours might return when we were one that now are two;
And O if we could be once more the twain we used to be,
Your people might despise again the gifts you gave to me.

Buthaina, shall I never be alone with you again?
We two were filled with love as clouds are over-filled with rain;
Within your net a lad you caught (the lad was I), and love
Grew with me as I grew to be the man you know not of.

Buthaina, all my life have I desired that you shall speak,
The bloom of youth that once was fair is fading from my cheek;
I will not hear you if you dare to leave me, or deny—
My love remains immortal though, as mortal, I must die.

And similarly does Ibn Dawoud assert: In depriving myself of you, love, it is my dearest wish to guard my wounded heart and my brimming eyes. True it is I asked of you the communion that would have calmed my blood, but fear not, beloved, I am quieted. Do not fulfill your vow to be mine, lest forgetfulness come at last—and I would fain play the miser with my sobs.

The Book of the Planet Venus is dedicated to a schoolmate who inspired in Ibn Dawoud a passionate devotion that was to last through life. Our author was in great distress because of his forbidden love for Ibn-Jami and because he found himself at first unable to renounce it. So, as a solace to his troubled soul, he constructed from 'Odhrite verses (known to him since childhood) an ideal of living in which the desires of his heart would accord with the practical exigencies of his faith. Stanzas like the following went with him always: We two were left on this evening behind the tents of the Tribe. And we were overtaken by the night immovable under a scented cloak of the Yemen while first the shadows fell and then the dew. At the thought of God far away from us, our hearts began to throb within us and we were moved to rid ourselves of the ardent heat of youth. Yet we returned again to the tents, having but scarcely calmed the soul's thirst between our lips and watered by chaste reserve. This delicate and troubled poem especially in the imperfect embrace of the closing line betrays admirably the sensitiveness of Ibn Dawoud.

Only one part (the first) of the *Planet Venus* has been preserved to us, but the contents of the entire book are presaged in the dedication to Ibn-Jami with which it begins. Says Ibn Dawoud, I have given my volume a hundred chapters of one hundred verses each. In the first fifty rubrics I recall the various aspects of love: its laws, its variations, and its true worth. In the fifty others I present an anthology —necessarily much restricted in its choice—from the vast swarms of poets who have praised love. I had at first intended to include quotations from the Book of God and from the maxims of his prophets, in order thus to justify the divine doctrine of love. But love does not enter into the ritual of the Cult which is based solely upon proofs for that in which one places faith. . . . Love is the act of the elect, the privilege of delicate natures; it is an intellectual affinity. . . . Following the natural order of the characteristics of love, my book indicates at the outset the essence of love and its causes; next, the amorous states consequent on established love—the very abandon and apartness of it, as well as the fixed point to which the transport and tenderness of mutual passion carry it. Lastly, having told what fidelity during life is, I discuss that faithfulness which lasts beyond the grave.

The titles of the individual chapters of the *Planet Venus* are illuminating:

1. He who gazes further will be in longer pain.
2. In the state of love, intelligence is the captive, but desire dominates them both.
3. He who regards his evil as a remedy will never achieve a cure.
4. He is not prudent who does not take his ache to the doctor.
5. To speak one's mind is to invite affront.
6. To humiliate oneself in friendship is the merest politeness.
7. He who sees his joy endure thinks less of it.
8. Where seductive grace abides, let there be chastity.
9. It is ungracious to fatigue friendship with cavilings.
10. Horrid suspicion is born of too great egotism.
11. The rendezvous once reached, what matters the spy?
12. He who is refused interviews, repays the score with few gifts.

13. He who is cut off from friendships stoops to concealments.
14. He who is refused an interview contents himself with the messenger.
15. He who is encompassed by friends is denounced by those of his own time.
16. He who does not recover from a fault is ignorant of how to guard friendship faithfully.
17. To censure one's brother for a mistake exposes one naturally to boredom and hatred.
18. Neighboring dwellings, distant hearts—that is worse than to live in houses far apart.
19. He who pardons has not blamed; he who excuses himself has not sinned.
20. When perfidy has come it is easier to be on one's guard.
21. The more one fears separation, the more insatiable is the desire.
22. Very few whom love has not blamed have thought of consoling themselves.
23. He who has more love than he can endure will suffer every treason of his beloved.
24. He who grows used to absences exposes himself to suffering.
25. In the farewells to the departing one there is the anticipatory savor of the return.
26. Departure was invented only to torture lovers.
27. Absence of the beloved friend gives free rein to sorrow.
28. He who has not the experience of being loved weeps on the trails of former encampments.
29. When one is deprived of a beloved presence, of what use is it to seek a dwelling place?
30. He who is deprived of the desired being tells his passion to the passing winds.
31. The flashes of lightning are dear to the maddened and desiring lover.
32. The sparks of the braziers are dear to the exhausted and exalted lover.
33. The plaint of the dove is familiar to the lonely soul lost in love.
34. He who undergoes the test of separation and abandonment does naught but regret the peace and even the quarreling of former days.
35. The cries of the lost camel are familiar to every passionate lover.
36. He who no longer shares rendezvous becomes the prey of dreams.
37. He who is deprived of seeing seeks satisfaction in tokens.
38. He who no longer may behold the tokens themselves contents himself with remembrances.

39. Old gossips, with their imaginations and illusions, are the source of all weakness and weariness.
40. Abridge your sleep, prolong your night.
41. When endurance is vanquished the tears break forth.
42. A wasting body is slight proof of a real sorrow.
43. It is long to follow the route of endurance, difficult to hide the secret of love.
44. Here are the secrets that are betrayed by those whose patience weakens.
45. Love that is not drawn by interest will not be repulsed by blame.
46. He who progresses in love sees the growth of his sorrow.
47. As time grows dim, friendships are discarded.
48. He who loves without hoping for reward can count on himself alone.
49. Constancy in a covenant knows only the beginning and the very distant.
50. A little fidelity beyond the grave is more than much of it during life.

From the above one sees how the *Planet Venus* is no simple anthology of poetry, as criticism before Massignon surmised—it is rather a most precious record of sentimental life in ninth-century Arabia. No document can show better than this *ars amandi* of Ibn Dawoud how cultivated minds in Bagdad felt regarding the eternal riddle of love, at the moment when the heretic Al Hallaj undertook his public attack upon it. We have before us the old Greek theory of love (physical fatality, a natural force inevitable and blind, without reason and without end), the $\delta\eta\xi\iota\theta\upsilon\mu o\nu\ \xi\rho\omega\tau o\varsigma\ \alpha\nu\theta o\varsigma$ so dear to Sophocles and Empedocles. But a theory of love purified as it would have been understood was lived and sung by the fabled Bedouin poets of the tribe of the Banou 'Odhrah.

Ibn Dawoud is the authentic precursor of Ibn Qozman of Cordova (died 1160), who, almost three centuries before the latter, had sung of courtly love in strains, the themes of which (popularized by new meters that charm the ear of Northern Europe) are very deeply to influence and reshape the lyrics of Provence and France and Germany. From courtly themes, as set down by Ibn Dawoud by the end of the ninth century, are derived the quite Arabian topics of the gay science of William IX of Poitou, the sweet new style of Dante's master, Guido Guinizelli of Bologna.

So far as we know, it is in Arabia that there was the first systematization of platonic love. This was the result of a refined deviation of idealism which started in an inversion of the cult of divine love. It was the only idea acceptable to many theologians, since the Islamic dogma dissuades man from loving God.

Far from seeing in love the soaring of the soul toward the Divine, the superior desire of an exalted spirit, Ibn Dawoud, with a more exact sense of the disciplined ritualism of Islam, isolated from love all devotion due to God. According to our poet love, instead of uniting us to Him, is nothing but a blind fatality of the physical order, common to humanity—the rôle of the elect soul is to suffer it without yielding to its blandishments. In pages of wholly Greek inspiration, in which he exposes the four theories of the origin of love (magnetic, astrological, physiological, mystical), Ibn Dawoud indicates his preference by beginning with the myth placed on the lips of Aristophanes, in the Platonic *Banquet:*

Certain adepts at philosophy have declared that God created every spirit with round form like a sphere. He then divided it into two parts, placing each half in a body. Now each body that encounters the other half of its spirit is loved by it because of primitive affinity, and thus it comes that human characters associate with one another in accordance with the necessity of their natures. These are the words written by Jamil: Love chained my spirit to hers ere we were yet created, and even before our weaning, in the cradle itself. Love waxed as did we, forever increasing in stature; though we die, nothing shall dissolve our part. Surviving through every change, love will visit us in the shadow of the tomb and even beneath its stone.

Here for the first time in the roster of poetry we have the formulation of what we are accustomed to call medieval love.[3] Before this we have had it indicated somewhat in Latin by Petronius and in Greek by his contemporary Meleager. In the latter poet the austerity of the old spirit is gone and love has become a religion, curiously touched with the hot breath of the East. Like the romancers of the thirteenth century, Meleager, in the purest manner of Platonism, reduces his ritual of love to an actual theology. But in both Greek and Latin *Anthologies* there is no clarity of mood or nobility of theme in the examples of amatory epigram which represent the generations after Augustus—the style is delicate, exotic, fantastic—the atmosphere is loaded with a steam of perfumes—no subtlety or fluctuation of passion is left unregistered, but the emotion is buried in masses of conceits. For a moment Meleager or Petronius can be piercingly simple, but the very next instant the fantastic mood descends again upon them and their fellows, and feeling dissolves in a mist of metaphors. We shall not find any codification of romantic love in either of the great *Anthologies*.[4]

But, curiously enough, we do find the most perfect possible pattern for one of the two main aspects of Platonic (or romantic) love[5] in the life and writings of Fortunatus. Born not long after the year 530 near Treviso in Upper Italy, this poet studied ancient letters and law at Ravenna. He became afflicted with a disease of the eyes which he cured by anointing them with oil from a lamp in the chapel of St. Martin. As this pious act brought him full recovery from his complaint, Fortunatus set out on a pilgrimage to France to pay homage at the sepulcher of his benefactor in Tours. He came to Poitiers and was sheltered by St. Radegunde, who had managed to secure a divorce from the king, Chlothaire, and was living with her foster-daughter, Agnes, abbess of the convent there.[6] With them, says Rand, Fortunatus lived in a charming intimacy for twenty years, up to the very hour of their deaths. He is a troubadour with as deep a devotion as ever knight had for his lady. He uses to Queen Radegunde the language of a lover, and his love is rare and pure—*cælesti affectu, non crimine corporis ullo*. This Merovingian poet signals the first appearance of chivalry in western Europe, where it was never repeated in truer form. Naturally Fortunatus is inconsolable when his inspiratrix goes into Lenten retirement. This was an heroic season for him, though Agnes probably saw to it that he did not starve. And when she shone out on the world again!

TO QUEEN RADEGUNDE ON HER RETREAT

Heavy with God, my friend, your mind you turn
To feed the soul and let the body burn.

You that are life to all your sisterhood
Recur to that retreat which you found good,
Keeping today your eternal vow—and we
In spirit shall go after willingly.
For from our eyes you take away the light
So quickly, that for lack of you my sight
Is darkened as with clouds more heavy than night.
Excluding us, your cell you enter in;
Yet, though you shut us out, we are within.
It is most right that fleeing the brief days
You hide away—but to each one who stays
This month is longer than the lagging year.
But you put time beneath your feet as though
You'd not be seen by temporal lover so,
(For such, when I behold you, do I seem)
Yet that one vow together we shall dream;
My soul shall follow after yours and slip
Where in the flesh there is no fellowship!   (1)

TO QUEEN RADEGUNDE ON HER RETURN

What face comes here, so glorious with light,
And what delays lengthened so long my night?
Those joys you took with you, you now return—
And for two Easters shall my candles burn.
As in their manner seeds in furrowed fields
Spring up, to me the sight of you now yields
New harvest; and I pluck ripe fruits again
And bind together sheaves of peaceful grain.
The work of August is in April done;
And while the buds and tendrils in the sun
Put forth—my autumn's here, my grapes are won.
The apples and high pear-trees in their kind
Send forth their vernal odors on the wind;
While they yet bud, my trees are giving fruit;
And, as bare fields put forth no early shoot,
But yet with later burgeoning may burn,
I am your field, and sprout when you return.   (2)

We must remember, when we visualize the quiet sojourn of Fortunatus in the nunnery of Poitiers, that the years of it were filled with the most savage conflicts within the Frankish empire, yet that there is scarce a trace of this anywhere in his poems. We find no mention of the murder of Sigebert and Chilperich, no word of the fierce vendetta between

Fredegunde and Brunhilde. The picture our poet draws for us of a calm spot of earth where a few people dwell together in peace and contentment is significant and in a certain way prophetic of the time to come.

The poetry of Fortunatus should not be regarded as a slender and thinning rivulet of verse that trickles tardily from classical tradition to lose itself in the sands of the early Middle Ages. For of his own volition this artist brushed impatiently aside the themes and the method of portrayal that antiquity loved, although reminders of these were about him on every hand (as they were about Boethius), in order that he might devote himself to a fairly happy and first-hand delineation of the real medieval human beings and affairs with which he came in contact. He is as temperamental and as individual in outlook as Gregory of Tours. Therefore I believe Wilhelm Meyer and Rand justified in terming Fortunatus not the last poet of antiquity, but a first prophetic poet of the ages that were to come. Because he found the right way in which to view the changeful events and environments of sixth-century Gaul, the Carolingian poets are heavily in debt to Fortunatus—and by far the greatest obligation that they owe him lies in the healthy realism with which they in their turn treat the personalities, the occurrences, and the social relations of their day.

Long before the sixth century the component elements of society in western Europe had been disintegrated by the Romans in their decadence and by the barbarians in their insolence of material success. To the followers of Christ nothing seemed left but separation from a nature whose vices had become incurable; in the corruption of all pagan systems, Christian asceticism led logically to the cloister and the hermitage. But the conventual life was a virtual abandonment of social problems.

From this policy of despair, says Symonds, this helplessness to cope with evil and this hopelessness of good on earth, emerged a new and nobler synthesis, the merit of which belongs in no small measure to Germanic converts to the Christian faith. The earliest Middle Ages proclaimed through chivalry the truth, for the first time fully manifest in Fortunatus, that woman is the mediating and ennobling element in human life. Not in escape into the cloister, not in self-abandonment to vice, but in the fellow service of free men and women must be found the solution of social problems.

Since Ambrose and Prudentius a new humanism has been at work writing sacred poems and hymns, not for the liturgy of the church, but to fill the framework of Pindaric and Horatian hymns with Christian feeling and belief and Christian story. It is the purpose of this humanism to show that the new faith has a wealth of material just as poetic as the facts and fables of ancient tradition. Pagan culture is not superseded, but included. The concepts represented by the hymns of Prudentius and Fortunatus cannot dispense with the ancient authors who had contributed to their making. To see the color and warmth gained in sixth-century verse by wedding ancient myth with Christian fable, we need but to contrast the *Vexilla regis prodeunt* of Fortunatus with the comparatively lean and harsh appeal of Gregory the Great to the Comforter in his *Veni, creator spiritus:*

VENI CREATOR SPIRITUS

Come, Holy Ghost, to us descending,
On the minds of men attending,
Fill with Thy supernal flame
That same bosom Thou didst frame.

Thou who art our great Defender,
Thou the gift which God did tender,
Fount whence light and mercy roll,
Unction of the wounded soul,

God's right hand Thou art, and seven
Are the gifts Thou hadst in heaven,
Word that to our Lord doth reach,
In men's mouths Thou puttest speech.

With Thy glory fill our senses;
In our hearts Thy love intense is
Power eternal to avail
In the day when flesh is frail.

All our foes afar repelling,
Send Thy peace to be our dwelling;

> If Thou goest on before
> Harm will shun us evermore.
>
> Bring Thy rich rewards of pleasure,
> Bring Thy grace for men to treasure,
> Drop the chain and break the rod,
> Bind us in the truce of God.
>
> Bid us know the Father through Thee,
> Bid us know the Son who knew Thee
> For that Holy Spirit we
> Trust into eternity.
>
> Praise the Father and the Son
> And the Spirit three and one—
> Send, O Christ, unto the lost
> The benefaction of the Ghost. (3)

Against this gray performance of Gregory's the ensuing verses of Fortunatus stand forth not as a hymn but as an intimate poem of reflection, in which description, narrative, and allegorical exposition are all germane, written for a moment of the day when thoughtful song would be appropriate. The poet allegorizes the moment, he shows its moral significance, he calls up a typical example, and through it all he lets us hear the echo of the hymn itself, as though it stole in from the chapel near by. It is almost, says Rand, as if the poet preferred to keep to his couch and ponder on the sacred meaning of the moment, instead of arising and taking part in the service. Despite the *sensus historicus, allegoricus, tropologicus,* and *anagogicus,* Fortunatus' marching song of one Christian's faith is naive, instead of sentimental, appeals to us as unpondered, immediate, real:

VEXILLA REGIS PRODEUNT

> The banners of the king advance,
> The cross with mystery doth flame,
> And from the tree the Flesh of flesh,
> Word Incarnate, hangs in shame.
>
> The lance's edge hath pierced His side,
> O look on Him that for our good

Cleansed us of the stain of sin,
Washed out with water and with blood.

Now is fulfilled what was foretold
By David in prophetic song:
Suspended from the rood Our God
Will rule. To Him shall nations throng.

O glorious and radiant tree
In royal crimson richly decked,
His sacred limbs to touch and hold
Thee did Our Lord, fair rood, elect.

Thou blessèd cross upon whose arms
The body of the Savior fell;
As with a balance thou didst weigh
The Christ that bore us out of Hell.

Thy wood is all a sweet perfume,
Thou art like nectar very sweet;
Rejoicing in thy fruit thou mak'st
A perfect triumph more complete.

Altar and sacred victim, hail!
In Thy passion is our glory.
Life from death thou bringest back,
Life in death shall be our story.

Hail thou cross, O hail thou only
Hope that agony may win;
To believers bring salvation,
Take the sinner from his sin!   (4)

The mythology of Mary is already built when Fortunatus wrote his two great hymns to celebrate the arrival at Poitiers of a piece of the Holy Cross, and incidentally to honor his inspiratrices, Radegunde and Agnes. This mythology of Mary (Mariolatry) gave religious sanction to chivalrous enthusiasm; and a cult of woman sprang into being which, although it was romantic and visionary, conditioned not alone the very shape and pressure of medieval literature, but the actual basis of modern domestic and civil life as well. In fact, so far as we now know to the contrary, it was in a triangular love affair of an exquisite and subtle sort that a Merovingian reënacted the *modus vivendi* of the modern world.

Embodied in all the poems which deal with the long service of Fortunatus for his two ladies is the Petrarchist aspect of Platonic love, which theoretically excludes the sensual appetites from the worshipful homage man pays to woman. It was not wife or mistress but liege lady who inspired the troubadour and the knight. Dante had children by Gemma, Petrarch fathered the brood of an unknown concubine, but it was the sainted Beatrice and the unattainable Laura who received immortal praise from these poets. By a process equally logical Fortunatus, in his love for Radegunde and Agnes, discovered in actual human life his correlative for that worship of the incarnate deity which was the essence of a religion that had exalted to the throne of heaven a Virgin and a Mother. This combination of Mariolatry and love-vassalage is the origin of Romantic Love.

But the Platonic aspect of romantic (or medieval) love also flourished from indestructible roots throughout the age of poetry which followed Fortunatus—we find its positive traces in the cult of friendship, in the panegyric, in love-missive, in capitulary, beyond the peradventure of a doubt. The Franks attached as high a value as did Socrates to the association of friends, an older and a younger, in a comradeship intense enough to merit the name of love. With due regard to the difference between the plastic ideal of ancient religion in the stream of neo-Platonism and the romantic ideal of early medieval Christianity, this Platonic conception of *paiderastia* is a close analogue to the chivalrous devotion to women. This love of man and boy (and no less of woman and girl), judged by its ideal, is a fine and noble thing, no more apt to sink in the mire of phallicism than modern love itself. Alcuin bears witness to both aspects of romantic love:

SONG TO A NIGHTINGALE

O nightingale, what cunning stole you from
My land and, envious, struck my pleasure dumb?
You filled my heart with what the muses say
And charmed the sadness from my soul away.
O therefore let a host of flying birds
From every hand complain with me in words
Such as Pierian poets use! You were

Sad colored, but in singing, I aver,
You were not sad. From out your little throat
Your voice poured forth an endless happy note
That tangled all the muses in your singing;
And ever from your mouth God's praise went ringing.
Though nights were black, your most admirèd voice
In holy song ceased never to rejoice,
My beauty and my beautiful! Though they
With undiminished voices sing alway,
Shall cherubim and seraphim give praise
As you were wont to do? Man has no joy
Such as he knows who makes it his employ
By day and night to praise like this the Lord.
Ah, food and drink to you were things abhorred
Being less sweet than song; to you less sweet
Were crowds that other songsters might find meet.
Nature and nature's kind, creative God
(For Him your praises had no period)
Gave you this charge: being dead with wine and sleep,
You were to instruct us so that we might keep
No more this drowsy state but rather wake,
And from our minds the seal of slumber break.
That which you did, not having soul or sense,
Teach us to do with nobler diligence.
We that have senses and are rational
Should do that thing to which your voice doth call;
Then thanks and praise throughout all time shall rise
In heavenly realms beyond the eternal skies.   (5)

TO THE CUCKOO

Now from the topmost boughs resounds the song of the cuckoo,
And the parti-colored world brings to blossom the buds of the flowers;
Now the young vine puts forth from the shoot the wine-bearing jewels,
And now in the golden land the nightingale, never-tiring,
Pours its melody forth, uplifting our ears to its music.   (6)

Before we turn aside from the purely Platonic aspect of romantic love in Carolingian days, it is helpful to cite two famous poems which are most remarkable medieval exemplars of that mystically ennobling idea of *paiderastia* which stirred the hearts of Achilles and Patroclus. Walahfrid Strabo's song to his friend is otherwise noteworthy for its romantic note of moonlight and its atmospheric apartness.

MOONLIGHT

Now while the moonlight down pure air is shining
Thou art perhaps beneath its glorious rays,
Under that white torch in the sky divining,
As in a glass thy friend of other days.

Perhaps thou thinkest how its single splendor
Binds in one body our divided hearts;
Divided? Rather say by friendship tender
Bound with a bond of trust that never parts.

And if thine eyes should still deny thee greeting
Of thy friend's form and face, at least believe
To such as we have been, even light so fleeting
Is yet a pledge of love, and do not grieve.

Thy faithful friend transmits to thee his verses;
As a fixed chain running 'twixt me and thee
So may our love be, while my prayer rehearses
Hope that the years may treat thee tenderly. (7)

And Gottschalk the heretic, none other than the author of the *Eclogue of Theodulus,* sends from his exile of more than a thousand years ago a love-message to his boy, which is living evidence of how a lad's sympathy raised a poet's soul from the eclipse of night and taught it to sing a hymn of joy for the mercies of God:

A SONG IN EXILE

O young my lad, you would have me sing—
    Why, O why?
What song, my boy, do you seek to wring
    From such as I?
Singing is sweet, but not from me
Who am exiled deep in the distant sea—
    Why will you make me sing?

O little my son, it were better far
    I weep my wrongs—
Tears from a broken heart, they are
    More than songs.
And O belovèd, it can not be
You seek such singing as this from me—
    Why will you make me sing?

You must know, little brother, that I desire
    Your sympathy;
Child, let not the help of you tire—
    Pity me!
A generous heart and a soul brought low,
Yours and mine—I would have it so—
    Why will you make me sing?

You are young, and hard are the words of youth!
    Little you know,
Though you give yourself to heaven's high truth,
    This is my woe—
Exile is long and a weary way,
And I suffer by night and endure by day—
    Why will you make me sing?

But since you desire that I sing to you,
    Comrade mine,
And whatever manner I use will do:
    A theme divine
I choose, and the Father I sing, and the Son
And the Spirit proceeding from both as from one—
    Why will you make me sing?

Thou art the Blessèd One, O Lord,
    Paraclete,
Born of the Father, Incarnate Word,
    O Thou complete,
Thou God that is one, Thou God that is three,
Thou art holy and just, Thou wilt pity me—
    From a full heart now I sing.

Sweetly I sing of my own accord;
    Hear me, boy,
What time I sing of our gracious Lord
    A song of joy.
A song of the soul, a song of the lips,
A song by day and at night's eclipse—
    He is a merciful King!   (8)

Chapter IX

IRISH CULTURE IN THE SIXTH CENTURY

Before we proceed to study Carolingian art, to ascertain how it carried forward the romantic attitudes bequeathed by Merovingian poets and their models, we must pause to consider more fully several pertinent matters of literary technique and transmission which have been hinted at above. Of much presumptive influence on both pattern and weave of Carolingian poetry were Irish writings[1] from at least the seventh century on; likewise the mimes and minstrels, with their popular Latin verses and vernacular folksongs in German and French; no less, the monks and clerks with their syllabizing rhythmic Latin prose and liturgic song; also the contributions of various sorts from Islam and the Near East generally. As to this last, there is much evidence of Arabic influence on early medieval poetry which is accepted as valid by nearly all orientalists—the difficulty seems to lie in persuading the European medieval archæologists that it is so.

It is wrong to regard the Irish during the earliest centuries of the Christian Era as an outlawed race far removed from the pale of southern civilization and severed from close association with the world of Mediterranean culture. The truth is rather that at no period in its recorded history has Ireland been a backwater off the stream of human progress. About the year 500 before Christ the Carthaginian traveler Himilco made a voyage around the west coast of Europe and wrote a log of his journey, from which I quote some famous passages concerned with Erin:

> The land of Europe nourishes
> On its level sward the generous Iberian race,
> People who border on the icy northern ocean
> And, scattered widely, occupy the cultivated soil.
> Here stand the pillars of much-enduring Hercules,
> Swept by the cold north blast unmoved they stand;

Here proudly a peak soars above the ranges
Whose rocky top bends straight toward the south wind.
And the wide bay yawns under its ominous brow
Where the islands, the Oestrymnides, rear their heads.
Scattered they lie and rich are they in metals,
Both tin and lead. A vigorous race inhabits them,
Of haughty soul, yet shrewd in all their dickerings.
And in their skiffs they plough the turbid sea
And the stormy pit of monster-tenanted ocean.
These people do not build their keels of pine
Nor do they round their barks from sturdy fir,
But with a wondrous skill surpassing common practice
They fashion their skiffs of rough skins firmly tied
And in such hidebound craft skim o'er the mighty deep.
From here a two days' voyage the Sacred Island lies,
Rich in its greensward, o'er the billows it rises
Peopled thickly by the ancient folk of the Hierni.
Beside them lies the broad isle of the Albiones,
Near—all too near—the hardy race of Britain.
And here it is, to the bounds of the Oestrymnides
The Tyrians are wont to voyage the seas.   (1)

Overseas then from Spain and from Gaul, from the mouths of the Garonne and the Loire, and from Armorican ports, Gaelic settlers thronged into Ireland. For centuries this intercourse between western Europe and the Sacred Island can be traced, nor did it ever appear to die down. The immigrants did not stream across Britain but over the open highway of the sea—no longer in barks fashioned of hides, but in vessels built to outride the Atlantic storms, with high decks like caravels and stiff leathern sails.

How amazing is this early record of man's annihilation of distance! Particularly when we recall that the crucial feature in the struggle to win dim horizons was the gaining of a water route two thousand years before the prows of ploughing ships could be driven with any near approach to that safety and precision finally brought about by improvements in the art of navigation, and by the extended use of the mariner's compass. What visions must have confronted the apprehensive mind of the sailor on new stretches of ocean waste, when at night, beneath the northern stars, he dreamed of man's final conquest of the sea and read the scroll of the future when

> Instructed ships shall sail to rich commerce
> By which remotest regions are allied,
> Which makes one city of the universe,
> Where some may gain and all may be supplied.
>
> Then we upon our globe's last verge shall go,
> And view the ocean leaning on the sky;
> From thence our rolling neighbors we shall know
> And on the lunar world securely pry.

It was in the fourth century before Christ, about the time that Aristotle died, that Pytheas of Marseilles was commissioned by the chamber of commerce of his city to discover the hidden source of the enormous wealth of the Carthaginian bankers who held a monopoly of the tin and amber trades because they carefully preserved the secret of the origin of these materials. On his successful return from this expedition, Pytheas published a full report of it, and from that time the whole northwest of Europe was an open book to the Greek merchants of the Mediterranean. Relics of many sorts, both linguistic and antiquarian, prove the growing intimacy of Gaul with Ireland—as one instance, in lieu of many: it was an invasion from the continent in the third century B. C. which gave Leinster its ancient district name of Laigen, from the broad-headed lances the Gaulish intruders carried. And an old Irish poem tells of the traditions of Laigen under its legendary kings:

> The sweet strain heard there every hour,
> The wine-barque on the purple flood—
> Showers of silver flashing bright,
> Torques of gold from distant Gaul. . . .

Two hundred years before Christ we know Italy was exporting her wine to Ireland, and some four long centuries thereafter, when wine was being grown in the vineyards of Provence, a goodly share of it was consigned to the same ports, transported thither by shrewd merchants of Marseilles, first down the quiet river valleys, then across the Channel. Wine and gold coins went up from Italy and Gaul—tin and amber came back. Thus at the time of the Roman empire Irish commerce with Europe was as settled a matter as ever it has been since. Tacitus (98 A.D.) informs us that its harbors and cities were well known to the merchants of his day. And in the following century when Irish princes acquired the habit of sending to Gaul for mercenaries to fight their wars, Ptolemy of Alexandria published a curiously exact and detailed list of the river mouths, mountains, and port-towns of Ireland adequate for the navigation of his time.

We surmise quite surely that Hellenistic-Roman culture and art, which had spread from northern Italy to Marseilles, crossed the Irish seas with the ships of Aquitaine carrying the wine of Bordeaux. We learn how eager Irish youths of the fourth century A.D. went in search of knowledge to Narbonne, where Greek was spoken as a living tongue. We see how Pelagius could so learn his Greek in Ireland in the year 415 that he could carry on in Jerusalem a debate with Orosius the Spaniard in a tongue for which the latter required the services of an interpreter. Ovid and Vergil were read in Ireland well before the fifth century; and it is no longer remarkable that in the year 595 the Irish saint Columban commanded Greek, an idiom which Gregory the Great could not master, although he had twice been papal nuncio in Constantinople.

Now because Ireland had always lain outside the uttermost confines of the Roman yoke, she succeeded from the beginning in keeping intact her own language, customs, history, and law. So, when we come to confront the earliest remains of vernacular Irish poetry, we must not be surprised if in their rhythms we often catch the glint of a self-conscious artistry which cannot be explained by the stiff and sometimes stupid canons of Græco-Roman prosody. In some districts of Gaul racial pride had been washed away in seas of blood by Roman conquerors, but Ireland, during all the Dark Ages, suffered no violent breach in the traditions of her past. She had uninterrupted intercourse with the southern world, without losing her own civilization. She was one of three vigorous nations which kept their national institutions intact and which the love of literature reached so early that they left behind a record of their pagan culture in vernacular poetry and prose. The other two races were the Anglo-Saxons and the Icelanders, both of whom were to come strongly under the initiating influence of the Irish.

When, in the early fifth century, the helpless province of Gaul was being overrun by the Huns and Vandals and Goths and Alans, whole districts of this Roman colony being devastated and sucked dry, Ireland was safe even though on the mainland almost all the ancient lines of communication were broken or closed. Even the Saxon conquest of Britain, which barred all passage through it for nearly one hundred and fifty years (449-597), made small difference to Ireland, since she troubled herself but little about the neighboring isle. Traders from Gaul still sailed the western coast of Erin, creeping up the Shannon to Roscommon and Loch Ce—and on the eastern side their ships passed by the Irish sea to what are now Down and Antrim, Iona and Cantyre.

Owing to the sacking of populous and fertile regions in Gaul, a host of learned men fled with other refugees across the Channel to Ireland, for this was a Celtic country inhabited by a people of nearly related descent who spoke a language apparently not greatly different from their own. They came drifting over from the Loire and the Garonne, or through Brittany to trading ports, and established a new home of classical studies. The rhetors mentioned by St. Patrick were perhaps among the number of these immigrants. The teaching staff of the chief university of Gaul— Burdigala (now Bordeaux)—seem to have founded a settlement and school of learning at Bordgal in Mide which preserved the name of their old college in a new land. Trained in the best traditions of fourth-century Latin oratory and grammar, they handed on the classical traditions of the humanities which had been rudely broken on the Continent. According to the roseate view of Zimmer, from the fifth to the seventh century in Ireland the great increase of learning brought about a sort of early renaissance: all Latin authors old and new were studied, together with grammar, metrics, chronology, astronomy. The tradition of solid hard work and devoted pursuit of knowledge to the limit of scholarship gave Irish universities the renown of possessing the acme of Latin learning. Along with Vergil, Ovid, Horace, Tacitus, Sallust, and the rest, students read the new works from Gaul and Spain—Orosius and Isidore, Jerome and Victorinus—writers of a later Latin that carried on a vital tradition and remained the living tongue of thought and education.

Only in Ireland apparently had the culture from overseas found a secure footing—there seems to have been in Britain no similar flowering of classical and romantic elements during the fifth and sixth centuries. Between the first settlement of Britain by the Saxons and the mission of Augustine lie 150 years which are no whit less important for the later history of Wales than for that of England. If we knew the true record of this Age of Arthur and his Knights of the Round Table, it would doubtless be no less picturesque than that which the deft hand of fable has woven around the dim figures of that distant day. But were it not for Gildas, this period would be wrapped in all but total darkness. There is a mass of traditional material, it is true, embodied in the triads, the lives of the Welsh saints, the *Mabinogion*, and the narrative of Geoffrey of Monmouth, which probably has a more substantial basis than is commonly supposed—and in this connection the works of sixth-century bards mentioned by Nennius (fragmentary bits of which may be preserved in much later Welsh idiom) should not be overlooked.

But the clue to the interpretation of this ancient Welsh and British evidence has not been discovered—the touchstone that will enable us to separate, in this strange medley, fiction from fact, legend from history. For, as Alfred Nutt points out, Welsh is unfortunate in not possessing (like Irish) a considerable mass of written matter known to be older than the year 906, and in some cases dating from the eighth century. In Irish we thus control an element of comparison which allows us to detect that many texts, preserved to us only in MSS of the eleventh and later centuries, belong to a far earlier period of time. In Welsh the elements of comparison are so slight as to yield only the faintest of clues. In default of linguistic evidence we are thus for the most part thrown upon internal testimony gained from the subject matter.

Now in most texts of a historical character such testimony is often as valid as paleographical or linguistic evidence—for instance, a reference to the Normans must indicate a date after the eleventh century for the passage in which it occurs. But many of the Welsh poets have been at obvious pains to disguise their historical allusions in a form penetrable only by the initiate. It is also certain that for two centuries at least (roughly speaking, the twelfth and the thirteenth) the bards were trained to cast their poems in conventional molds. New was added to old, old was recast without thought of forgery in our sense of that word, but none the less there was also a certain amount of deliberate intention to deceive. Finally, there are a number of poems that are destitute of historic references in the ordinary sense of explicit facts. Accordingly, we can make no use here, no matter how sparing a one, of Welsh pages of tradition, in spite of their vast potential importance to the story of later European poetry.

This importance derives from the chance that led marauding expeditions of Saxons in South Britain (from the fifth to the seventh century) continually to drive hordes of British Celts to the shores of Armorica which lay straight across the Channel from them and was but sparsely settled by Romance-speaking peoples. In their new-found home, which was called after them Britannia Minor (Bretagne), these British Celts retained their own speech. Now part of the intellectual baggage these fugitives brought with them were ancient British and Celtic prose sagas and traditional poetry of several sorts. Above all else there accompanied them to Armorica the figure of the national legendary British hero, Arthur Pendragon, who, later decked out in the chivalric robings of medieval romance, was destined to play his rôle in twelfth and thirteenth-century poetry. And I have a fancy, too, that the original foundation of many a famous Breton lay may have crossed the Channel to avoid the raiding and plundering Saxon.[2]

Guesswork, however, no matter how close to the truth it later be found to be, is not our present affair. It is high time to resume the interrupted thread of the discourse and tell how Ireland at the end of the sixth century and the beginning of the seventh, sent forth numerous apostles to settle in the Merovingian kingdom of the Franks and among other German tribes, to establish missionary stations in which the noblest secular culture was fostered side by side with Christianity.

A marked characteristic of the Irish monk was his *consuetudo perigrinandi:* his confirmed yearning for new horizons. Singly or in groups of three, seven, or twelve, these clerks of God were seized by the itch to separate themselves from the enormous colonies of monks and artisans and laybrothers (for such the ancient Irish monasteries really were) and to seek ascetic seclusion from the world in foreign parts. It is a mistake, in view of our knowledge of Celtic wanderlust, to believe the prime impulse that motivated Gaelic pilgrimage was a missionary one.

At first these clerks were content to explore and colonize the small islands of their native lakes and rivers which lay at no great distance from the monastic *civitas* of their allegiance. Thereafter they began to investigate the numerous larger islands which swam in the northern fog off the Irish coasts; *mari eremum quærere* was the favorite term for this pleasure: to seek retirement on the sea. And when these attainable lands were no longer worthy the notice of a professional anchorite, a new hazard was added to the game by setting forth in frail boats called coracles, to search out some desert rock on the uncharted ocean. Two Irish songs from the late seventh or early eighth century indicate with sufficient clarity the news that sea-rovers brought back from those Isles of the Happy to stay-at-homes clustered about the peat fire:

> Once when Bran, son of Feval, was with his warriors in his royal fort, they suddenly saw a woman in strange raiment upon the floor of the house. No one knew whence she had come or how she had entered, for the ramparts were closed. Then she sang these quatrains to Bran while all the host were listening:

> > I know a spot beyond the edge of the ocean
> > Where all day long sea-horses gleam and rise,
> > And the white surges with perpetual motion
> > Circle the land that on four pillars lies.

Columns of bronze, white underneath our island,
Glitter unchanged across the happy years,
A fairer land than mortal plain or highland
It is, where flowers fall instead of tears.

For there an ancient tree is green with singing
Where birds among the blossoms call the hours,
And music sweeter than the birds is ringing,
And men drink wine more fragrant than the flowers.

And there a hero from the sunrise riding
Illumines with his face the level land;
His horse across the snowy sea-plain striding
Drips blood along the waves and on the strand.

And golden chariots thunder up behind him,
Which with the sea-tides sway unto the sun,
Chariots of silver (whoso looks will blind him),
Chariots of bronze to drive where games are won.

Go westward then and seaward past men's trouble.
And fifty islands such as mine will rise,
As large as Erin is, or thrice, or double,
And each as marvelous as Paradise.

Therefore sleep not, nor drink your drowsy potion,
Lest sloth corrupt you as the rust your swords,
But rise and sail across the crystal ocean
Where in far seas fair women wait their lords.

Thus it was that Irish clerks soon came to the Hebrides, the Orkneys, the Shetland Isles, and Iceland itself. In the vivid phrase of sixth-century Gildas: The dark hulls of their rude skiffs termed coracles might be seen creeping across the glassy surface of the main like so many insects awakened from torpor by the heat of the noonday sun, and making with one accord for some familiar haunt. Whoever, like Bran, saw in the blue flames of the winter's fire the chorus of many-hued women on a pure white cliff over the range of the sea in a land against which laughter peals, that dreamer set him forth in fair weather for the land of Evin's apple-tree, whose mane dripped with crystal spray.

Then on the morrow Bran went upon the sea. When he had been drifting for two days and two nights, he saw a man in a chariot coming toward him across the waters: it was Manannan, son of Ler, who sang these couplets to Bran:

To Bran around his coracle the billows crawl the crystal sea;
But from my car their crimson swell a field of flowers is to me.

You watch, O Bran, with craning throat sea-horses glisten to the sun;
But in a land of light I note where honey-colored rivers run.

You see the speckled salmon leap from out the ocean's womb and play;
They are my calves, my snowy sheep, whom god or mortal dare not slay.

The ocean multitudinous with color is your shining space;
But golden stairs lead down to us in silver halls of joy and grace.

And there immortal lovers play nor want for wine or happiness;
For under hedges man and maid shall kiss for aye and not transgress.

And we are older than the world, and we are younger than your clay—
Bran, from your purpose be not swirled until to us you come away!

In the third century of our era the southwestern regions of Britain were constantly ravaged by Irish sea-rovers and to a large extent finally settled by them. In this way is explained the presence in Wales and the Cornish peninsula of a substantial Goidelic element in the population; unmistakably evidenced by tombstone inscriptions that contain Irish names written in Ogham. Thus, from the districts north and south of Severn Bay, Irish settlers accompanied British fugitives to Armorica. And they made further expeditions into Frankish territory, advancing to the foot of the Alps, soon thereafter crossing them—so that Bobbio or perhaps Tarentum on the one hand, and Iceland on the other, ultimately set the limits of this Irish search for the pot of gold beyond the rainbow's end.

It was only by way of afterthought that the Irish helped lay rubble and basement of medieval Christian culture. For just as the Irish peripatetics had gone to Iceland with no original thought of missionary enterprise, so their later expeditions to Brittany and the kingdom of the Franks had no such ulterior purpose. But the sad state of things from a Christian's point of view in the Frankish realm proved too much for Columban of Luxeuil and his associates; so they expanded their first aims and became emissaries and teachers to a half-pagan people among whom they had initially planned to dwell only to lead a life of contemplation.

Columba (born in Ulster 521) and Columban (born in Leinster 543) have often been confused even by people who should know better. The former was the apostle to Caledonia—at the age of forty-two he left Ireland with twelve followers and founded a monastery on Iona (or Hy), a small island off the west coast of Scotland. By the time of his death in 597 twenty-three mission stations among the Scots and eighteen in the country of the Picts had been established.

Now there are a goodly number of Irish vernacular poems ascribed to Columba or Colum Cille (Dove of the Church), as he is most frequently called, but such verses are not found either in MSS or in linguistic dress, which necessarily presupposes an earlier date than the eleventh century. They do not, therefore, warrant inclusion here. But a Latin hymn, the famous *Altus prosator* (The High Creator, Ancient of Days and Unbegotten), was certainly written by him, and its measures roll majestically forward on their appointed course to acclaim him a master of style:

ALTUS PROSATOR

Ancient of Days, Creator High, Unending, Unbeginning God,
Who shall throughout time's period be infinite eternally,
With whom is Christ, Thine only Son, with whom the Holy Ghost shall be
In glory co-eternally, perpetual God in unison,
The Deity whom we proclaim is not three deities but one,
Three persons though we wonder on, our saving faith is in His name.

Beneficent the angels and archangels, the authorities,
The powers, principalities, and thrones are ordered by His hand.
Lest the majestic goodness of His trinity inactive stand,
Creations such as these He planned to hold the largess of His love.
They have their offices to show, as in His mighty word they move,
The riches of celestial love, the privilege His hands bestow.

Celestial glory in His face, with archangelic splendor crowned,
Out of the heaven's highest round of light and sempiternal space,
Though God had made him, Lucifer the arrogant fell to disgrace.
And rebel angels lost their place, whom vanity lured on to err.
Because the rest in glorious and princely kingdoms faithful were,
Their captain sinned the deeplier, for pride had made him envious.

Down to dark cells of divers make, into the deep abyss of hell,
The Dragon great and terrible, the ancient, foul, and subtle Snake,
A third part of the shining stars drew with him in his slimy wake!
Our Adversary, whose mistake hurled headlong to eternal wars
Apostate angels, in his den imprisoned under horrid bars,
Is crueler than human scars, and subtler than are beasts or men.

(2)

The unforgettable stanzas of Columba were sung for generations in continental schools and monasteries, finding perhaps their most famous setting in the Latin rhythmic poem of Hrabanus Maurus on *The Catholic Faith*.

Columban never set foot in Scotland—he was the apostle of culture and light to Burgundy, Switzerland, and Italy. Columba, as we have seen, spent his life among the Pictish pagans of North Britain; Columban labored among the heathen of Central Europe.

He was the greatest of all the teachers sent forth from Irish shores. He had received his first training in Christian doctrine and classical letters on one of the islands of Lough Erne, but while yet a young man he migrated to Bangor, then at the height of its fame and, with its thousands of students from abroad and at home, a beacon light of learning surely, and of piety perhaps.

Nothing is more dangerous to a proper understanding of the transmission of culture from ancient days to ours than an undervaluation of the rôle played by ancient Irish monasteries and monastic schools. We are far too ready to depreciate early medieval study and investigation because the men of those far-away times knew nothing of steampower, electricity, gunpowder, wireless, aviation, and a hundred other inventions and discoveries which add to the hardships of life. Monastic schools like that of Bangor were not important—as are some religious houses today, it may be—as places of doctrinal propagandism. They were primarily essential to the world as centers of ambitious and initiating energy.

Such institutions as Bangor were schools, all the way from kindergarten to university, hospitals, hotels, publishing houses, libraries, law-courts, art academies, and conservatories of music. They were houses of refuge, places of pilgrimage, marts for barter and exchange, centers of culture, social foci, newspaper offices, and distilleries. A score of other public and practical things were they: garrison, granary, orphan asylum, frontier fort, postoffice, savings bank, and general store for surrounding agricultural districts. We carelessly imagine the early monasteries as charnel houses of cant and ritual—whereas they were the best-oiled machines for the advancement of science, the livest accelerators of human thinking, precedent to the University of Paris.

I am most willing to grant that neither in the scholar's cell nor in the oratory of the monk are in any age adventurous policies for the advancement of the world's welfare ordinarily planned. So the monastery schools and abbeys in Ireland (and elsewhere before the spread of Cluny), in so far as they represented merely teaching and letters, were probably little more effective in molding the social campaigns of their age than were royal courts. But call a university school like sixth-century Bangor the inevitable rendezvous for free thought and liberal thinkers, stamp it the asylum for refugee politicians and men of letters, name it the open forum for convivial wits, sea-rovers, discoverers, and explorers, journalists and pamphleteers generally—and you are on the warm trail that leads to the proper perspective of things. For at Bangor dwelt, for short or long, top-sergeants in the army of intelligentsia—so far as we know, in the heyday of its flourishing, it was the incubator of mentality north of Constantinople. All that the world of its day had to offer in the way of curious speculation on things celestial and mundane, all that was eager and whimsical, wise and disquieting in sixth-century philosophy, religion, and politics had here their central abiding-place.

From the days of Bangor all through the Middle Ages droves of artisans, tradespeople, and laborers settled within the college precincts—so much so that these establishments grew to be aggregations of craftsmen, merchants, and textile-workers as large as a thriving town. We know, for instance, that in the ninth century the Abbey of St. Riquier was the nucleus of twenty-five hundred houses, which would argue a population of well over ten thousand souls. The part of the ecclesiastical settlement given over to laymen for purely commercial purposes was so large that they were perforce grouped by streets and lanes. The enumeration of their various activities specially mentions: wholesale merchants, smiths, shield-makers, saddlers, bakers, shoemakers, butchers, fullers, furriers, wine-merchants, and beer-sellers. The cartulary of St. Vincent in the eleventh century adds other crafts to these: carpenters, weavers, workers in gold and silver, drapers, linen-merchants, leather dealers, tailors, cobblers, waxmakers, salt merchants, and glaziers.

In fact, so far as we can judge from a study of industrial development and expansion from the fifth to the eleventh century, western Europe underwent no specific Dark Ages. Quite the contrary, if we believe Usher, who finds this very period one of active economic growth. There was certainly no breakup in occupational organization brought about by the fall of Rome. A certain measure of superficial decay ensued, but only because the domination of Roman policy had forced a premature industrial growth that could not be continued: in Gaul, for instance, there were eight great establishments with government subsidy which were engaged in the manufacture of weapons and munitions of war. After the passing of the empire all such forced industrial effort would inevitably flow into channels more in accord with the genuine needs of the community.

The flux of commerce toward Rome declined in the Dark Ages, of course, but inasmuch as this had never been a genuinely reciprocal trade, it was hardly a retrograde movement. Changes took place in those industries which catered primarily to the wealthy city-dwellers of the empire. Fewer objects of luxury were made—former refinements of execution and manufacture disappeared. Certain commercial arts were lost or neglected. And yet Usher insists that the transition from the restraints and compulsions of the older system to the freer regime of the Middle Ages involved construction as well as destruction. All the fundamental specializations of occupational life maintained themselves, sheltered (even during the period of greatest disorder) on the vast estates of the feudal lords and in the monasteries.

In schools like Bangor the range of studious activity was a wide one. Verily, it was a thoroughly equipped and vigorous seat of learning in the latter half of the sixth century that could dispatch a trained and elegant scholar like Columban to convert the pagans of France. The proofs of his learning are evident to any student of his writings. The scholarship of them is manifest; so is their facile grace, as instanced by the following *celeuma* or boating song, quite certainly of his manufacture:

PLY THE OAR!

Heia, fellows! Echo, resounding, sends back our heia!
Placid lies the wide-spread floor of the sea; the tempest,
Calmed by the serene face of ocean's arbiter, slumbers;
Under their sliding weight, conquered, the waves are quiet.

Heia, fellows! Echo, resounding, sends back our heia!
Beat with your equal oar-stroke, steadily shake the keelson!
Soon the smiling peace of sea and sky shall permit us,
Under our bellying sail, to run with the wind's swift motion.

Heia, fellows! Echo, resounding, sends back our heia!
So that our emulous prow may cut the waves like a dolphin,
Row till the timbers groan and the ship leap under your muscles—
Backward our whitened path flows in a lengthening furrow.

Heia, fellows! Echo, resounding, sends back our heia!
Over the waves play the Phorci: sing we, however, heia!
Stirred by our strokes the ocean foams; however, sing heia!
Voices unwearying, echo along the shore—sing heia!   (3)

Columban wrote other good Latin verses, full of quaint metrical conceits, in both the classical and the monkish rhyming style. Allusions to pagan and Christian antiquity abound in his poems. Where but in Ireland did he acquire this scholarship? His life on the continent was one of rough, practical, all-absorbing effort which left small time for such studies. And even if time and leisure permitted, the opportunity was wanting; there were no library facilities, for the continent at that moment was plunged in utter darkness, literary as well as spiritual. We must, I think, reasonably conclude that men like Columban gained their extensive acquaintance with the classics, and their eloquent scholarship at such abbeys as those of Bangor and Lough Erne. Towards the end of the seventh century the Irish schools were famous throughout Europe: Hy, Lismore, Bangor, Clonfert, Clonard, and Armagh—the last-named at this period had seven thousand students. Aldhelm celebrates their literary renown, claiming whole fleets of ships transported the legion of Breton students thither. Exaggeration? Hardly.

About the year 590 Columban left Ireland with twelve disciples and traversed Gaul. Welcomed by Gontran of Burgundy, he is invested with the old Roman castle of Anagratum (Annegray), where the largest and most famous of the early monasteries soon rears its head. Crowds soon flock to the Irish teacher, for the great foundations of Luxeuil and Fontaines follow in rapid succession, and Columban numbers among his pupils scores of the children of the noblest Franks and Burgundians.

Luxeuil was, of course, only a new type of an institution with which Gaul had been familiar for more than two hundred years. Monasticism had been definitely introduced into Gaul towards the middle of the fourth century, and the manner of life it offered had at once attracted to it a multitude of votaries. During the fifth century no less than eighty new monasteries were established in the district along the Rhone and the Saone, and somewhere near twice that number in the rest of Gaul. When, in the year 486, Chlodwig led a band of barbarous and heathen Franks across the Rhine and founded his kingdom, it was found that this invasion, instead of demolishing the existent system of religious houses, only brought new patrons to it. Not only Chlodwig but Childebert I themselves founded and endowed a goodly number of monasteries (both for men and for women), and the noble class were not slow to follow in the royal footsteps. Princesses enrolled themselves as nuns

(Radegunde, Chrodield, Basina) and devoted their patrimony to convents.

And still, despite the fact that all Gaul was so strewn with monasteries that no district was neglected—that in the densest forest, in the wildest desert rose the hymn and rang the axe of the monk—that Maur, thirty years before the arrival of Columban, had founded at Glanfeuil the rule of Benedict of Nursia—the spirit of Christianity and culture had as yet no abiding hold upon the popular mind. Kellett reminds us that the first Catholic king accepted baptism because in a desperate strait the Christian god seemed mightier than Thor or Wotan—nor did his conversion prevent his murdering his nephew and stealing the crown. Gregory of Tours tells how in Neustria, where the Franks were supposedly more under the sway of Christ than in Austrasia, a royal wanton could murder her queen, marry the king, and slay a protesting bishop at the altar of his church.

The sixth and last of Thierry's narratives of the Merovingian times gives us a picture of the career of Leudaste, a parvenu of the sixth century, the son of a Gallo-Roman serf, yet raised by an act of royal favor to the rank of the chiefs of the conquerors of Gaul. The life-story of Leudaste almost transcends belief; nevertheless, intimately connected as it is with that of many celebrated persons of his day, it apparently offers us only a typical episode of the general trend of existence in this age. The unadorned tale of our parvenu's adventures solves several problems about which scholars hold divided opinions: (1) What was the condition of the native Gaul and the serf under Frankish rule? (2) How were Gaulish cities then governed, which were under the ambiguous rule of count and bishop? (3) What were the mutual relations of two rival, if not invariably hostile, powers—Gallo-Roman and Frank?

Other points of controversy regarding sixth-century backgrounds have been set beyond serious debate by the descriptions of Gregory of Tours; in the history of Bishop Prætextatus we have the portrait of a Gallo-Frankish council, in the sketch of young Merowig we get the drawing of outlaw life and the interior of religious sanctuaries. The tale of Galeswintha paints conjugal amenities and domestic customs in the environment of palace and court, the narrative of Sighebert instructs us in the very sources of the national feud between jealous Frankish kingdoms—we learn of Fredegonda the pattern of primitive barbarism, Hilperic who acquires the polish of civilization but none of its subtle virtues, Mummolus, who (like an earlier Petronius) corrupts himself deliberately in order to belong to his age. Princesses who had assumed the veil hire bullies to do murder on an episcopal council. Kings have what number of wives and concubines they will, with dowager queens encouraging their convenient lust. Witchcraft and sorcery are held in honor. Incestuous marriages are frequent. Festival banquets in memory of old heathen deities cause no popular censure. Human sacrifices are not unknown. Drunkenness is a prescriptive right, a national vice.

Hopeless as this picture is, it does not faithfully reflect the end of organized society in a civilized world—on the contrary, we find here only the confusion that is to be expected whenever history repeats itself and, for the time being, submerges ancient culture beneath great masses of primitive peoples. The first effect of this is always to smother all traditional expressions and apparently to extinguish them. But such primitive peoples are like the tarry screenings of a mine-run grade of bituminous coal suddenly heaped on the red glow of a furnace bed—if they do not put out the existent fire, they later act as the best sort of fuel for it, and under the forcing of a rightly applied draught the fire works its way up through the new material, licks at it with fierce tongues of flame, and the blaze brought about by the initially obstructive fuel is greater than ever before.

This is exactly what happened in the West in the fifth and sixth centuries. To start with, the Goths and Vandals and Saxons and Franks had no more realizing sense of the values of classical civilization than if they were the brutes they seem, but by not later than the end of the eighth century, there had set in that extraordinary development in human history which we call western culture. And of this the sixth century is both the critical age and the turning point. For although the Franks were only nominally Christians and knew little of the realities of religion and its humaner educating symbols, they were already arbiters of the western world and were soon to be its masters. The work of making this fierce race Christian in very deed, of destroying the last vestige of heathenism among them, of restoring the authority of the storied past was the yeoman work of two powers—monasticism and the papacy. And as to the first of these powers, the whole responsibility for actual initiative lay with Irish scholars. They alone brought breadth of intellectual viewpoint and freedom of training to Gaul—they introduced imagination and spiritual force into a world well-nigh sunk in materialism.

Characteristic of the Irish confessors was their earnest, single-hearted pursuit of learning in the widest sense attainable, and their solid hard work as scholars. The foundations of Columban long remained centers of art and science amid Burgundian and Lombard barbarism. The settlements of his comrade, Gall, rose into the proud abbey which still retains his name, and which for centuries was the beacon-light of learning in western Europe. The sister abbey of Reichenau, the rival of Gall in power and wisdom, owes its establishment on an island in Lake Constance to the teaching of an Irish scholar. Under the shelter of these great houses, and of such as these, learning was planted in a multitude of lesser societies, scattered throughout the entire territory of German infiltration. And quite uniformly the impulse which led to their formation as schools as well as monasteries is directly due to the energy of Irish travelers.

It is little surprising to find our masterful and fearless Columban at war with the Gaulish bishops of his time who were addicted to lechery, theft, and inebriety. Luckily, we have recorded for us in five versified epistles the atrabilious correspondence said to have been exchanged by two Frankish bishops in the year 665: Importunus of Paris and Chrodebert of Tours. I know no better mirror of the conditions prevailing in the human comedy of the Merovingian age, fifty years after our Irish missionary has moved the scene of his activities to pastures new, than that furnished by the passages of this amazing minstrelsy.

In the case of the sixth-century Welsh bards, and again when referring to Irish songs ascribed to Colum Cille, I have said we were not warranted in using material ascribed to the sixth century and earlier times, unless the evidence makes it practically certain that no possibility of archaizing forgery exists. It is now time to take inventory of ancient Gaelic literature in Ireland with a view to determining how rich and how varied was the stock of poetry that lived in favored Erin, while much of the remainder of Europe was in a relatively inchoate or semi-barbarous state of culture.

The sixth and seventh centuries were the golden age of Irish letters. During the fourth and fifth centuries Ireland had become, if not the sole legatee, at least the outstanding inheritor of a classical culture which, our previous chapters have insisted, was well on its way towards Christianized modernism. Ireland had apparently made such wise use of her opportunity to derive spiritual profit from a continental debâcle in which she had not deeply shared, that a great period of humanism brought her the culmination of a national poetry full five hundred years before the vernacular efflorescence in France and Germany. In a turbulent world overrun by illiterate barbarians, Ireland was not only the haven of rest, it was the great seminary of Christian and classical learning—at once the university and the literary market of unsatisfactory generations.

It was during this period that the repertory of bards and story-tellers was first written down in the cloisters and schools. Unfortunately, not a single tale, and but two or three short poems, have descended to us from these early centuries in contemporary MSS. In Ireland itself most old books were destroyed during the Viking terror that burst upon the island towards the close of the eighth century. Perhaps it is hardly fair to fasten upon the Northmen the unshared responsibility for the loss of Irish MSS, but— wherever the blame may lie—the old books were destroyed, except for the least bit that chance preserved in continental parchments. It is not until the eleventh century that we begin to have an almost unbroken series of hundreds of MSS in which all that had escaped destruction was collected and arranged. Many of the tales and poems thus preserved were undoubtedly composed in the eighth century—some few perhaps in the seventh. And as Irish scholarship advances, it is not unlikely that fragments of poetry will be found which, from linguistic and internal evidence, may be claimed for the sixth century.

Ireland did not employ poetry as the vehicle of epic narrative—there are no ancient Irish epics and ballads. So much was prose the natural medium for Gaelic story that, when in later centuries the Arthurian romances were done into Gaelic, they were all turned from poetry to prose. At the same time, most Irish tales and stories are interspersed with lyrics placed in the mouths of the principal heroes—after the manner of the cantefable, most familiar to modern readers from the French story of Aucassin and Nicolete.

In his indispensable catalogue of Irish epic literature published forty years ago, de Jubainville listed five hundred and fifty separate titles of tales and poems, four hundred of which have been preserved in MSS. With what has been discovered since, it would now be easy to add another one hundred tales which we possess in MSS form, and at least another one hundred which we know only by title. But even this aggregate of five hundred tales by no means represents the whole extent of medieval fiction in our possession, because quite a large number of MSS remain still unexplored. Besides, if we were to add to our list of purely imaginative pieces the extant MSS of historical narrative and religious legend which fairly swim in romantic episode and atmosphere, our total of five hundred would be again increased, perhaps by half.

Whoever wishes to obtain insight into the spirit (as well as the form) of ancient Irish romance may turn to very excellent English renderings of the *Death of Cuchulinn*, the *Cattle Raid of Cooley*, the *Voyage of Maelduin*, the *Destruction of DaDerga's Hostel*, and the *Silva Gaedelica*. But in reading them the uninitiated must remember that scarcely a single Irish tale of any length has reached us in its original form—in the shape current anciently among the people and recited by fili or shanachie. What we have is late redactions patched together from various sources: fragmentary, diffuse, and self-contradictory. Before the modern reader can visualize what these romances were in the Golden Age, he must somehow recast them in their original condition and reinvest them with a primitive consistency—not by any means an impossible task when several versions of the same tale have come down to us.

If we do this, and compare the result with the vernacular epics of France, England, and Germany of five or six centuries later, we shall discover that even at this advanced period those countries have little or nothing wherewith to compare the Irish romance before the time of Charles the Great. We shall feel that even the rich treasure of Anglo-Saxon story is quite thrown into the shade when compared in wealth or variety with that of Ireland. It was, likely enough, the anti-national spirit of continental Christianity which led to the neglect of vernacular story on the mainland of Europe, while it was probably Irish influence and Irish example that taught the Anglian monk to value his native literature, to write it down and preserve it.

So much for the early romances in Erin. Now for the lyrics!

Chapter X

IRISH LYRICS AND BALLADS

In his remarkable study of Irish influences on the poetry of the Scandinavian peninsula, Axel Olrik[1] tells us how, from the western parts of Norway, from Hordaland and Rogaland, bold mariners thrust forth on the great seas far to the south of the Orkney and Shetland Isles and came upon the Gaels—the Celtic race whose culture had undergone a rich and unique development. In the year 617 the Irish coast was laid waste by a heathen Viking horde, presumably Norwegians. Then ensued a period of peace while the Scottish islands were receiving their permanent Norse immigration, but when the Viking Age properly began, these Northmen delivered their concerted blows against Erin.

At that moment the poetry of this ancient Ireland exhibited a wondrous glory of color seemingly born of its luxuriant soil and gilded by a sun that broke in riotous splendor through its enclouding mists. Delight in woman's beauty veins old Irish song: she is pictured white as snow, black as coal, red as blood, with rosy feet peering through silver-fretted sandals. In these verses one finds a joy in the red-gold sheen of an apple, in the softly rustling whispers of sacred branches of silver. One finds a yearning for the sea whereon with their white-foaming manes rush the steeds of Manannan, the ruler of the ocean. One feels a constant longing for distant horizons where the land of the blessed is lighted by the last rays of a declining sun.

On the continent of Europe the Romish church and culture had tended to bring about the neglect of vernacular poetry and its utter submergence beneath an anti-national gloze. But in Ireland Christianity itself served only to widen and enrich the racial world of poetic fancy—and we behold in it a strange interweaving of the forces of the new God and the battalions of traditional heroes and animistic beings.

Over the heads of this strangely gifted race the first storm clouds of the Viking terror broke. First there were marauding raids upon the monastic islands and coasts; then the abbot was driven out of Armagh—where the most famous cathedral of Ireland was located—and castle keeps were erected at strategic points throughout the interior. We have in the *Rigsthula* a poem from this time whose verses are sprinkled with Irish words and whose whole content is based on the world of Celtic phantasy. A new manner in northern poetry begins to sprout from Irish sowing, a style at once more concise and plastic than the older one. Something of this may be easily read in the prophetic *Völuspa*, but the fact emerges clearly in the youngest poem of Helgi Hundingsbani—here are ships with sails tightly furled, scudding before the whistling gale—here are long billowed waves pounding the gunwales, as if the whole world were falling together—here are the valkyries of Odin riding upon the battlefield:

> There were northern lights over Logafjoll,
> And forth from the glory shot flashes—
> He saw high-helmeted girls rush riding,
> Blotches of blood on their breast-plates;
> And from the tips of their spears dripped fire.

Chadwick believes that the great transformation which came in northern poetic art may be due in part to the vast widening of Scandinavian experience at this time, but Olrik claims it is due to Irish models. The Norsemen enter the Viking Age with epic verse and emerge from it with a prose narrative permeated with lyric. They enter this time with heroic lays, using the elegiac phraseology of reminiscence, and appear at its further marge with an artfully polished prose which describes with equal readiness the world of fact or of faery, achieves successful delineation of detail, and understands minutely every variation of psychological mood. It would indeed seem that the *thulir* had learned this art in Irish schools.

Now it is at least possible that the Anglian monk and scop may have likewise learned from Irish example to value their national literature, for in several ways they seem to give willing testimony of their indebtedness to Gaelic art. Leach finds (with how much justification, I am not sure) that the Anglo-Saxon poet was slower in weaving the fabric of imaginative episode than was his Celtic fellow and was, therefore, prone to filch from the latter's larder his store of narrative themes. I can only say that the critic who, like myself, believes in the lightning quickness of the Celtic mind[2] will not think Leach's guess an unreasonable one. Beside the matter of its themes, I have long felt that old English poetry is unoriginal in the form of its verse-structure, which is flowing, continuous, discursive, and prevailingly non-stanzaic. Of course it is permitted us to assume the Anglian monk and scop did not borrow these factors from startlingly similar arrangements of rhythmic prose and of specifically lyric passages in Gaelic romance, but rather invented them out of whole cloth or had them indirectly from Roman Gaul or from lost Cymric models. I see no reason, however, why we should turn our back on known facts only to indulge ourselves with pure assumption. Furthermore, I prefer to consider the brooding quality of Anglo-Saxon poetry—its violet mist, its minor key—an echo of Gaelic minstrelsy rather than an original creation of the English temperament which through the long centuries it has never exactly reproduced elsewhere.

The very flaws of *Beowulf* are redolent to me of the periphrastic Irish manner at its worst—the heavy ornamentation of style with figurative phrases, the plethora of different terms for every unimportant thing, the over-use of conventional epithets which fairly swarm in a vocabulary learned by rote, the familiar encrustation of the verse with splendid words that ever threaten its eloquence. Here *Beowulf* most often shows itself to me but the poor copy of a fair Gaelic model. And as for *Widsith*, the whole catalogue of imaginary travels (57-89) and the lists of mytho-historical characters (14-35, 111-124) appear to me but negligible transcripts of second-rate Irish *rosc*.

This *rosc* has survived to us in the fine eighth-century *Deer's Cry* of St. Patrick, and the *Song of Amergin*—an apostrophe to the consummate glory of poetry. But such verses were continued by many later poets—the best-known of these are pseudo-Taliesin's "I am a wonder whose source is not known"—until all realizing sense for the meaning of this ancient hymnic material had vanished from the Celtic world, and nothing was left of *rosc* but its outer mask. This later form was popular in boastings before mortal combat, in lists of magic transformations, and—at its lowest estate— in stereotyped folderols of imaginary travels, like Glewlwyd Gavaelvawr's speech to the champion of Britain. It was at this point of final befuddlement that the poet of *Widsith* used it to such disporportionate length that, if we dismiss the two-thirds of his piece occupied by this Gaelic *rosc*, there is woefully little left of the "heroic English lay."

It is true that Celtic influence shows less visibly in other Anglo-Saxon poems, like the *Wanderer*, the *Seafarer*, the *Ruin*, the *Wife's Complaint*, and the *Lament of Deor;* still I conceive that they may indicate Gaelic prototypes surely enough in their curious modernity of effect. Certainly their appeal is closer to us than that of most subsequent English poetry for centuries yet to come. And I read Irish provenience also in their peculiar type of reflective sentiment, their mirroring the mood of a time when bolder poetical attack seems impossible, their sense of the vanity of human affairs, their melancholy regret for departed glories[3]—every amateur of Gaelic (and Cymric) poetry will recognize these hallowed tags. Still, they are no more lyrical than are the Norse lays of the Viking period—theirs is the elegiac note of Ossian, and at best they sound like remote bagpipes in a British fog.[4]

In fact, there is scarcely a line in either Anglo-Saxon or Old Norse poetry that can conveniently be termed lyrical. Even if one should be hardy enough to believe that ancient northern rhapsodic verse grew out of a more primitive lyric type—"a song in chorus with narrative stuff in it, like the later choral ballads"—there have descended to us no remnants of such earlier minstrelsy from which to conjure. It is best here as elsewhere to acknowledge the flat truth: both Old English and Old Norse are quite wanting in lyric flair, even though they do contain a few elegies whose stiff lines are never once keyed to concert pitch. The sort of lyric found at the close of the Middle Ages in the folk-songs, popular ballads, and carols of the fifteenth century is not dimly adumbrated by any verse of early northern literature transmitted to us. And this is the more remarkable because long before the end of the Viking Age the Irish had created a great place for themselves in the history of European letters through their early development of rhyme, their masterly treatment of sound-groups, their intricate system of verse-forms, the vivid immediacy of their imaginative pictures, their unbelievably fine power of observation, and their fluency in the use of the erotic note. Unfortunately, the great mass of older Irish lyric poetry is preserved to us, like that of Greece and Rome, exclusively in fragments scattered as citations through works of the most varied character—many of them listed as examples of usage in glossaries, others quoted as illustrations in handbooks of metrics and grammar. Others, again, are found in annals having to do with famous personalities and events. Besides these, we find lyric tags on the margins of manuscripts, sometimes with special reference to the context of the adjacent passage, but more often indicative of some fugitive conceit or memory that troubled the copyist, or merely to try the scribe's quill before he continued his transcription. A few of the quatrains of such isolated content are doubtless the impromptu creation of the person who wrote them down. To collect all the *disjecta membra* of so great and flourishing a genre as the Irish lyric after it has once been submerged, transcends the opportunity of any individual—for a complete and well-planned corpus of it we must await the unselfish labors of long years yet to come.

Meyer, however, lived long enough to publish a suggestive anthology of medieval Irish lyric fragments, contenting himself with the period 800-1100 because of the inordinate richness of the material after that date. Their content is uncommonly variegated. The æsthetic value of the poems is undoubtedly outweighed by their historical importance—as, for instance, in the verses of the Viking period, with their Norse loanwords and graphic references to the customs and physical appearance of the Northmen. And yet their beauty, as judged by modern taste, is far from negligible. Most of these lyric fragments are the work of professional poets of two classes: the highly respected *filid* (court poets, artists who have learned their trade in schools of rhetoric) and the much less highly regarded bards. Many of these fragments—particularly songs of compliment and disdain—are difficult to grasp because in Irish poems that deal with persons it was customary never to repeat the name of the object of the poet's flattery or contempt. Instead, every sort of paraphrase is used to characterize this person's descent, rank, place of dwelling, and so forth. Very noteworthy, too, are the frequent negative expressions resorted to: you are not the fawn of a sick stag; he is no fruit of a withered tree—these are very emphatic even when the intention is an ironic one. Acervation of adjective attributes and short intercalations of patch-phrases occur so often as to be a hallmark of Irish lyric style, but these are necessary for the continuous alliteration, especially that of the linked sort, lasting deep into the ninth century.

Whatever the future may bring forth in the way of a better understanding of early Irish lyrics, it is now high time for us to present a carefully chosen group of illustrative English renderings of old Gaelic poetry. I have deliberately kept my reader waiting for them until, by a process of elimination of other possible factors, my argument might hope to have established the likelihood that a certain new note we shall later observe in Carolingian poetry had its source in the specifically Gaelic contribution of Irish monks and minstrels, and could not reasonably be traced to any other origin extraneous to Carolingian France.

THE SONG OF CREDE

These are arrows that murder sleep
    Every hour the cold night through;
Love all day is pain to me—
    Hero of Roiny, where are you?

It came to me out of a foreign land,
    Stronger than all, my love for the dead;
Bloom and color have fled for me,
    And oh! my peace is fled!

Speech was sweeter from him than song,
    (God's songs are sweeter, it may be!)
But his lips were flame, and no braggart's lips,
    And he was slender to lie with me.

Ah, why am I not as I was, a child,
    A timid child still passionless?
Age has me now, and I am paid
    For all my loving waywardness.

Gooary is my father. I
    Have all that Aidne has to yield.
What are my people now to me?—
    My heart is in Irluachair's field.

Around the sides of Colman's Church
    They chant in Aidne stave on stave;
They praise Dinertach's name—and he
    Is a spent flame, and in his grave!

Chaste Christ! What sorrow is like mine?
    My heart is weary, and fate is strong;
These are arrows that murder sleep
    Every hour the cold night long.

LAMENT OF THE OLD WOMAN OF BEARE

Ebb-tide is flowing to the sea,
And my old age uncovers me.
Though I may grieve thereat,
Happiness comes out of fat!

I am the Woman Old of Beare;
The smocks were new I used to wear,
Now—though I shake with cold—
I have no new smock, nor none old.

You girls around me, you have not
Loved, save for the gain you've got;
Had you lived with me—then
It was not gold we loved, but men.

My body has dropped bitterly
Into the mean abode you see;
Christ in good time shall yet
Come and command them to deliver it.

These arms of mine that, when they're seen,
Look thin and bony—why, a queen
I was. And they were rings
Of beauty round the necks of kings.

Now these same arms so bony and thin
When they are seen—it would be sin
Unfit my name, and truth's,
To lift them over comely youths.

But let you girls be glad and woo
Lads that May Day brings back to you;
With me let sorrow lag,
For I am wretched, and a hag.

I hear no sweet speech, not the least;
No sheep dies for my wedding feast;
My hair is all but gray—
I keep it meanly veiled alway.

Why should I think it good or bad
That my poor scarf is colored sad?
Time was my every veil
Was rainbow-hued, and we drank ale!

Time was kings sat on Femen's Stone:
From Bregon, Ronan's Chair is gone;
Them long since storms were flaying—
Their tombs are crumbled slabs decaying.

The great sea-waves, they talk out loud,
Winter has risen like a cloud;
Fermuid I shall not see
Coming this day to visit me.

Those kings—I know what they are doing;
Across the reeds of Alma going
They row and row. The deep
Is a cold house, and they asleep.

Well, I have had my day with kings,
Drunk wine with them, and worn fine rings—
Today I drink in rags
Whey-water among shriveled hags.

I cry Amen! and Woe is me!—
Acorns at length drop from their tree—

A feast by candle-light—
And then the church's gloom all night.

The flood wave had me long ago,
And now ebb-tide has me in flow;
One bore me on its swell—
I know its fellow's tricks too well.

I scarcely recognize a place
Of many I knew that like a face
Were known to me and good.
All ebbs. There's no more flood.

THE HERMIT'S SONG

I wish, O eternal and ancient King, Thou Son of the living God,
For a hut to dwell in, a little hut, hidden where none has trod.

And near it a little lark should sing, a blithe little bird, all gray;
By the grace of the Ghost a clear pool there might wash my sins away.

A wood of beauty should bound it in a stone-throw on every side,
And the living voices of birds therein should live and be multiplied.

The door might face to the sun, and a brook should lie on the forest floor,
And the land be gracious to plants and seeds that should grow in front of my door.

And goodly comrades to chant the hours, sensible men each one,
Humble souls and obedient hearts, should pray to the King of the Sun.

A pleasant church with a linen cloth where Christ sits by the board,
And shining candles to shed their light on the pure white words of the Lord.

One house where all might go for the care of the soul and the body's care,
And say no evil or ribald thing, and speak with no braggart air.

This is the husbandry I would take, the desire which I cannot hide—
Leek and salmon and trout and bees, and a hen or two beside.

Raiment and food for my need, and I to be sitting there—
These gifts I ask from our fair Lord King—these, and a place for prayer.

A SONG OF THE SEA

Bold across high borders leaping, storms convulse the Plain of Ler,
Winds arise across the ocean, savage winter slays the year;
And the blast is sharp like a spear.

When the wind sets in from eastward all the billows vigil keep,
Its desire goes past us westward where the sunset comes to sleep
On the broad green breast of the deep.

When the wind sets in from northward driving with it fierce and
    strong
Waves like battle pouring southward, all the surge is led along
Under skies that are charmed by song.

When the wind sets in from westward over tides that salty be,
Its desire goes past us eastward to the Sunrise Tree
And the broad long waste of the sea.

But sweeping over Saxon shields the wind that's from the south
Strikes Caladnet and the islands, and with seas that know not
    drouth
Chokes the gray-green Shannon's mouth.

At the mouths of rivers surges break and whiten into cream;
Winds are round Cantire and wintry all the lands of Alba gleam,
And Slieve-Dremon empties forth its stream.

Son of God, Lord of Hosts, from the surges horrible,
Lord of Feasts, hear and save us from the tempest and the swell,
And the blasts of winds out of Hell!

SUMMER HAS GONE

 My words for you: stags bellow on—
 Snows of winter—a summer gone.

 Winds high and cold, and a low, cold sun
 Fades from the sky where wild seas run.

 Deep-red bracken, its shape awry—
 The wild goose raises his ancient cry.

 Cold that tangles the wings of birds—
 Season of ice—these are my words.

THE PHILOLOGIAN AND HIS CAT

Pangur is proof the arts of cats
    And men are in alliance;
His mind is set on catching rats,
    And mine on snaring science.

I make my book, the world forgot,
    A kind of endless class-time;
My hobby Pangur envies not—
    He likes more childish pastime.

When we're at home time quickly flies—
    Around us no one bustles;
Untiringly we exercise
    Our intellectual muscles.

Caught in his diplomatic net,
    A mouse jumps down his gullet;
And sometimes I can half-way get
    A problem when I mull it.

He watches with his shining eye
    The wall that guards his earnings;
As for my eyesight—well, I try
    To match my stare with learning's.

His joy is in his lightning leap;
    Me—I'm a mental wizard;
My claws are sunk in problems deep,
    His, in a mousie's gizzard.

As comrades we admit we shine,
    For each observes his station;
He practices his special line,
    And I, my avocation.

Our rivalry you'll find is nice,
    If in the scale you weigh us:
Each day Pangur goes hunting mice,
    I bring forth light from chaos.

ST. BROCCAN'S HYMN IN PRAISE OF ST. BRIGIT

Brigit had a snowy soul,
Strife and envy left her whole;

Brigit was no speckled snake,
Sold not Christ for money's sake.

Wonderful was every word
That her congregation heard;
She was pitiful and kind,
And the poor had all her mind.

Once a lad asked alms to save him,
And her seven sheep she gave him;
Trusted God in her distress,
And her flock was no way less.

Once they brought a sinning nun
To her for her benison;
And the nun was maid once more—
Salt from stone, a goodly store!

Once a wild boar in the north
Killed our swine or drove them forth;
Brigit touched him—he became
Like our other pigs, and tame.

Robbers nine whose swords she had
Blessèd, stained with blood each blade;
Brigit prayed with all her soul,
And the wounded was made whole.

Wonder was it when she stayed
With a widow who had made
Shuttle serve for kitchen wood,
And had killed her calf for food.

Brigit saw the sacrifice:
Morning came, and in a trice
Made the loom as good as new,
And restored the calfkin too.

Holy Brigit, pray for us
And in danger stay with us,
Guard us in our pain, and rise
With our souls to Paradise!

THE CHURCH BELL AT NIGHT

Sweet little bell, struck on a windy night,
I would liefer keep tryst with thee
Than be
With a woman foolish and light.

THE HOSTS OF FAERY

White shields they carry in white hands,
With silver emblems palely glowing;
Also blue swords that glitter, going
Where stout horns sound in mighty lands.

In serried ranks to dreamy wars,
Immortal captains following after,
The blue spears march, and like soft laughter
Their hair is, and their brows are stars.

And stricken foemen know the cost
Of ravaged lands when that war's ended
To which came marching on their splendid,
Invincible, avenging host!

They have the dreaded strength of kings
Who fathered them, and queens for mother;
And on the head of each and other
The gold locks lie in yellow rings.

Their slim, smooth bodies bend and shine,
And their bright eyes are starry blue
O'er teeth that have the ivory's hue
And thin lips like a streak of wine.

And they are excellent in slaying,
And any ale-house where they sing
With cunning melody will ring—
And they are skilled in fidchell playing.

THE SCRIBE

The trees like a hedge surround me,
    And a blackbird sings to me,
And on my book and around me
    The birds spill melody.

From the topmost twig in the bushes falls
    The gray-frock cuckoo's glee;
O it's good to write in the dear Lord's sight
    Under the greenwood tree.

THE CRY OF LIADIN AFTER CURITHER[5]

Curither

Liadin, since I left you, days
Are like long months, and every month
Is longer than slow-footed years.

Liadin

Oh, little joy and little praise
Is mine for the poor oath I swore
Since his torn heart was wet with tears.

And, saving the dread fear of heaven,
It were sheer madness not to do
The joy we two might share and part.

How worthless is my vow, being given,
I that was gentler in old days
Now twist with pain Curither's heart.

Yes, I am Liadin, that one
Who loved Curither, I am she,
And they that say as much, say truth.

But that short hour was shortly done,
Curither is not now with me,
Nor the sweet company of youth.

Why, when he sang it was as though
The forest sang in hearing him,
And the sweet-voiced empurpled sea.

I would that none of this were so,
That naught of all which I have done
Had torn his heart with grief for me.

I have no further thought to hide—
Curither has my very soul,
And all things dear beside grow dim.

This roaring flame—Oh, I have died
At the mere hearing of his name,
And I must live, denying him.

THE CRUCIFIXION

At the cry of the first bird
They began to crucify Thee, O Swan!
Never shall lament cease because of that.
It was like the parting of day from night.

Ah, sore was the suffering borne
By the body of Mary's Son,
But sorer still to Him was the grief
Which for His sake
Came upon His Mother.

THE VIKING TERROR

The bitter wind tosses tonight with wailing
   Ocean's white hair upon the wintry sea;
I have no fear of Norland warriors sailing
   Fierce toward the sands of Ireland, and to me.

FLIGHTINESS OF THOUGHT

I am ashamed of thoughts that idly go astray.
I shall have danger from them on the Judgment Day.

They wander wicked ways at quiet psalm-singing,
They fret in God's great eyes, they think an evil thing.

In companies of women, throngs of wickedness,
Through woods and cities, swifter than swift wind they pass.

Unferried, never missing step, they cross the sea,
And in one bound from heaven to earth they shortly flee.

Upon a race of folly hither and yon they roam,
And after dizziness they come at length back home.

Though one should bind them or put shackles on their feet,
No resting spell shall make them constant or more meet.

Nor whip nor sword-edge serves to keep them under hasp;
Like slippery eels they glide and slip beyond my grasp.

Lock nor deep-bolted dungeon nor earthly chain may serve,
Nor fort nor sea nor barren desert makes them swerve.

Belovèd and chaste Christ, Thine eyes are clear to see—
Come with Thy sevenfold grace and keep them nearer Thee!

Chapter XI

ROMANESQUE AND THE NEAR EAST

On the basis of the MSS which have survived to us, eleven of the nineteen centuries that separate us from the Augustan Age couched their outstanding documents of culture and high imagination in Latin. Only from the twelfth century on do the vernacular idioms begin to assume their preponderant position in the stream of literary utterance. There are but two notable exceptions to this otherwise unvarying rule: Gaelic and Arabic.

I have presented the matter of Gaelic poetry at such length in earlier pages of this book, because it offers us a corporate body of popularizing native verse in central and northern Europe previous to the Provençal outburst. And by envisioning these Irish rhythms thoroughly we can understand how galling a strait-jacket continental Latin meters had put upon the romantic or insular temperament. It was not until Irish song was driven to the mainland of Europe through a truly Celtic combination of wanderlust and missionizing zeal (reinforced by Norse raids at home), that an untoward destiny placed its muse beneath the killing yoke of medieval Romish culture. From that luckless moment Erin lived no longer in the dreams of mankind as the unforgotten holy island of Breton legend which was anchored in an unknown sea of Paradise by diamond cables, where diaphanous saints wore the shapes of white birds. For, whatever other debt native erotic poetry has had to pay the Roman genius, it certainly owed it that sense of disciplined form which has legislated out of existence all the irregular impulses of its whimsical and imaginative art and replaced them with mechanical expressions of dignity and precision. Poured cooling into a classical mold, poetry of whatever sort, from the Carolingians until well towards the close of the tenth century, is apt to contain no personal outcry, no passionate description of the mood of the writer, no ironic reaction upon the societal life of his age, no philosophy based on immediate experience, no silhouette or adumbration of the ethical strivings of individual man, not even this man's past emotions recollected in tranquillity—but only the borrowed and therefore tawdry plumage of Classical Rome and Silver Latinity.

We have already found (and shall discover again) that the centuries intermediate between Fortunatus and Gerbert of Rheims had on rare occasions a plenitude of power, especially in descriptive and narrative verse, outside the pale of classical imitation, but the prevailing rule of poetic composition and theme treatment is hopelessly attached to Augustan fashions.

But long before the end of the first Christian millennium there emerges another body of popularizing vernacular verse besides the Irish—one which, like the latter, had grown to ripeness beyond the uttermost confines of Greek and Roman sway and which, more even than the Gaelic, was *extra anni solisque vias*, beyond the known and computable world.[1] This is the Arabic poetry of the Ignorance that came to its zenith in the latter half of the sixth century.

Now this poetry was preserved as a sacred relic by Islam when in a savage burst of disinterested faith it had launched forth, poor and free, upon the conquest of the earth, having no homeland save its tents and the infinity of a dream which it pursued in the gallop of its horses, in the wind that flared the burnooses and carried the clouds of dust—Islam, throughout Dark and Middle Ages, the true champion of the never-attained idea which, the more one seeks to grasp it, plunges one only the more deeply into the future. According to Faure, when Justinian had closed the schools of Athens and had driven the artists and scholars from the empire[2]—at about the period that Gregory the Great burned the Palatine library—it was with Sassanian king Chosroes that almost all of them took refuge. History has magnificent strokes of chance. The Arabs, masters of Iran, found there the treasures snatched from the general ruin, and it was these collections that permitted scholars to initiate the new Europe into the thoughts of antiquity. While in most places the shadows were lengthening across the Occident, the caliphs were opening universities, digging canals, tracing gardens, reviving the study of science and medicine, and covering the conquered lands with caravansaries, mosques, and palaces. Against the lowering background of the history of these times we see their works as in a dazzling fairy-tale, a story from the *Thousand and One Nights*.

It seems to Faure the miracle of the Arabian mind that it remained itself everywhere, without, however, of itself creating anything in the regions that were swept under its dominion. Anarchic, nomadic, and a unit—as little bounded by moral as by material frontiers—through that very fact, Islam could adapt its genius to that of conquered peoples and at the same time persuade them to become absorbed in the unity of that genius. Coptic in Egypt, Berber in the Moghreb and in Spain, Persian in Persia, Indian in India—Islam allows the vanquished races to express according to their nature the new enthusiasm it knew so well how to impart.

Surely it is not inapposite to pause for a paragraph and say that it seems no remote hypothesis which would have Arabic first absorb, and then bring to the western world, hints of that burgeoning of Sanskrit lyric and drama and court epic which is so distinctive a phenomenon of early medieval India from the fifth century forward for almost six hundred years, and which found its high-water level during just the period that was the glory of Irish and Arabic letters. It is a little startling for the modern mind to read, for instance, Bhartrihari's first hundred stanzas devoted to woman and meet in the tender verses that depict her charm a peculiarly melting and sympathetic quality such as we find in our English romantic poetry—and meet again a treatment of love and nature in the Hindu poet which is in many ways more akin to our own sentiment than are the classics. Love, to be sure, is without the Platonic mania that infests modern poetry, but otherwise is expressed with the same wistful tenderness so familiar to contemporary art, and so foreign to the simpler, more virile temper of Greece and Rome. And as to natural description in Bhartrihari, More reminds us that this is not introduced merely to give a locality for the action, as ordinarily in the classics, but is more closely identified with the mood of the agent and becomes highly symbolical, as in writers like our own Hawthorne. The classical authors did not as a rule search for this sympathetic spirit in external nature, nor read in her varying aspects the expression of their own changeful moods; but one need read only the first *Century* of Bhartrihari to see how in this respect Indian poetry approaches the methods of medieval romance. Nature is here burdened with human meaning; birds and flowers, hills, sky, winds, and streams, all the earth is redolent of passion. In the springtime the song of the cuckoo brings torture to those who are separated; in a myriad places the lotus flower multiplies the one beloved face; the acoka tree may not open its swelling buds until touched by the maiden's foot.[3]

The best productions of the Indian drama are nearly a dozen in number and date from the fifth to the eighth century. They are the compositions of Kalidasa and Bhavabhuti or of authors who masquerade under the name of a royal patron such as Shudraka. These dramas show certain affinities with Greek comedy but afford many more striking points of resemblance to the work of Elizabethan playrights and, in particular, of Shakespeare. The aim of the Indian theater is not to portray types of character, but individual persons; nor do they observe the unities of time and place. They are given to introducing romantic and fabulous elements, says Macdonell; they mix prose with verse; they blend comic elements with serious situations, and delight in puns and distortions of words. The character of the clown (*vidushaka*) is a close parallel to the fool in Shakespeare. Also common to both are several contrivances intended to further the action, such as the writing of letters, the staging of a play within a play, the restoration of the dead to life, and the use of intoxication as a humorous device. In the light of such a series of coincidences (and many more unstated) must we continue to believe Hindu influence on western art to be absolutely beyond the realm of probability, and ascribe to ethnologic parallelism this instructive instance of how similar developments in lyric and drama can arise independently?[4]

Mackail characterizes the moment that saw the culmination of Irish and Arabic poetry as a time when, but for it, the Dark Ages were settling over Europe and poetry was growing faint and dim. In the East, it seems, the illusive brilliance of Justinian's era—the first attempt at a classical renaissance—had passed away as quickly as it rose. In the West but little tradition of letters survived; monastic chroniclers had ordinarily mere wretchedness to record. In Italy we see the extinction of the Gothic kingdom and with it, apparently, all hopes of a new Europe; beyond the Alps one meets the sanguinary annals of the Franks. Only in two countries was there outstanding imaginative life and independence of spirit; neither into Ireland nor into Arabia had Roman despotism ever effectively penetrated, and from these two remote soils, unbroken and virgin, there rose a curious flowerage of delicate and exquisite song.[5]

A few examples of ancient Arabian lyrical poetry, inclusive of idyllic and elegiac moods, will sufficiently indicate the types we have in mind, because Lyall, and more recently Nicholson, have found remarkably excellent English renderings of songs from the two great literatures of Islam—Arabic and Persian.[6]

THE FEUD

Shahl the Mountain Crag (about 450 A. D.)

We had forgiven the sons of Hind:
"They are our brethren (so said we),
The old days may return and find
They are the men they used to be."

But when the wrong stood clear and plain,
And naked wrath was bare today—
Our hatred wrought us bitter pain,
And as they slew us, we did slay.

So strode we out as lions stalk
At dawn the desert, angry-eyed;
Our blows beat down their empty talk,
We shamed their pomp and broke their pride.

With fools a man may be too kind—
Their folly flouts him but the more;
Battle will bring thee peace of mind
Where kindness only leaves thee sore.

THE SONG OF THE DWARF

Jahdar (Sixth Century)

As his comrades were shaving their heads and vowing to conquer or die in the impending fight, Jahdar, an ill-favored manikin with flowing locks, said to his people, "Disfigure me not through baldness. Leave my locks, for the first of the foe to ride forth from the glen tomorrow. I shall answer for him."

To wife and daughter
  Henceforth I am dead,
With dust of my hair
  For ointment shed.

Come close, dark horsemen
  That hither ride—
Shave if you can
  My lovelocks' pride.

A mother wots well
  Of the son she bore
(Held in her bosom
  She smelt him o'er),

Where warriors meet
  In the battle's van,
If he be a coward
  Or a man!

THE ASSIGNATION

Imra al Kais (died about 540 A. D.)

O many the tents that gave their riches to me of old!
I took my delight therein, I emptied their cups of gold—
And passing unseen the guards that, had they beheld, had slain
(For death, if they dared to kill, alone would have paid the stain),
I entered their tents what hour the Pleiades golden bright
Unfolded, a girdle of stars like gems in the belt of night.
I entered.—Within the tent beside the curtain she stood;
Lightly for sleep she was clad; she saw me and found me good,

And she spoke to me, saying, "Lo! The risk—is it naught to thee?
Thy madness I know of old—What brings thee once more to me?"
... I took her and led her forth. And trailing her robe in sand
She wiped with her broidered skirt our footprints from out that land
To where, below their tents, the edge of the valley sank
In hillocks of windy dunes and many a yellow bank. ...
And there to myself I drew her, seizing her side-locks both—
Full-ankled and bosomed deep, a woman and nothing loth.
Her color was fair to see, her grace was the desert's grace,
Her breast was luscious and smooth and bright as a mirror's face:
O virginal pale white pearl, full fed from untrodden springs,
The waters are crystal and pure that nourish such lucent things!
The cheeks that I saw aslant were gentle and soft as dawn—
The antelope hath such eyes when beside her there stands a fawn—
Her neck that was spotless and lovely, under the band she bare
Seemed snowy beneath her neckcloth, parting the coal-black hair
That down on her shoulders fallen (as from the palm-trees height
The ripening clusters hang) rivaled the deep midnight. ...

THE SCOFFER

Tarafa (about 560 A. D.)

Canst thou not make me immortal, thou that blamest me so
For desiring battle and loving the pleasures that fly?
Else, if thou lackest power to ward me from Death, I must go
To scatter my riches ere I behold him and die.

These are a triad of pleasures that make of my youth a delight
(And saving for these let me die and make lament for me)—
One is the foam of the wine wherein water is poured, and not bright,
But ruddy, and drunk away from the crowd should it be;

And one is the rescuing charge on the back of a valiant mare,
Running as wolves that from pools I have frightened away;
And one is to lie in her tent while the rain drips down from its hair
With an amorous woman beguiling the tedious day.

DESOLATION

Labid (about 600 A. D.)

Waste is the land where once the people of Mina alighted to dwell
    and remain,
Waste and desolate now, and Rajam and Ghawl and the valley of
    Raiyan are bare,
Save that as writing half-worn from a stone, a lonely relic that
    seems more plain

Because of the ruin around and above it, remembers once they
 were sojourners there.

Over the land that ruin has taken since once it knew music and
 mourning and mirth,
The sacred moons and the secular months have passed till the years
 are many they tell,
There where once in the spring the rains fell soft from the heavens
 to bless the earth,
There where the clouds of the thunder burst into floods or faded to
 showers that fell.

The clouds of the morning and evening have come, the clouds of
 day-time and night-time have gone,
Losing and leaving their darkness in thunders that speak to each
 other a speech that is blind,
Till, in the pale-growing grasses that thrive in this place, the deer
 and the ostrich alone
Move on the desolate slopes of the vale, bringing fearlessly forth,
 each one in its kind.

And there the wild cattle may browse and suckle beside them their
 new-born calves, and 'tis there
The half-grown heifers may wander in troops, not leaving too
 distant the statelier kine;
There, of the houses of men, by the torrents of rain discovered, the
 stones lie bare,
Bright and distinct as the tracing of figures wherewith the wrist
 of a woman may shine.

Yea, as the soot is pricked in her arm till the pattern is shown
 distinct and clear,
So are these stones from the dwellings of men, but they that builded
 are whither gone?
Nay, what avails it to ask of the deaf and the speechless to answer
 the riddle, and hear,
They that utter mysterious riddles in language the tongue of a man
 hath not known?

THE ETERNAL FEMININE

Maisun (about 680 A. D.)

I prefer a tent where the wind blows round me
To high palaces;
And a cloak of wool
To sorrowful ceremonial garments.

The crusts I ate in that tent
Were better than fine bread—
And O the wind's song on the hill-path
Drowns out your tambourines!

Likewise to tame cats
I prefer watchdogs that bark—
And a desert horseman
To you, you fat barbarian!

To those of my readers who are rightly skeptical regarding the ascription to feminine authors of most lyric verses which, since Lesbian Sappho, have been put into the lips of women, I can only say that Maisun was born and bred in the desert and that I cannot easily imagine another sex than hers alluding in exactly the scornful terms of the third stanza above either to husband Muawiya, who wed Maisun as governor of Syria and again later when Caliph took her to Damascus, or for that matter to any other unwanted and overstuffed mate.

DRINKING SONG

Abu Nuwas (died about 810 A. D.)

Youth and I together ran headlong after pleasure,
Acting all the sins that man doth in any measure;
But among the gifts of time none to heaven is nigher
Than the ascending liquid chime struck from lute or lyre.

Often at Dhi Tuluh where tents with sunshine laden
Lifted skyward, at my prayer sang to me a maiden—
"Spend your youth ere it be gone, Spring's a shadow going,
And at evening and at dawn, drink—the river's flowing!

"Pour into your cup the wine, sparkling, cool, and ruddy—
Clear though miser's gold may shine, yet to this it's muddy.
Once a Persian emperor chose the wine we drink of;—
Hue and fragrance so concur, 'tis doubly dear to think of.

"I have pawned my soul, I swear, pledging it for liquor,
Kiss my mouth that's red and fair like this cup of ichor;
Terror for my bargain may some time come upon me,
But I've put my soul away—joys of sense have won me."

And for good last a bit of woman worship embedded in the manner of neo-Platonistic formula which, two centuries later, was to form a conventional pattern of troubadour romanticism, a song of that Dakiki (died 975) who began the *Book of Kings*, the Persian national flower of chivalrous story which was completed by Firdusi:

LOVE'S LITANY

I would that all the earth might know no dawn,
My mouth from hers would never be withdrawn!

Round my pierced heart her scorpion hair is curled
Till I fear not the scorpions of the world;
Under her lip one dimple like a star
Glistens, and I have watched it from afar
As I have watched the starshine pale to morn.
She is the body of beauty that, once born,
Love takes it for his image, and my soul
Takes on her form because of love's control.

O God, if I must live without her, I
Pray you to be kind to me and let me die!

Mackail points out that neither Irish nor Arabic verse had the chance to develop further in its native soil. The poetry of pagan Ireland was crushed out or driven underground by Christianity, and this country bade fair to flood the western world, not with poets, but with missionaries; the triumph of Islam in Arabia might have done something similar but that its normal effect in this way was merged in a much vaster movement. Arabia emptied itself out bodily over half the known world; until then, it had been a blank in history, but within a single generation it issued in the storm of conquest that broke the Persian empire and hurled the armies of Heraclius into irretrievable rout— within two generations it had spread its dominion from the Oxus to the Guadalquivir. An immense exhaustion followed that incredible effort.

According to Arab critics, good poetry was written down to the end of the second century after the hegira—but from the establishment of the Abbasid caliphate soon after the end of the first century (750 A. D.), it took on a distinctly Persian flavor, ceased to be purely Arabic, and became cosmopolitan. The golden age of Islam in the reign of Haroun al Raschid was one of splendid culture on the brink of decay—a culture that had lost its vitalizing force. All the best of the Arabs, says Blunt, had passed outside the desert borders and had become city-dwellers in Syria, Irak, Persia, and Egypt. Their old ways of thought had been exchanged for new ones; they were no longer Bedouins; their insularity had gone. So far as the rules of the art go, good verse was written, but the special desert flavor of the old is lacking: that splendid realism in regard to natural things, that plainness of speech, and that naiveté of passion which distinguish pre-Islamic from all other poetry, and which the West finds of such priceless value. While in western Europe to the very borders of the Irish Sea racial pride had been washed away in blood, during all the Dark Ages Arabia suffered no violent breach in the traditions of her past, except what she brought upon herself through a new religion and worldconquest. And all this time she had uninterrupted intercourse with the Mediterranean countries without losing her own civilization.

Now, in the present shape of our knowledge (or, rather, of the use to which we are willing to put our knowledge), it is difficult to state what may have been the fertilizing contacts between eastern and western poetry from the fifth century of the Christian Era onwards to the time of the Crusades. Contacts galore there were, but were they impregnating on the West, of their seeds did new conceptions come to European poetry?

We know, for instance, just what tangible things the people of the West got from the Arabs during the Middle Ages: coffee, asparagus, buckwheat, cotton, flax, hemp, lemons, mulberries, olives, palms, rice, saffron, and sugar. Manufactured articles of luxury, also: confectionery, damask, gauze, crystal and plate-glass, linen, morocco, muslin, paper, silk stuffs embossed with gold and silver, syrups, taffeta, and velvet. Likewise, the rudiments of algebra, chemistry, and trigonometry, magic, talismans, and the Arabic numerals which were of such value in simplifying complex calculation.

The Arabs (as Seignobos tells us) had condensed and transmitted to the West all known science and invention from the ancient oriental world, such as Greece, Persia, India, and China. Through Arab channels the Occident thus had its opportunity to become again civilized after centuries of barbarism. And certainly, even if our ideas and our arts derive from a more remote antiquity, most of the inventions that make life the more agreeably livable come to us from the Arabs.[7]

Of course, we cannot watch through a clear lens the flux and refluence of culture in occidental and oriental minglings during the Dark Ages, as we have been able to study in previous chapters the relational attitudes of Ireland and Gaul. But at least no one should be longer content with the indolent notion that fertilizing contacts between Arabic and Latin lie outside the probability of the situation at almost any period during the so-called ecclesiastical centuries. Rather does such concourse of influences appear to be the necessary outgrowth of conditions after the year 632, when Arabia intervened in the history of the modern world and began the victorious march which ended in the existence of a new Mohammedan empire of greater territorial reach than that of Alexander—for it stretched from central Asia over Persia, Syria, and Egypt, all along the northern African shores up to the Pyrenees. In fact, the power of Islam was carried beyond the Pyrenees into the province of Septimania (or Gothia), the remnant of the Gaulish dominions of the Visigothic kings—so that for more than forty years (713-755) Narbonne, Arles, and Nîmes, all became Moorish cities. This fact (so conceivably important to explain Arabic influence in Gaul) is quite generally forgotten. A great portion of the earth's surface that Alexander had won for Hellenism, or Constantine assigned to Christ, passed under the new Semitic power—a sway by no means as alien in form and belief to the Christian realm of our Carolingian day as is commonly imagined.

For what people forget (Bevan[8] tells us) is that the peoples of the nearer East, after the wave of Mohammedan conquest had subsided, showed a quicker susceptibility to the old Hellenistic civilization on its scientific side than the rude northern races of Europe. Aristotle was reverenced and studied in Mohammedan lands from central Asia to the Atlantic, and in the ninth century was better understood in Balkh or Samarkand than anywhere in Europe, at least before the thirteenth century. Old Greek books on the different sciences were translated from the Syriac into Arabic in the golden prime of the Abbasid caliphate under Haroun al Raschid, a contemporary of Charles the Great. And in consequence there was the best teaching in all the world in the schools of Bagdad: mathematics, astronomy, zoölogy, botany, chemistry, grammar, and logic—wherefore the Mohammedan East made an advance in rationalist science which the West did not overtake previous to the Italian renascence.

From the eighth to the twelfth century we are apt to find sorry conditions of life and culture throughout the Christian West: miserable small towns, tumbledown peasant burrows, rude fortresses, countrysides ever disturbed by local wars—a land in which one could not journey a single day without risk to life and property. Exactly the opposite was true of the East: there loomed the rounded domes and minarets of Cairo, Bagdad, and Damascus—and all the other cities of the *Thousand and One Nights*—with their palaces of marble, their workshops, schools, and bazaars, their gardens whole leagues in extent. There were the surge and the spray of merchant caravans on the highroad between Spain and Persia in a Moslem and Byzantine world that was far richer, better policed, and more enlightened than the Christian West. It is small wonder if, from the ninth century on, our European brothers often confessed themselves inferior in culture to the unbeliever, marveled at the wonders of such an Orient, and attended Arabic schools in crowds.

Two testimonies of this last fact have been recently presented by Wiener. The first of these is in the introduction to the notorious *Hisperica famina* and runs as follows: "I notice a large number of young men dressed in elegant attire and pretending to be archers, crowding to the cities of Spain in order to study rhetoric. One might think they were preparing to wage battle, and why should they not, if one remembers the boastful way in which the rhetoricians speak of their wisdom? No one has ever seen such assemblies of dandies as listen to this flashy diction of the schools. Behold that young man over there who has left his native heath to study poetry; one might think, from the noise he is making, that he was cutting down an oak, preparing to forge a golden ornament, or playing some odd musical instrument." The elegant attire of our quotation refers to the Arab costume affected by the young bloods, and they are said to seem like archers because of the quiver-shaped box suspended from a girdle in which they carried, perhaps a sword and scabbard, but quite as probably the tablets, quills, and galls with which they made their lecture-notes.[9]

The other quotation given by Wiener is from Albarus (ninth century): "All the Christian youths, fair of face, eloquent in speech, conspicuous in apparel and bearing, learned in gentle science, perfected in Arabic rhetoric—these people spend their days in ardently studying Arabic books. Gathered together for the purpose of profound wisdom, they yet spend themselves in voluptuous praise of pagan literature—ignoring the beauties of ecclesiastical truth, and despising the holy church streams whose source is in Paradise. For shame! These young clerks do not know their own Latin language, so that, in the whole college of Christ, perhaps one in a thousand may be found who can write a decent letter to a brother. And an innumerable crowd of these dandies explain most subtly their Arabic preciosity of diction which lends metrical decoration to the end of their verses with monorhyme."

Now, the *Hisperica famina*, the *Lorica*, the *Rubisca*, and the *Adelphus adelpha* are written in a mixture of outlandish Latin, hybrid Greek, and Semitic (Arabic) words—as strange and artificial a jargon as was ever invented, but one apparently taught, and in use, in Gaulish and Spanish schools from the fifth century on, if we believe the testimony of Vergilius Maro the Grammarian, who listed twelve different ways of writing Latin (arrived at by clipping words, turning them upside down, adding or inserting syllables, etc.), and if we study Aldhelm, Gildas, and other early Christian writers. The hybrid Greek formations clutter passages in the Church Fathers, though by no means so smotheringly as in Hisperic speech—and patristic literature also employed mongrel Semitic (Arabic) roots, but never any great number at a time.

It is because of the presence of Arabic words, first in the language of the Spanish Goths, and afterwards in the sister tongues of Germanic races who acknowledged the hegemony of Gothic, that Wiener feels warranted in the assertion that their mediation of Arabic language and literature is the chief contribution of the Goths to Europe. His tentative story of the manner of this mediation is as follows:

After the dispersion of the Goths by the Arabs they scattered among their Germanic kin, where they were gladly received, not only because of their historic reputation for superior intelligence and power, but also because they now brought with them the new learning and arts of their Moslem conquerors: the science of drainage and intensive agriculture; the novel building methods just acquired from the East; Hindu and Greek medicine and mathematics gained from commercial contacts with the extreme eastern parts of the empire. No wonder then (says Wiener) that Alcuin should in the beginning of the ninth century have spoken of the Goths as a nation favored by God; that Charles the Great should have considered it a chief duty to throw open waste lands for their colonies and also to combat the Arian heresy (which was supported by their notable learning) by employing Alcuin, the best educated man of his day, in that struggle.

From this point it is argued (with little knowledge of the subject) that the new calligraphic schools of France, whose influence spread almost at once to Ireland and England, received their impetus from the Visigoths, and that Fleury, especially, became a seminary of Gothic learning. Attention is next directed to the drainage canals which, about the middle of the eighth century, were laid out in the north of Italy, either by Arabs or by Arabicized Goths. It was apparently about the same time a Gothic church was established at Ravenna, where the Goths preserved the Spanish tradition, though under the influence of the Greek church.

This, Wiener asserts, is evidenced by the Gothic calendar and the Greek synaxaries which preserved the memory of Gothic martyrdom at Cordova during the Arab invasion.

Another witness to the influence of the Visigoths in the ninth and tenth centuries is the large number of Spanish works which have been found in northern Italy. It is for this reason that a number of Gothic MSS have been preserved at Bobbio and Milan, and that frequent interpolations were made in various unexpected places—as in Jordanes, in the preface of the code of Lombard laws, and in the chronicle of Paul the Deacon, where an Arab tradition seems to have become the basis of what has been generally regarded as a bit of genuine Germanic mythology.

About the year 760 Goths were exerting such an influence upon the monastic school of St. Gall that the accustomed geographical denominations began to yield to new words which, for all we know to the contrary, are of Arabico-Gothic manufacture. These names spread northward along the Rhine, increase greatly in number, and some of them in the ninth century take their place permanently in the Anglo-Saxon vocabulary.

Well, from such evidences as are listed in the previous paragraphs and from other similar testimony that might be gathered to the same purpose, what are we going to deduce as to the direct influence of Arabic—whether through Spanish Goths or not—first upon the development of Latin poetry before the end of the ninth century; second, upon the rhymed poetry of Romance, Celtic, and Germanic peoples? Shall we say that Arabic science and poetry aroused the national consciousness of German and Romance peoples and caused a poetic efflorescence in their native tongues? Shall we presume that because of the introduction of Arabic prosody a new tonic versification and rhyme on a universal scale (and not sporadically as in Latin) swept old metric forms out of existence and brought about the birth of modern shapes of verse? Shall we imagine that the second sound-shifting which separated High German from Low German, may have been effected by the *viva voce* teaching of linguistically untutored Spanish Goths in the classrooms of St. Gall?

To be candid, I am grieviously tempted to say no to every question above suggested, for in common with most other critics I am unready to grant as proven the rather definite and large claims which Wiener has seen fit to rest upon evidence that is often uncertain and speculative. But the more one reflects, the more one is disinclined to utter an uncompromising negative. For the fact remains that vernacular transmission of some sort is needed to account for Arabic influences in western Europe well before the tenth century, and every circumstance seems to indicate that the Goths are the likeliest agents for them. Let us see.

The first acquaintance of the West with most of Aristotle's writings was due to the Arabs of Spain. Aristotle had long been studied in Syria and Arabia, and the knowledge of his works, which had passed from Constantinople to the east, had subsequently followed the course of Arab conquest along the northern coast of Africa till it reached, first Spain, and then France. But more than four centuries were required for all the Arabic translations of Aristotle executed at Bagdad in the first half of the ninth century to spread in Latin form across France and Germany, and even then it was in meager abridgment or curtailing that some of the most important treatises (like the *Poetics*) were known to the Middle Ages. Bearing such facts in mind, if we discover that distinct traces of Arabic initiative appear in western forms of thought and expression well before the end of the tenth century, we can hardly dismiss the matter with either a shrug as a mere coincidence, nor explain the Arabic heritage during the Dark Ages as one due to chance contact with oriental strays of knowledge on the part of western Europeans. A more definite idea of translation or adaptation of the Arabic original by somebody is necessary to explain the transmission. Therefore, why not the Goths as the logical choice?

It has been indicated above that the *Lay of Hildebrand* is an example of the new artistic poetry created by the Goths during the period of migration; a similar contention as to the origin of the *Elder Edda* can hardly longer be avoided—indeed, the whole development of later northern poetry, as Naumann suggests, is but the living out to the full of what had been begun by Bosporian Goths before their dispersal. Then why should we balk at according to their brothers of a later date an important share in bringing Arabian rhythms and rhymes to the poetry of the German and Romance races? Why should we consider these things native growths, derived from the Latin? Of course, accentual rhymed verse was in certain specific forms native to Latin—we see it beneath the surface of the classical period; we see it emerge in the third and fourth centuries when, to quote Mackail, the quantitative meters imposed on Italy by the genius of Greece were beginning to give way with the loosening of classical civilization and culture. Accentual rhymed or assonant verse has already attained a decisive predominance before the vernacular tongues of the West begin to develop substantive bodies of poetry of their own. But it is no less certain that in this predominance Arab influence had a substantial, if not a decisive, share. In this, Arabic music (much as we hear it nowadays) probably had its quota, for it must be noted that while the native Latin rhythms were falling or trochaic, those of the new vernacular poetry are rising or iambic; the one can thus hardly be the direct descendant or derivative of the other.

To my mind it would be most unwise to deny to Arabic culture a creative influence in furthering the racial, vernacular spirit in Carolingian Europe—and equally foolish to neglect the patent fact that the Goths (whether of Mœsia, Italy, or Spain) were the most poetically gifted of all the Germanic peoples and, therefore, quite likely at any moment of their history to have furnished the mediatory channel for a continuation of ancient and eastern civilization down into the Middle Ages.

From their first appearance in history Gothic was the channel through which Latin mercantile and humanistic phrases passed into Germanic currency—for in very early days the Goths were fairly woven into the fabric of Mediterranean life. The Gothic Bible of Ulfilas presents to us a language that is apt for all the subtler reaches of New Testament story—arguments that the Zulu Bible lends itself with equal ease to Christian metaphysics, because their whole essence dwells in the prototype, and not in the Zulu imitation, emanate from minds which are inconversant with the question involved. The successor of Alaric (as reported to us by the eavesdropping Orosius who overheard a captain of the Narbonne guards conversing with St. Jerome in his cell at Bethlehem) had ideas regarding the self-determination of the Goths and their attitude toward the prostrate western empire, which might be copied with profit by the masters of European destiny at the present moment. And Ataulf's idyl with Galla Placidia is a fairer story than anything surviving to us in Greek romance. The fashion of heroic poetry in a vernacular tongue, if not its very self, is sprung from the peninsular Goths: it was two of their number who (according to Priscus) sang before Attila of his victories; and I feel sure that it was a Gothic scop and not an Italian *scurra* who is represented by the *citharœdus* that, Cassiodorus informs us, Theodoric sent northward at Clodowech's request. Goths, whether from east or west of Europe, were the interpreters and singers during the barbarian centuries, of that romantic opera for which later times have invented the curious name of epic. The Goths exerted a creative influence on Lombard balladry, as we learn from the Alboin stories in Paul the Deacon—and the Ælfwine of *Widsith*. And most convincing of all indications of Gothic literary supremacy is the fact that the major part of Teutonic popular legendary epic material which has descended to us is of Gothic origin: Ermanrich, the Harlungs, Dietrich, Heime, Witig, Hervör, Hildebrand, and perhaps Walter of Aquitania; except for the Frankish tale of *Sigfried*, the *Nibelungen* story is a poetic creation of the Burgundians, a race, if not related to, at least most closely associated with, the Goths. Theodulfus, reputedly the most elegant versifier of the Palace School, was a Spanish Goth.

Now, that Wiener has insisted upon the truth of Gothic mediation of eastern culture during the eighth and ninth centuries in western Europe is very much to his credit, for in this he has become an uncompromising oracular mouthpiece of the truth; and that few "proper" people seem just now to believe in his contention only adds to the great service he has rendered scholarship. I venture to predict that twenty years from now all "proper" people will be preaching Wiener's tenets. That many of his Arabic etymologies are not Arabic does not disturb my belief that Wiener is speaking verity—for luckily the strength of a case in world-tribunals does not depend on the ability of any one lawyer for the defense to marshal his evidence properly. In such a connection I seem to recall the terrible *faux pas* and the distortions of evidence, in spite of which the viewpoints of Sophus Bugge regarding the obligation of northern mythology to Christian models won their way to the front.

Wiener's emphasis on Arabico-Gothic influence during the formative centuries which preceded the vernacular efflorescence in medieval Europe is specially necessary to offset the blithe preaching of many modern scholars that early medieval Latin poetry is an integral body of traditional Roman matter, by the superficial study of which one may arrive at an adequate estimation of the western rationalizing genius before the time of Abelard. How tragic a misconception can arise from this attitude of scholarship is indicated by Robinson's study of the relation of medieval intelligence to social reform in a popular book devoted to the making of the modern mind. Herein Robinson says that by the end of the Christian Era, which culminates in Augustine (A. D. 430), a great part of the critical Greek books had disappeared in western Europe, and that except for Lucian no single pagan writer later than Juvenal can be easily recalled. Worldly knowledge, says Robinson, was reduced to slender compendiums on which later students were forced to place pitiful reliance—scientific, literary, and historical information was scarcely to be had. And the western world, so far as it thought at all, devoted its attention to mystical ideas and religion—a world intellectually bankrupt before the German invasions and their disorders plunged it into still deeper ignorance and mental obscurity.

After he has thus dismissed with a few contemptuous phrases the four centuries which were possibly the most important ones in recorded human history, Robinson handles the seven hundred succeeding years in a sentence. From Augustine to Abelard, he says, the prosperous villas disappeared, towns vanished or shriveled up, libraries were burned or rotted away, schools were closed (to be reopened here and there, after Charlemagne's educational edict, in an especially enterprising monastery or by some exceptional bishop who did not spend his entire time in fighting).

Of course such writing as Robinson's is vicious and false as I hope more than one chapter of this book will sufficiently establish. With regard to the last phrase of the preceding paragraph, for example, I may say that at one time, soon after Charlemagne's educational edict, we know there were in France more than five hundred abbeys and colleges (*ecclesiæ collegiatæ*) which were going concerns, many of which offered undoubtedly as good a curriculum of study as the average twentieth-century institution of learning. But the real point of issue, after all, is not whether one man's characterization of an epoch be acceptable or not—the question is rather how can generalization so eminently out of touch with the facts in a case be possible. And the only answer is, I imagine, because the field under academic investigation is many hundred times too broad and long, too kaleidoscopic in its transformational planes, too infinitely varied in its cultural possibilities, as not hopelessly to befuddle that historian who, like Robinson, views it *en bloc*.

I wish now to return from my excursion into the possibilities of Arabico-Gothic influence on Carolingian civilization through the intervention of clerk and scholar from such schools as Cordova, in order to view again the impressive list of tangible commodities which the West had from the East, and which I have printed on page 199 above. If these staples of the body and the mind were really brought directly to bear upon the customary ongoing of the life of villein, artisan, clerk, and bourgeois—if they did not remain, previous to the twelfth century at least, blind forces of sporadic influence merely upon the numerically few—then indeed, was the existence of the western world much ameliorated by them, then presumably it was our old friends, the merchant and the soldier, who brought about the long-delayed meeting of two disparate worlds, from which contact the nations of the West became civilized.

It is easy to exaggerate the part actually played by business men and doughboys in introducing oriental novelties to France and Germany—whereas it is quite certain that the crusaders and their camp-followers from Palestine scarcely came into clash with any one but the Turkish warriors, themselves newcomers in the Moslem world and almost barbarians. And as to the Frankish principalities that the crusading adventurers found already intrenched in Syria, these consisted only of an aristocracy maintained by French knights and Italian merchants, which never had emigrants enough to people the country and which, besides, did not draw the constant body of recruits necessary to the upkeep of their estates from western Europe. These Frankish soldiers of fortune grew quickly rich, lived in luxury surrounded by a corrupt population, contracted every known Syrian vice (of which there are many), and for the two centuries of their sway in Africa were anything but the intermediaries of frictive influence on the Occident.

In the course of my narrative I so often portray the occupation and attitude of monks that I may expect my reader to know fairly well what manner of man the medieval ecclesiastic is. I wonder, however, if that reader apprehends what a typical knight is like. Is this medieval figure a chivalrous, courteous person of adventuring temper who spends his time saying his prayers, making reverent love to the madonna, carving the heads of infidels? Perish the thought. The knight, in the temperate words of Carlyle, is a small landowner, holding his strip of soil on condition of military service to some lord. Primarily he is not a soldier but a small tiller of the earth—a squireen who is normally much more concerned about his crops and his pigs than with his lord's affairs. The authentic knight is ignorant, rather brutal and turbulent, prone to quarrel with his neighbor—but with no native taste for national wars and the prolonged absence from his farm that such frays involve, unless there be a braw bit of plunder likely. He is a matter-of-fact soul, little inclined to romantic adventure for its own sake. So, despite the pretty superstitions of swashbuckling narrative from Chaucer and Spenser to the romantic revival, this medieval member of the militia is much like ourselves. It is a fair assumption, when we are confronted by some importation from the East into early medieval Europe, that it was not brought about by a soldier, whether of high or low degree.

And even when we turn from the warrior to the peddler as a carrier of oriental wares to the West, though we may find here the field of influence more sharply defined and apparently of a directer sort, even then we are forced to make an arbitrary choice among several possible sources—for, quite generally, we are unable to guess whether an invention from the Orient reaches us through crusaders, Italian merchants, Saracens of Sicily, or Moors of Spain.

One most specific and influential way by which eastern poetry and story-telling reached Carolingian Europe is all too readily forgotten: I mean the slave-trade between the Jews of France and the Moors of Spain. In the year 826 we find Archbishop Agobard in his tract *De Insolentia Judæorum* forbidding the Christians of his diocese from selling slaves to the Jews for exportation to the Arabs in Spain; and—curiously enough—in the controversy that followed, the emperor supported the side of the Jews. Under Louis the Pious, particularly after his marriage to Judith, his second empress, the position of the Semitic race might fairly be held to menace Christianity. Poole recalls to us that Charles the Great had shown these people tolerance, and that Louis had added his personal favor—under him they enjoyed unparalleled prosperity. For they formed a peculiar nation under his protection, secure against both the nobles and the church; and their privileges were guarded by an imperial officer denominated king of the Jews—Rey Juif.

Free from military service, these Jews were indispensable to the commerce and the foreign relations of the empire; and on account of their financial skill it was common practice to intrust the farming of the taxes to their hands. They had rights from which Christians were excluded, said and did whatever they wished, and had the weekly markets held on the Christian Sunday so that they could hold inviolate the observance of their own Sabbath. They owned their own synagogues and schools, and held their city property and country lands in fee-simple. They planted vineyards and set up mills and factories in full assurance of community assent. Their wives and daughters were welcomed at court with marked distinction, and they were separated from the throng only by the more sumptuous display of their apparel. The empress Judith was singularly attached to them, and the courtiers, not slow to see which way the wind was blowing, attended the synagogue and made fain to admire the preaching of the *darshanim* above that of their own clergy.

Now it is just at this time that a great mass of fables and stories and droll tales (fabliaux) find, so far as we know, their first wide dissemination in medieval literature. Some of these popular narratives are evidently indigenous in origin and workmanship, as is easily guessed from their scenes and themes; but others are certainly of oriental lineage, for they derive from themes that are famous in the older traditions of the south and east.

For the first sort of storiette and fairy-tale no explanation is needed—they are quite simply the work of monks and clerks and minstrels who invented them and gave them literary form. But for the second sort (romance, adventure, gallantry, and magic) a problem is felt to exist. Oriental yarns in Europe two hundred and fifty years before the first crusade are felt to be an anachronism. Led astray, therefore, by the whimsical notion that the ninth century was unlettered, uncreative, and untraveled—tormented by their inability to explain the presence of oriental themes in western Europe long before any well-known route of immigration is open—critics have succumbed. They have either assumed more constant and vital lines of literary transmission between East and West than political alliances seem to warrant—such as one due to the Carolingian overlordship of Italy, or later to the Byzantine minglings of the Ottos—or they have clutched at the slippery Italian mimus to stop the gap between, say, the Carolingian renascence and the period of chivalry.

As a matter of fact, neither of these theories of source is in the least needful—the formula for such literary carryings westward would be Arabic and Greek originals brought westward by travelers, pilots, tradesmen, and transmuted on the way into a tongue and a fashion intelligible to the new European audience. There is certainly no time during the Dark Ages when the part of Greece as an intermediary between Orient and Occident is not of high importance for the history of literary intercourse and the distribution of popular stories of all kinds. Ker assures us that after Greek had ceased to exercise any distinctly literary influence on the West other than that which had long been known, if not exhausted, in the rhetorical schools, it continued to provide new matters for amusement and edification: saints' lives and fables, romances like that of Alexander and Apollonius of Tyre; while doubtless in many easy ways, without writing or literary form, Greece helped to carry westward the themes of eastern stories for the future profit of minstrels. It gave the *Physiologus* to all the modern tongues; it translated the Buddha into the legend of Barlaam and Josaphat.

Chapter XII

THE CAROLINGIAN LYRIC

I may not speak for another, but I believe the inevitable sensation which comes from first reading in the volumes of the *Poetæ ævi Karolini* is one of bitter disappointment. It is perhaps as if one's hand had reached out half unconsciously for a book of poems and had picked up a table of logarithms instead. The reader rightly feels that it must have been a sorry kind of poetry which devoted itself so largely to epitaphs, inscriptions on church gates, riddles, acrostics, book-titles, and the like. The whole is at first blush about as lively as a collection of burial urns. And there are unfortunately many readers who close the covers of these volumes never to return to them.

Small blame to such! For the purpose of appreciative comment and æsthetic criticism, the poetry of A. D. 580-880 is still an insoluble mass. It consists chiefly, though not entirely, of religious and didactic utterance and seems to contain but the *disjecta membra* of what in a happier age might be twenty different genres:

1. Platitudinous narratives on the Fall of Troy and the Deeds of Alexander.
2. Legendary records of the gesta of secular and churchly notables.
3. Visions and miracles for the tuition of lay minds.
4. Apothegms, maxims, proverbs, and exempla.
5. Gnomic and mnemonic verses.
6. Fables and moralizing tales.
7. Eulogies of sovereigns and pontiffs.
8. Birthday greetings and letters of condolence.
9. Obituaries of rulers, ecclesiastical princes, and saints.
10. Epic poems, like those of Abbo and Ermoldus.
11. Rhyming and metrical prose in praise of continence, chess, early rising, mathematics, godly walks, grammar, and science.

12. Alphabetical stanzas, acrostics, centos.
13. Catalogues of beasts and birds, teachings of natural history.
14. Exegetical and doctrinal verse.
15. Epigrams, epitaphs, devout inscriptions for portal, altar, and tomb.
16. Versified letters, admonitory in tone.
17. Puzzles, rebuses, enigmas, and riddles, etymologizing puns.
18. Hymns to the Virgin, odes to the saints.
19. Philosophizing distichs on the evils of this world and the glories of the next.
20. Monastery rolls, necrologies, and church histories.
21. Confessional outpourings on petty infractions of creed and flightiness of thought.
22. Elucidations of gospel symbols, and patristic tradition.
23. Eclogues and conflictus.
24. Folderol of incantation and magical charms.

The above list of embryonic types contained in the *Poetæ ævi Karolini* is by no means complete, and yet it is long enough to suggest the fairly distinguishable genera of poetry represented by the writing of the Palace School and similar confraternities in the eighth and ninth centuries. Now there is a good reason why all this sorry balladry should be gathered, edited, and published—for it has much to teach us as to the ways of European culture at the close of the Dark Ages. But why should we call this monkish rhetoric poetry? And why, in the name of sense, should we study the temper of a great age in such an offscouring of dullness? And yet this is just what scholarship has done.

It has encountered an enormous pile of poetic slag that is devoid of all personal appeal, empty of *joie de vivre*, stripped of local color, descriptive of no living scene. As a consequence, scholars have found this material as unatmospheric as a Leyden jar. And yet, in spite of this, they have hunted in it for traces of its immediate origin and for the smell of the soil from which it sprang. They have rummaged through a body of verse choked with learned allusion, the emanation of an inane tradition, and have sought to discover there specific indications of the place of its birth or its adoption. One might as well hope to track down seventeenth-century Italy in the withered moss of the *Adriatic Rosamund*. It is no wonder that some minds conceive the Carolingian age as a literary Sahara which separates ancient from modern times. Conversely, it is no wonder that these same minds believe Carolingian metrical strophes the fit expression of a period which historians still assert was one of debâcle and cataclysm. Let us follow such a portrayal:

What is the course of the night of the ninth century? asks Funck-Brentano. Dimly the records afford a glimpse of a people scattered and without guidance. The barbarians commit the most cruel outrages, sacking town and village, laying waste the fields. They burn churches to the ground and depart with a host of captives. Skimming over the sea like pirates, the Normans penetrate to the center of France— Chartres is sacked, Autun overgrown with weeds. The country as far as the Loire is destroyed so completely that wild animals now roam the sites of prosperous towns, and the plain where once the harvests ripened knows now but the thistle and the sharp-thorned briar. Once resplendent in her wealth and glory, Paris is but a heap of ashes.[1]

Funck-Brentano warms to his theme. Nay, he continues, in the little country villages the houses crumble to dust, church walls are full of cracks, their roofs gape wide, the tabernacles are overgrown with weeds while ivy clings to their capitals. The house of God is become a den where foxes burrow and birds of prey have their nests, where one may see the lidless eyes of the owl shine unblinkingly through spiders' webs. Powerless to resist the barbarian invaders, many men-at-arms join them. Private wars become common; three men cannot meet two without putting them to death; men destroy one another as do the fish of the sea. When conducting his army across a territory from which his enemy is deriving supplies, a leader ravages the land with such fury that he does not leave her poor hut to an old woman in her second childhood. There is no longer any trade—only unceasing terror. In their fear of events men build only of wood. Architecture is no more. To avoid silver, richly illuminated manuscripts, enamels, cloisonnes, resplendent colors, gold and silver plate, and costly jewels. The pageant of Byzantine glory is such that even today we visualize sixth-century oriental art in a jeweled iridescence, in a shimmer of gold.

Nevertheless, this art was to all outward seeming a lifeless and monotonous one, incapable of transformation or renewal. Like Byzantine literature it remained firmly attached to classical tradition, constantly returning to classical models for fresh sources of inspiration and occasionally for fresh methods; like Byzantine literature, it had received an even deeper imprint from Christianity, which brought it under the conventionalizing guardianship of ecclesiastical ideas. Because of all this, and also because it was, like literature, an official art, Byzantine symbolism often lacked freshness, spontaneity, and life. It decorated, rather than interpreted, existence, developed form instead of idea, was often both an imitation and a copy. In its excessive attachment to classical tradition and its docility to the church, Byzantine art (like Byzantine writing) was too quickly apt to translate even its fertile discoveries into immutable formula.

There is not a word in the above paragraph that might not be used equally well of Carolingian literature, particularly in an enumeration of the outstanding characteristics of its rhetorical utterance. So much is it true that the shape and direction of western poetry in the ninth century bespeak the same canonical and ritualistic ideas as those of Byzantine utterance, that one must either believe the latter to have had a regnant influence over Carolingian poetry, or posit for them both so exact a parallelism in experience and development as to transcend the bounds of likelihood and the possibilities of chance. But at the present moment I am not stirred to marshal any philological evidence of this claim regarding the amazing coincidence in manner and expression between the poetry of Byzantium and of Aix-la-Chapelle. It is good mathematical philosophy to describe one set of related facts in terms of another which shows identity of relationship among its salients; and there is slight chance of mistake or confusion in employing this pro-interest him. For, as he grows accustomed to the absence of rhyme, to the dearth of theme, to the stilted manner that is characteristic of even the best of this writing—with its unimaginative borrowings from classical imagery and its tireless reminiscences of biblical phrasing—the reader becomes conscious that, while real beauty and earnestness is ever lacking, while the deep issues of life are never touched by this poetry, there is yet before him a body of adequate diction, a certain level dignity, a smooth, if shallow, surface of expression. How great a step in advance is marked by these things, he alone knows who has labored, say, with the phrases of Vergilius Maro and the befuddled *Hisperica famina*, or—truth to tell—with the Merovingian barbarisms of Gregory of Tours. In fact, the voluble euphuism of Venantius Fortunatus, much as Carolingian poets owe to it, does not offer the sure foundation for coming lyricality that the frosted but rather sumptuous measures of ninth-century rhetoric do. To quote almost at random from the better-known material of this time, here are the opening words of the *epitaphium Chlodarii pueri regis:*

> Hoc satus in viridi servatur flosculus arvo,
> Pulchrior en lacte candidiorque nive,
> Donec altipotens veniat per sæcula judex,
> Qui metet ostrifluas falce perenne rosas.
> Hunc tua, Jordanis, sacrata protulit unda,
> Pampinus Engadi rore beavit eum.
> Livida purpureis vaccinia cincta rosetis
> Vernat ut et rosola gliscit in omne decus,
> Pallida ceu sandix inter viburna refulgit,
> Et nitit imbrifluus Cynthius altus aquis,
> Ut rubit obriza flagranti cocta camino,
> Et rutilat vario Indus honore lapis.

A thousand times at least as I have read such lines as these I have felt how wrong it was to compare their rudimentary colors and their conventionalized starkness of expression either with the voluptuous sleekness of Horace and Catullus or yet with the lean grace of William of Poitou and Vogelweide. It is rather in the world of Frankish ivory figurines and Byzantine mosaic and Gregorian music that this verse finds its background and its being. Let us see if we cannot gain a better angle of observation from which to criticize our Carolingian show-pieces of poetry by some study of the directive processes and the intention of Byzantine art as it was adapted in the western Europe of the eighth and ninth centuries.

Byzantine art, as it found its definite formula and attained its apogee in the reign of Justinian, was one of the most brilliant expressions of eastern civilization. From the sixth century onward a knowledge of this art and an admiration for it were carried to the uttermost parts of the known world. Through Syria and by the Red Sea the eastern Empire was in communication with the Far East, and either directly, or by way of the Persians and later of the Arabs, it came into touch with Ceylon and China. Through the Black and Caspian seas, spices, aromatic essences, and precious stones, reached it from Central Asia. Towards the north, trade-routes extended even to the Scandinavians and Russians, who supplied Byzantium with furs, honey, wax, and slaves. The Byzantine merchants, Syrians (especially in the fifth and sixth centuries), and Armenians penetrated to Africa, Italy, Spain, and Gaul. Under the protection of the imperial fleet, the Byzantine merchant marine dominated the Mediterranean until the eleventh century, merchandise, and the instruments and objects of art pouring through the markets of the Byzantine capital to the most distant lands and cities. Paul the Silentiary, a poet of the sixth century, pleasantly describes the trading vessels of the universe, sailing full of hope to and from the queenly city. Western merchants, first of all from Amalfi and Venice, later from Pisa and Genoa, Catalans and Celts from beyond the Alps played an ever increasing part in this great disseminative activity.[2]

Everywhere in Byzantine art we find a love of stupendous luxury and prodigious splendor. Precious marbles and mosaics, magnificent work in gold and silver, and wonderful hangings—all intended to enhance the beauty of religious rites, to glorify the majesty of the sovereign, and to give pleasure to the court and the grandees. In public and private life there is nothing but sumptuous tissues shot through with purple and gold, finely carved ivories, bronzes inlaid with the violence of anarchy, the peasant has abandoned his ravaged fields. People have fled to hide in the depths of the forest or among inaccessible mountains. Ties which united the inhabitants of the country are burst asunder; custom and legal usage no longer avail. Society is without governance. Everybody lives in a moated grange or castle. Except for the people in these fortified keeps, one may walk the length and breadth of ninth-century France and not meet a living human being.

Thus bravely, Funck-Brentano marches to meet his end in a logical absurdity. Why does he do this? Because he derives from a study of his sources of information a certain sum total of facts which he interprets to suit his argument, which is, that French feudalism can be explained only by assuming that throughout the Dark Ages the colter of barbarian savagery disembowled mountains and deracinated pines. Now in order to avoid the untoward end of my predecessor in the Carolingian field, I approach my task of analyzing ninth-century poetry without conscious bias. I study the literary fruits of this epoch as such, and not for the purpose of set contrast with those of another time. I have nothing to prove except that which is evident. I realize that Carolingian court-poetry, the expression of a definite and numerically very restricted caste, is almost all that has come down to us from the era of Charles the Great and his successors. I find that this great mass of metrical writing does not follow speech-stress, but imitates rather hollowly an artificial prosody and classical models. Therefore I do not expect this great mass to indicate much the sway and thud of vernacular emotion, so easy to sense in purely lyrical material wherever found. Therefore, I draw no prejudiced picture of mental anarchy because of a stilted sort of Carolingian rhetoric which expends itself largely on epitaphs, inscriptions on church gates, riddles, acrostics, book titles, and the like. A large portion of this rhetoric I relegate to the philological cellar from which it has been exhumed. The remainder is easily arranged for convenient study.

First, if the reader be patient and continue his search duly through the broad acreage of measured Carolingian lines, he begins to gain insight into various matters that cess of association in the instance before us. For neither Byzantine nor Carolingian art is a primitive or fresh art—both of them are heavily overlaid, richly embroidered, and highly endowed with maze and convolution. Both of them are picturesque rather than dramatic, charming rather than emotional, pathetic rather than impassioned, harmonious rather than skillful—iconography rather than living art. They are traditional, not realistic. Each teaches us to gauge the other.

The story of the development of music[3] in the eighth and ninth centuries furnishes us with another *point d'appui*, from which to regard appreciatingly the weaving of the fabric of Carolingian rhetorical poetry. Musically speaking, the work of the Latin church down to the eighth century at least, limited itself to the reanimation and the rehabilitation of the dying art of the Greeks. Western Christian music, therefore, equally with its Greek prototype, illustrates strictly the melodic principle—that phase of music in which the effect to be obtained from the resources of pure sound is perceived only as consisting in certain arrangements of consecutive simple tones. The aim of the composer is single; it excludes polyphonic as well as harmonic relations; its outcome is coherent individual utterance, or melody. This is the music of ancient Greece and is still the music of all eastern peoples.

Wooldridge indicates that the Greek practice of magadizing (singing in octaves, as when men and children sing the same melody), in which lies the fundamental principle of polyphony, was continued in the Latin church. Indeed, it is likely that the simultaneous enunciation of the melody by the voices of men and young boys was recognized by the Christian West, as by the Greeks, as a distinct musical effect arising from a series of repetitions of the consonance of the octave. But apparently no advance beyond the Greek position with regard to the practice of magadizing was made in the west during the early period in the history of the church. We look in vain through the treatises on music by Christian writers down to the seventh century for any clear proof of the definite acceptance of magadizing as an artistic device. Likewise we find no definite acknowledgment by these writers of any change in principle, as, for instance, the transfer of the idea of consonance from melody to harmony, which is actually involved in the deliberate adoption of magadizing as a set means towards a new end.

It is, however, in the eighth and ninth centuries—a period usually considered as sterile in respect of literary production as it is fruitful and significant for music—that these necessary first steps forward in the direction of polyphony were made. For in the earliest treatises written after the reawakening of conscious critical effort towards the close of the ninth century, we meet with distinct references to a form of musical art called organizing. This is the practice of symphonious singing and playing that consists in the singing of concords by concurrent voices. We find also at last a definition of consonance which reveals surely that view of its nature in which it is seen as existing not between intervals, but between simultaneous sounds.

What a different view this musical background gives us of the coming-to-be of Latin lyricality in the tenth and eleventh centuries as well as of the hidden essence and reality in our Carolingian verse! For this poetry, which, till now, like the Byzantine has seemed so lacking in freshness, spontaneity, and life—a garment so stiff with jewels that it can stand alone without indwelling personality to sustain it—this very poetry suddenly shows itself to us so docile to the purposes of recreation that within two hundred years it will be made to undergo an efflorescence, a birth into new guises that shall not end until, in the twelfth century, Carolingian poetry meets apotheosis in the goliards, in the archpoet, in the amazing vernacular poets of chivalry and love. If a great body of Carolingian ore is so smelted in the fires of fancy that it gains a golden embodiment, regains a new vigor, experiences an unlooked-for revival, and, combining the various tendencies under whose influence it has first been shaped, succeeds in assuming original forms respondent to the real genius of the peoples of western Europe—how shall we dare to call this Carolingian ore intractable to the uses of poetic art, inert and dull, immutable?

That it should at first seem immutable to us is due to the identity of tone that rings from most of it. The reason for this common tone in almost everything composed in Carolingian Latin is that its authors deliberately employed in its manufacture a bookish or priestly Latin learned in school on the dead body of routine grammatical tradition, rather than (even if only by alternation) the spoken Latin in which they chattered, joked, and quarreled, the argot that was the vehicle of their arguments, their story telling, and their pictorial thinking. It is a misfortune that no great poet or singer appeared in this age to lend the weight of his authority to the creation of a literary language compounded of these two vocabularies: the one of inheritance, the other of actuality. Because of the lack of some great example of this sort, it was not the fashion among lesser men of that day to devote high artistic effort to the profane themes of everyday life, nor yet to write in the vivid language of actual existence of the mighty themes their age considered alone worthy of poetic immortalization. This was all to come, thank heaven, very soon thereafter.

And the moment that the wind of favor veered away from the re-mumbling of an obscure tradition in Carolingian verse, the moment the latter ceased to stuff its content with echoes, ceased to shoulder the staggering burden of a useless past, ceased to rattle bones long dry—that very moment we have no longer monastic copying of biblical and classical fustian, we have a permanent mutation in literary expression. And that mutation was both instanced and brought about by various impregnating phenomena: by the development of popular Latin verse through the influence of hymnody; by the development of church music away from sheer melody towards polyphony and harmony; by a better acquaintance with Byzantine art; by the adaptation of the sequence to profane uses; and by the syllabizing of rhetorical prose engendered by the stress-groupings in vernacular speech and music. The foredoomed result was that, as had already been done by some Carolingian clerks and schoolmen, all poets now brought their inventive power and their significant ideas to bear upon their writing in such a way as to adjust it to contemporary thought and feeling—and the tenth-century renascence of Latin letters ensued.

All through Carolingian poetry there are hints enough of an occasional tendency to depart from the Romanesque mode of classical copying. We meet them perhaps most clearly in the nature-introductions, or in a few lines on outdoor nature tucked away here and there among the longer narratives, and at times even in whole songs devoted to pastoral scenes. Self-conscious they are still, like the *De cuculo* attributed to Alcuin, the eclogue of Naso, or the *Carmen philomelaicum* of Paulus Albarus, but they stir the sense with pleasant anticipation of what is to come, when poetry shall leave the leading-strings of doctrinal theology and begin to wander through the earth alone:

>   Lumine candoris clarent hic lilia celi,
>   Fulbe rose florens imitant his purpura terre
>   Et viole pariter stellarum vice coruscant.
>   Dum vario redolent pariter unite colore,
>   Albeole renitent ceu unio lilia conclis,
>   Instar et gipsæ conplectens colla puelle
>   Lactea. . . .

Work such as this may be more or less of the forging of mastersong, but there is undeniable excellence indwelling in it. Men's minds are not yet ripe perhaps for what another century is to bring into vogue—a real personalizing of joy in nature and experience written by poets who are alive to the finger tips. And yet, when that desirable springtime is at hand in Latin verse, it is only the expected fruition of forces already at work in the world of the Palace School, for swelling lines such as these of the *Planctus Karoli* tell of what is coming:

PLANCTUS DE OBITU KAROLI

>   From the day's beginning to the sunset west
>   Let a sound of sorrow shake the deep's vast breast.
>   Heu mihi misero!
>
>   Grief grown giant-like shadows land and darkens sea,
>   Woe unparalleled, sorrowful exceedingly.
>   Heu mihi misero!

Romans and Frankish men, allies that trusted us,
Now huge affliction leaves you ever dolorous.
        Heu mihi misero!

Old men, children, every mighty potentate,
Mourn; and matrons, weep for Cæsar's fallen state.
        Heu mihi misero!

Torrents of tears ceaselessly flow and fall—
The wide world weeps at Charles's burial.
        Heu mihi misero!

Virgins and widowed wives, the pilgrim, the fatherless,
Charles was their father and their aid in distress.
        Heu mihi misero!

The orderly skies, them, O Christ, Thou governest—
In that realm, O grant to Charles Thy rest.
        Heu mihi misero!

This prayer Thy faithful, yea all believers make,
Virgins and old men and widows for Charles's sake.
        Heu mihi misero!

What now is Charles, the serene and royal?
A stone—and a name—and the heaped-up soil.
        Heu mihi misero!

O Holy Spirit, thou that dost govern all,
Take to thy requiem this soul majestical.
        Heu mihi misero!

Rome and the Roman race, woe to ye, yea and woe!
Charles the ever glorious now lies low.
        Heu mihi misero!

Woe to thee, Italia, beautiful in thy despair,
And the girdle of thy cities that shows so fair.
        Heu mihi misero!

Since thy hurts are dire, O France, endure and weep,
Thou shalt never know a hurt more deep.
        Heu mihi misero!

Charles the august, the eloquent, the king,
To Aachen they have carried him, a lifeless thing.
        Heu mihi misero!

And now night brings to my bed dire dreams—
And the day returns—and no sun beams.
   Heu mihi misero!

Yea, the world is broken, the Christian's hope is fled,
The prince we revered, that prince is dead.
   Heu mihi misero!

Cease, O Columban, and dry thine eyes—
For him that was thy lord let thy prayers arise.
   Heu mihi misero!

Father of all that is, thou our God,
Mercifully grant to him thy fair abode.
   Heu mihi misero!

Lord of battles, Lord of all men as well,
Duke of the heavens, yea and of infernal hell,
   Heu mihi misero!

Where thy apostles are, even in thy holy place
Take Charles our emperor, Christ, into grace.
   Heu mihi misero! (1)

 This was composed not later than the year 815 and some thirty years thereafter the persecuted and outlawed Gottschalk could swing into verses like those to a young boy who has asked for a poem. Among all ninth-century writings his song is remarkable for its lyrical unity of mood and its sad refrain. The rhyme, if not quite pure, is abundant and catching. The nearest metrical affinity of the accentual lines would be trochaic dimeter.

 So far as I know, there is everywhere still current the feeling among students of Carolingian poetry that the academic vogue of meter in the early Middle Ages prevented the growth of a more natural Latin poetry. It is argued by critics that the forms of classical Latin poetry had a beautiful fitness for the thought and feeling which they enframed, but that these same ancient measures were highly unsuited to the Christian and romantic sentiment of the medieval period, and that therefore another vehicle than metrical verse would have been developed to express this thoroughly declassicized medieval attitude, even if metrical quantity had remained a vital element of the Latin poetic language, instead of passing away during the early Christian centuries and remaining only as a school convention for the time of Charlemagne and the centuries thereafter.

Now I have no objection to the statement, made after an examination of the facts of poetic record, that accentual verse is less obviously academic than its metrical counterpart, seems more fit to act as the carrier of modern spiritual emotion, and is therefore the true medieval style. But to insist that this must be so, is to reason in advance of the facts of record. Besides which, it clouds the issue of all appreciative study of poetry by making the outer garb of it the chief distinguishing factor. It is no accident of exterior clothing that makes or unmakes for us the poetry of Dante, Shakespeare, or Goethe—not terza rima, blank verse, iambic pentameter, doggerel—but the spirit and the content of their thought. To identify these elements with the clothes they wear, both begs and beggars the question. Why should it be otherwise with the Carolingian poets?

So I shall leave aside from my further survey of Carolingian poetry (at least until a later book on the subject) any classification of my materials on the basis of external form— meter or rhythm—and let the verse translations incline my reader to a delight or a disbelief in the poetry of the age of Charles the Great as a separate, and not unworthy, contribution to the range of modern literature.

A LOVE MESSAGE FOR BROTHER ZACHARY

From your jocund lip and fluent mouth we drew, as it were,
    liquids suffused with dew that fell from heaven;
Like liquid honey from yellow fountains they overflowed to
    moisten my very fibers with their much sweetness,
O Zachary my brother,
O venerated priest of God,
Thou dweller in Britain, thou nursling of the Latin land,
Thou ornament of Ireland, mighty trumpet,
Far famous friend from the resounding ocean shore!
A winnower of the church, a flail, thou dost discern
From the full ears the windy chaff and sendest
Unto the stars of splendid heaven the harvest of thy wheat,
Plunging the chaff into the flame-bearing pots of hell.
Wherefore with running pen, sharp-pointed and from our full
    heart we send thee so many greetings

As mother earth, wet to its vernal seeds, brings tender flowers to
    bear from the greening roots,
As earth has rosebuds growing in garden beds,
Or crocuses paling in flower or purpureate violets growing red,
Or shells on those shores where the Gallic sea buries its wave-wet
    sands.   (2)

It might have been polite to the memory of the author of the above tender missive to arrange it in the form of a typical præludium to a sermon, for in writing these lines Paulinus of Aquileia, an Irish priest, won his parodistic atmosphere by deliberately imitating such a form. English can hardly attain the air of arch-sobriety instinct in these hifalutin verses.

THE BATTLE OF FONTENOY

A third of night must pass ere dawn should bring the morn
When, not upon the sabbath but on Saturn's day,
Hell laughed at broken trust, brother from brother torn,

And war cried out upon the fearful battle fray,
And brother, brother killed; and kindred slew their kin;
And fathers to their sons no mercy dared to pay.

More fearful strife in Martian fields did ne'er begin—
O broken Christian rule that blood shall not be shed,
Over what slaughtered troops did throated Cerebus grin!

Lothair, by God's all-powerful hand being wisely led,
Battled his way toward victory boldly with his sword.
(Had others fought as well, concord were even now dead!)

But even as Iscariot betrayed the Lord,
So thee thy dukes, my king, unto the sword betrayed—
Think how the wolf deceived the lamb. Trust no man's word.

The peasants call it Fontenoy where fountains played,
Fountains of blood that wrought the ruin of the Franks,
And on those fields and woods and marshland, horror stayed.

Nor dew, nor storm, nor any shower shall wash the banks
Where they that mothers, fathers, sisters, brothers weep,
The strong, the skillful, fell in battle's ordered ranks.

But him whose treason in these lines shall never sleep,
I, Engelbert, beheld him fighting amid the rest;
The foremost rank, alone of many, did he keep.

I saw the valley depths, I saw the plain of test
Where that strong king Lothair beat down and broke his foes,
Until they fled unto the river, sore-distressed.

And the twin camps of Charles and Louis, the tale goes,
Were whitened with the linen vestments of the dead
As fields grow white with autumn birds before the snows.

By verse or music let not praise be sung or said
For that great battle. East and west and south and north
Weep for those fallen on that day. A curse be sped

With it, and with the numbered year that brought it forth!
Let it be utterly forgot by all men's minds—
By twilight and by dawn, and by the sun's bright worth.

Let it be night, most bitter night, deep night that blinds—
That fated day when fell the strong man skilled in war
Whom father, mother, sister, brother no more finds!

O loss and lamentation! Naked the dead are;
And wolf and crow and vulture devour the flesh of these—
O horror!—unburied limbs lie naked to each star.

Let me not tell of woe or mourning more, but cease;
And let each man that may, restrain his flow of tears,
Praying that in the bosom of the Lord their souls have peace.
(3)

ALCUIN'S EXPOSITION OF THE SONG OF SONGS

Within this book sang Solomon with his admired sweetness
Poems passing wonder of the bridegroom and the bride;
The church and Christ he praised and sang, remembering in his
    music
The faithful who attend upon that marriage feast beside.
Wherefore, O youths, I ask you note and in your memories hold it,
The song of Maro's sweeter but with falsehood very rife,
And frivolous and vain it is, and evil to your hearing;
While *these* are precepts unto truth and to perennial life! (4)

PENANCE

    Grant me, O Lord that art the world's redemption,
        Thou light of everlasting day,
    Out of thy mercy, penance and exemption—
        Pity me, pray!

The burdens of accomplished sin are on me—
    Hide me from them and their control!
For I am stricken, and their weight upon me
    Tortures my soul.

I am not worthy even in desolation
    To lift, O Christ, ashamèd eyes
Unto the golden stars whose northward station
    Is Paradise.

But thou art clement, thou dost see in sorrow
    The pitiful river of my tears;
Out of thy mighty mercy thou wilt borrow
    Peace for my fears.

A heart swept free of sin's adulterate legions
    My debt of gratitude shall be,
When I shall pay in sempiternal regions
    My thanks to thee.

Therefore, my pitying Lord, with sorrow soften
    This adamantine heart of mine;
Come, Great Physician, medicine me often
    With drink divine.

Thy Father's royal throne, O thou hast near it
    Thy seat, and past time's period
Thou that art one with Him and with the Spirit
    Reignest with God.   (5)

TO LOTHAIR THE EMPEROR

Thou, our emperor,
Thou art benignant,
Who with thy father's
Scepter dost govern
Benignantly, lawfully,
Ruling with mercy.

Thee the Eternal
Lord of the universe
Chose, when he bade thee
Grasp the paternal
Reins and thy father's
Imperial scepter.

Thee from the dangers
Laid for thy downfall,
Thee did He save, and
Over and over
Out of the bloody
Slaughter of battle
Brought thee victorious.

Then in Rome's pinnacle,
Yea, in the golden
City he crowned thee,
Naming thee Cæsar—
Mighty dominion,
The world is thy empire.

Then the Italian
Land thou didst stabilize,
Thou with thy army—
And France before thee,
Regent and ruler,
Shook, and the whole earth
Fears and adores thee.

Now through the heavens
Five times the sun has
Run since thou tookest
Empire upon thee,
Cæsar thou splendid
In name and in arms!

Now may the Lord Christ
Ever and ever
Cherish thee wholly—
Now mayst thou worship Him
While the imperial
Purple strikes terror
Through thy domain!   (6)

THE MONK'S TALE OF THE VICTORY OF PIPPIN THE KING OVER THE AVARIAN RACE

Now all the people Christ hath made are children of the living Lord;
With hills and rocks, with field and stream the men He made are
 in accord;
And latterly to God He brought the Avarian race, a tribe abhorred.

They had wrought evil overmuch since first they sprang from out
    the void,
They burned both church and chapterhouse where monks were
    piously employed,
They smashed the earthen pots therein, and gold and silver they
    destroyed.

Their stealing vestments from the dead not even sacred tombs
    could stem;
The linen of the priests they tore, the levites' garments, hem
    from hem;
And from the nuns they stripped their clothes, the devil so per-
    suading them.

King Pippin that is son of Christ, he moved against them foot
    and horse;
The Lord He sent Saint Peter down, prince of the apostolic force,
To guide him on his marching there, and to direct his battle course.

Now Pippin our most Catholic king, the Lord with daring girt him
    round;
Beside the chalky Danube's flood he pitched his camp upon the
    ground
The enemy surrounded him—where'er he looked, a foe he found.

But Unguimeri our foeman shook and spake as boldly as he durst
Unto the queen Catina then, of all men's wives the most accursed,
And to her king, his liege, he said, "Do you, Cacanus, fear the
    worst!

"Your kingdom now hath seen its end, and longer you shall never
    reign;
God gave long since to Christian hands your governance of hill
    and plain—
Pippin shall now abolish you, that Catholic prince with all his
    train.

"King Pippin with his train draws nigh, he shall despoil you of
    your state—
Your people by that mighty host, they shall be slaughtered, small
    and great—
Your fortresses in plain and hill and forest he shall desolate.

"Go now and hasten, take with you presents and gifts magnificent;
Go now, adore that mighty lord, perhaps his anger will relent;
Bring cheerfully your gold and gems, he will not slay you in his
    tent."

When King Cacanus heard him speak, he stood completely
    terrified;
And with his Tarcan first-born then he sprang upon his mule to
    ride
And offer homage to our king and bring his costly gifts beside.

And to our king he said, "All hail, thou prince of princes, thou
    art lord;
Into thy hands I give my realm with field and forest, fall and ford;
And all the folk that dwell therein beneath the shadow of thy
    sword.

"My folk submit themselves to thee, now let thy clemency appear,
But spare our first-born, Lord," he said, "let not thine anger come
    so near,
We bow our heads beneath thy yoke—give not our nation to the
    spear!"

Now, faithful Christians that we be, let us deliver thanks to God—
He hath confirmed our governance of the Avarian stream and sod,
And over all the pagan tribes his mighty victories have trod.

And long live Pippin that great king, in fear and favor of our Lord,
And may he as a father reign until old age shall grant accord
Of sons that shall maintain in death and life the power of his
    sword!
    Gloria æterna patri, gloria sit filio! (7)

BONIFACE TO HIS SISTER IN CHRIST

I have sent to you, Sister, the ten golden fruits
That grew on life's tree from its nourishing flowers;
They hung from its branches, its tenderer shoots,
When the Life-tree was drooping in death's bitter bowers.
As the taste of their nectar shall honey your tongue
And the smell of the nard in your nostrils be sweet,
In your soul shall the joys of the spirit be sung,
Of the pleasures of paradise then shall you eat.
Fruit like to these apples in heaven shall fall,
And the bliss of the skies you shall taste of and know,
But on alien trees there are apples of gall,
On the pestilent death-tree they ripen and grow.
For tasting them Adam was smitten with death—
(They were poisoned before by the venomous snake,
By the gall of that serpent, the touch of his breath!)
Such fruit let the hands of a maid never take.
To touch it is sin, to taste thereof, evil,

For black with their plague shall the teeth shriek in pain
That holiest bonds have been broke by the devil
And heavenly riches were squandered in vain!   (8)

A BALLAD OF KING HEROD
(To be sung at Christmas)

When our Lord was born to us
    The king was much amazèd;
Magi brought their gifts to Him;
    A star their way had blazèd.

And King Herod questioned them
    Where the Child should lay Him,
Asking them to name the place
    So that he might slay Him.

When the Magi worshiped Him,
    They sought another road out;
From the wicked presence of
    That bad king they strode out.

Then King Herod burning with
    Uncontrollèd fury
Sent his soldiers forth to slay
    All the babes in Jewry.

So they did his wicked wish—
    Every child was killèd—
Babes of two and babes of less
    All in death lay stillèd.

If a mother bore a boy,
    Then the boy was slain—
From their mother's breast and from
    Cradles they were ta'en.

Why do you rage, O wicked one,
    Cruel and depravèd?
The very babe that you required,
    Christ alone was savèd.

And he pierced the mother's breast,
    Cut that tender blossom
So that blood instead of milk
    Fell from her soft bosom.

To the children martyred there
    Let us now be praying,
For before God's altar they
    Joyfully are playing.

Sainted children, hear us now—
    All our prayers are due you;
So we shall forever sing
    Joyful praises to you.   (9)

ELEGY FOR LOTHAIR THE FIRST

Prince, thou wert once so great as earth is wide,
Now art thou shut within this narrow cell.
O let each man his fall from thee foretell—
By glory death has never been defied.

Ye prosperous, from this prince's mortal doom
Mark how man's pomp may come to desolation,
Having in death no further splendid station
Than this thou closest with thee in thy tomb.

With sudden grief, O Rome, shalt thou go crying,
O world where sires illustrious dwelt of yore!
Rome, made infirm by Leo's death before,
Now mourns, imperial prince, thy sudden dying.

Those laws the fathers founded in old days
Which by long lapse of years had grown so dim,
Are as they were. They were remade by him
Who sought to reëstablish Roman ways.

Thou kep'st the appointed time thy royal state
Honoring all places with thy peaceful law,
Yet with that bow which none save thee could draw
Thou wert among the Roman archers great.

Thou didst against thy foes so boldly sweep,
And hadst thy conquered enemies so dear
That he who mourns thee not shall rightly fear,
And he that feared thee shall most rightly weep.

ENVOI

O Prince, who does not mourn thee, being dead?
What country did not fear thee, being alive?
And that same race thy terrors once could drive
Makes lament, prince, that now thy life is fled.

O Roman name, now midnight falls on thee,
Weep, weep again thy light now lost in heaven.
Break down thy arches! To thy foemen given,
Now must thou yield, O Rome, the victory.   (10)

ANTICHRIST

Let him who will, now hear the song that cometh from my tongue;
The glory and the fame of God on high shall now be sung—
How Antichrist shall come before the judgment trump has rung.

The Lord permits that Antichrist shall come to trouble man;
In Babylon he shall be born among the tribe of Dan,
The devil for his father and the Hebrews for his clan.

And thirty years shall he be hid unknown to all the race,
Then he shall reign for two and one and half a yearly space;
And power shall be his within that time of our disgrace.

Ye people, now take heed to what the apostles teach and say,
Let none by his epistles be seduced and led astray,
By preaching, or by signs, or by vainglorious array.

Then Enoch and Elias, sent of God, shall come—and lo!
Unto their deaths the both of them in that same year shall go,
For Antichrist shall murder them (our Father wills it so).

The bodies of those holy ones in death three days shall lie,
And the third day they shall arise by power from the sky
And preach unto the populace the devil to defy.

Ascending into heaven they shall cry to God for sign
That vengeance shall be wrought because their blood was spilled like wine,
And justice shall be meted out upon that soul malign.

For Jesus Christ our Lord who saves the people by His word
Shall send from out his very mouth a sharp and gleaming sword;
Himself shall kill the Antichrist, perdition's son abhorred.

Then peace shall come upon the earth for forty days to be,
And then the Lord shall come to us for all men's eyes to see,
And tribes and men and nations shall be judged eternally.   (11)

THE DESTRUCTION OF JERUSALEM

At the cross the Jews disgraced Him and their land, the Eternal One,
Maker of the sea and earth, of rivers and of starry space;
But Vespasian's vengeance sought them in the prowess of his son
When the princes came together to destroy that savage race.

By Jerusalem did Titus take in hand the cares of war,
There upon the Jews preparing utter vengeance and disgrace;
And he stormed against the wicked with a lion's angry roar
When the princes came together to destroy that savage race.

Camps he made against their ramparts, clamor shook the hated town,
Round Jerusalem his legions closed on Easter's day of grace;
Over Palestine to plunder it he sent his troopers down
When the princes came together to destroy that savage race.

During two times twenty circles of the sun had time gone by
Since to heaven from earth ascending Christ with angels took his place
At the right hand of the Father to be throned and rule the sky
When the princes came together to destroy that savage race.

* * * * *

Giving to the sword their bodies, rushing wildly here and there,
Pain and anguish overcame them, none escaping, high or base,
And like pallid ghosts and horrid on each other they did stare
When the princes came together to destroy that savage race.

Horribly they yawned in dying, horribly like dogs insane
Gnawing at their very entrails, on the skins of plants they graze
While they die, and round them flying here and there the souls remain
When the princes came together to destroy that savage race.

In that warfare child and mother fought and kindred fought with kin,
With their jaws and with their fingers tearing at each other's face;
Bits of food from each and other did they seek to snatch and win
When the princes came together to destroy that savage race. (12)

TALE OF THE IRON CHARLES

Some years before, it happened that one of the foremost princes, Otker by name, had incurred the anger of the terrible emperor and had taken refuge with this same Desiderius. Hearing now that the terrible Charlemagne was drawing nigh, they ascended a mighty tower whence they could see far and wide and observe whoever was coming.

And first the baggage-train appeared, baggage coming more swiftly than the expeditions of Julius Cæsar or of Darius. And Desiderius spoke to Otker, saying:

"Is this not Charles in that great host?"

"Not yet," Otker answered him.

And then they saw an enormous army, brought together from the ends of the empire, so Desiderius said to him:

"Surely Charles moves joyfully in forces such as these."

"He is not with us yet—not yet," the other answered him.

"What shall we do if yet more men come with him?" said Desiderius, beginning to tremble.

And Otker said, "What he is like, that you shall see when he cometh. And as to what he will do with us, I know not."

And behold, upon their speaking together there appeared Charles's school that never knows any rest. And seeing them, the astonished Desiderius made inquiry:

"This then is Charles?"

"Not yet—not yet," answered Otker.

And after this they beheld the bishops and the abbots and the priests and the clerks, with their attendants about them. And Desiderius, having beheld them, being now scarcely desirous of daylight but rather desiring death, stammered amid his sobs:

"Let us two go down and hide in the earth, away from the face of his anger that is so terrible an enemy."

But Otker, fear-stricken (in happier times he had once been accustomed to these things and familiar with the retinue of the incomparable Charlemagne) answered him, saying:

"When you shall behold the very earth of the fields agleam with iron, and the Po and the Ticino running iron-colored with their waves and overflowing the walls of the towns, then is there expectation of Charles's coming."

And scarcely had he finished these words when there appeared in the western sky, as it were, a dawn overshadowed by ominous clouds such as changed to darkness the brightest daylight.

And then the Iron Charles appeared.

He was crowned with an iron helm, he was clad in iron gloves, he was bound with an iron breastplate, his shoulders were decked in iron, in his left hand he bore upright an iron spear, and his right hand was laid on his iron sword, the ever invincible sword. And as to his thighs, which, to mount on their horses, other men leave bare, these were sheathed in iron greaves. Upon his shield there was naught but iron. Also in spirit and color his horse was iron. And they that went beside him on either side, and they that followed him, and they that went before in all things likewise were clad in iron.

    And Otker, casting one glance at him, said to Desiderius, "This now is Charles, he whom you desired to see."

    And he fell half-lifeless to the floor.

THE MONK OF ANGERS

Angers,   one hears,   has a monk of mighty thirst,
His name   the same   as Adam's was, of men the first;
Men think   his drink   runs to such vast quantities
No man   else can   run a score as large as his.

    Praise him, praise him, praise him, praise him!
    Sing we Bacchus' praises now!

They say   each day   he cries out for wine to drink;
Daylight   nor night   sees him pause or makes him shrink;
That sot   does not   cease until he staggers by,
Like a   tree that's
    wheeling   reeling   underneath a blowing sky.

    Praise him, praise him, praise him, praise him!
    Sing we Bacchus' praises now!

I swear   he'll bear   his carcase to eternity
So stained   and grained   with life-preserving wine is he;
He'll keep!   Don't steep   his body with embalmer's myrrh—
No spice   so nice   as alcohol, I do aver!

    Praise him, praise him, praise him, praise him!
    Sing we Bacchus' praises now!

He'll sup   no cup   politely like another man;
He passes   mere glasses   for a larger drinking can,
He'll ask   a cask   and, lifting it gigantically,
He'll drink   and swink,   surpassing mere mortality!

    Praise him, praise him, praise him, praise him!
    Sing we Bacchus' praises now!

Shed tears,   Angers,   if death should get him in his grip;
No other   such brother   in all your city's fellowship!
Who'll quaff   and laugh   and soak in wine as he has done?
Make eternal his diurnal   deeds in stone or paint, my son!

    Praise him, praise him, praise him, praise him!
    Sing we Bacchus' praises now!   (13)

FAREWELL TO HIS CELL

Thee, O my cell, belovèd spot, that to me
Wert habitation, thee I bid goodbye,
A long farewell unto eternity!
Thee trees with echoing branches go about,
And woods that are forever filled with flowers;
Around thee all the meadows shall be green
With wholesome herbs, and these the cunning hand
Of the physician, for his work of healing,
These shall he seek and find. And circlewise
A river belts thee in with flowery banks
Where jocund fishermen spread forth their nets;
And all the cloisters of thy gardens are
Fragrant with branches bearing fruit, and with
White lilies mixing with the crimson rose.
And birds chant matins every morning there,
Praising their maker in the face of God.   (14)

In the midst of all the pomp and circumstance of the verses that fill the *Monumenta Germaniæ Historica* one stumbles upon the little obituary note that follows. Its author seems to have felt it was a pathetic thing to have died a little girl amid such human greatness, and to have been born so needlessly. Its stately Latin lines have the true Roman dignity and reticence—rhyme would ruin its dry brevity:

ADELEID

Within this sepulcher
A little girl lies buried;
She was called at baptism Adeleid.
Charles was her father, Charles the Mighty,
Noble in wit, intrepid in the midst of arms,
The bearer of the two diadems.
While her powerful sire conquered the Italian kingdom,
She had, near the high walls of Pavia, her birth.
Nearing the Rhone
She was snatched from the threshold of life.
Far distant,
Her mother's heart was stricken with sorrow.

She died, never beholding
The triumph of her father,
And now in the kingdom of the blessed,
The Infinite Father
Has her.   (15)

THE CAROLINGIAN LYRIC 241

An enormous amount of clever sifting still remains to be done before critics can be finally persuaded of the subversive influence Carolingian ballads exercised on the development of medieval secular poetry. This work of winnowing has already been so well done in sacred song that we have been finally induced to lay aside from hymnody all consideration of those genres of ecclesiastical writing which are impertinent to its descent: church narratives partly lyrical in tone, extended paraphrases of Gospel story, retellings of Old Testament prophecy, didactic verse, apologetic poetry, polemic diatribes sprung from partisan dispute, sectarian homilies, versified sermons, and all their debatable and puzzling ilk. But as yet no Aristotle and no Horace have furnished us with an *ars poetica* to aid in clearing the turgid Carolingian pool.

All the more necessary, then, for us to disregard the external form of Carolingian ballads and to occupy ourselves with the spirit and the musicality of their content. A single case in point will illustrate this: In Neumann's history of music there is a modern transcription, as well as a reproduction, of the neumes of the planctus on the death of Charles the Great. These show us how markedly the phrasal organization of the musical setting follows the accentual pulse of the poem. We learn therefore that this planctus is no real metrical offering, but popularizing accentual verse, at a time, too, when we had thought the Gregorian chant (which ignores the connection between verbal accent and musical phrase and accent) was too firmly fastened on Carolingian technique to permit the possibility of such a thing. The fact that other popularizing Carolingian pieces have a very real union with sung tunes is growing increasingly manifest.

Another real contribution to our better appreciation of Carolingian verse that must soon be made, to amplify and personalize Henry Osborn Taylor's very interesting chapters on the early medieval mind, lies in the direction of biography. When we understand the living background of Carolingian writing as well as we do that of the Victorian, then we shall no longer busy ourselves too vainly with matters of sheer mechanical versification but rather look for the message it contains. I have recently had to revise my views somewhat regarding my favorite author of the eighth century, Paul the Deacon, just because I have visualized the story of his life—as Scheffel did Ekkehard's—and have made him an actual, breathing figure in my gallery of friends, instead of a ghost from the unrealized past.

Paul was the son of Warnefrid, a Lombard nobleman of Friuli. Friuli was the meeting ground of a thousand wonderful tales. Paul was a young Walter Scott aflame for every local legend. When we first hear of this youth, he is occupying an important secretarial post at the court of Desiderius in Pavia—the Poitou of four centuries later. When Adelperga, daughter to Desiderius, marries Duke Arichis of Benevento, Paul follows this blue-stocking to her new home —Ekkehard again, and Hadewig of the Hohentwiel. It is at her prompting that Paul writes his not very Roman history, in which he extols his lady for her humanism and her love of poetry. And now that he has established his claim as a man of letters, he enters Monte Cassino, where he is to spend the rest of his life except for a few years, when he answers the call of Charles (782) to a lectureship at the Palace School, traveling with Charles on his journeyings, which were far and swift—a good experience for a university professor of sorts. Together with another famous Italian scholar and poet—the grammarian Peter of Pisa whom he knew in the schools of Pavia—Paul works bravely to hasten the revival of classical studies on which the Frankish emperor is bent. He arouses much admiration in Aix for the extent of his knowledge, especially of the Greek tongue, and for the elegance of his verse. Some of Paul's poetry is not unpleasing to modern taste: the impassioned petition for his captive brother, the three fables, or the distichs on Lake Como, in which the religious mood is mingled with a sincerer feeling for the charm of nature than ever breathes from Petrarch's Latin. And finally, just as we should hope, Paul's most intriguing bid for fame is his vivid history of the Lombards, written after his return to the peaceful shades of Monte Cassino.

I offer the bald synopsis of Paul's life only as illustrative evidence that further vivification of the personal side of Carolingian writing than any yet undertaken will do away with the notion, tentatively entertained by Henry Taylor, that the men who carried eighth-century classical tradition were slender in numbers, that the places (like Tours, Rheims, Fulda) where open-minded laymen might then thrive were few. In the light of fuller biographical revelation, I prophesy we shall not regard as scant the rays of enlightening influence "the few devotees of culture cast on the vast encompassing ignorance of their day." And then we shall not regard as too romantic the claims of Heinrich Zimmer for what the Celtic missionaries brought to France—a love for landscape and for all its animate inhabitants. For we shall find in Latin, too, that the saints of forest and mountain freely adopted animals as their companions and familiars, that wrens and fowls, badgers and even wolves, became disciples to the Carolingian hermits—and we shall strain to believe that other holy men than Colman MacDuagh taught flies to mark their places in the psalter. In Carolingian Latin we shall come to realize that multiplication of nature in which the Celt discovered the unity of God—there we shall find that birds and breezes and billows seem but the straying thoughts of that same deity whose eternal calm is shown in the mountains and fair hills of the continental home adopted by the inspired outcasts of Erin. Then we shall come to trust more to the fertile valley and wild summit of eighth-century France as quickening causes of its Latin poetry, and less to its hexameters, pentameters, trochaic septenars, iambic senars, and sapphic strophes.

Chapter XIII

ROMANESQUE MIMES, MONKS, AND MINSTRELS

It can hardly be chance that has permitted to descend to us from the seventh century two absolutely new types of satirical verse, except for the survival of which, this century, both in prose and poetry, would offer us only Hobson's choice of an ungolden mean between pomp on the one hand and bareness on the other. Except for what is to follow as exemplification of seventh-century Romanesque, the period belongs to Isidore, Julian, and Fredegarius, to Aldhelm, Bede, and Adamnan, and might be called the Awkward Age, for it has yielded us neither of the desiderata of writing—neither very bad good books nor very good bad ones. It is an age of the professors in Italy as well as the Northumbrian school of York, where pellets of learning are being prepared for later dispensing by Carolingian doctors of logic —pellets indicative of a mild intellectual catarrh. Boniface, with his house of Fulda, and Gall and Columban were preparing mighty brews for the future but these were powerless against seventh-century gravedo. Careful sifting of all its poetry and prose give us but two instances that sparkle. These I subjoin.

The first piece is a dramatic skit with lively dialogue written in elegiac distichs and hexameters against which the coarseness of its utterance stands out in clear-cut parodistic relief. Since one guess as to its intention is as good as another, I choose most earnestly to believe it the jest of a keen monastic mind intent on paying its respects to an age which had seen fit to substitute nonsense for art. Its scene is the refectory after dinner.

TERENCE AND THE BUFFOON[1]

At the opening of the play, the Buffoon rises in his place among the spectators and from the middle of the pit addresses Terence when he walks upon the stage.

Buffoon:—
    Get off the stage with those old tricks of yours,
    Give o'er, surcease, stop, quit, my ancient poet!
    Come clean, step down, friend Terence! None endures
    Your wornout songs—they're musty and we know it.
    I tell you, get the hook for your old plays,
    You ancient idiot, put your rhymes in storage—
    You couldn't teach a man to cool his porridge;
    Believe me, no one loves your dusty lays.

Terence:—
    By Hercules, who was that wretch, I ask,
    That twisted up his muddy web of words,
    Being violent against me? Who dared mouth
    Such phrases? Is he one who, shameless, comes
    From provinces remote that he hurls forth
    Such harsh cacophony with laughter at me?
    My very bowels he hath deeply pierced
    With his sharp spear! I must consider where
    I shall discover him and seek him out.
    With all his vehemence, if he's at hand
    And will present himself, with open mind
    Will I repay my proper debt to him.

    Then the person who represents the Buffoon is pointed out to the poet. On hearing the words of Terence,

Buffoon:—
    You want me? Here I am. You want to pay me?
    I'll let you. I'll be here and bring the bill,
    And I don't dodge the settling of accounts.

Terence:—
    Why do you gnash your teeth against my verses?
    Who are you, wicked man? Temerarious coward,
    Whence come you that you vainly waste on me
    This tedious speech, these wordy butcheries?
    Presumptuous fool, it is not fit that you
    Should thus corrupt and taint the sacred muses.

Buffoon:—
    You ask me who I am, hey? Well, I'll tell you—
    A better man than you, you ancient piece
    Of thin senility. Why, I'm a youth,
    A tyro, something worth your while, a tree
    Well-fed and fruitful, you old sterile stump!
    Old idiot, if you'd only just shut up,
    You'd find it rather profitable business.

Terence:—
>What senseless thing is this! You are, you say,
>A better man than I am. Being young,
>Do what I do, who am so old and weak!
>A good tree must abound with goodly fruits.
>What is your harvest? I, a sapless trunk,
>Give out a better fruitage than do you.

Buffoon (to himself):—
>That sounds like truth to me, but I won't say so.
>   *(to Terence):—*
>What are you up to now? What's that you're trying
>To say? Why, that's the way an old man speaks
>Who falls in his dotage after many years
>And has a second childhood—in his mind.

So back and forth they argue through eight more speeches, neither convincing the other. The last word belongs to the poet:

Terence:—
>My boy, trust not to boastful youth. Proud words
>Fail oft, and humble speech doth oft rise up.
>O, if my ancient strength were in my breast,
>I should receive your prayer as infamy,
>Which you hurl at me with such speech as wounds
>My spirit. . . .(1)

This first piece, which might be justly entitled The Parting of the Ways of Poetry, was written free-hand by some young clerk who was, to borrow a phrase of Goethe's, *verteufelt human*. This scholar's Latin is not the pattern of Vergil or Horace made boorish by the decay of culture, degenerate by the mangling of time—it is the breath of the quivering nostrils of a poet, Celt, or Frank, or wandered like Fortunatus from upper Italy. This Romanesque which "shameless comes from provinces remote" to Rome is his thieves' cant, his beggars' whine, his polyglot provision against starving. He uses it for gain, as others of his clan—the janglers and harlots and merry-andrews—do their merchandise. But more than jargon is our poet's Latin, more than the vehicle of his longing for meat and ale and lust. His spirit moves in it to unutterable invective and satire; he feels in it. This Gael or Frank or Mantuan has made Latin his own journalese patter, has adapted it to his temperament, to his measure of the time and its thought. Young Juvenal come to judgment.

Crasser—and no doubt deliberately so—in its obscenity and its barbarisms is the second piece, made up of not less than five letters pretendedly exchanged by bishops Importunus of Paris and Chrodebert of Tours, as of the year of grace 665.

EPISCOPAL COURTESIES

I

Importunus to Chrodebert, Greeting:—
    Saintly Brother and Bishop, my lord Chrodebert,
    We hear you assert
    The wheat that we sent you, you couldn't make use of.
    We desire to indulge in a little abuse of
    Deeds done of your mind, that none of your kind
    Shall find the jokes funny that you seem to find.
    What you did to friend Grimald, the king's majordomo,
    Was somewhat beneath a dignified homo,
    When in the reign of King Sigebert you
    Walked off with his wife, his one little ewe;
    And throughout the realm he found ever after
    His honor had turned into laughter,
    And then with the people who come from Touraine
    You sent her away
    In a nunnery to stay—
    And a choice congregation of virgins (!) were they,
    Assembled in—well, I won't be *too* plain.
    You read with her all of the Bible,
    Your residence there was so chaste,
    I'll not waste
    Further words or lay myself open to libel,
    Who is neither for God nor for men—why, he—
    You fled from the nuns to a monastery.
    Be damned to you then, and be done with it. There is
    My seal: Importunus, writing from Paris. (2)

II

My Lord Chrodebert:—
    As priest you are godless, as bishop you're evil,
    As saint you live under the laws of the devil.
    If any one doubts me, I'll give him the facts—
    I desiderate here undeniable acts:
    You pray not to God, you believe not His Son;

You do ill to your enemies, one after one;
You're so self-sufficient,
You think you're omniscient,
But you lie, as we know.
You fear not the Son,
You do not His will,
Your actions all show
You are laboring still
For him you *do* love, and by whom you're undone.
And when your monastic progenitor got you,
He had no delight in Our Lord. Let it spot you
That the work of your mother, the nun, was unholy!
Your father thereafter
(It moves me to laughter!)
Thrust you out on the world, roly-poly.
If he taught you and fed you,
He was afterwards sorry—
The Word never led you,
And this is your story:
You shine not except in a liquorish glory!
On Grimwald damnation,
Remember, you brought,
But God won't forget all the good that he wrought
For your sake—
And pray, what return did you make?
You slept with his wife against all the laws
Of the church and of men, and you put her away
In a nunnery to stay,
And *not* for the cause of devotion, I say,
And we know you are damned, forever and aye—
And you stole all his money, his silver and gold,
Which he gave you for reasons I've never been told.
Why, how did you dare
To steal all his ware,
Then seek for him here, and inquire for him there?
Your wicked endeavor
Is not even clever!
If she's got a good face,
You'll love up a girl
From any old place,
And not out of charity
Or any such rarity.
While you keep such a life,
You can never be saved, with long cunning and strife.
That's enough, is it not? Now take my advice,
And suffer castration,
And then you won't perish at God's great assize
With men who commit fornication.

For additional sins I could strike to your heart,
But you'd best send me something now on your part.
Let these letters go out
For miles round about.
Remember me now with affection, my dear.
I send this to your home;
If the rider who brings it
You see, let him come
And give you my counsel. And if it comes near,
Read it and lay up these things in your heart.
And if it stings, it
Belongs in a place lower down, in the rear. (3)

Against these two "Gothic" pieces of the seventh century let us put a backing of poetic example and technic as it was taught by two of the universal schoolbooks of that age: Boethius's *Consolation of Philosophy* and Bede's *Metrical Art*. Choosing one of the most "modern" songs that interlard the first of these books, we find the following poem on the Variability of Fortune:

VARIABILITY OF FORTUNE

When from the Pole the roseate steeds of Apollo
    Come, shaking light in their train,
The pale-faced stars that darken and dull and wane
    Grow dim in the flames that follow;
Now Zephyr encarnadines in vernal roses
    The meadow with soft sweet breath,
But when Auster insane and strong threatens the world with death,
    No bush a flower discloses.
Often serenely shining the tranquil ocean
    Is quiet and waveless and still,
And often impetuous Boreas has his will
    In the wild sea's wild commotion.
Some form in the flow of the world is always dying,
    And varying Time is strange.
O trust that the fallen fortunes of man will change,
    Trust even in goods that are flying!
From everlasting this law hath stood that was made:
    All things that are born must fade. (4)

Choosing almost at random from Bede's treatise on prosody, we find a passage in which the author shows he has no scruples about the "modern" sort of composition employed by the vulgar writers in their rhythmic verses that neglect quantity but still preserve the outer form of classical meters—in fact, he rather admires such poets.

Now let us contrast, two and two, our selections: on the one hand, *Terence and the Buffoon* and *Importunus and Chrodebert* have the "Gothic" qualities that offend every renascence of antiquity, have in rich measure the imaginative gifts that marked medieval poetry for favor with the romantic schools; on the other hand, with Boethius and with Bede, just the opposite is true. So in the seventh century we find poetry in division against itself; we find a divorce of Mercury and Philology undreamt of at the consummation of their *Nuptials* by Martianus Capella. How may one best account for such duplicity in Romanesque literature?

The first modern critic to attempt its explanation concisely was Wilhelm Scherer who, fifty years ago, asserted the rôle played by the Roman mime in the development of medieval poetry. Little by little the conviction grew that after the fall of the empire Italian mimes spread northward throughout Europe, bringing new elements to the life and literature they found there. And so the picture took shape which represents the repertory and the art of twelfth-century minstrels as the resultant of two forces: the lofty epic idealism of scop and jongleur; the vulgar but contagious realism of Roman mime and joculator.

There is something in this theory of continuance and new birth through the mingling of two elements, either of which might soon have proved sterile but for fructification from a new seed, which satisfies the uncritical imagination, so that we may not wonder at the quick adoption of it. Medievalists are now possessed of a thread which will lead them through the dim chambers of the Dark Ages, as they seek an explanation of hardly understood poetic phenomena. They cling therefore tenaciously to this tenuous thread, in secret dread of its breaking, but openly smiling whenever the classicist is heard to demand that the Roman mime be dead along with the ashes of that empire which had cherished him. The medievalist remembers that this very empire led a ghostly but real existence far into modern times. Why, then, he asks, should these interminable fun-makers have yielded up their spirit at just the moment when the fall of Rome opened to them new fields of effort?

A full generation after Scherer's pronouncement that the metamorphosed Italian mime was the solitary pilgrim in a sad sort of poetic wandering from Rome to Canterbury, the only one to propagate entertainment, spin edifying yarns, and carol snatches of song learned in many lands, comes the book of Reich and with it a Roman mime who, like Selkirk, is monarch of all he surveys. In places untrodden of Caliban and Ariel there lurks the mime, sole carrier of the poetic bacillus through the Dark Ages. Anything in thirty centuries of the world's literature, says Reich, which is dramatic is mime, unless it be classic or a copying of classic form. The whole spiritual world of expression has become with a wave of Reich's hand either mime or non-mime. To other convenient totalities which sum the universe (day and night, land and sea, time and eternity) a new unit has thus been added.

Nonsense? In a way. And yet Reich's book cannot be disregarded, for here and there—as we have found to be the case with Wiener—he has reached a speculative explanation for a recurrent element in early medieval poetry which is definitely puzzling because, in our fragmentary and hit-or-miss knowledge of the literary growths from the fourth to the tenth century, we have not yet secured an adequate number of anchorage points to enable us to build up in their midst a relationed and warrantable system of poetic development. Winterfeld was certainly not converted to Reich's doctrine of an ever-present Roman mime until he had rejected as unusable a dozen other possibilities of linking the age of Augustus to that of Charles the Great and the Ottos. I gladly forgive Winterfeld for trading the cloistered clerk for the mime, the professional man of letters for the jack of all trades, the better to explain a continuity from the *Satyricon*, the *True History*, and the *Golden Ass* to the *Tales* of the St. Gall monk, the tabloid *Dramas* of Roswith, the *College History* of Ekkehard, and the *Ruodlieb*. It was the counsel of despair that led him in the ardor of new conversion to ascribe to an unseen mime what he could not trust a half-misunderstood monk to accomplish, viz., to cultivate every form of creative expression known to medieval times, and to give to each that impetus that brought it to its zenith.

Now, so far as I have observed, all medieval archæologists who study early European literature longitudinally rather than in cross-section, still assign the parentage of poetry to the descendants of the Roman mime, nor is there any overt sign in the sky of scholarship that they will cease to do so. Particularly in the scheme of Latin transmission until the close of the Middle Ages such archæologists adhere to the term *mime* for what we would rather denominate by such terms as monk and poet, real, romantic, and Romanesque. Almost twenty years ago I felt this neither a wise not a helpful thing to do, and therefore published the result of an examination of Latin literary records in the earlier period of western European poetry (A.D. 550-1050), to show that the living utterance of those days did not necessarily derive even by indirection from the southern mime. Today I am increasingly aware that Romanesque poetry owes provably little to hypothetical mimi and provably most to other impulses that affect the instinctive and native Latin art of the changing medieval generations. Therefore I cannot avoid again considering the pretensions of this mime (a lord of hosts who confronts us in a hundred forms) to the authorship of the writing I more gladly ascribe to peddler and beggar, artist and professor, scribe and journeyman and prentice, vagrom monk and dilettante of letters, scop and soldier and missionary, tourist clerk and sightseer, peripatetic artisan, philosopher and hireling, and all the rest of the goodly company of story-tellers who must have found amusement in literature without using it as a professional means of livelihood. The philological evidence on which the following chapter is based may be conveniently found in the pages of *Modern Philology*. In my ensuing discussion of mime, minstrel, and monk I can therefore restrict myself to the more philosophical aspects of our testimonies in the case at issue. And before we proceed another inch, it is desirable to define the word *mime* (or *mimus*).

As used by critics, it means three things:

1. A dramatic performance popular in Rome previous to the fall of empire.
2. Any sort of realistic imitation of life—skit, dance, poem, topical song, gag, juggling, pantomime, acrobatic feat, trained animals—in short, Roman vaudeville or variety show.
3. A Roman vaudeville artist or entertainer.

It is quite useless to speak of *mimus* as the source of anything else unless we know at each step exactly what is meant by the term. Let us, therefore, discover at once what we may about it.

1. Mimus: Dramatic Performance

Luckily, we need not pause overlong with this type of mimus, for there is no such thing—it is purely the invention of Hermann Reich, who, when Grenfell published the synopsis of a story discovered in Oxyrhynchos (a small Egyptian town), seized upon this as proof that his drama had existed and restated his position as follows: From the time of the great Alexander there arose in the larger Hellenic cities of the Orient the great mimic drama, growing out of the sung and recited mimes. This so-called mimic hypothesis mingled prose and lyric parts, arias and *cantica*. It soon won the stage of Rome and became latinized. Philistion is the classic of the Greek hypothesis, Publilius Syrus and Decimus Laberius are the great names in the Latin derivative. Throughout the Græco-Roman empire in Europe, Asia, and Africa, people received the mimic drama with acclaim; rulers and emperors cherished it, and later even the church fathers could not drive it from popular favor.

This is Reich's contention, but the facts in the case do not bear it out. That the great mimic hypothesis should flourish as early as the third century B. C., but had to wait three centuries to find its classic in Philistion, deserves no confutation. It is urgently important to point out that Reich's constructions, for the most part, do not withstand examination. For, as Sudhaus points out, a pronounced conservative tendency and a clarity as to the requisites and the aims of their art enabled the mimes to remain what they were and prevented their merging with the higher drama. As numerous utterances prove, the mime was always conscious that his main task was character portrayal. Doubtless for the entertainment of audiences, he did play comedy, produce spectacular pieces, and give such farces as the *Charition* (discovered at Oxyrhynchos), which might be termed a scurrilous *Iphigenia*, but not a real mime. He never forgot, however, that the depiction of character and manners was his true field, and our piece (Oxyrhynchos 413) shows how, despite a comprehensive action, the whole object of a mime could be made the sustaining of a single character-rôle. If one lays aside pure jugglery and the low types of mimesis, the mime is nothing but *ethopoia*. It is no drama, for how could a form be drama which can do without any sustaining progressive action? Action, which is everything for a drama, is only incidental to the mime; it may even be excluded entirely.

The opening chapter of a famous book of Chambers is entitled "The Fall of the Theaters," and he employs therein without definition the words farce, mime, spectacle, performance, stage, theater, plot, and actor. But an examination of his sources shows quickly that there is no evidence that any mimic drama was ever acted in any playhouse in Rome. Theorize about the matter we can, but proofs are lacking, nor will further study uncover such evidence. Surely the mimes are no dramatic type, says Wilamowitz. The narrator makes his appearance either in the market-place or in a private dwelling, later in the place which is called theater, a word that means nothing more than an elevated spot where his actions can be the better viewed by the spectators. The narrator can be as well compared with the fun-makers of the West as he can with the aristocratic rhapsodists of the East, who likewise recited pieces of Archilochus and Hipponax. He imitates with drastic comic effect various voices, as is demanded by the dramatic action of his narrative. God forgive those who believe this sort of thing was really played!

2. *Mimus: Roman Vaudeville*

Whatever the mime may have been in the beginning, by the early centuries of the Christian Era it had degenerated until it pandered to the worst instincts of humanity. A survival of better things we have in the recited mimus like those of Sophron, Herodas, and Theocritus, as well as in the songs like the erotic fragment of Grenfell (page 64 above), but *pægnion* was the word for everything beneath the legitimate or dramatic type. If any sort of show was fated to endure across the fifth century into the western world of the early Middle Ages, surely it was *pægnion*.

For one might be blind and yet enjoy himself. There was music, both vocal and instrumental, there was the squealing and grunting as of pigs, there was the imitation of every animal's bleat, squawk, or bellow. One could be deaf and not miss overmuch, for there were sketches from all types of low-life and side-street, knock-down farce, take-offs, and acrobatic turns. One need not even understand the jargon of the players for an evening's treat, but could go like the modern tourist to follies or review, *tingeltangel* or *variété*, sure of his reward. Who would not laugh if mine host Trimalchio blew out his fat cheeks like a bugler, or if a slave made music on a lamp and swallowed fire? Who would not be startled by the unspeakable lasciviousness of Theodora's pantomime which, to judge by Pompeian frescoes, was nothing rare? Whose face would not burn at the nakedness of person and pantomime and words which Plutarch claimed to intoxicate and stupefy the spirit more than strong wines?

3. Mimus: Roman Entertainer

The preceding section on *pægnion* has told us what to expect of these entertainers. Whatever they may have been in far earlier times, in the fifth and sixth centuries the profession of mimus was colored by admixture of every kind. *Histrio, prestigiator, scenicus, tragœdus, comœdus, thymelicus, scurra, saltator*, and *mimus*, are so variously glossed by contemporary chroniclers that we are at a total loss how to separate the *artes lubricæ* they practiced. Sidonius, who must be expected to know, says that the *histriones* falsely boasted of doing the same thing as Philistion. Cassiodorus specifically refers to a certain Sabinus as actor, horse-tamer, and charioteer, to a Thomas as charioteer, crook, and wizard.

The mimes were dramatic performers of one sort and another, reciters of obscenest jokes, charioteers and circus hands, high-jumpers, dancers, magicians, sleight-of-hand workers, and ill-doers generally. We are transported from the stage, from the realm of private theatricals, from recitation in the circle of friends, for sociable entertainment, and for the amusement of a dinner party, to the realm of side-show and fair, to the circus tent, to the harlequin's booth, to the lascivious pleasures of drunken carousal and brothel. Let us not be misled to conceive the matter otherwise. The men appear in motley or clowning dress, the women more or less naked. One indulges in the absurdest rodomontade and boasting, another gives imitations of human customs and characters, a third portrays lewd scenes: to the accompaniment of cymbals and drum a man or woman enters and plays the rôle of prostitute, pander, adulterer, or drunkard. A fourth is conjurer. Any sort of coarse comedy, grimacing, imitation of the cries of animals is welcome.

Such then, is the Roman mimus, performance and performer, that Gauls and Germans knew from the earliest days of our era. By the fifth century mime was an old tale to them, and known to them undoubtedly in three different ways: (1) from personal acquaintance in Italy; (2) from hearsay and from graphic description of returning tourists; (3) from personal acquaintance in Gaul and Germany, whither, sallying forth from Roman frontier towns in the earliest historical times, penetrating ever farther, the mimus had followed the steps of the southern merchant. Some Roman mimes probably outlasted the sixth century a while and continued their profession in Romance territory as late even as the age of Charles the Great, though by no means so long in strictly Germanic districts. Some European minstrels doubtless owed certain tricks and turns directly to inherited mimic tradition, especially during the fifth and sixth centuries—but that the two (minstrel and mime) were for a dozen generations largely identical, I do not believe. And nothing in the records makes this creed imperative or even appealing.

It has often been asserted by students of literary progress that hunting in the documents of the Dark Ages for traces of Latin *mimi* is love's labor lost. Their work has been stated to be as perishable as the other ephemeral gayeties of the banquets and festivals they enlivened. Nothing more of the songs of the mimes has survived, such students insist, than of the instinctive skill of their brothers, the acrobats. In last analysis, it is said, there are in the present state of our knowledge regarding early medieval conditions two things we may never hope to know: first, whether there exists a relationship between the Latin poems preserved to us and the work of the Roman mimes; second, if this relationship actually exist, of what sort is it? If the mimes sang, many critics believe their songs have been buried with them in the tomb, and whatever remained of them in the memory of their contemporaries was scattered, distorted beyond recognition, and lost.

I frankly admit being bored by *obiter dicta* such as the above, since but few students know what a careful search in proper places will bring about. Almost to a man they have not undertaken it. I am as impatient as any other of that unfortunate tendency in modern investigation: namely, to examine with brave display of erudition every stray bit of philological evidence that exists regarding the Roman mimus, and then to jump to any conclusion that suits the irresponsible whim of the historian. But on the other hand, not to examine whatever evidence we possess as to the existence of Latin entertainers during the Dark Ages, and then to denominate them straight out the fathers of early medieval jongleurs (and Faral for one does this) strikes the objective observer as a high-handed proceeding.

How can Faral be so sure that the work of the mimi was as perishable as the gayety of the banquets they enlivened—unless he look about him to make sure? A priori, there is no more reason why an eighth or ninth-century chronicle should not indicate the repertory of Roman mimes, than why a thirteenth-century Provençal novel should tell us so much about the activity of the jongleurs. If the mimi did sing the popular songs and tell the popular stories of their day, as the later jongleurs did, why, then, it seems imperative that we rummage through the literary records of that earlier day, almost sure that we shall stumble across traces of mimic tradition in their descriptions.

To discover what the jongleur was doing in later medieval times, one has but to turn to *Flamenca* and learn how he played on every conceivable musical instrument and had at his tongue's tip the popular songs and stories of Europe; but we can only theorize as to what the mimus was doing in the previous centuries by way of song and story. Faral asserts that at this epoch the mimus was doing what the jongleur did after him, only that the former's repertoire was more restricted. And I say that Faral has no right to an opinion in the matter because, in his search for mimus, he confessedly places no reliance on the literary records, because he trusts solely and implicitly in the historical documents of the dark ages.

Now, these historical documents are unfortunately silent as to what songs and stories Latin mimi brought into the West, and they are untrustworthy sources for any other specific statement regarding mimic activity. We have seen above, and we shall see again below, how little value may be accorded the indiscriminate lists of various classes of entertainers contained in the chronicles Faral prizes so highly.

Long ago Paul Meyer assigned to the mimi the beginnings of medieval literature, and Léon Gautier agreed with him. They knew that testimonies which followed one another closely in chronicles from the end of the Roman empire far into the Middle Ages taught of the existence of groups of individuals designated by the classic names of *scurræ, thymelici, joculatores*. These names crossed (without disappearing) the distress of Merovingian and Carolingian days. The same names are met with later, flourishing throughout Gaul in the eleventh century.

Let us see what Meyer and Gautier have done. Without specifying in any case just what the work of these mimi was, they assert this labor of theirs was the point of departure for medieval Provençal and French literature. But this is bad argument. For, if we make one thing the literary source of another, if we make the activities of Roman mimi the source of the functioning of medieval jongleurs, then we should mean the first thing is the direct and ascertainable cause of the second thing, begets it, stands to it in the relation of progenitor to offspring. We should not mean, quotha, that vaguely, and despite utter lack of any proof of the fact, the first thing is in a loose and general sort of way (perhaps in its age!) what the second thing may conceivably have been in its time.

If we find, that is, in the work of any medieval jongleur forms, phrases, types of expression, themes, technique, character portrayal, attitudes, ideas which are identical, or largely coincident with, the utterance of Roman mimi, then and only then, can we make the latter spiritual ancestors of the minstrel. But if (as is true of Meyer and Gautier) all these matters with which the profession of jongleur has to do are referred back to fifth-century Rome, simply and only because the Latin words for entertainer are not done away with in the records that mark the interim between that time and the epoch of the jongleur, then we have no right to derive the medieval minstrel from the loins of the mime. Why, if such illogical derivation be permitted, we can trace back our medieval minstrel to an antiquity more hoar even than that indicated by the mimic dances to the phallic, fat-bellied spirits of fertility in Homer's day—for certain dialogue songs in the *Rigveda* are almost certainly texts of very ancient mimic musical performances and owe their inclusion in the canon to their use as mysteries or cult-dramas; likewise, hymns in the burlesque manner like *Drunken Indra* are typically mimic. It is indeed a long line of honorable descent if one be permitted to trace his way (as Reich suggests) back from Hauptmann's *Sunken Bell* to dances which occurred centuries before the mimic songs in the *Rigveda*. But who would call the author of such a mimic poem from, say, 1500 B.C., a spiritual source of our contemporary dramatist?

Of course the ancient names for entertainer continue all through the Dark Ages and deep into medieval times: we hear them all again and again; why should we not? Mimus had meant, and long continued to mean, entertainer, juggler, minstrel, poet. If a man of high or low degree chanced to be regarded by the common people of seventh, eighth, or ninth centuries as an acceptable poet, that man was dubbed mimus. Of course the names continue. We hear of mime in sixteenth-century France (in the farce *Maistre Mimin*), and much has been made of this fact. Why not make as great commotion over the circumstance that we have mimes and minstrels and jugglers in the twentieth century? Could not the continuance of these classnames, then, be made to mean that we today owe all our realistic portrayal in literature, all our magic of the theater, directly to the saltimbanques who set Trimalchio's dinner-table in a roar?

Names continue. All words endure which symbolize general concepts. We hear of comedy and tragedy all the way from barbarian Rome to this very moment that is passing—likewise of epic and romance and lyric. Yet comedy and tragedy during the Middle Ages were completely lost sight of *except* in name; epic is dead ages ago, and yet its name is on the lips of all as if it existed today; romances in current magazines are very different things from medieval ones. Who will claim there is a constant tradition of any great division or type of literature from the dim past to now, merely because of a title? These types have come and gone, risen and faded and fallen —the pressure of a changing world of fashion has differently shaped them. Church and popular festival, old religion and new philosophy, time of reform and season of indulgence, ephemeral fads and enduring psychological verities—these are all mirrored somewhat in the realistic prose and poetry of whatever period separates us from the dead past. And this sort of thing we owe by direct tradition to Roman saltimbanques? I doubt it.

More than half a century ago Zimmer contended that *scop* meant not alone the dignified epic singer of antiquity, the harp-playing vassal who sat above the salt at royal banquets, but also one who entertained his audience with quip and joke. We likewise know that *mimus* signified, not alone the Roman vaudeville artist, but *minstrel*, in the widest sense of the word. When such is the case, how can critics depose that descendants of Latin vaudeville performers were the ancestors of jongleurs? It is true that we do know more or less about the monkey tricks of early mimi, as we do about those of later jongleurs. And in a certain way we can trace the stunts of the one back to the other, for in *Flamenca* we find our old favorite turns of Empire days still in vogue. But it is not of the circus performer or the variety actor that we are thinking when we speak of jongleur as the child of mimus—we are thinking of the creative artist, the maker, the poet, the fashioner and preserver of specially literary themes and types. Faral seems to forget this salient fact, or he would willfully blind our eyes to it, for he does nothing toward narrowing and limiting his definition either of mimus or jongleur. On the contrary he deliberately enlarges it.

Strenuous objection should be had to this broadening of the meaning of jongleurs to include all whose profession it was to divert humanity, if this definition is to be at once used to prove that medieval spielmann and jongleur derive straight from Latin mimus—for such enlargement surely clouds the issue. Remember, if you please, that when Faral says that jongleurs are mimes pure and simple, his readers naturally imagine he is claiming for the best of medieval art, for music, song, and story that enchanted western Europe, a Roman origin. And Faral's readers think this because they conceive of jongleurs as did Diez: all those who make a profession of poetry or of music—they are not remotely dreaming that jongleurs include the crowded category of tumblers, acrobats, and performers of nondescript acts.

I at least am not seeking the origin of the skill that permitted medieval trapeze experts to swing by their toes or their teeth, which taught balance on the slack wire, which sent swords and stones and flame down living throats, which distorted the human frame into bow-knots, which, with a touch of the practiced hand, kept a circle of ten gilt balls in the air without one falling to earth. Neither I, nor any other reader of Faral, cares tuppence at the present juncture whether the monkey tricks and the circus art of the early Middle Ages came straight from Rome or from Sparta or from Thebes. What we do care for at this moment is to tear aside the veil from the apparent mystery which enshrouds the birth in early medieval Europe of the vernacular and realistic art of that jongleur who sang songs and told stories the world will not forget.

Now if we confuse this sort of artist with every contemporary parasite and clown, or if we believe this creating artist got all his vital and abundant art from earlier generations of professional jesters and fools, who had infinitely enlarged the roster of their primitive acts, which they had varied and made more complex—then let us say that figs grow from thistles and bricks are made from chaff. It is an old artifice of the schools, this one of which we find Faral guilty: to enlarge one's definition until it includes everything intended, thereafter gravely to derive from so swollen a concept whatever one wishes, and to strut from the stage with a wave of the hand. But this is legerdemain.

We have seen that mimus as rightly used may mean: (1) vaudeville; (2) actor or entertainer. What then does Reich mean when he says that everything dramatic in the world's literature that is not classic or imitated from classical models is mimus? What does Winterfeld intend when he asserts that only through the continued existence of the mimus may we hope to envision the development of the centuries?

In such statements they do not restrict the term mimus —and it is very important to realize this—to any one type of performance like recited poem or song or gymnastic, nor yet to any one sort of performer. They make mimus betoken a certain literary attitude; they make it synonymous with realism. According to Reich, anything dramatic without reference to form is mimus; Winterfeld says that the art of profane narration and real life itself are mimus. The latter bids us call mimus every realistic and living portrayal in prose and poetry during the Dark Ages.

It is not common sense to make *mimus* in any age connote *biologia*. It is wrong to surrender bodily all the creative genetic literature for centuries to the commonplace crowd of motley vaudeville artists who may have swept northward from Italy during the barbarian conquest and occupation. For in the first place we are prone to forget the homely Aristotelian truth that the impulse to play and to imitate is among the most elemental stirrings of the human soul, and that this common impulse, sometimes quite innocently, creates similar types of vaudeville among peoples which have never come into close cultural contact. And secondly, I fancy the authors and reciters of mimes during the empire would have been the last to claim to create works of any artistic, far less of any literary merit. They furnished, as do our manufacturers of hits, salable stuff for a Roman season. Their audience were the nobles who shouted themselves hoarse over the bear-mimes and the dog-shows, over the meaningless and sterile clatter of circus and vaudeville: the crowd of philistines, spear-carriers, shopkeepers, and barbarians who held the reins of government. It is absurd to trace the life-giving roots of this creative literature of Carolingian and later times to the purely conventional art of these people.

For vaudeville art is conventional. In the more than two thousand years that we have known it, the canons of this art have been but seldom violated—mimi have always been doing much the same thing in the identical old way. Their jokes bloom perennial, the business of the old hands at the game may be seen on the stage of any variety theater or in the circus ring today. It is nothing less than a miracle how little their repertory and tricks have changed from their passing across the threshold of history till now: topical song, suggestive dance, portrayal of low-life, dialect recital, boasting, repartee, juggling, sleight of hand, buffoonery, and slapstick.

But if it be wrong to surrender creative realistic literature to the mimi, it is no better, I believe, to accord it bag and baggage to the scop. The scop I regard as that minstrel, singing to the harp at the courts of German kings, who, during the period of invasions of the empire by East German peoples (350-550 A. D., the so-called heroic age), created the legendary tales which were to become the material for romances in later times, passing into the *Eddas*, the *Nibelungen Lay*, and many other poems. With a scop as a legendary figure caught in the mists of prehistoric Europe, the coryphæus of an immensely ancient traditional type of epic poetry which is presumably a common Germanic heritage from the Aryan past, I can have at the present moment no concern. As a matter of fact, I have never believed in him or his product, nor need any one who is irreligiously inclined towards romantic German propagandism.

However this be, Kögel believes that with the rise of the Frankish empire and the consequent downfall of the smaller courts the honorable estate of the older poets had come into disrepute. The impoverished descendants of the old scopas are now rumored to lead a vagrant existence in German territory, to be compelled to reckon with the tastes of a new audience, the commoner herd, and thus driven to include farcical elements in their repertory. Thus, the poor old scop is supposed to have become a merry-andrew (*joculator*, *mimus*, *scurra*) and to have so fostered the more vulgar type of narrative that a great mass of fabliaux and short stories suddenly appears in the second half of the ninth century.

I am thankful for Kögel's word, *suddenly*. For if the creative realistic writing of the late ninth and early tenth centuries had not appeared suddenly; if it had come into being fearfully, painfully, step by step—then I should almost be persuaded that it was due to the gradual elevation of the repertory of the mimus, or the rhythmic degeneration of the scop, or the slow awakening from a long sleep on the part of the monk. But there is nothing gradual about it—this medieval renaissance. The most superficial examination of earlier records suffices to teach us that in the ninth century realistic narrative literature came into existence with a single bound—just as at a later time the drama did. For this phenomenon, nothing that we know of the opportunity confronting either mimus or scop, nothing we know about their ability to answer to a new opportunity in the ninth century, offers a sufficient explanation. If the impulse to novel types of realistic narrative is to come, it presumably must come from without. The mode or manner of this mutation in literature we know; but what is the cause of it?

It means little to me when Paris derives his minstrel from mimus and scop, when Hertz and Schönbach call him offspring of mimus, scop, and vagrant clerk. For none of these scholars makes clear the time, the reason, or the occasion of such a merging, except to posit it as possible—wittingly or not, they dodge the main issue. If two or three differing traditions ever unite in a single new art-form, then we may be sure some specific impulse is necessary to bring about this commingling. Merely to call attention to the opportunity for such a junction of varied elements, without assigning a valid reason therefor, accomplishes nothing. In any age of which we have record there has been constant opportunity to marry divergent forms of artistic expression and, as the legitimate child of such wedlock, to secure a new literary genus. But only rarely has this happened, because the proper occasion was lacking.

To photograph life in art requires genius: it demands the immediate personal vision. Another thing is necessary before a realistic scene can take lasting shape in a conscious literary product: a diction suited to the purposes of the author. Of these two requisites for a living art, genius is, of course, the greater and the rarer. Shall we deny this visualizing power in the Dark Ages to the monk and the nun (as critics do) and accord it to the mimus or the scop? Should we believe the vaudeville artist could lay aside his slap-stick and write the tales of the monk of St. Gall or tell Roswitha's legend of the founding of Gandersheim? Not I.

It should never be forgotten that, prior to the tenth century at least, cultured Gaulish and German poets felt impelled to express most of their thoughts in a foreign medium, Latin—a medium which many of them did not command freely, and for two reasons. First, before a wider dissemination of higher education than then existed, there would be few who could attain the stylistic ease that characterized the writing of later men of letters; second, in the ninth and tenth centuries, simplicity and correctness were rarely striven for, bombast and a rhetoric of word inflation being the goal. Ecclesiastics and schoolmen generally had, of course, no such conception of the mission of poetry as prevailed in a later age. Verses and letters were written to gain fluency of expression in the Latin tongue, to inculcate grammatical principles, to acquire an epistolary style—and were, therefore, decked out with every sort of pompous quirl and flourish. Verse-making had a practical aim, or was but a sort of play in academic metrics—content mattered little, formula was all. A flowery diction was attempted, verses were overloaded with scholastic erudition until they staggered and fell, and even the slightest structures, such as epitaphs and inscriptions, confront us with the most unlikely quotations from the *Song of Songs*, Vergil, and Ovid. Such monastic copying of biblical and classical tradition which leaned entirely on the materials, emotions, forms, and ideas of the past, manifested practically no power of either observation or invention. This was the work of monks. It was, at heart, not Gaulish or Germanic or Roman —it was curiously unracial.

Now, from the work of such clerks as these, no future can reasonably be expected—first as last, their labors will consist of the dull multiplication of known facts. So the critic has felt himself justified in dismissing all monks from his study of the living sources of medieval literature. The critic then turns to the scopas whom he accredits with having continued a dignified line of expression marked by lofty idealism; he turns to the mimus who, he knows, maintained an undignified line of utterance marked by a vulgar and contagious realism. He then but adds the two together and gains as his total the repertory and art of European medieval minstrelsy. Why not? It is as easy as that. And in a sense this is the truth.

There were two types of expression more or less separate; the two things united. But who united them? Who was it that took the stereotyped facts and figures of Gaulish and Germanic poetry, the formulated themes and tricks of lighter entertainment, and, for the first known time in western European history, combined the two in a way that secured a mutation of permanent influence? To this question there can be but one answer: this answer is written large and clear in a hundred records. It was the monks.

I find no surer indication that it is not mimus or scop, but monk, to whom we owe the re-creation of realistic art in the ninth and tenth centuries, than that it is just the monks and their work which furnished all the bases of the medieval renaissance of which we shall hear in a later chapter. Notker, Froumund, Gerbert, Ekkehard, Walahfrid, Rabanus, Fulbert, Roswitha, Gottschalk, the author of *Ruodlieb* and of *Ecbasis*—it is such spirits, struggling with an inept Latin, who gave direction to the glories of a later and vernacular literature; they were the torchbearers. Popular proverbs and tales, *volkslieder* sung on the streets, saws of the humblest minstrel, fables from distant lands—it was not the patter of Italian vaudeville artists that brought them into manuscripts and held there forever—it was the toilsome, loving labor of these same monks. Do I seem not to take sufficiently into account the poetic coherence and the artistic beauty of the humble models which these monks began to incorporate into work of their own? In answer, let me say that I believe any effectiveness which popular Gaulish and German art of the Dark Ages possessed, was not due to the spasmodic effort of unalert, unlettered, and unimaginative men dwelling in some isolated community. No, it was in a crowded center of culture where stirred throngs gathered, that the throes of composition brought forth an enduring and popular art of profane narration. And for the time we are considering, such centers were presumably found only in the monasteries.

It was a great thing these ecclesiastics did, uniting diverse elements that had hitherto been separate; finding expression for the humbler and more realistic elements of vernacular tradition in a Latin diction learned from long occupation with biblical and classical models. For this combination, made in the monasteries, established a new mutation in literary form that gave life and meaning to European literature.

Mutations of permanent influence in literature can be achieved only by writers with exceptional opportunities. Such chances in the ninth and tenth centuries lay in monastic culture and environment; they did not lie—in the nature of things they could hardly lie at that time—outside them. The moment these monks, clerks, and lay-brothers brought their inventive power, their significant ideas, to bear upon their writings in such a way as to adjust them to the demands of contemporary thought and feeling—that moment we have no longer monastic copying of biblical and classical tradition, we have permanent mutations in literary expression that yield (as we shall later see) the novel in hexameters, the romance in hexameters, drama, legend quick with dialogue, the short story, the beast fable, fabliau, historical poem, and lyric, and a swelling list of satires, parodies, hymns, and sacred ballads that have laid aside their traditional adherence to an older art and breathe the life of their day. In the light of this magnificent catalogue of novelties, it is little edifying to note how Kögel ascribes to the wandering minstrels whatever note of simplicity or realism he discovers in tenth-century poetry. He says the poet of *Christ and the Samaritan Woman* knows how to relate his theme straightforwardly and graphically and thus shows contact with the minstrels; he acknowledges the author of *De Heinrico* is a clerk, one who knows how to write concisely since he has learned his art from the minstrels; likewise, he feels sure the poet of *Clerk and Nun* must have had his theme from some wandering singer. This is the old stupid formula with a vengeance: "dull, verbose, incoherent," spell monk; "witty, simple, graphic," spell minstrel. Will some one tell me why? This formula has been proven wrong a hundred times, never perhaps more strikingly than by the *Song of Waltharius*.

The surprising list of new forms in ninth and tenth-century art informs us clearly that the monks and the monastic schools had given Europe the four prerequisites for a body of splendid modern poetry: the artist with imagination and feeling; the desire to portray real life in simple form; models which the unscholarly might amplify; an audience eager for the author's work. And yet Winterfeld contends that only through the continued existence of the mimus may we understand the development of the medieval centuries. Why, where is now his mimus vanished? Surely, when the culture of the ninth century cherished in the monastic schools was lighting the way to the modern art of profane narration, if there existed a solitary descendant of the old Italian vaudeville performer in Gaul or Germany, then just so surely do we know what his mimus was doing. He was mouthing, gesticulating, dancing, squawking, playing on some strange instrument, eating fire, swallowing a sword, engaging in lascivious pantomime with an unclothed mima, juggling with gold balls, playing the stupid, bragging absurdly, taking off his audience, pounding somebody's head with a make-believe club, balancing a table on his chin, or doing something else equally delightful and original. But I feel sure this mimus of the Dark Ages was sublimely unconscious he would ever be called upon to father medieval jongleur and minstrel.

The point is the following: In the ninth and tenth centuries such a modification appears in western literature that we have begun to leave the Dark Ages behind and have come to the threshold of the modern world. This is indeed a metamorphosis. We can ascribe the change to causes unknown to us and then invent whatever picture suits our idle whim—or we can seek and find the reason for the change in certain definitely known facts. I prefer the latter course.

Notker and Roswitha owe their best work to the mime, says Winterfeld. I should put it differently and say that when these artists depart from an over-ornamented style and the traditional method which their day used for recording facts and themes—then they owed their best work, neither to a mime nor to any model of their own day, but to themselves. It was possible to be one's self in prose and poetry before the year 1000, though it must be admitted the deed seems to have been difficult of accomplishment. Here and there in the hisperic weave we find threads of a color so bright, so near the hues of everyday life, that there is nothing dull or dark or medieval about them. Before Notker ever wrote his college history, Gregory of Tours had written things that Ker says might go straight into a ballad; Gregory the Great had provided great treasure of vivid legend in his *Dialogues*; Ermoldus had so pictured a siege of Barcelona that it was instinct with dramatic truth.

When we read Notker we know what we shall find—a struggling poet, narrow in view, awkward in performance, incoherent in statement; and yet one that may at any happy moment of forgetfulness of self hold us by the simple force of his portrayal. Listen to what such a clerk as he writes in his poem on Doomsday, whish is paraphrased from Latin verses ascribed both to Bede and Alcuin, verses from which it is no long stride to the conventional dream-poets and to such openings as are offered by the beginning of the *Piers Plowman* vision:

Alone I sat in the shade of a grove,
In the deeps of a holt, bedecked with shadows,
There where the waterbrooks wavered and ran
In the midst of the place—so I make my song—
And winsome blooms there waxed and blossomed,
All massed amid a meadow peerless.
And the trees of the forest trembled and murmured
For a horror of winds, and the welkin was stirred,
And my heavy heart was harassed amain.
Then I suddenly, sad and fearful,
Sat me to sing this sorrowful verse. . . .

Winterfeld would have ascribed these verses to a Roman mimus or to his lineal descendant![2]

Chapter XIV

THE CAMBRIDGE SONGS[1]

Among all the possibilities of origin for European lighter verse previous to the vernacular outburst of the twelfth century, none is more sympathetic to the mind than the hypothesis that Latin folk-songs preceded any strictly native models of popular balladry. Of course the school (monastery, episcopal school, college of rhetoric) was the workshop in which the pattern for practically every bit of Latin verse during the Dark Ages was made; besides, for centuries, the school furnished the constant logical background without which neither churchly nor vagabond lyric can properly be conceived. In other words, not only didactic and epic Latin poetry (including satirical and narrative forms) were never successfully able to deny that they were college-born and bred, but the same fact is true of the more "popular" rhythms: erotic lyric and folk ballad, apostrophe and ode, elegy and pastoral, burlesque and topical song, dance couplet and drinking round, secularized hymn and parodistic sequence. To sum the matter sharply, it may be said that all the apparently casual, naive, and artless types of lyric poetry in the Latin Middle Ages, as well as all the pretentiously artful, artistic, and artificial lyric forms, were children of learned institutions in town and country, and not the spawn of loosely-knit and unlettered communities.

Not that this statement of fact changes the situation overmuch from the one propounded by earlier folkloristic theorists, but it does place the original blame for composing lyric poetry of any sort whatever upon the individual product of learning, rather than upon the denizen of an undrained swamp or a forest primeval, the isolated dweller in mountain regions and valleys undisturbed by passing feet. The arts and crafts in Gaul and western Europe generally during the Dark Ages were focused in the monastic cities (or families) in so far as they were not carried on by alumni of such institutions at the courts, in great baronial estates and manors possessing a school system, and in the thriving commercial marts. Many an eighth-century monk besides St. Œngus witnessed the old royal encampments eclipsed by new monastic establishments, saw the ancient pagan fortresses lying waste, while once-solitary hermits' cells became like Rome for the multitude of their inhabitants.

Such generative centers of disciplined work as the vast monastic families of the eighth century and later, were lamps of learning lucid and mighty for their time. They were highly organized and privileged stations of labor, tillage, milling, water-power, and winter storage. In the course of a generation or two they quite invariably became trading communities of commercial activity and wealth, and of patrons of the arts of peace. On monastic lands, as in a civil jurisdiction, joint husbandry was carried on by the guild or family. Groups of workers who made over their land and accepted service under church protection were undoubtedly bound not to desert the monastic territory. Tenants of special monasteries that were exempt from taxes had every advantage of good roads, drainage, and fences. Small gifts rained on the monasteries to protect donors from pestilence, famine, murrain, child mortality, storms, fires, earthquakes, eclipses, and other very tangible evils. Great grants of land, fair tribute of wealth and noble treasure were bestowed for benefits in need, life insurance in this world and the next. With their estates and confederations, their armies of dependents (*familiæ*), their men of learning and authority, their sculptors, illuminators, and carvers, poets and musicians, their physicians, their metal-workers, braziers, and smiths, their spreading agricultural communities, and their increasing trade-connections—the leading monasteries of the eighth to the eleventh century were states in themselves.[2]

Why then should we be inclined to deny such centers of all existent culture the patterning of the *volkslied*? The answer to this question is perfectly evident: We are slow to grant the origin of Latin folk-song to the monastery because in practically no possible instance does this song, as it floats down to us, represent the original version of it, particularly if the surviving ballad be the popularized text of some widely disseminated piece. By "popularized" I mean spread abroad through much singing and recitation. On the contrary, such a poem, once created in school as the result of conscious artistic effort, passes out of its academic or learned environment to a hazard of new fortunes on the open road. And once at large, if it be fated to endure—if it have nimble wit and ribald theme, singable refrain and catching melody, plasticity and sentimental appeal, if it lends itself easily to drastic mimesis—why, then this song attains to forms undreamed of by its father. A twist of phrase and a minor key— we have a hymn of it. A change of tempo and a pious mien— we have a roaring parody.

Church hymnody and school rhetoric are undoubted sponsors in baptism for the stanzas of joculators and goliards, no matter if the somewhat bawdy populace that furnished an audience and a livelihood for these entertainers were responsible for subversive changes often amounting to complete alteration of the technique, intent, and manner of the songs they had more or less unconsciously stolen and adapted. It is very important that we realize these facts, for otherwise we shall continue to lay all our bases for medieval and modern poetizing in the vaudeville, mimic performances, and popular festivals of lewd rustics, who had no more artistic initiative than a ham sandwich. The clowns at country fairs, the *stupidi* of rural circuses, alien vagabonds and harlequins and savages were not the creators of medieval poetry, but without question they were its disseminators, continuators, shapers, interpreters, and popularizers. And this is in all conscience enough to grant the *mirabile vulgus* of the Dark Ages, without throwing in the head and the tail of all realistic poetry from Homer to Henry.

We have no reason to disbelieve that there was a plethora of popular Latin verse in the eighth and ninth centuries—lighter erotic and ironic singable lyrics quite free from the quibbles and formulæ of the more mechanical cultured poetry—although little enough of it naturally survived in the written collections of MS material. Sufficient hints of such types of composition both in Latin and the vernacular have come down to us from various sources:

The lines of King Miro's minstrel recovered from the prose of Gregory of Tours heads the list:

> Heu, misero succurite
> Oppresso mi subvenite,
> Adpenso relevamini
> Et pro me sancti Martini
> Virtutem deprecamini,
> Qui tali plaga adfligor,
> Tali exitu crucior,
> Incisione disjungor.

Recovered from the prose of the *Gesta Karoli* is the mocking rhyme on an unlucky brother-in-law of Charles the Great:

> Nu habet Uodalrih
> Firloran erono gilih
> Ostar enti uuestar
> Sid irstarp sin suester.

We have already recorded the gentle tilt of bishops Chrodebert and Importunus and the cynical lines on the capacity (in at least one direction) of an abbot of Angers. Suggestive remnants of mocking songs—the jilting of Liubene's daughter; *Hug timidus*; the man from Chur—inform us further of popular lyricality in Carolingian days, as does the spring song of a ninth-century monk writing in his cell:

> The woodland meadow encloses me,
> The song of the blackbirds echoes in my ears as I sit at my parchment....
> From the tree-summits the cuckoo in his gray cowl calls to me with clear voice—
> O in truth it is goodly writing here under the forest's roof!

But none the less, it is not until the tenth century, as our records run, that realism in the modern acceptance of that term, enters into Latin poetry and obsesses it. Then a modification in European literature appears which shows that we have left "dark ages" behind and are come to the threshold of the modern world. Suddenly we are conscious in Latin poetry of full-throated laughter at the miraculous element in traditional doctrine, at the grotesque commingling of impossibilities in this strange life of ours—we meet a real joy in ineffable nonsense, a mad zeal in the construction of madcap edifices, a sheer delight in falsehood for its own sake. Not since late Hellenistic Greek and Silver Latinity (when even patristic writing caught the infection of it) have we heard this note of hilarity in song until it sounds forth to us from tenth-century poetry.

Let us follow a few typical instances of this stark change of mood displayed by tenth-century verse. From this time we have five rhythmical tales, each of which deals lightly with superstitious belief in the world of miracle and magic. Four of them are translated in their entirety; because of its length we must be content only to indicate the fifth.[3] Our first example is a fabliau of irrefutable stamp which precedes the earliest French example of its stripe by one hundred and fifty years. On reading it we may recall that the comic yarns of Germany have never received due acknowledgment from other nations, although the latter have ever stood ready to suck the juice from them without a word of thanks.

THE SNOW CHILD

Listen, my people, and be attentive and hear
Of the jest and the manner of jesting,
How a Swabian woman lied to her man, and her husband lied to her.

Carrying riches over the sea in ships, yea, departing from Constance
His home he left, this worthy man from Swabia,
Also his wife, a lusty woman overmuch.

Scarcely his ship had cut the sea when a fearful tempest arose,
The deep was troubled, fire flashed from heaven, the floods were lifted up,
And lo! after many days the south-wind came,
Throwing him up in a far country, an exile upon that shore.

Verily the wife was not idle in the house meanwhile;
She called unto her players and singers,
She had a company of young men;
Rejoicing in whom, the memory of her exile passed from her,
And the next night there was begotten upon her a male child
Whom in her season she shamefully brought forth.

Now when the space of two years had passed, the aforesaid traveler returned,
And the unfaithful wife went to meet him, bearing with her the child,
And the man kissed her, saying,
Whose is the child? Speak now, lest I be wroth with thee.

Wherefore the woman, fearing her husband, was moved to deceive him in this,
Saying unto him: My husband,
One day I went among the mountains,
And being thirsty with snow did I quench my thirst,
Wherefore I grew heavy with child,
With this man-child was I made pregnant.
Languishing for thy love I swooned away with desire,
I wandered with naked feet, in the snow and ice I went;
Bearing with me this child, the fruit of my womb,
Even as I beheld thy sails bellying with the wind,
Or as I saw the swelling prow of thy ship.

Then after five years, yea and more, had passed over,
Once again the merchant prepared his ships, building him vessels anew;
He spread his sails and went forth
Taking with him the male child of the snow.

And when he had crossed the sea he brought the child forth from the ship,
Trading him to a merchant for gold, for a hundred gold pieces he sold him;
And the child being sold, he returned home with his gain.

And entering into his house he spoke to his wife, saying,
Now must thou take heart, my spouse;
My dear love, seek thou now to be comforted,
For I have lost thy son in whom thou tookest no greater delight than did I.

For a tempest arose, a mighty wind smote us,
Driving us upon the sands, among the shallows of the sea,
And the sun grew hot, shining fiercely upon us,
Wherefore thy child that was fathered of the snow
Melted away.

Thus the Swabian tricked his deceitful spouse;
Thus out of fraud cometh forth fraud,
Him whom the snow brings forth, rightly the sun melts down. (1)

After the manner of the Vulgate *The Snow Child* tells a story fit for the *Decamerone*. With considerably less circumlocution the hero of the sequence *How the Swabian Made the King Say, You're a Liar* relates a monstrous falsehood and is rewarded with the hand of the ruler's daughter. Ker rightly finds the malice of the first of these two verse yarns different from anything in vernacular literature prior to Boccaccio and Chaucer, for the biblical tone and the swollen rhythm refine the mischief of the tale most whimsically. *The Snow Child* is self-conscious, is amused at its own craft—a quality quite unlike the ingenuous simplicity of the French merry tales, not to speak of the churlish heaviness of the worst of that genre. Here is its companion piece:

THE SWABIAN AND THE HARE

I'll tell you a tuneful tale of lies,
Now learn it from me, you children wise,
And when you sing them this song hereafter
Your hearers shall split their sides with laughter.

There once was a king and he had a daughter,
A lovely liberal girl was she;
So he made a rule that whoever sought her
Under this rule should be:

Any rascal that's present and skilled in sin
Who shall continue
His lies, will win you,
Provided there ring from me the king
A word that proves I'm taken in.

Hearing this, up spoke the Swabian
Who wasn't in any respect a Fabian:
Alone, he said, with arrow and bow
Lately a-hunting I did go.
Among the beasts I spied a rabbit,
My flying arrow just did stab it.
I cleaned it as soon as it ceased to stagger
And cut off its bloody head with my dagger.
I picked up the head
With this hand here,
And it poured me forth
From the left-hand ear
A hundred pecks of honey clear.

And out of the other ear, if you please,
There fell an equal amount of peas;
And these
I tied up at once inside his skin,
Then to cut up the body did I begin.
Up under his tail
What next did I feel,
But a letter signed
With the royal seal!
And it said in the letter, my lord, that I
Am master here, and a servant you—

That, roared the king, is a whacking lie,
The letter is false, and you are too!

And the Swabian, having fooled her pa,
Became the royal son-in-law.   (2)

The third song is a recasting in Latin Adonic rhyming couplets of a favorite subject originally treated in a German folk-tale. In it the old prank of the cunning Swabian who stole and ate the liver is combined with reference to some impostor punished by Archbishop Heriger of Mainz (913-927). The song recalls curiously more than one of Hans Sachs's stories.

HERIGER

1

Heriger, bishop
  Of old Mayence,
Met with a prophet
  Who made pretence
He'd been carried to hell
  And had come back thence.

2

The things were many
  That he'd found out;
And he added that hell
  Was walled about
With a thicket of trees
  Like a rampart stout.

3

Heriger laughingly
  Said, That's fine!
I'll send to that pasture
  My keeper of swine;
Lean hogs driven hellward
  With fat will shine.

4

So the liar went on:
  I was borne thru the air
To Christ's high temple.
  I saw Him where
He was sitting and eating
  And drinking there.

5

John the Baptist
  As butler is fine;
He summons the saints
  When it's time to dine,
And hands around goblets
  Of sparkling wine.

6

[Through scribal oversight six verses are omitted from the poem at this point; they refer to St. Peter as cook.]

7

But Heriger told him,
  Our Lord is wise
To make John butler,
  For I surmise
He never takes liquor
  In any guise.

8

But you're just lying
  When you relate
That Peter is sunk
  To a cook's estate.
His rank is higher—
  He guards the gate.

9

Now tell me truly
  Did God, as was meet,
Give you in heaven
  A proper seat?
Were you much honored—
  What did you eat?

10

The prophet responded:
  I sat in a nook;
A piece of the liver
  I stole from the cook;
And when I had eaten
  My departure I took.

11

Then Heriger sent him
  To stand in a fen,
Tied him with thongs
  To a sapling, and when
He'd beaten him soundly,
  He spoke again:

12

If Jesus should ever
  Ask you to a meal,
And you sit at his table,
  You'd better conceal,
The next time you go there,
  Your impulse to steal! (3)

With the next example we turn away from a successful skit like the foregoing—which is the earliest known example of that happy-go-lucky attitude toward the saints and their celestial abode so popular in later centuries—and study another satirical poem, this time devoted to an old maid's affection for her pet she-ass. Like *Heriger*, it is written in rhyming couplets of five syllables each, it undoubtedly mirrors some actual occurrence, and it conveys the impression of being an actual impromptu. Its author was either an indifferent Latinist or was somehow bound by a vernacular original, for his German constructions show through. The nunnery referred to is Homburg on the Unstrut river, near Langensalza in Thuringia.

Although the author of *Elfrida* strives for the epic manner and emotional intensity of depiction in order to point his rude wit, he is a good bit of a bungler—for not every clerk and minstrel who wrote had the true gift of poetry. The song is printed, although it is not very interesting, because it is of the type we are treating, and a good-bad instance of a thing is every whit as instructive as a bad-good one.

ELFRIDA

In Hohenburg convent
    It came to pass
That there browsed in the pasture
    A brave little ass;
To his mistress Elfrida
    Faithful he was.

Out in the meadows
    What did he spy
But a hungry wolf
    One day running by!
So he showed him his tail
    And guarded his eye.

The teeth of the wolf
    In his tail he feels,
So he fights with a lifted
    Pair of heels—
And the wolf a long, long
    Battle he deals.

But when he felt his
    Strength running out,
He lifted his voice
    In a moribund shout,
Calling his mistress
    To please come out.

Hearing the desperate
    Cry of her ass,
To her sisters Elfrida
    Spoke. "Alas,
Run and aid me in
    This dire pass!"

"The dear brute I sent
    To the fields for a bite;
I hear him crying
    In terrible plight—
I know with a savage
    Wolf he doth fight."

The sorrowing sisters to
    Elfrida ran,
And many a woman
    And many a man
Go forth to capture
    The wolf if they can.

Adele that was sister to
    Elfrida came,
Sister Agatha
    Did the same,
And they all went out
    The tumult to tame.

But the wolf had broken
    The ass's side,
And eaten him up—
    Blood, bones and hide—
And then he had hid in
    The forest wide.

So all the sisterhood
  In despair
Beat their bosoms and
  Tore their hair,
Seeing the innocent
  Ass lie there.

The little body
  Elfrida bore,
Greatly lamenting
  And sorrowing sore,
Hoping to bring him to
  Life once more.

The gentle Adele and
  Fritherun dear
Both came with her to
  Bring her cheer,
Telling Elfrida to
  Shed no tear.

"Dear sister, weep not
  This dolorous pass.
The wolf will not hear your
  Crying, alas!
And God will give you
  Another ass." (4)

 Because of the two sequences already given (*Snow Child*; *Swabian and Hare*) and because of the further use of this form by the Cambridge Songs (as in *Kaiser Otto*), Wilhelm Meyer believed it was the discovery of this type that developed the personality of ninth and tenth-century poets, furnished new content for their writing, freed popularizing poetry from the classical strait-jacket and from Romanesque uniformity, led it back to the well-spring of all poetic beauty—to music—and introduced a natural and unhampered evolution of poetry *ab ovo*, not Latin poetry alone, but French and German and English poetry as well.

 This view of Meyer's prevails quite generally today, but is none the less an inversion of the true picture. It puts the cart before the horse. A purely practical device which substitutes separate syllables for a reiterated single vowel was not the biogerm of lyric efflorescence. The sequence did not cause lyric poetry—but lyric poets did develop to profane uses the sequence form, as they did a score of other ecclesiastical types that burgeoned suddenly when the faculty of song met and mated with the need of singing.

 This factor, says Taylor, wrought with power—the human need and cognate faculty of song stimulated by religious sentiment and emotion. Music shaped the composition of the lines, molded them to rhythm, insisted upon sonorousness in words, promoted their assonance, and—to meet the stress and mark the ending of musical periods—compelled words to rhyme. The exigencies of melody evoked finished verse—through the inspiration of its meaning and its new vocal capability, verse aided the evolution of melody. Each quickened by the other and molding the other, verse and melody attained a perfected strophic unison.

Still, I insist that it is not wise to stress heavily the importance of the sequence for the development of popular Latin poetry previous to the twelfth century when, in its final forms, this type becomes so glorious a representative of the hymn, when profane and unforgettable student-songs appear in molds parodied from innocent intrusions on the liturgy. For although tenth-century sequences do seem to become verse before our very eyes, although in them we do seem to follow the central current of the evolution of medieval Latin poetry from Romanesque to realism, although they do seem the spontaneous children of the Middle Ages and see the light in the closing years of the ninth century— yet the sequence forms required a long period of growth before they attained the glory of their climacteric. And meanwhile, often enough, they acted as a bane and not as a blessing for the growth of sturdy and beautiful song. There is evidence enough of this unhappy truth in the MS of the Cambridge Songs, nowhere perhaps more apparent than in the grotesque ballad on *Kaiser Otto* which, whether we relish the fact or not, stands forth naked in the accentual swing of the Jesse James type of versification: "The dirty little coward; he shot Mr. Howard"—than which classic it is provably worse:

KAISER OTTO

It was the mighty Kaiser Otto
That gave this song its name.

Otto was asleep, he put his limbs to rest
When the palace one night caught fire,
And the counts they were afraid to wake him from his sleep
So they saved him by playing their lyre,
And the dukes give that name to this song.

For when he was aroused he gave his soldiers hope,
And he was a terror to the foe;
The Hungarians, they said, were by the river's bed,
City, farm, and village lie in woe,
And many a mother cried for her boy,
And sons for their mothers did cry.

Then Otto, he said, have the Parthians forgot me?
I have waited on my officers too long;
For while I linger here, disaster comes more near—
Let us delay no more, but come with me to war—
We will fight this Parthian foe.

Then Cuonrat the brave (there was no braver man),
He said, "Let the soldier die whom this war shall terrify!
Go put your armor on, for our enemies are in arms,
And I the banner will bear
And first shed the blood of the foe!"

And roused by his words they grew eager for the fight;
And for their arms they called and at the foe they bawled,
And when the war-horns blew they flocked to the banners,
A hundred Teutons charging on a thousand of the foe!

A few fled away but there were more of them that died;
And the Franks kept the field, and the Parthians did yield,
And the bodies of the dead dammed the stream,
And the Lech, running red with blood,
Told the Danube of the rout of the foe.

Though with his little band the Parthians he did beat,
And though after and before he won battles many more,
Yet his soldiers all wept when he died,
But he left to his son the kingdom he had won,
And he left the good old customs and his name.

The ballad goes on in the same rambling, inchoate way to refer clumsily to the two subsequent Ottos, and concludes in true folk fashion:

Let us now put an end to this tune
Or people will say that they were not brave that way;
And since even noble Vergil were not equal to this story,
We will sing no more of this song. (5)

Better than the type of tenth-century sequence represented by *Kaiser Otto* and the *De Heinrico* is the transitional species represented in the MS of the Cambridge Songs by at least six pieces:

No. 5 (Resurrection) the præludium of an Easter sermon used as a separate ode.
No. 6 (To the Virgin) a similar rhythmic apostrophe.

Nos. 15 and 19, songs of compliment to Conrad II and
  Heribert, Archbishop of Cologne.
No. 23 (Daughter of Proterius) the oldest instance of
  the tale recording man's compact with the devil
  as in Faust.
No. 24 (Lantfrid and Cobbo) a variant of the Damon
  and Pythias theme.

These pieces, largely unsyllabized, are dithyrambic prose rather then poetry. The last two of them are very effective in the rough form in which they are cast; and for the purpose of indicating at least the partial origin of medieval balladry in a *rhetoricus sermo*, free from any definite setting in musical pattern, nothing could be more happy than the survival of these Gothic tales.

But after all, the great sign in the days of the Ottos that the mutation in poetry has come, and that modern verse has been born, does not lie in any of the twelve pieces thus far treated. We do not find the cleft which has so long divided written literature from naive expression healed by any or by all of the twelve. In vain should we summon Latin *leiche*, macaronic strophes, clerical *eulogia* and *planctus*, rough-hewn ballads and hymns of compliment, religious odes, comic legends, lying tales, facetiæ, fabliaux, and pederastic pieces from the *Cambridge Songs*, to prove that the great appointed dawn of modern singing is at hand. All these tenth-century types do not yet surely prophesy that later climactic moment, when suddenly as at sunrise the whole earth had grown vocal. Immensely interesting are the following three poems but nothing necessarily new in the world:

O ROMA NOBILIS

Rome, thou imperial queen of the universe,
Over all cities thou regent most excellent;
Martyrdom's blood is thy roseate curse,
The virgins' white lives are thy lilies all redolent!
With blessing and benison thee do we hail,
Through the long centuries thou shalt prevail.

Thou, the omnipotent porter of paradise,
Take, O thou Peter, the voice of our prayer;

From Israel's judging when thou shalt arise,
Be not irate nor implacable there—
From temporal troubles to thee do we cry—
Hear thou our suffrages mercifully!

Sinners, we pray to thee, Paul, and petition thee;
Philosophy fled from the work of thy soul!
The steward of the Master whose love did physician thee,
Grant of that grace our appropriate dole,
That we, being filled with the words of the wise,
Shall feed upon knowledge and to thee arise.   (6)

TO THE FLEEING BOY

O thou eidolon of Venus adorable,
Perfect thy body and nowhere deplorable!
The sun and the stars and the sea and the firmament,
These are like thee, and the Lord made them permanent.
Treacherous death shall not injure one hair of thee,
Clotho the thread-spinner, she shall take care of thee.

Heartily, lad, I implore her and prayerfully
Ask that Lachesis shall treasure thee carefully,
Sister of Atropos—let her love cover thee,
Neptune companion, and Thetis watch over thee,
When on the river thou sailest forgetting me!
How canst thou fly without ever regretting me,
Me that for sight of my lover am fretting me?

Stones from the substance of hard earth maternal, he
Threw o'er his shoulder who made men supernally;
One of these stones is that boy who disdainfully
Scorns the entreaties I utter, ah, painfully!
Joy that was mine is my rival's tomorrow,
While I for my fawn like a stricken deer sorrow!   (7)

LITTLE JOHN THE MONK

Among the church biographies
I found a waggish anecdote,
A story so appropriate,
I'll tell it you in prosody.

Said John, a monk diminutive
In size but not in probity,
To one of his fraternity,
An elder in the hermitage—

"I'd like to live as angels do,
In heavenly security,
Unfed, unclad, dispensing with
The labors of mortality."

"Take care," the brother answered him,
"Don't jump at things so easily.
My friend, you may wish afterward
You never had begun the scheme."

"Success or failure," answered John,
"Depends upon initiative."—
He stopped and took his clothing off
And went into the wilderness.

And there he lived for seven days
Enduring foods gramineous,
Upon the eighth his belly won
And sent him to the hermitage.

'Twas late and all the doors were shut,
And in their cells the brothers were,
When, feeble with debility,
He whimpered, "Brother, open it.

"Before your noted doorway here
Sits brother John the indigent.
Don't spit your pious words on one
Brought back by dire necessity."

Behind the door they answered him:
"Dear brother John's an angel now,
He's looking through the pearly gates—
Mankind no longer bothers him."

And as they wouldn't open up,
John's night was not a happy one,
But he would have his way, and so
'Twas thus he had to pay for it.

They took him in when morning came—
The things they said were blistering;
But as they gave him crusts to eat,
Our John was very meek with them.

And when he had got warm again,
He said his Benedicite,

> And then although his arms were weak
> They let him try to hoe a bit.
>
> And thus for too much levity
> And lack of sense they punished him—
> And though he's not an angel, yet
> They say he's famed for charity.   (8)

Songs like the above, graceful and light-heeled as they are, may be honestly accounted marsh lights playing fitfully across the supposed gloom of the tenth century, and little more. But with the three songs that follow we have reached the goal for which our whole book has been but a record of the human strivings of younger Perceval towards his grail—we have entered into the fullness of a world of poetry that is our own. One is the song of May festival in which the nightingale assumes her symbolic role as a personification of the unnamed love of Fulbert of Chartres, as a priestess of mystic love:

THE NIGHTINGALE

> When spring leads out new buds across the wold,
>   And leaves on greening branches swell,
> Sweet odors burn, and flowery seeds unfold,
>   Then laugheth Philomel.
>
> Her own sweet voice she knows, and from her throat
>   With measured pause she stops and sings,
> And pausing, sings again her liquid note
>   Of idle, summery things.
>
> All day and night she singeth, giving sleep
>   Amid melodious intervals,
> And lovelier solace shall no wanderer reap
>   Than her sweet-throated calls.
>
> Her voice is clearer than the zither's note,
>   When, grove and forest glade along,
> Her measured music stops such tunes as float
>   From birds of lowlier song.
>
> Then, soaring to the high tops of the trees
>   Which she makes glorious with her wings,
> Because of all the springtime joy she sees,
>   She gladly sits and sings.   (9)

One is a beautiful and tender love song. A lover in his rooms awaits the coming of a tardy mistress. He has prepared for her a spread of spices and wines like unto Porphyro's. A choir boy and a singing girl are chanting sweet melodies to the music of lute and lyre; slaves are bearing goblets of colored wine; the lover bursts forth with the impassioned prayer:

COME, SWEET FRIEND

Come, sweet friend, and be with me,
Darling of my heart, my treasure!
Come now into my chamber—see,
It is fresh-decked and fit for pleasure.

I have put cushions in the seats,
And hung bright cloths about the room,
Set fragrant herbs to mix their sweets
With flowers fresh-plucked and all in bloom.

There's a fair table set for dining
And laden down with dishes rare
And ruby wine in goblets shining—
Everything you ask is there.

And you shall hear soft symphonies
Blowing, and flute-music, too;
With a skilled boy a maiden vies
In singing songs to pleasure you.

He plucks the cithern with his quill,
Her lute accompanies the lass;
The servants bring tall cups they fill
With wine less ruddy than the glass.

But banquets please me not so much
As the dear converse coming after;
And freely to possess and touch
Is more than food and wine and laughter.

Come then, sweet sister, soul's elect,
Of all things dearest, most divine,
Your eyes, my soul's best part, reflect
Within their light, the light in mine.

> I lived in sylvan solitudes,
> And loved all solitary places;
> I fled, among the secret woods,
> Tumult, and men, and thronging faces.
>
> But now, my dearest, stay no more,
> Let us be studious of love!
> I can not live without you, nor
> Lack the sweet end and crown thereof.
>
> You can not now postpone the employ
> Which you must come to, spite of staying!
> Quickly perfect our promised joy,
> In me there is no more delaying!   (10)

Now, in the light of such songs as the foregoing, it is only the fault of the historians and the literary critics that, when we try to picture to ourselves the intellectual state of Europe as at the year 975, certain almost stereotyped ideas immediately suggest themselves: We think of Europe as immersed in a gross mental lethargy, passively witnessing the gradual extinction of arts and sciences which Greece and Rome had splendidly inaugurated, allowing libraries and monuments of antique civilization to crumble into dust, while the nations trembled under a dull and brooding terror of coming judgment, shrank from natural enjoyment as from deadly sin, or yielded themselves with brutal eagerness to the satisfaction of vulgar appetites. It seems to me to smack of malfeasance in his office as historian of medieval Latin poetry that Max Manitius publishes his recent monograph on the *Culture, Learning and Literature of the Occident from 800 to 1100* without mentioning with a single word the MS of *Cambridge Songs*, without elucidation of their invaluable testimony for eleventh-century life, and with the statement that the sole exemplar of realistic profane poetry of this time is the novel, *Ruodlieb*, written about 1050 by a monk of Tegernsee.

It is, therefore, with something like a shock to preconceived opinions that we first become acquainted with a document like the *Vernal Sighs of a Woman*, which makes manifest that the ineradicable appetites and natural instincts of medieval humankind were no less vigorous in fact (though sometimes less articulate and self-assertive) than they had been in the age of Greece and Rome, than they were to be in the Renaissance. At any rate, here we have a girl who is sick at heart—her love or her baby or her faith in life is gone. She says so simply and rhythmically. If she had been Alcuin or Wipo or Ekkehard, you may be sure we should have had a school-poem of the business. But she was herself. Let us be unsurprised:

LIGHTLY BLOWS THE WIND OF SUMMER

Lightly blows the wind of summer,
And the sun, the warm new-comer,
Shines on earth, whose bosom bare
Melts in that dissolving air.

Now the ruddy spring goes out
With her festal robes about,
Shaking o'er the world her flowers
And her leaves on forest bowers.

Now the beasts their lairs are finding,
And sweet birds their nests are binding,
Singing in the greenwood trees
Of the joys of marriages.

Why must I behold this mirth,
Hear this rapture in the earth—
Why, when sound and sight denying,
All my heart is given to sighing?

For, alas, alone I sit,
Thinking wanly over it;
If my head lifts from my knee,
Then I neither hear nor see.

O thou spirit of the spring,
Hear me, help me—everything,
Flower and seed and frond are there—
But my soul is sick with care.   (11)

I am mindful of the folly of guessing the sex of the author of a medieval lyric, and so I may not be sure that a suffering woman wrote our plaintive song—yet it seems to me subtly feminine in imagery and presentment, and I believe in its author we have a contemporary sister of Roswitha of Gandersheim, or a predecessor of Héloïse and Marie de France. So sang then a heart-sick girl (or some clerk for her) about the year 1000. There is nothing of the church or school about the song—nor yet aught of the stock phrase of classical imitation or minstrel cant. Hers is the formula as old as the hills, as new as tomorrow, and as wide as the breath of man: Earth rejoices—my love is dead. Winterfeld called the poem a jewel of the modern lyric that is just awakening. I cannot see why it is necessarily modern or why it is just awakening. It is medieval.

With this song in our ears, the story in outline of the earlier medieval lyric, the Romanesque, comes to an end. And because of this long preamble to the tale of Goliard Verse and Latin Minnesong, we may now proceed with an easier conscience and a lighter heart to this second part of our study which will appear in another volume, and will attempt a differentiation between professional goliard songs and popular Latin love-poetry.

It may be that some, even much, of the foregoing book might have been omitted on the assumption that it repeated certain things already sufficiently known. But where the material is so vast as that of earlier medieval Latin poetry, where no sure lines of lyric demarcation have hitherto been laid down, where a new type of Romanesque begins to emerge from traditional classical and biblical backgrounds, where doctors (of philosophy) so carefully disagree as to all the symptoms of what I have labeled Romanesque poetry, where the vehicle in which many of its songs are written still unhappily remains so difficult a thing for us to read—why, I have been afraid not to go deeper into the foundations, not to circle more widely through kindred lyric expressions from Erin to Araby than I otherwise should ever have thought of doing. Despite this fact I pray that my reader will regard this volume as an attempt at appreciation and not at erudition. It is just because erudition has until now played so large a part in the criticism of early medieval songs, because the cultured amateur has not more easily commanded them, that profound misunderstandings regarding their nature and their scope have been so long current.

NOTES TO CHAPTER I

[1] See F. Haverfield's *The Roman Occupation of Britain*, revised by G. Macdonald (Oxford, 1924), pp. 171 ff.

[2] See B. W. Henderson's article on the Roman provincial system in *A Companion to Latin Studies* (Cambridge, 3d edit., 1921), pp. 398 ff.

[3] See T. G. Tucker, *Life in the Roman World of Nero and St. Paul* (New York, 1922), pp. 37-8.

[4] Tucker, *op. cit.*, p. 38.

[5] Rome alone seems to have possessed any such medium of communication as a newspaper. It was the custom in that city, as early as the first century of our era, to publish daily upon a white bulletin board an official report of such local news as was of general interest. Numerous copies of this *Roman Daily Advertiser* were carried swiftly into Gaul, as into every other portion of the empire, and were read with great curiosity, since male subscribers followed with keen eagerness whatever occurred in the capital and their womenfolk were mad to learn of the latest fashions and gossip of Rome. Of course, officially, the postal service was solely for government business, but doubtless the term was not too rigidly defined. See Ludwig Friedlander's *Town Life in Italy During the First Century* (Boston, 1902), p. 9.

[6] We shall never know anything adequate of the greatest work of the first century after Christ, for the chief witnesses of this age fixed all their interest in Rome—and it was not in Rome that the work was being done. Nor was it in the East where the seedling of Christianity was preparing for transplantation. If we could bargain with the writers of the first century, we should forego a great part of their laments over what was dead in Rome and Italy for a glimpse of what was growing in Africa, Gaul, and Spain. The Romanizing of the western provinces in particular was probably the most brilliant service ever rendered to civilization. Our side of Europe was twice saved from destruction, and very narrowly saved, by the vigorous Romanization of Gaul. There is something ludicrous, pathetic, and yet consoling in the thought that Roman Gaul was being made with marvelous rapidity all the while that morbid and sensational declaimers in Rome were painting the world as a crowd of profligate slaves. At the fall of the Republic fifty years before Christ, Toulouse was a mere military outpost in the backwoods. A century later it was a celebrated seat of learning. Cordova, formerly an ordinary place of trade, rose in even less time to send from a single house three leaders of the front rank to rule the literature of the capital: Lucan and the two Senecas. See *Collected Literary Essays*, by A. W. Verrall (Cambridge, 1913), pp. 3 f.

[7] See *The Roman Occupation of Britain* (1924), p. 173.

[8] See L. W. Lyde's *The Continent of Europe* (London, 1913), pp. 191 ff, and R. C. Bosanquet's article on provincial roads and travel in *A Companion to Latin Studies* (Cambridge, 3d edit., 1921), pp. 411-435.

[9] See S. Baring-Gould's *In Troubadour Land* (London, 1891), p. 246.

[10] See Bosanquet and Lyde, as above cited.

[11] *Ibid.*

[12] See G. Ferrero's essay on the development of Gaul in his *Characters and Events in Roman History* (New York, 1909), pp. 71-99.

[13] See Ramsay's *St. Paul the Traveler* (London, 1905).

[14] This bipartite division into "artistic" and "popular" songs really settles nothing as to the ultimate origin of a poetic model. At best such division may hope only to help define the manner of immediate transmission of verse. Who does not suspect a popular source for more than one elegy of Catullus, ode of Horace, eclogue of Vergil? (See Kirby Smith's rendering of the *Copa* in *Martial the Epigrammatist*, Johns Hopkins Press, 1920, p. 170). Even in the way of lyric types which seem to have a definite provenience in the Middle Ages, nothing is modern. It would seem, for example, that the *aube* or lovers' waking-song found its earliest beginning in the Provençal *alba* of the troubadours. And yet Athenæus, writing in the third century of our era, quotes a Locrian prototype:

> Now by the gods, what ails you? Don't
> Betray us—I implore you won't!
> But rise before he comes, or he
> Will do great harm to you—to me!
> Poor wretched me—oh look—the day
> Shines through the doorway—go, I pray!

Critics are right in doubting that just this version of the song is, in the strict sense of the words, either old or popular. But, as Kirby Smith says, this *alba* is older than the troubadours by a thousand years, and the mere existence of it is enough in itself to suggest that even in ancient Greece there were popular prototypes of those epigrams of second and third century B. C., which Ovid had before him.

[15] See W. Warde Fowler's note on the disappearance of the earliest Latin poetry (*Roman Essays and Interpretations*, Oxford, 1920, pp. 171 f.) and the most interesting parallel therein cited.

In the first half of the eighteenth century Germany and Italy invaded musical England in the person of Handel, a German by birth and an Italian by training. As a result, ancient English national music vanished almost entirely from the minds of Englishmen. It could not wholly disappear from the world, for it was in MS and in print and some of it survived in the cathedral services. The obliteration was less complete than with the old Latin songs. But none the less Handel was the Ennius of English musical history. So effectually did he and his great German successors wipe out the memory of the English music of the fifteenth and sixteenth centuries, that not even the all-pervading German research of today has ever reached it. The Germans know as little of it as the Greeks knew of the old Latin poetry; like the learned scholars of the Roman empire they remain unconscious of a fine field of inquiry.

[16] See W. P. Ker, *The Dark Ages* (New York, 1911), pp. 201 f. There seem to be two ways in which Latin was made available for popular poetry. Irregular Latin verse might be either in the classical forms used irregularly, or in forms not classical at all. But in both cases there is the common feature that quantity is neglected or, at any rate, not treated under the old rules. In both cases there is a rebellion against the Greek tradition of prosody introduced at Rome by the founders of Latin poetry under the Republic. This emancipation from the Greek rule of good verse sometimes, but not always, went with a strong metrical emphasis on

the accent, like that which in Greece itself was replacing the old verse measures with the new *political* line, the verse of the Greek ballads. In Latin there was more excuse for it than in Greek, because it was a return to the natural genius of the language. This of course does not make things any better from the classical point of view; but it increases the dignity of Romanesque Latin among modern accentual forms of verse, if it can in any way be traced back to the Saturnian Age. A pedigree of this sort has been attempted by some scholars (see Stengel's article on Romance versification in the second volume of *Gröbers Grundriss*, and Garrod's fine note in the *Oxford Book of Latin Verse*, pp. 505-512).

But whether Saturnian verse died out after the beginning of classical Latin poetry or survived in country places and came back in a new form first in Romanesque and later in French and Provençal, it is certain that the old Latin rhythms, before the Greek forms were introduced, had more likeness to modern verse in their accent than popular Greek (Romaic) verse has. It is known also that when the common people adopted classical measures they used them accentually, for in Latin the tunes of common speech interfered with the strict use of prosody. The Latin poets wrote like Homer as nearly as they could, but they could not escape from their language. In Vergil and Ovid there are traces of the Italian Faun—vestiges of the old poetic diction, an emphasis which is not Greek but comes down from the ancient days before the *vates* and the Camenæ had made way for the Greek Muses. Greek meters were brought into agreement with the accent of Latin speech.

[17] See W. P. Ker, *op. cit.*, p. 203. The accentual effect here is the same as in the rhythm of Tiberianus, and the regard for quantity equally distinct, though not quite so thorough-going. In the interval there were many poets who kept the same sort of measure, among them Prudentius and Fortunatus. In this particular kind of trochaic verse it proved to be fairly easy to adapt the Greek form to popular use without spoiling its original character altogether. It was the favorite verse for popular songs, like the quoted lampoons of Cæsar's army; it was much employed in hymns, divided into two versicles like the eights and sevens of the hymn-books. From William of Poitou to *Locksley Hall* and *A Toccata of Galuppi*, and later ("Where the dawn comes up like thunder"), it has been at the service of modern poets and yet has never lost its ancient character. Trochaic verse is such—so widely distributed and so much at home—that Latin verses of this sort appeal to every one familiarly. Latin poets very early gave them their modern quality by trusting a good deal to the accent.

[18] In his *Oxford Book of Latin Verse* (1921, p. x), H. W. Garrod tells very clearly the story of their origin. The first Latin poets, he says, are the priests. But behind the priests are the people—moved by the same religious beliefs and fears but inclined, as happens everywhere, to make of their holy day a holiday. And thus a different species of Latin verse, known to us chiefly in connection with the harvest home and with marriage ceremonial—the so-called fescennine poetry—arises. This poetry is dictated by much the same needs as that of the priests. It is a charm against *fascinum* (the evil eye) and hence, fescennine. The principal constituent element in this body of verse is obscene mockery. This obscenity was magical. But just as it takes two to make a quarrel, so the obscene mockery of the fescennine verses required two principals. And here in the improvisations of the harvest home we must seek the origins of two important types of Latin poetry—drama and satire.

NOTES TO CHAPTER II

[1] It is difficult to estimate the share oriental influences had in transforming the methods of government in Gaul, and in corrupting, or at any rate modifying, the character of the Gauls among whom the Orientals settled. But in his *Syria As a Roman Province* (Oxford, 1916, p. 178), E. S. Bouchier presents a convenient summary of this matter. Syrian influences in Gaul were presented mainly through the medium of Greek literature, art, or religion, and only as at least externally Greek were they at all widely accepted. It cannot be said that prior to the Arab conquests of the seventh century the captured Orient took prisoner the fierce conqueror, as Greece had done to Rome towards the end of the Republic. Rather the undying spirit of Greece had seized on fresh instruments by which to act on the western European world, undergoing some modifications in the process but still quite recognizable. No Gallo-Romans, unless like St. Jerome they had a special interest in the origins of Christianity, would learn the Aramaic language, or be readily brought into contact with the wild fancies of oriental myths except in a much sobered Greek version. The Syrian cults which spread to Gaul had lost the extravagances which characterized the shrines of Hierapolis and Aphaca; and the gods had been sufficiently syncretized to pass without much violence as Jupiter, Apollo, or Venus. When a true Syrian worship was presented in the West in an undisguised form (as by Elagabalus at Rome), it was received with laughter or contempt. Even in the case of Christianity it is almost certain, humanly speaking, that it would have remained an insignificant local sect if the genius of Hellenized Jews from outside Syria—Paul of Tarsus, Barnabas of Cyprus, Appollos of Alexandria, and many more—had not let fall the more exclusive features, asceticism, circumcision, and community of property, and formed its doctrine into a system capable of philosophical expression.

[2] It will be recalled that in his *L'enseignement des lettres classiques d'Ausone à Alcuin* (Paris, 1905, pp. 268 ff.) Roger places but small faith in the reputed flourishing of Greek letters from the fourth to the seventh century either in Brittany or in Ireland. He concludes that if in the sixth and seventh centuries Greek was not quite unknown to the Irish, then they knew it only as the teachers of following centuries did. The best of their knowledge probably sprang from collections of glosses in their possession—to warrant the attribution of a fuller command of Greek to Columban, say, or to Gildas, requires the authority of more definite documents than we now have. I do not object to Roger's decision; it is everything except human.

[3] See T. R. Glover, *Life and Letters in the Fourth Century* (Cambridge, 1901), pp. 125 ff; *Travel and Travellers of the Middle Ages*, ed. A. P. Newton (New York, 1926), chapters ii and iii.

[4] See Franz Cumont, *The Oriental Religions in Roman Paganism*, with an introductory essay by Grant Showerman (Chicago, 1911), pp. x, 196 ff.

[5] For a discussion of this whole matter of Gothic influence on early Christian art in Gaul, see Josef Strzygowski's epoch-making book on *Altai-Iran und Völkerwanderung* (Leipzig, 1917), especially chap. v, sec. 3Be, pp. 287-294. His theories are open to the correction that Romans possessed the dome and the vault several

centuries before the collapse of the Empire of the West; and that dome and vault were standard in Byzantine architecture.

[6] The best summary I know of the social and political conditions making for the growth and spread of Gothic art and civilization is in the twelfth chapter of G. W. S. Friedrichsen's *The Gothic Version of the Gospels. A Study of its Style and Textual History* (Oxford, 1926), pp. 162-168. From this summary, with (I hope) some permissible alteration in order to gain a closer argument for my immediate subject, I excerpt the following picture:

So long as the Goths in Italy were but the mercenaries of the empire and their sojourn there conditioned by the terms of their service, their art and ideas are likely not to have had much, if any, influence upon Roman life; the same restriction applies in the case of auxiliaries on foreign service with the legions in Gaul, and to those Ostrogoths who, since the debâcle of the Hunnish dominion, had trekked restlessly through the Balkan provinces until Theodoric the Amal led them into the fair Ausonian fields.

But the beginning of the fifth century saw a complete change in the relationship between the Goths and the Latin-speaking world. The foreign mercenaries were now masters of the soil; billets now were settled homes, and by the grace of Cæsar erstwhile settlements became mighty kingdoms. In 412 Athaulf led his Visigoths into Gaul, where the kingdom of Toulouse maintained itself until Chlovis drove its rulers across the Pyrenees into Spain. Athaulf, who set out to obliterate the Roman name, eventually came to desire nothing more than that his people should live under Roman forms of government; and his marriage to Placidia, the daughter of Theodosius, may be said to symbolize the civic and political union of Visigoth and Roman.

Since 476, under Odoacer, the Goths had been settled in northern Italy, and when n 493 Theodoric the Ostrogoth rode triumphing into Ravenna, it was as virtual king of Italy. From this time forth the Goth was master of Rome, and if the conquered Latin was to enjoy the same subject rights as the victorious Goth, it was by grace of the benevolent despotism of Theodoricus Rex. When, therefore, we approach the time of the efflorescence of all the arts in Ravenna—say, the second quarter of the sixth century—the Burgundian and the Visigoth had enjoyed over one hundred years of settled rule in Gaul and Spain; three generations of Vandals had indulged themselves as masters of luxurious Carthage; and in Italy the Ostrogoth had learned to appreciate, at least since 493, the amenities of the *Romana civilitas*.

[7] See J. Strzygowski, *loc. cit.* In his *Origin of Christian Church Art* (Oxford, 1923, p. 77), Strzygowski says: "The regions which first followed Persia in employing vaulted roofs for their basilicas were not those in immediate relations with the Mediterranean area and its essentially Græco-Roman culture, but those connected through an active commerce with the main sources of vaulted architecture in the East. The decisive influence in dissemination seems to have been that exercised by the mass migration of the Goths westward from the Black Sea. This people and the craftsmen who went with them built vaulted structures in groups where hitherto there had been only single, if conspicuous, examples, as at Milan."

[8] See Ernest Barker's *The Crusades* (London, 1923), p. 104.

[9] For the whole matter of the decline of university education in the last century of paganism, see J. W. H. Walden, *The Universities of Ancient Greece* (New

York, 1909), pp. 109-129. At this time the important university centers in the East were Athens, Alexandria, Antioch, Bertyrus, Constantinople, and Nicomedia. After Julian's death there were still sophists at Athens but their vogue was much diminished—in the fifth century there was danger that Athens would relapse into a quiet rural village. Alexandria suffered greatly in the year 391, when the library in the Serapeum was destroyed, but scholars never failed to flock thither, and for another century at least her university was famous for philosophy, mathematics, and astronomy. In the fifth century Antioch still maintained her school of sophistry and Bertyrus hers of law, though the palmy days of both were gone. In 425 the university of Constantinople was put on a new basis and continued to offer courses in philosophy, law, rhetoric, and grammar (in Latin and Greek). In the fifth century Cæsarea (Cappadocia) was the seat of grammatical and rhetorical disciplines, while at Ancyra (Galatia) there was a school of philosophy. An important station of sophistry toward the end of the century was Gaza in Palestine.

[10] Oddly enough it was in the very days that Julian's envoys to Delphi returned with the prophetic response:

Tell ye the king: To the ground hath fallen the glorious dwelling—
Now no longer hath Phœbus a cell, or a laurel prophetic;
Hushed is the voiceful spring, and quenched the oracular fountain,

that the last stronghold of the pagan faith, the neo-Platonic school at Athens, was making ready the most powerful message that the ancient world had for the Middle Ages. Tinged with eastern mysticism, touching (according to St. Augustine) every fundamental truth except the doctrine of the Incarnation, conjunct in authority with the Hebrew prophets, the foundation of angelology, encyclopedic for Jews, Arabs, and Christians—neo-Platonism flowed like an engulfing stream of imagistic thought across a thousand otherwise sterile fields of medieval expression. See Walden, *op. cit.*, pp. 125 f; A. E. Taylor, *Platonism and Its Influence* (Boston, 1924), opening chapter.

NOTES TO CHAPTER III

[1] See C. H. Haskins's essay on the spread of ideas in the Middle Ages, *Speculum*, I (1926), 19 ff.

[2] See V. L. P. Thomsen, *Über den Einfluss der germanischen Sprachen auf die finnisch-lappischen* (Halle, 1870).

[3] In his most important survey of oldest Germanic literature (*Die altgermanische Dichtung*, 1923, pp. 20 f.) Andreas Heusler summarizes certain notable Gothic contributions to western European art. About the year 200 in Scythian South Russia the Goths became neighbors and rulers of peoples who dwelt at a far remove from the main mass of the Germans. In this region the Goths made first-hand acquaintance with a simplified offshoot of the Greek ethos. As a result their artistic expression changed utterly. A new type of decoration based upon interlacing convolutions representing the conventionalized limbs of dragons and birds ("animalized line-ornament") was thereafter passed on to their kindred tribes by the Goths of the Black Sea district. And for several centuries throughout Europe this animal decoration was the hallmark of Germanic artistic heritage. Its finest development, and the longest survival of this form, occurred in northern territory.

Other matters than such arts-and-crafts patterning wandered back to the stay-at-homes in distant Scandinavia: the runic script appears to have reached northern territory not later than the third century and to have been transmitted southwards again to the West Germans (see von Friesen's article in Hoops, *Reallexikon*). Mythical conceptions, too, were carried back from the Black Sea, and traditional fables like that of Loki in Fetters, originally an earthquake giant and cousin german to Prometheus (see Axel Olrik, *Ragnarök*, 1922, chap. v), although we must not forget the chances are rather against the acceptance of the Caucasus district as a germinating center of such materials and favor their spread from some culturally more significant region, perhaps from Greece itself (see Kaarle Krohn, *Die folkloristiche Methode*, Oslo, 1926). It may be permissible to add as Gothic transmission such cult-rites as the Complaint for Dead Balder, if this prove a descendant of Semitic Tamuz and Adonis planctus (see Neckel, *Die Überlieferungen vom Gotte Balder*, 1920, passim). And it is not impossible that the hieratic type of Othin worship may derive from Gothic Southeast rather than from the German-Celtic divide at the Rhine.

But one question outweighs in importance all the foregoing. Just what was the state of affairs that conditioned the apparently new creation of the Goths: laudatory ode and heroic song—not to forget the very office of court-poet itself? For with Gothic heroic song, and in its unstrophic measures, heroic legend came to the other Germanic nations. But this source no longer points to the older Gothic home in the Far East between Don and Dniester—this the Goths sent forth from their later settlements at the time of Attila and Theodoric. (See Heusler, *op. cit.*, pp. 149 ff.).

At a much later period, in the ninth to the eleventh centuries, the Russian and Byzantine East again loom on the horizon of North Germanic peoples through the forays and trade settlements of the Varangians (the Vikings of the Orient), as well as through their service in the household regiment of Eastern Roman emperors. But this connection brought the Norsemen little besides a core of novelistic material. (See F. R. Schröder, *Germanisch-romanische Monatsschrift*, 1920, pp. 204 ff., 281 ff.).

[4] See Hans Naumann's summarizing essay in *Deutsche Vierteljahrsschrift für Literaturwissenschaft und Geistesgeschichte*, III (1925), 642 ff., entitled "Die neue Perspektive. Ein Literaturbericht zum frühgermanischen Altertum." He says (p. 645): "So far as we can determine the character of Old German, it meets us as a sober primitive peasant tongue distinctly practical in inclination, a sheerly natural phenomenon prone to avoid every imaginative flight. Early contact of Old German with Roman institutions on the Rhine and the Danube seems to have changed its manner but little, only increasing its practical and technical vocabulary. Subversive alteration came first with the Gothic, which was the earliest Germanic language to take on a loftier culture. This newer Gothic had two aims—the founding of a Christianized ecclesiastical idiom of a Hellenistic cast and a highly literary tone—the minting of that 'poetic speech about 600' which was the garment of heroic song."

[5] Starting with theories of epic style developed by W. P. Ker in *Epic and Romance* (2d edit., London, 1908) and Andreas Heusler in *Lied und Epos in germanischer Sagendichtung* (Dortmund, 1905), Jan de Vries insists upon the development of such balladry in its northern home, in the north of Germany on the boundaries of the Danish kingdom. In his *Traditie en Persoonlijkheid in de oudger-*

maansche epische kunst (Arnhem, 1926, pp. 11-13) de Vries says it is no chance that we find the oldest traces of this poetry in just the above-named region, for that was the Ionia of the Germanic tribes. From the earliest days of historical surmise the great importance of the Dano-German border zone is manifest. Since even in the Stone and Bronze ages this district was a center of Germanic culture. (Query: How does de Vries know this culture was Germanic?) De Vries goes on to say that several recent investigations have proved the origin in this North Sea littoral of various phenomena of epic poetry which thereafter spread across a large part of the Germanic peoples—like the ancient meters that arose first in southern Denmark, Schleswig, and Holstein, later to appear in the strophic verse-structure of Scandinavian poetry as well as in the alliterating poetry of Anglo-Saxon, Old Saxon, and Old High German. (See R. C. Boer, *Studien over de metriek van het alliteratievers*, Amsterdam, 1916, pp. 227 ff.) According to de Vries, the Hildebrandslied already displays such degeneration of metrical structure in alliterative verse that it must be regarded as the end of a poetical era of development, not as the beginning of one. It is obvious to de Vries that such a German, epic, alliterating verse parallels in its early growth, development, and decay, a similar earlier body of poetry that existed on the North Sea coastal territory.

De Vries adds that the agreement of linguistic formulæ and conventionalized symbolism in Anglo-Saxon and Old Norse poetry harks back to a tradition of style developed much earlier than our oldest preserved examples. He believes Magnus Olsen's brilliant explanation of the Eggjum runestone gives us a glimpse of creative artistry long antecedent to the oldest Eddic ballads, which must have an unwearying poetic tradition of centuries behind them because of their self-conscious and consistent periphrastic glossaries. (See Olsen, *Eggjum-stenens indskrift med de ældre runer*, Christiania, 1919.) But let us not bury ourselves in guesses regarding the content and origin of this primitive northern balladry, counsels de Vries. It is impossible to build a bridge back to Tacitus. Germanic songs certainly existed in the day of Tacitus, they are in decay in the eighth century, and doubtless continuity of some sort exists. We cannot say anything definite about the form of this missing epic poetry. The oldest alliterative verse is trochaic trimeter which agrees with Germanic speech rhythm; therefore this verse may have arisen from a stylized prose. Furthermore, in passages which seem to belong to the oldest strata of the Edda, we have a mingling of prose and poetry—as we have in early Celtic and in the traditions of the Toradjas of central Celebes—so it does not seem rash to guess that the primitive Germanic epic form was a *chantefable*. Of the heroes who were celebrated by it, we know nothing.

[6] See J. B. Bury's *History of the Later Roman Empire* (London, 1923), I, 98.

[7] See Otto Seeck, *Geschichte der Untergang der antiken Welt* (Berlin, 1910), vol. IV.

[8] Of course, even earlier, Ovid's ladies were wearing German wigs.

[9] See O. M. Dalton's *The Letters of Sidonius* (Oxford, 1915), I, liv ff.

[10] See F. J. C. Hearnshaw's Introduction to *Mediæval Contributions to Modern Civilization* (New York, 1922), p. 17.

[11] E. A. Freeman, "The Franks and the Gauls" in *Western Europe in the Fifth Century (Historical Essays, Series 1)*; Samuel Dill, *Roman Society in the Last Century of the Western Empire* (London, 2d edit., 1921), particularly Bks. iv and v.

NOTES TO CHAPTER IV

[1] The analogy is fertile in many ways, says Mackail, most strikingly of all in the way in which both of these bodies of epic romance ignore history, forget difference of race and severance of language, fail even to mention the cataclysm which separates that actual or imagined past from the present. For instance, we do not find in Arthurian literature any allusion to the Norman conquest of Great Britain. This literature and its whole environment are shut off from the world of the twelfth century by an absolute barrier. There is no hint that the medieval world, whether by slow change or violent shock, has somehow been made out of the Arthurian world—the question how one came from the other does not even rise. So also it is with Homer. In both cases, too, the seed-ground of the new poetry is in a grouping of countries around a central sea. And that sea is not only a highway of commerce and migration, but the fluid medium through which the movements of the human mind spread and communicated themselves so readily that they appear at the same moment and independently in many different quarters. In Homer as in Arthur there is the individuality of an age but not of a country. See J. W. Mackail, *Lectures on Greek Poetry* (London, 1909).

[2] The modern man of culture is denied the possession of a great field of poetry because of his imperfect comprehension of the daughters of the old common Latin tongue. For example, how rarely can an English speaking person enjoy to the full the halfsaid thing—equivoque, innuendo, nuance, hidden shrug, and stifled sigh— in French, Italian, or Spanish verse.

[3] At this point it would but cloud the issue to add as side-line ancestry those eighth and ninth-century Arabic schools which, while not a part of western civilization proper, were still active teachers of poetic creation in the Middle Ages.

[4] And in this procedure we must not be dismayed, if at times we notice a marked divergence in character between ancient and Romanesque verse, so that for the moment all idea of an essential unity between the two seems to be in abeyance. In his essay on Science and Philosophy as Unifying Forces (see Marvin's *The Unity of Western Civilization*, Oxford, 1915, pp. 162 ff.), L. T. Hobhouse clears this difficulty for us neatly:

There are three sorts of integrality of connection between the old and the new world of ideas—a unity of character—the unity involved in continuous descent from a common origin—the unity of effective interconnection and mutual dependence. These senses of the term unity are confused by many writers but should be clearly distinguished before any useful inquiry can be made.

The unity of character in poetry is a different thing from continuity of historical development, since in the course of a few decades a civilization may radically change its character; it may even lose all the specific features of its own family and come into closer resemblance with others of quite distinct parentage.

Again, unity of character is not the same thing as the effective interconnection and coöperation of different centers. On the contrary, such coöperation is of most value where there is a marked difference in character, where the lack of a quality in one body is counteracted by a surplus in another.

Thus these three forms of poetic unity are distinct, but if distinct, they are not unrelated. Naturally, where there is a common origin for poetry, many traits of the primitive unity of character are likely to persist, and where there is effective intercommunication many differences will be rubbed off. At least, we may be assured that the poetry of Europe, like its philosophy and its science, has gone backward and forward as a unity, and will continue so to do.

[5] Rather than attempt a synthesis of my own, I reproduce the gist of Alexander von Humboldt's famous exordium from his *Ansichten der Natur*.

[6] See A. Lang's chapter on heroic and romantic myths, in vol. II of his *Myth, Ritual and Religion* (London, 1899), pp. 300 ff.

[7] Walter Headlam, *A Book of Greek Verse* (Cambridge, 1907).

NOTES TO CHAPTER V

[1] See Mackail, *Select Epigrams from the Greek Anthology*, p. 32: The literary treatment of the passion of love is one of the matters in which the ancient world stands farthest apart from the modern world. Perhaps the action of love on human lives differs but little from one age to another, but the form in which it is expressed was altered in western Europe in the Middle Ages, and ever since we have spoken a different language. Strangely enough in this regard, the *Nealce* of Petronius finds its closest parallels in the lyrics of the Elizabethan Age.

[2] Immediately following the epigrams assigned to Seneca, Codex Vossianus, Q. 86, gives sixteen epigrams, each headed by the word *item*. Of these, two are quoted by Fulgentius as the work of Petronius. Especially in view of the fact that they all bear a marked family resemblance to one another, there is, therefore, a strong presumption that they are all by the author of the *Satyricon*. Further, there are eleven epigrams published by Binet in his edition of Petronius (Poitiers, 1579) from a MS originally in the cathedral library of Beauvais, but now lost. The first of the series is quoted by Fulgentius as being by Petronius, and there is no reason for doubting the accuracy of Binet or his MS as to the rest. These poems are followed by eight other epigrams, the first two of which Binet ascribes to Petronius on stylistic grounds, but without MS authority. Lastly, four epigrams are preserved by Codex Vossianus F., iii, under the title Petronii; of these, the first two are found in the extant portions of the *Satyricon*. The evidence for the Petronian authorship of these thirty-seven poems is not conclusive, but the evidence against such authorship is of the slightest. See Bæhrens, *Poetæ Latini Minores*, IV, 74-89, 90-100, 101-108, 120, 121; Haseltine's edition of Petronius (Loeb Library), and especially H. E. Butler, *Post-Augustan Poetry from Seneca to Juvenal* (Oxford, 1909), pp. 134 f.

[3] Propertius, in whose Umbrian blood there was possibly some admixture of the Celtic, speaks of himself as *mollis in omnes*. H. W. Garrod, *The Oxford Book of Latin Verse* (Oxford, 1921), p. xviii. Of the makers of Roman poetry very few indeed are Roman. Livius and Ennius were half-Greeks from Calabria. Nævius and Lucilius were natives of Campania. Accius and Plautus—and later Propertius—were Umbrian. Cæcilius was an Insubrian Gaul. Catullus, Bibaculus, Ticidas, Cinna, Vergil, were Transpadanes. Asinius Gallus came from Gallia Narbonensis, Horace from Apulia. Of the considerable poets of the empire, Lucan, Seneca, Martial, are of Spanish birth. A Spanish origin has been conjectured for Silius. Claudian is an Alexandrian, Ausonius a Gaul, Statius and Juvenal are Campanians,

Persius an Etrurian. Rome's rôle in the world is the absorption of outlying genius. See Garrod, *op. cit.*, pp. xv f.

⁴ The subtle and moving effects in the *Eclogues* of this *molle ingenium* are well characterized by Mackail when he speaks of the note of brooding pity which pierces the immature and tremulous cadences of Vergil's earliest period. We are passed out of classicism into what we call romanticism. The Celtic spirit—for that is what it is—is overmastering. It constantly girds a poet and carries him whither he would not. See Garrod, *op. cit.*, p. xix.

⁵ The argument all through here is Garrod's.

⁶ *Lydia*, poem, verses 104 to 183 (end) of *Diræ*. Despite its attribution to Valerius Cato by Ellis (*Amer. Jour. Philol.*, 1882, pp. 271-284; *ibid.*, 1890, pp. 1-15), its publication in 1907 in the Oxford text of *Appendix Vergiliana*, and the opinion of Lindsay (*Class. Rev.*, 1918, p. 62), most Latinists today join with Tyrrell in considering it the work of an unknown poet contemporary with Petronius. See Tenney Frank, *Vergil* (New York, 1922), p. 131.

⁷ E. E. Sikes, *Roman Poetry* (New York, 1923), p. 9. The reader will, of course, recognize my restatement of Lanson's famous passage in the preceding paragraph on romanticism.

⁸ Somehow I cannot feel with Sikes that Quintilian's failure to say a word in this connection of Catullus is primarily due to his ranking the latter as a writer of lampoon and epigram, and therefore technically outside the lyrical canon. It would seem more reasonable to presume that Quintilian and other critics of the early Empire found Catullus too prone to be guided by his emotions, too apt to be unreticent and self-revelatory, too preoccupied with his sex and his soul, too slow to subordinate reason to feeling, too little restrained by the rules governing an artistic if corrupt generation, to be considered in the first flight of aspirants for lyric fame. But see Sikes, *op. cit.*, pp. 9 ff.

Nepos in "Atticus," lists Lucretius and Catullus as the leading poets of the late Republic, and Velleius Paterculus some sixty years later (circa 30 A. D.) lists Lucretius, Catullus, and Varro in the same connection. This may or may not be significant of critical insight. Sikes himself declares that an urban life, highly artificial and conventional, dominated by "good taste," shrinking from any form of eccentricity, could not foster the intensity of personal emotion which overflows in lyrical utterance. Sikes grants that the statement that the Augustans were intent on repressing "enthusiasm" may seem in flat opposition to the subjective poetry of the elegiac writers who are chiefly occupied with their own loves or (as in Ovid's *Tristia*) their own misfortunes. But he contends rightly that Propertius and Ovid were not minded to be *lyrical*; they made no song of either their passion or their woe; they may have felt deeply and truly, but their feeling was restrained by the code of refinement and good breeding. The elegy must conform to the character of a Roman gentleman, who may be a profligate but must never forget to be an artist. Since Roman art was typical rather than personal, the lover must not emphasize the individuality of his mistress or himself. Celia or Delia or Corinna, says Sikes, is any mistress for any lover.

NOTES TO CHAPTER VI

[1] See de Labriolle, *History and Literature of Christianity from Tertullian to Boethius* (New York, 1925), pp. 39 ff. and 52 ff. No important work of Latin Christian literature appears before the end of the second century. The reasons for this are simple. Cicero had said *Græca leguntur in omnibus fere gentibus; latina suis finibus, exiguis sane, continenter*. And since his days, increasingly during the early centuries of the Empire, though Latin was the official language of the state, Greek had become the Mediterranean dialect. To some its popularity might seem to threaten the continuance of the Latin tongue, though, when we note that tombstones in remote country districts in the western provinces bear Latin inscriptions, the alarm, as we now see, was needless. Yet Greek on the higher cultural level had made a thorough conquest of the Roman world; it was in everyday use throughout the West. Orient and Occident were linked together by extensive commercial intercourse. From Greece, from the Euxine, from Syria, and from Egypt, merchandise streamed into Brindisi, Ostia, and Pozzuoli; and was sent by land to Rome, and redistributed across Spain, Africa, and Gaul. The cults, customs, arts, ideas, and speech of Levantine merchants infested the West.

Greek had been spoken for a long time in southern Gaul. The traces left by the Phocæans had not been entirely effaced, and the infusion of Greek elements was continually replenishing this linguistic foundation. Emigrants from Asia and Syria were constantly ascending the Rhone and the Saone, carrying with them portable bazaars of assorted goods, or establishing general stores on the banks of these rivers. Claudius, Nero, and Hadrian did what they could to encourage the general use of Greek. Favorinus of Arles (A. D. 70-80) lectured at Rome in Greek, as Apuleius did at Carthage a little later. Elienus of Preneste, who never left Italy, rendered his books in Greek, and passed as a native Athenian. The stoic Cornutus, who numbered among his pupils Persius and Lucan, made use of Greek exclusively for his philosophic essays. In fact, the setback from Greek to Latin was not strong until the fourth century, when men like Rufinus and Jerome translated the most notable productions of Greek Christian thought into Latin for the use of the western world. A great gain was then made for the Roman vocabulary—the poverty of which had been deplored by Lucretius and Seneca—and Latin then enriched itself by superabundant additions to its stock.

See de Labriolle, *op. cit.*, p. 518. After Boethius, Cassiodorus, and Isidore of Seville, the framework of the intellectual life of the Middle Ages was established for a long time. A natural line of demarcation at this point closes the history of Latin Christian literature, in his argument. But this dismissal of de Labriolle's seems to me—to say the least—blithe.

[2] A mere listing of the poets of these centuries shows their sterility from the classicist's viewpoint: Paccius, Codrus, Rubrenus Lappa, Voconius Victor, Parthenius, Catullus, Brutianus, Cerrinus, Marrius Atinas, Titinius Capito, Manlius Vopiscus, Faustus, Julius Cerealis, Caninius Rufus, Atticus, Helvidius, Nardus, Collinus, Valerius Pudens, Sulpicius Maximus, Pollius Felix, Novius Vindex, Atedius Melior, Faustinus, Rufus, Stertinius Avitus, Septimius Severus, Canius Rufus, Passennus Paulus, Calpurnius Piso, Sentius Augurinus, Silius Proculus,

Cluvienus, Varro, Vergilius Romanus, Pomponius Bassulus, Lentulus, Hostilius—such are the small fry that swam about in the turbid waters of epic and idyl, lyric and elegy before the reign of Hadrian. Nor does the matter grow better thereafter: Annianus, Septimius Serenus, Paconius, Alfius Avitus, Marianus, Julius Paulus, Marullus, Aemilius Severianus, Sulpicius Apollinaris, Terentianus Maurus, Serenus Sammonicus, Albinus, Vespa, Pentadius, Paulus Quæstor, Chalcidius—these are the stars of lesser magnitude before Ausonius. When compared with Augustan models, a sorry list indeed.

[3] In his *Latin Literature* (New York, 1895), p. 32, Mackail etches the picture of Greek ascendancy on our mind: Though two centuries were still to pass before the foundation of Constantinople, the center of gravity of the huge fabric of government was already passing from Italy to the Balkan peninsula. *Italy itself was becoming one of the western provinces.* Nature seemed to have fixed the eastern limit of the Latin language at the Adriatic, and even in Italy the Greek tongue was equally familiar with Latin to the educated classes. From Plutarch to Lucian, Greek authors completely predominate over the Latin. Although the tradition of the classical Roman manner took long to die away, the classical Roman writers themselves completely cease with Suetonius (died 160). A new Latin, *that of the Middle Ages*, was already rising to take the place of the speech handed down by the Republic to the Empire. The one unassailable fortress of Latin, *par excellence*, was the extraordinary body of legal literature.

[4] See H. E. Butler, *Post-Augustan Poetry* (Oxford, 1909), the first chapter of which deals with the decline of Roman poetry after the principate of Augustus.

[5] See H. W. Garrod, *Oxford Book of Latin Verse* (Oxford, 1921), p. xv.

[6] See H. E. Butler, *op. cit.*, pp. 1, 10, 12.

[7] See H. W. Garrod, *op. cit.*, p. xvi.

[8] See Bouchier, *Life and Roman Letters in Roman Africa* (Oxford, 1913), chapter v, on Fronto and his circle.

[9] See Mackail, *Latin Literature*, p. 238: Alike in the naive and almost childlike simplicity of its general structure, and in its minute and intricate ornament, like that of a diapered wall or a figured tapestry where hardly an inch of space is ever left blank—this *elocutio novella* is much more akin to the manner of the thirteenth or fourteenth-century Romance idiom than to that of classical Roman. In its delicacy of phrasing and its romantic flavor it can be seen best of all perhaps in the English rendition by Walter Pater of Fronto's allegory of the Creation of Sleep (*Marius the Epicurean*, chapter xiii).

[10] See Mackail, *Latin Literature*, p. 240: The first thing in the style of Apuleius that strikes a reader accustomed to classical Latin is not daring tropes, nor accumulation of sonorous phrases, but the perpetual refinement of diction which keeps curiously weighing and rejecting words, giving every other one an altered value or an unaccustomed setting. In Apuleius the simple organism of archaic prose is artificially imitated by breaking up all the structure into which the language had been wrought through the handling of centuries. In the ordinary sense of the word, half the phrases of the *Metamorphoses* are barely Latin. The story is mere groundwork which Apuleius overlays with fantastic embroidery—it appeals to him, of course, as a professed mystic and a dabbler in magic, but mainly as a *décadent*, whose art seeks out strange experiences and romantic passions no less than novel

rhythms and exotic diction—a brooding sense of magic is over the whole. See also Bouchier, *Life and Letters in Roman Africa*, p. 65.

[11] See Mackail, *Latin Literature*, p. 258: Much of the pronunciation of modern Italian may be traced in Commodian's remarkable accentuation of some words; like Italian, our poet throws the accent back from a long syllable, slides it forward upon a short one. Assonance is used freely but there is no more rhyming than occurs in poetry of the late empire. Not only in pronunciation but in grammatical inflection do the beginnings of Italian appear—case-forms of the different declensions merge, inflections dwindle away before the free use of prepositions, as we find also in the *Pervigilium Veneris*.

[12] We find what we should expect, viz., that in the various Christian poems produced in Africa from the middle of the third century, often by men of some education, measures and accentuation of a popular type are introduced in preference to the display of classical learning, which the Church long discountenanced. See Bouchier, *Life and Letters in Roman Africa*, p. 89.

[13] See Mackail, *Latin Literature*, p. 264: Up to the age of Constantine Gaul had enjoyed practical immunity from barbarian invasion and had had only a moderate share of the civil wars which throughout the third century desolated all parts of the empire. In wealth and civilization and in the arts of peace Gaul probably held the foremost place among the provinces. Marseilles, Narbonne Toulouse, Bordeaux, Autun, Rheims, and Treves, all possessed flourishing schools of oratory. The last-named city came to be a frequent seat of the imperial government of the western provinces and, like Milan, a more important center of public life than Rome.

[14] See Ker, *Dark Ages*, pp. 204 ff: Here is a successful transition from Classical to Romanesque and medieval form. Iambic dimeter becomes an octosyllabic line without strict rule of quantity; yet for all that it may preserve its identity. Between the correct verse *A solis ortus cardine* and the irregular rhythmic line *Rex æterne domine*, there is indeed, an enormous technical difference, but not such as to destroy the identity of type at the back of both; not even though the rhythmical verse drop out the opening syllable and put spondees where they ought not to be. It has been remarked by W. M. Lindsay that lines from some of the early tragedians read almost like those from a Christian accentual hymn, for instance, Ennius's *O magna templa caelitum commixta stellis splendidis*.

The hymns of Ambrose and his school, in iambic dimeter, are in the same position with regard to later accentual hymns in this verse as we have seen the *Pervigilium Veneris* to be in relation to later accentual trochaics. The Ambrosian hymns began by respecting quantity and accent together, and were followed by rhythmical poems which neglected the classical quantities. It should be observed that Ambrose does not consistently make accent coincide with quantity in his hymns— variations are frequent. But in the great majority of his verses the word-accent falls on the strong syllable of an iambic foot.

[15] See Benedetto Croce's *History; Its Theory and Practice* (New York, 1921), pp. 202 f.

[16] Croce, *op. cit.*, p. 214.

[17] See Ker, *Dark Ages*, p. 136: The *Dialogues* were translated into Anglo-Saxon and French. They are a series of stories intended to correspond in the West to the *Vitæ Patrum*, the lives of the saints in the desert, the widely read collection

of miracles whose vogue appeared to Gregory rather unjust to the fame of the holy men of Italy. It is not meditation, speculation, or devotion that unbends the mind of Gregory in his *Dialogues*—it is memoirs, the record of occurrences. The author makes up for his well-known scorn of polite literature by the stores of legend with which his book is filled, legend that represents, as no mere history could, the common mind of the sixth century. It has no limits, no scruples. It tells how St. Benedict in a vision saw the whole world brought together in one glance; how Father Equitius charged the devil to depart out of a nun; how the hermit of Lipari saw Theodoric the Great on the day of his death carried in bonds between Pope John and Symmachus and thrown in the Volcano; how the anchorite of Samnium took a stick to the bears that came for his beehives.

The other books of Gregory were studied everywhere in the Middle Ages: the *Pastoral Care*, the *Homilies*, the *Moralia*, a commentary on Job. This last is one of the reservoirs in the history of literature—a comprehensive book that gathers the results of older sources and in its turn becomes the main source for everything beneath it in order of time.

[18] Although on several occasions he wrote with remarkable insight and touch of the epigrammatists of the *Greek Anthology*, yet in his book on Latin literature Mackail makes no reference to the existence of a Roman counterpart of the famous Hellenistic collection. Likewise in his discussion of Petronius, Mackail has no word for those epigrams from the *Latin Anthology* with which we open our argument for the Romanesque lyric. In his book on the Silver Age, Summers accords the poems of Petronius found in the anthology the faint praise that damns. He says they are simply brief records of passing impressions or emotions and personal experiences, comparable with the sonnets of modern times or with the epigrams in the *Greek Anthology*. He acknowledges their elegance and polish, but says alas to the trifling nature of their contents, labeling them mere *vers de société*. Further, Summers excludes Petronius from his section on lyric and amatory verse, saying that neither the verses of Cæsius Bassus nor of any other lyric poet of the Silver Age have come down to us.

Until an authentic evaluation of the Roman anthology is published (in the manner of Mackail's introductory essay to selected poems from the *Greek Anthology*, and Paton's translations in the Loeb Library), investigators in the field of Romanesque verse will be slow to dare the announcement of their belief that Latin poetry was written in another than the classical Roman manner sooner, more definitely, and more extensively than they are as yet permitted to assert. It is safe to prophesy that a better understanding of the Latin anthology than is now current will show it to be a splendid thing and not a drab one. Is it true, for instance, that *inter eils goticum scapia matzia ia drincan, non audet quisquam dignos educere versus* in that fifth-century classical revival of Carthaginian society which, on the invitation of a Vandal prince, Octavianus, came afterwards to record? At any rate, we shall find in such materials new patterns of Romanesque.

NOTES TO CHAPTER VII

[1] To understand the importance of the dance in Greek life we must forget all the associations of the Latin word *saltatio*. To the Romans dancing meant jumping

with vigor, and they did not usually indulge in the amusement until drunk with wine: *nemo fere saltat sobrius nisi forte insanit*. Of moral, educational, and artistic purpose, the Roman dance had none. We must dismiss from our minds the maudlin revelry of a Roman banquet and the trivialities of a modern dance-hall, if we wish to visualize the universal application of Greek dancing as an art. Sometimes it was simple, like the figures once practiced by English May girls with their Jack in the Green—sometimes it was elaborate, involving years of study and muscles specially trained. But, unlike the Russian ballet, it was never barbarous. There was in the Greek dance no riot of color, noise, and gesture, which would probably have suited the taste of Imperial Rome. See F. A. Wright, *The Arts in Greece* (London, 1923), pp. 13 f.

[2] See Mackail, *Select Epigrams*, p. 57: There is another sense in which we may speak of the feeling for nature, and in regard to poetry it is perhaps the most important of all. But it no longer follows (as do the other attitudes towards the outer world) a sort of law of development in the human mind generally; it is confined to art, and among the arts is eminent in poetry beyond the rest. This is the romantic or magical note. It cannot be analyzed, perhaps it cannot be defined. The insufficiency of all attempted definitions of poetry is in great part due to the impossibility of their including this final quality, which like some volatile essence escapes the moment the phial is touched. In the poetry of all ages, even in the periods where it has been most intellectual and least imaginative, come sudden lines like the *Cette obscure clarté qui tombe des étoiles* of Corneille, like the *Placed far amid the melancholy main* of Thomson, where the feeling cannot be called moral, and yet stirs us like the deepest moral criticism upon life, rising as far beyond the mere idealism of sentiment as it does beyond the utmost refinement of realistic art.

[3] I doubt if this difference in attitude toward the environing world should be made a criterion of different poetic faiths. It would rather seem a distinguishing characteristic of separate kinds of verse within one and the same age. Garrod (Introduction to *The Oxford Book of Latin Verse*, pp. xix ff.) shows beautifully how in the *Æneid* the fine spiritual steel of the Attic dramatists has already submitted to a strange softening process. Something melting and subduing, something neither Greek nor Roman has come in. We are passed out of classicism, are moving into what is called romanticism. Pain of the world and a note of brooding pity are suggested by an environment of nature in more than one Vergilian eclogue; nature parallelism—the whole emotional train of pathetic fallacy—is on a sudden subtly close to us. Similarly, Catullus (as in the *Letter to Hortulus*) employs the symbolism of natural objects with a delicacy and a tenderness that belong to the romantic, rather than the classic, literatures. But this is to be as much expected as that in Wordsworth and Keats we should not infrequently find a summoning up of the hard moral grandeur of Lucretius or of the casual serenity of Horace when the shapes of natural objects and scenes are being limned. We do not for this reason call poets of the Republic and the early Empire romantic figures in a romantic world—we call them classic; and the very opposite is true in our characterization of nineteenth-century English poets as determined by their attitudes toward external nature.

Literal minds often speak of the "evolution" of a poetic sense for nature, as if this were something that grew from an original grain of mustard seed to be the greatest of shrubs in the branches of which forest song-birds came to lodge. Rather does this intimate feeling for nature inhere in every poetic age of which we have full record—but comes to its broadest expression in landscape symbolism in such periods of lyrical efflorescence as the fourth century knew. Suppose, for instance, the *Latin Anthology* had not preserved for us the Petronian epigrams—then our record of the Silver Age would not have been "full" enough to indicate its possession of the romantic (Romanesque) type of envisioning nature.

[4] The case cannot be put more clearly than has been done by E. E. Sikes in the following statement, taken from his *Roman Poetry*, pp. 145 f.: Is Mme. de Staël right in attributing this change to the spirit of Christianity? If we confine the phrase to the actual dogmas of Christians, there is little warrant for the theory. It is often argued that a taste for natural beauty has been derived from the Christian view of the world as a thing of divine significance permeated by the presence of God. But Roman Stoicism held this belief and was yet unable to widen the ancient æsthetic values. The early Christians themselves were too much occupied in regarding the world *sub specie æternitatis* to admire the passing show of visible things. As late as the fifth and sixth centuries, cultivated and broad-minded Christians like Sidonius or Fortunatus retained a purely classical outlook on nature, while to the more ascetic holders of the faith all phenomenal beauty was repugnant. Nor could the change have arisen from the fusion of Hebraic thought with Greek and Latin Christianity. The book of Job is full of the wonders of creation, and the Psalmist delights in the hills that stand about Jerusalem—but the wonders and the delights are purely religious and untinged by æsthetic appreciation. A race which almost wholly rejected the arts of painting and sculpture could hardly have recognized nature as beautiful in and for herself.

Still, if early Christianity added little or nothing to the stock of æsthetic perceptions, it paved the way to a radical change in the function of art. As an immediate result, the medieval spirit produced only a contempt for the body in contrast with the soul—but this very change implied a recognition of the soul as an element without which art is purely formal. The mortification of the flesh turned the artist to the objects of spiritual vision—to the infinite, the eternal. Sophocles and Vergil in poetry, like Phidias and Praxiteles in sculpture, had striven for an ideal which could be completely apprehended and expressed. Their art aimed at a mark before their eyes. It is, of course, mere ignorance to call this mark unspiritual. All these great artists were concerned with the things of the spirit, whether it might be Phidias adding to the received religion in his conception of Zeus, or Vergil showing that the Roman empire was foreordained of God. But it is true that for the classic artist the spiritual rarely eludes the material, rarely soars into regions of infinity and eternity where the body may not follow. The medieval sculptor could no longer rest content with the symmetrical beauty of a Polyclitus. Dissatisfied with formal perfection, he grasped at something beyond the senses and therefore incapable of full expression. Art became symbolic, significant of the reality that underlies the objects of sense perception.

[5] Sikes, *op. cit.*, pp. 117, 125.
[6] *Ibid.*, p. 126.
[7] *Ibid.*, p. 137.
[8] *Ibid.*, p. 130.
[9] *Loc. cit.*

[10] It is not uninteresting to trace landscape in color through its parallel course to landscape in words, says F. T. Palgrave (*Landscape in Poetry*, New York, 1897, pp. 2 f.). Both painting and poetry are bound to exhibit nature as seen and penetrated by the artist's soul. The artist, in turn, frames his ideal landscape on the great lines of nature herself, after her laws and inner intention. Poet and painter thus revert to realism in its true essence through the union of observation and individual genius. In varying degrees nature must thus be generalized or modified: the result is either bare realistic photography or a mere catalogue of details. Whether rendered in words or colors, each fails to give the landscape that union with human feeling which art itself and the human soul are forever imperiously demanding. Many a skillful landscape picture and many a descriptive passage of poetry leave us cold because of their failure to record this marriage of man and nature.

Poetry renders the subject chosen in successive verbal pictures and brings before us images of scent and sound and movement. It thus seems to have great advantages over painting, because in regard to form the painter is confined to a single instant and can barely suggest motion. Besides, with the light and shade available as materials, the latter cannot exceed one octave in the long scale of nature ranging from absolute darkness to midday splendor. Add to this that the poet may prepare the reader's mind for his landscape and connect it with its underlying human sentiment, while the painter must produce his effect almost wholly by the canvas presented. And yet who will doubt that colors, even a single color, may place the scene before our eyes with a vivid, realizing truth which the genius of poetry is unable even to approach?

If landscape art in any real sense existed from Homer's day to the end of the first Christian millenium, evidence of the fact has barely survived in a few crumbled Græco-Roman frescoes. During this long period poetry seems to have had landscape almost singly for her portion. But from this time forward, first as a background for human figures, then from Titian to Turner, landscape appears in all the pictorial arts, itself, and by itself, an unfailing source of human pleasure.

[11] See Matthew Arnold's essay *On the Study of Celtic Literature.*

[12] See Edward Dickinson, *Music in the History of the Western Church* (New York, 1902), p. 40: The principle of ancient music to which the early Christian types conformed subordinated the musical setting to poetry and the dance figure. Harmony was virtually unknown in antiquity, and without a knowledge of part-writing no independent art of music or musical verse is possible. The song of antiquity was the most restricted of all melodic styles: the chant or recitative. The essential feature of both chant and recitative is that the tones are made to conform to the meter and accent of the text, the words of which are never repeated or prosodically modified out of deference to melodic phrases and periods. On the contrary, in true song the words are subordinated to the exigencies of musical laws of structure, and the musical phrase—not the word—is the ruling power. The principle adopted by the Christian fathers was that of the chant, and Christian music could not begin to move in the direction of modern artistic attainment until a new technical principle and a new conception of the relation between music and poetry could be introduced.

[13] Edward Dickinson, *ibid.*, p. 48.

[14] See William Fairweather's remarkable study of early Christianity in the tideway of Hellenism: *Jesus and the Greeks* (Edinburgh, 1924), pp. 194 f, 198 ff.

Philo's teaching left its mark unmistakably on the thought of the early centuries of our era, acting as a ferment in the intellectual life of the age, affecting paganism, Judaism, and Christianity alike. Neo-Pythagoreanism is at one with Philo in laying stress upon the ecstatic vision. Still more striking is the affinity between the speculative theories of Philo and neo-Platonism as set forth in Plotinus. Neo-Platonism was the outcome of the philosophical spirit of the third century and the culminating point in it. During the period when theosophy was in the ascendant neo-Platonism formed the last of the three great branches of Greek philosophy, and so fails to be distinguished on the one hand from neo-Pythagoreanism, which prepared the way for it, and on the other, from the system of Philo, which was a mixture of Old Testament revelation and Hellenic philosophy. It differed also from Gnosticism, which bore the colors of Christianity. All these systems, however, were founded on the widespread belief in a dualistic opposition between God and matter.

There were elements in neo-Platonism akin to Christianity. Its idealism drew men like Augustine to the contemplation of Christian ideas. It taught the doctrine of a Trinity, was familiar with the idea of redemption, shared the desire to overcome the sensuous and to attain the truth by divine help and revelation, Nevertheless, the two systems were at variance: the doctrines of the Incarnation. the resurrection of the body, and the creation of the world in time formed the boundary lines between the dogmatic of the Church and of neo-Platonism. On these topics no agreement could be reached. A conflict ensued, an excellent idea of the nature of which may be gathered from Kingsley's *Hypatia*; the Church gained the victory. Neo-Platonism failed in its claim to be the absolute religion, because it had no religious founder, appealed only to the cultured few, could not solve the problem of how to retain the ecstatic mood, and was too impractical to satisfy the intelligence of the masses. (Fairweather, *op. cit.*, pp. 317-327.)

[15] See R. C. Jebb's article on rhetoric and oratory in *Companion to Greek Studies* (Cambridge, 1916), pp. 157-165, and J. Sandys's like essay in *Companion to Latin Studies* (Cambridge, 1921), pp. 651 ff.

There was no end to this evil. Under ordinary circumstances, any thing like the growth of a style in diction that mirrored the personality of a speaker or an occasion is not to be looked for: *le style n'est pas l'homme* in such euphuistic moments. Perhaps no better example of this artificial manner of speech exists than in the *Banquet* of Plato where each person present eulogizes Eros in totally different diction—there were stated prescriptions for each kind of style. The result is music or imagist verse, rather than sensible and declarative utterance.

[16] Which, according to Wiener, should be translated: Vast joy stirs the hollow of my chest, I banish all sadness from my lungs, but contract the joyous storm in my arteries when I observe the worthy archers of wisdom who, with their throats, drink the noble draught of the urbane tenor and fashion serpent syllogisms of literature.

NOTES TO CHAPTER VIII

[1] For a splendid study of this Arab theory of Platonic love, see Louis Massignon's *Al-Hallaj, Martyr Mystique de l'Islam* (Paris, 1922), I, 169 ff.

² See Massignon, p. 174. Ibn Dawoud's father told him: He who loves and wastes away, who does not divulge the secret of his heart—he is a martyr. The precepts of religious law provide for the chastity of lovers, their withdrawal from pollution, the guarding of their virginity; but even otherwise it would still be the duty of each lover to remain inviolate, thus to perpetuate eternally the desire that possesses him no less than that which he inspires.

³ In his *Greeks and Barbarians* (p. 172), Thomson hunts in antiquity for examples of romantic passion—all for love and the world well lost—and finds them in the Greek Cleopatra, Medea, Orpheus, Daphnis, Sappho, Ibykos, Archilochus, Hermesianax, Apollonios. But none of these examples is from the greatest period of Greek literature, the Attic Age. Thomson says this is no accident, for it is in that age that the hostile spirit most effectually comes in. The capacity for romantic love was not at any time denied to the Greek nature. But what happened was this: the great age applied to love its doctrine of sophrosyne or self-mastery. As a result, love became terrible and to be shunned in exact proportion to its power over the soul. And on the Greek soul love had great power; no one should be mistaken about that. It is a famous saying of Plato that love is a form of madness; again, he says of Eros, Of old he has been called a tyrant. Sophocles compared love to a wild beast. Such language is habitual with the Attic poets. It is not at all the language of medieval romance; it does not say, All for Love. Indeed, when we consider it more closely, says Thomson, we find that it means the exact opposite of what the extreme romantic means. The Greek means that he has conquered, the romantic that he has surrendered. In ancient Greece men felt love as much as we do, but felt about it differently. They were for cool blood, we for bravado; they for self-mastery, we for ecstasy. They were Greeks, and we are Barbarians.

⁴ See Mackail, *Select Epigrams*, pp. 35 f.

⁵ Few modern writers reflect that in its origin Platonic love denoted an absorbing passion for young men. Numerous passages from the Platonic writings indicate the Platonist would have despised the Petrarchist as a vulgar woman-lover. The Petrarchist loathed the Platonist as a moral pariah. Yet in both its ancient and its medieval manifestations Platonic love was one and the same thing. Despite this fact, Plato's name is still connected with the ideal of passion purged from sensuality.

Much might be written about the mania of the Phædrus and the joy of medieval amorists, about the points of contact between the *paiderastia* exalted to the heavens by Plato and the love described by Dante in the most eminent example of medieval erotic mysticism, the *Vita Nuova*. The spiritual passion for Beatrice which raised Dante above vile things and led him to the beatific vision of the *Paradiso* bears no slight resemblance to the Eros of the *Symposium*. The emotional harmony between ancient and medieval mysticism rests upon something permanent in human nature, common alike to *paiderastia* and to chivalrous enthusiasm for woman.

Early Christianity divinized the spirit in its self-sufficing state, detached from the body and antagonistic to it. Woman regarded as a virgin and at the same time as mother, had been exalted to the throne of heaven. By a logical process the worship of woman became in actual human life the correlative for that worship of the incarnate deity which was the essence of religion. In like manner, the sensual appetites were theoretically excluded from Platonic *paiderastia*. It was the divine in human flesh, the radiant sight of the beloved that exalted the Greek lover. He sought less to stimulate desire by the contemplation of sensual charms than to attune his spirit with the spectacle of strength at rest in suavity. The physical perfection of a youth made vigorous by exercise suggested to his fancy all that the Greek loved best in moral qualities and was their living incarnation.

With due regard to the differences between the plastic ideal of ancient religion and the romantic ideal of medieval Christianity, this Platonic conception of *paiderastia* is a close analogue to the chivalrous devotion to women. The one veiled adultery, the other sodomy. That in both cases the conception was rarely realized in actual life only completes the parallel. See John Addington Symonds, *A Problem in Greek Ethics* (London, 1901), pp. 72 f.

[6] See E. K. Rand's charming and judicious essay on "The Brighter Aspects of the Merovingian Age" in *Proceedings of the Classical Association*, XVIII (London, 1922), 165-182.

NOTES TO CHAPTER IX

[1] The retelling of the main facts which concern the Irish literary efflorescence in the fifth and sixth centuries is based upon the well known essays and books of Haureau, Ozanam, Roger, Sandys, Mrs. A. S. Green, Zimmer, and Kuno Meyer. Specific notation of the source of each minor indebtedness seems beside the purpose of this book, particularly in its closing chapters, for the mere citation of the printed articles and monographs devoted to Celtic Revival, Influence of the Near East and Arabian Conquest, Carolingian Renascence, and the Cambridge Songs would add unbearably to the bulk of this simple portrayal of combinatory facts and seem (to me at least) highly irrelevant. The English versions of Irish poetry depend somewhat necessarily on Kuno Meyer's translations in his *Ancient Irish Poetry*.

[2] Gone, alas, without a trace, was the lyric part of the lay long before Armorican minstrels came to England in the train of the hundred Breton noblemen who had cast in their lot with William the Conqueror. Afterwards such singers continued to cross the Channel and to *recite* their lays throughout Britain for two centuries, much as itinerant Italian singers of the nineteenth century. In England they made a lay of Tristan from a *Welsh* theme, also a so-called lay about the viking career of Havelock the Dane. Other Celtic musicians—Irish, Welsh, and Cornish, no doubt—pressed their Breton cousins in this field; and French and English gleemen may likewise have been their imitators.

But as originally sung in Celtic, the lays were probably pure lyrics—musical utterances of moments of passion in the lives of Celtic personages real or imaginary.

Since few of his audience, however—on the roadside, at the inn, in cloister or manor-hall—could understand the Breton lay even during the early Middle Ages, the Armorican minstrel was fain to preface his singing with an explanation of the story. This elucidation, like the opera librettos of today, was presented in a language intelligible to the public. In the same way, Icelandic saga-men wove lucid prose about the complicated kennings of the ancient skalds, observing the fashion in which their Irish predecessors had interpreted in story form the cryptic lyric utterances of their bards. This story, which introduced the lyric or was interspersed between lyric passages, was doubtless originally distinguished by the name of *conte.* In the course of time the word *lai* came to include the *conte.* And not a single verse of the original Breton songs has come down to us in recognizable shape—the lays are represented only by the *contes.* From the eleventh century on, French and English poets took these short tales and developed them into narrative poems, for the most part in rhyming couplets. To these poems also, these romances in miniature, contemporaries naturally applied the word lay. See Henry G. Leach, *Angevin Britain and Scandinavia* (Harvard University Press, 1921), pp. 199 ff.

NOTES TO CHAPTER X

[1] *Nordisches Geistesleben* (Heidelberg, 1908), pp. 79 ff.

[2] At this point it is convenient to recall Havelock Ellis's comparison in his essay on the "Celtic Spirit in Literature," now reprinted in the 1926 edition of *A Study of British Genius*:

One's first feeling in turning from Celtic to Nordic literature is one of dullness and monotony. It deals with the same main themes, battle and love, but the two elements which are almost omnipresent in the products of the Celtic mind—supernatural invention and vivid detail—and add so much charm to the Celtic narration have almost entirely fallen out of the Nordic stories. When, however, we have become really acclimatized to the Nordic atmosphere, we perceive that the undoubted absence of these elements involves a distinction, but not necessarily a loss. We are simply in another world. There is atmosphere here also, as there always is in fine literary art, not indeed the atmosphere of twilight, but of starlit nights and of storm-swept days. Celtic literature takes us into a world where bright sensations, a restless invention, dominate from first to last. Profound human passion, with all its painful and stupid limitations, is not there—is not even conceivable there—for we are in a world where all things are possible. It may be noted that the Celtic story of Tristan and Yseult only assumed tragic vitality and significance when it had been molded by realistic Nordic hands. Nordic literature is dominated from first to last by emotion, and where emotion is, there is limitation, tension, pressure. If the fountain leaps high in the air, it is because of the oppression at its subterranean heart.

All Nordic literature impresses us as the expression of a people who are in the highest degree emotional, practical, serious—in a word intensely human. They do not feel as the Celtic man so easily feels, that after all the boundary between the real and the unreal is very vague, that the nimble invention can easily create a world for itself, that there is no misfortune so great that it may not be straightened out by a twist of the hand of the juggler who has learned to control it, and no feat so stupendous but that somewhere the charm to perform it may not be found. All Nordic literature is the record of some human passion to be humanly suffered, some human right to be humanly achieved, some human wrong to be humanly wreaked. But Nordic literature reaps the fruits of its abstention from the picturesque and the supernatural in the heroic magnificence which it is thus able to impart to its human figures—a magnificence which the Celtic hero who finds extra-human aid on every hand can never attain. There the Nordic poet at once reaches the springs of great art. It would be idle to search all Celtic literature for anything so poignant as the speech of dying Brynhild.

[3] The Celtic mind demands a great and invisible past of impossible magnificence; all Celtic literature is the search for the satisfaction of that demand. The memory of the splendor of Rome which had once been theirs long haunted the Celtic and especially the Cymric mind. H. Ellis, *op. cit.*, p. 218.

[4] When we have clearly defined for ourselves these precise qualities of the Celtic mind as it displays itself in literature—that in vision it regards the remote as remote, and in method is decorative—we begin to realize the truth that underlies many of the rhapsodical utterances of the writers on Celtic glamor. In this connection we hear much of the fairyland of twilight. The atmosphere into which all genuinely Celtic things brings us is quite accurately and precisely described as one of twilight. Twilight has the curious property of making the scenes it envelops appear at once both near and remote. The glowing high lights and dark shadows of full sunlight have disappeared, as also have the commonplace reflections from the clouds of dull daylight. We are left with a vision that is both delicate and precise. For a moment a kind of musical silence seems to fill the air; we are conscious of the presence of mystery; we feel as if we had caught a glimpse of a landscape in another world. This impression—fantastic as it may seem, and yet explicable by the conditions of the atmosphere during this brief period of diffused light—very exactly corresponds to the special impression which Celtic romance makes upon us. H. Ellis, *op. cit.*, p. 222.

[5] The ninth-century tale of Liadin and Curither and the fine poetry embedded in it may serve as an illustration of the light and delicate touch which speaks as highly for the moral standard of the people as for the skill of the poet. Unfortunately, the narrative is so abbreviated as to become occasionally obscure. It was evidently the chief object of the writer to preserve the quatrains, and to let his prose serve merely as a slight framework in which to set his poetry. He thus leaves a good deal to the imagination: one has, as it were, to read between the lines. This is more particularly the case with Liadin. The sweet longing, the fond regret, the bitter remorse and self-reproach of the words which the poet makes her utter contain more of the true elements of the story than the meager account of the narrator.

The theme of the story is the love of a poet and poetess. After an engagement to marry him, she takes the veil. It cannot be said to be clear at what point this occurs. If early, her act makes the plot a conflict between love and religion. The lovers then seek the direction of St. Cummine, perhaps without revealing Liadin's act of religion. He first imposes a light probation upon them, then, challenged by Liadin, allows them a perilous freedom. In the result he banishes Curither, who thenceforward renounces love and becomes a pilgrim. When she still seeks him he crosses the sea. Liadin returns to the scene of their penance and his prayers, and shortly dies. When all is over, Cummine lovingly lays the stone where she had mourned her love, and upon which she died, over the grave of the unhappy maiden. K. Meyer, *Liadin and Curither*, (London, 1902), pp. 7 and 8.

NOTES TO CHAPTER XI

[1] And perhaps for that very reason sought, as Celtic poetry did, the vision of the invisible world that lies on the farther side of a terrifying mist at the gates of the land of legend. Says Havelock Ellis (*op. cit.*, p. 219):

In nearly all poetry, it must be remembered, the element of remoteness is introduced. This element is essential not only for the attainment of any atmospheric effect, but also for all elaborate architectonic construction. In the *Arabian Nights*—the only great work which shows that special romantic quality which we find in the Celtic legends—not only is the ancient and highly idealized age of Haroun-al-Raschid used as a remote mist in which every story may be plunged to become iridescently beautiful, but the element of distance, of long journeys, of great mountains to be overpassed, and great deserts and seas to be traversed, is constantly used with elaborate skill. And when we are taken on board a bark of red sandalwood, with mast of fine amber and ropes of silk, we feel that we are bound for a land of romance exactly identical with the land that Maxen Wledig reached at the end of his long journey, or that Rhonabwy saw in his dream when he fell asleep on the yellow calfskin.

[2] It should be noted, however, that Faure's argument is open to the correction that not *all* the artists and scholars were banished. There was a renascence of a sort in his reign. Science and architecture flourished; Zeno and Anthemius engaged in philosophical disputes; Metrodorus the Grammarian was patronized by the Emperor, whose taste in architecture received the deference of Isidore the Milesian; and a crowd of court poets celebrated the splendors of the renovated capital. See Elie Faure's *History of Art*, II (New York, 1922), 207 ff.

[3] See Paul Elmer More's *A Century of Indian Epigrams* (London, 1905) p. iv; also A. W. Ryder's *Women's Eyes* (San Francisco, 1916). In short verses the Hindus excel. Their mastery of form, their play of fancy, their depth and tenderness of feeling are all exquisite. Of the many who wrote such verses, the greatest is Bhartrihari. He lived some fifteen hundred years ago as king of Ujjain, and lived most royally. At last he was roused from his carefree existence by an event that surprised and shocked him. He gave a magic fruit to a girl he loved. She loved another and passed the gift on to him. He presented it to his lady-love who in turn adored the king—

> The maid my true heart loves would not my true love be;
> She seeks another man; another maid loves he;
> And me another maid her own true love would see;
> O fie on her and him and Love and HER and me!

When Bhartrihari received the magic fruit from his wooer and learned of its travels, he was disgusted with the fleeting joys of this world. He gave up his kingdom and spent the rest of his life in a cave, writing poetry.

[4] Before Heinrich Zimmer studied the influence of Vergilius Maro on Irish literature, the writings of this Gaulish grammarian had not been taken any too seriously, and even the century to which this curious author belonged was a matter of vague surmise. Certain scholars put him as late as the ninth century, none placed him earlier than the end of the sixth. Zimmer proved that Vergilius lived in the fifth century and was an elder contemporary of his countryman Ennodius (473-521), who wrote scathing epigrams upon him, characterizing him as a *fatuus homullus* and censuring him for daring to usurp the sacred name of the great Augustan poet. The only reason for the late date previously assigned to Vergilius springs from the erroneous notion that he took many of his etymologies from Isidore. A study of these supposed borrowings (tabulated by Manitius, *Geschichte der lateinischen*

Literatur des Mittelalters, I, 120-127) shows that no literal agreement exists, such as might reasonably be expected if there had been copying either way. We may then assume that these etymologies were traditional and commonly taught in the schools of Gaul and Spain for hundreds of years.

Zimmer showed further that Vergilius' works were well known in ancient Ireland and that his absurd theories as to the twelve different kinds of Latin (clipping words, turning them upside down, adding or inserting syllables, and the like) were actually imitated by Irish clerks. Indeed, as Kuno Meyer asserted in 1913, Vergilius' theories had a lasting vogue in Ireland and led ultimately to the invention of a language which may still be heard spoken in the streets of Dublin: Shelta. This Shelta is an artificial jargon discovered by Charles Godfrey Leland (see his *The Gypsies*, pp. 354-372) and more fully described and traced to its Irish origin by John Sampson and Kuno Meyer in *Journal of the Gypsy Lore Society*, old series, II, 204 ff; "The Secret Languages of Ireland," new series, 1909.

[5] See J. W. Mackail's splendid essary on Arabian lyric, epic, and romantic poetry in his *Lectures on Poetry* (London, 1911), pp. 93-153.

[6] See C. J. Lyall's *Translations of Ancient Arabian Poetry* (London, 1885); R. A. Nicholson's *Translations of Eastern Poetry and Prose* (Cambridge, 1922). The English versions of Arabic verse depend chiefly on the latter's renderings.

[7] See Charles Seignobos, *History of Medieval and Modern Civilization* (New York, 1907), pp. 110-119.

[8] See E. R. Bevan's *The Land of the Two Rivers* (London, 1918).

[9] For all references to Wiener see his very stimulating book *Contributions Toward a History of Arabico-Gothic Culture*, vol. I (1917).

NOTES TO CHAPTER XII

[1] See F. Funck-Brentano's *The Middle Ages* (New York, 1923), p. 72. A complete refutation of the contentions of this unfortunate volume is offered by S. Singer in his fine essay on the Carolingian renascence, *Germanische-Romanische Montatsschrift* (1925), XIII, 187-201, 243-258.

[2] See Charles Diehl's article on Byzantine culture in the *Cambridge Medieval History*, vol. IV.

[3] See the *Oxford History of Music*, vol. I.

NOTES TO CHAPTER XIII

[1] The only MS of *Terentius et Delusor* is *Bibliothèque Nationale Lat. MS* 8069, of the late tenth or early eleventh century. The text is established by Winterfeld, *Hrotsvithæ Opera* (1902) xx; Chambers, *Medieval Stage* (1903) ii, 326. Strecker, *Poetæ Latini Aevi Carolini*, iv (1923). Various of its early editors dated the poem in the seventh century or inclined towards that date: Magnin, *Bibliothèque de l'Ecole des Chartes* (1840) i, 517; de Montaiglon, *L'Amateur des Livres* (1849); Riese, *Zeilschr. f. d. Gymnas.* xviii, 442; Sabbadini (1894). More recently the poem has been felt to be either tenth (Traube) or ninth century (Winterfeld), largely because it is felt to be indicative of a Terentian revival and therefore to be somehow of a piece with

the efforts of Roswitha. As such indication, however, is based upon rather subtle argumentation from the corrupted state of the text and from the homage paid to the *vetus poeta* by the *delusor* in his asides, it is neither clinching nor compelling.

[2] As I close this chapter, and in connection with it read again the preceding one, I note with some dismay that a querulous tone occasionally appears in them, especially with regard to certain pronouncements of Messrs. Wiener, Robinson, Reich, Faral, and Winterfeld. A first strong impulse urges me to recast the form of these slight essays on the influence in the West of Araby and the mimic tradition, so that their dialectic tendencies may vanish from view, and so that they may show the untroubled surface of a seemingly impartial attitude. Maturer judgment, however, will not permit me to do this. My decision to leave the two offending chapters in their present shape derives from the following reflection:

So far as I know, this book is the first to emphasize as a separate genre, a species of poetry apart alike from classical inheritance and from vernacular beginnings, the Romanesque lyric. True, I have used to repletion—if not to positive satiety—the phrases of behemoth and leviathan which affect the approaches to my literary integer, quoting so often the words of my torch-bearing predecessors on Dark Age trails (Mackail, Ker, and Garrod, for example), that in many a blue moment I have believed myself rather the cook of what others have prepared for me, than an analytic chemist of my subject. None the less, throughout my whole endeavor, there runs the idea of a new and dauntless entity in the world of human symbol—the Romanesque lyric. To incubate this and preserve its early stages from harm is my insistent purpose. When necessary to the proper accomplishment of this aim, I am within reason ready to fight.

Several times I have found the quiet progress of my disentanglement of Romanesque strands imperiled by the running about of persons saying unreflective and scarcely considered things apropos of the condition of poetry in Merovingian and Carolingian Gaul. Each time I have stopped my work to give patient audience to their claims I have come away largely unrewarded for my pains. But these men have published so pretentiously in the field of my effort and have so commanded the attention of unversed readers, that they cannot be dismissed by a lifting of the eyebrows or a mere wave of the hand. A sharp word seems necessary to dispossess them of positions they have not rightly won.

NOTES TO CHAPTER XIV

[1] Thus are invariably called the ten leaves (folios 432-41) which form the most important part of MS Gg. 5.35 in the library of the University of Cambridge. For full description of the MS, see Karl Breul's *The Cambridge Songs* (Cambridge, 1915), pp. 23 f, and K. Strecker's edition of the *Carmina Cantabrigiensia* (Berlin, 1926), Preface.

[2] See Alice S. Green's *History of the Irish State to 1014* (London, 1925), chap. XIII, "Monasteries and Industries."

[3] The Latin text of *Unibos* is in Grimm and Schmeller's *Lateinische Gedichte des 10 und 11. Jahrhunderts* (Göttingen, 1838); German translation in M. Heyne's *Altdeutsche lateinische Spielmannsdichtung* (Göttingen, 1900). See also F. v. der Leyen's essay on fables and minstrelsy, *Germanische-Romanische Monatsschrift* X (1922), 129 ff.

LATIN ORIGINALS OF LYRICS TRANSLATED IN THE TEXT

Chapter V

(1) ENCOURAGEMENT TO EXILE

Linque tuas sedes alienaque litora quaere,
O iuvenis: maior rerum tibi nascitur ordo.
Ne succumbe malis: te noverit ultimus Hister,
Te Boreas gelidus securaque regna Canopi,
Quique renascentem Phoebum cernuntque cadentem:
Maior in externa fit qui se temptat harena.
—*Petronius.*

(2) THE MALADY OF LOVE IS NERVES

Lecto compositus vix prima silentia noctis
   Carpebam et somno lumina victa dabam:
Cum me saevus Amor prensat sursumque capillis
   Excitat et lacerum pervigilare iubet.
'Tu famulus meus, 'inquit, 'ames cum mille puellas,
   Solus, io, solus, dure, iacere potes?'
Exsilio et pedibus nudis tunicaque soluta
   Omne iter incipio, nullum iter expedio.
Nunc proper, nunc ire piget, rursumque redire
   Paenitet et pudor est stare via media.
Ecce tacent voces hominum strepitusque viarum
   Et volucrum cantus turbaque fida canum:
Solus ego ex cunctis paveo somnumque torumque
   Et sequor imperium, magne Cupido, tuum.
—*Petronius.*

(3) NOBLESSE OBLIGE

Una est nobilitas argumentumque coloris
   Ingenui timidas non habuisse manus.
—*Petronius.*

(4) ILLUSION

Fallunt nos oculi vagique sensus
Oppressa ratione mentiuntur.
Nam turris, prope quae quadrata surgit,

Detritis procul angulis rotatur.
Hyblaeum refugit satur liquorem
Et naris casiam frequenter odit.
Hoc illo magis aut minus placere
Non posset, nisi lite destinata
Pugnarent dubio tenore sensus.
                    —*Petronius.*

(5) WE ARE SUCH STUFF AS DREAMS

Somnia, quae mentes ludunt volitantibus umbris,
Non delubra deum nec ab aethere numina mittunt,
Sed sibi quisque facit. Nam cum prostrata sopore
Urguet membra quies et mens sine pondere ludit,
Quidquid luce fuit, tenebris agit. Oppida bello
Qui quatit et flammis miserandas eruit urbes,
Tela videt versasque acies et funera regum
Atque exundantes profuso sanguine campos.
Qui causas orare solent, legesque forumque
Et pavidi cernunt inclusum corte tribunal.
Condit avarus opes defossumque invenit aurum.
Venator saltus canibus quatit. Eripit undis
Aut premit eversam periturus navita puppem.
Scribit amatori meretrix, dat adultera munus:
Et canis in somnis leporis vestigia lustrat.
In noctis spatium miserorum vulnera durant:
. . . .
                    —*Petronius.*

(6) NEALCE

Sit nox illa diu nobis dilecta, Nealce,
    Quae te prima meo pectore composuit;
Sit torus et lecti genius secretaque lampas,
    Quis tenera in nostrum veneris arbitrium.
Ergo age duremus, quamvis adoleverit aetas,
    Utamurque annis, quos mora parva teret.
Fas et iura sinunt veteres extendere amores:
    Fac, cito quod coeptum est, non cito desinere.
                    —*Petronius.*

(7) REMEMBERED SHORES

O litus vita mihi dulcius, o mare! felix,
    Cui licet ad terras ire subinde tuas!
O formosa dies! hoc quondam rure solebam
    Naidos armatas sollicitare manus.

Hic fontis lacus est, illic sinus egerit algas:
  Haec statio est tacitis fida cupidinibus.
Pervixi; neque enim fortuna malignior umquam
  Eripiet nobis, quod prior hora dedit.
—*Petronius.*

(8) APOSTROPHE TO SLEEP

Crimini quo merui, iuvenis, placidissime divum,
Quove errore miser, donis ut solus egerem,
Somne, tuis? Tacet omne pecus volucresque feraeque
Et simulant fessos curvata cacumina somnos,
Nec trucibus fluviis idem sonus; occidit horror
Aequoris, et terris maria acclinata quiescunt.
Septima iam rediens Phoebe mihi respicit aegras
Stare genas; totidem Oetaeae Paphiaeque revisunt
Lampades et totiens nostros Tithonia questus
Praeterit et gelido spargit miserata flagello.
Unde ego sufficiam? . . . .
. . . .
At nunc heu! si aliquis longa sub nocte puellae
Bracchia nexa tenens ultro te, Somne, repellit,
Inde veni! nec te totas infundere pennas
Luminibus compello meis (hoc turba precetur
Laetior): extremo me tange cacumine virgae
(Sufficit) aut leviter suspenso poplite transi.
—*Statius.*

(9) LYDIA

Invideo vobis, agri formosaque prata,
Hoc formosa magis, mea quod formosa puella
In vobis tacite nostrum suspirat amorem.
Vos nunc illa videt, vobis mea Lydia ludit,
Vos nunc adloquitur, vos nunc adridet ocellis,
Et mea submissa meditatur carmina voce,
Cantat et hinc, teneram mihi quae cantabat in aurem.
Invideo vobis, agri: discetis amare.
O fortunati nimium nimiumque beati,
In quibus illa pedis nivei vestigia ponet
Aut roseis viridem digitis decerpserit uvam
(Dulci namque tumet nondum vitecula Baccho)
Aut inter varios Venerem spirantia flores
Membra reclinarit teneramque inliserit herbam
Et secreta meos furtim narrabit amores!
Gaudebunt silvae, gaudebunt mollia prata
Et gelidi fontes, aviumque silentia fient;
Tardabunt rivi labentes currere lymphae,

Dum mea iocundas exponat cura querellas.
Invideo vobis, agri: mea gaudia habetis,
Et vobis nunc est, mea quae ante voluptas.
At mihi tabescunt morientia membra dolore
Et calor infuso decedit frigore mortis,
Quod mea non mecum domina est. . . . .
—*Appendix Vergiliana, ii. "Dirate."*

Chapter VI

(1) MORNING HYMN

Lucis largitor splendide,
Cuius sereno lumine
Post lapsa noctis tempora
Dies refusus panditur;

Tu verus mundi Lucifer,
Non is, qui parvi sideris
Venturae lucis nuntius
Angusto fulget lumine,

Sed toto sole clarior,
Lux ipse totus et dies,
Interna nostri pectoris
Illuminans praecordia:

Adesto, rerum conditor,
Paternae lucis gloria,
Cuius admota gratia
Nostra patescunt corpora;

Tuoque plena spiritu,
Secum Deum gestantia,
Ne rapientis perfidi
Diris pateant fraudibus.

. . . .

Haec spes precantis animae,
Haec sunt votiva munera,
Ut matutina nobis sit
Lux in noctis custodiam.
—(?)*Hilarius.*

(2) ÆTERNE RERUM CONDITOR

Æterne rerum conditor,
Noctem diemque qui regis,
Et temporum das tempora
Ut alleves fastidium;

Praeco diei iam sonat,
Noctis profundae pervigil,
Nocturna lux viantibus,
A nocte noctem segregans.

Hoc excitatus lucifer
Solvit polum caligine,
Hoc omnis errorum chorus
Viam nocendi deserit.

Hoc nauta vires colligit
Pontique mitescunt freta,
Hoc ipsa petra ecclesiae
Canente culpam diluit.

Surgamus ergo strenue!
Gallus iacentes excitat,
Et somnolentos increpat,
Gallus negantes arguit.

Gallo canente spes redit,
Aegris salus refunditur,
Mucro latronis conditur,
Lapsis fides revertitur.

Iesu, labentes respice,
Et nos videndo corrige,
Si respicis, lapsus cadunt,
Fletuque culpa solvitur.

Tu lux refulge sensibus,
Mentisque somnum discute,
Te nostra vox primum sonet
Et ore psallamus tibi.
—*Ambrose.*

(3) A WOODLAND SCENE

Amnis ibat inter arva valle fusus frigida,
Luce ridens calculorum, flore pictus herbido.

Caerulas superne laurus, et virecta myrtea
Leniter motabat aura blandiente sibilo.
Subter autem molle gramen flore adulto creverat:
Et croco solum rubebat et lucebat liliis
Et nemus fragrabat omne violarum suspiritu.
Inter ista dona veris gemmeasque gratias
Omnium regina odorum vel colorum Lucifer
Auriflora praeminebat, flamma Diones, rosa,
Roscidum nemus rigebat inter uda gramina:
Fonte crebro murmurabant hinc et inde rivuli,
Antra muscus et virentes intus myrtus vinxerant,
Qua fluenta labibunda guttis ibant lucidis.
Has per umbras omnis ales plus conora quam putes
Cantibus vernis strepebat et susurris dulcibus;
His loquentis murmur amnis concinebat frondibus,
Quis melos vocalis aurae musa zephyri moveret.
Sic euntem per virecta pulcra odora et musica
Ales amnis aura lucus flos et umbra iuverat.
—*Tiberianus.*

(4) THE NIGHT-WATCH OF VENUS

Cras amet qui nunquam amavit quique amavit cras amet:
Ver novum, ver iam canorum, ver renatus orbis est;
Vere concordant amores, vere nubunt alites,
Et nemus comam resolvit de maritis imbribus.

Cras amet qui nunquam amavit quique amavit cras amet.

Cras amorum copulatrix inter umbras arborum
Implicat casas virentes de flagello myrteo:
Cras canoris feriatos ducit in silvis choros;
Cras Dione iura dicit fulta sublimit thoro.

Cras amet qui nunquam amavit quique amavit cras amet.

Cras erit cum primus aether copulavit nuptias:
Tunc cruore de superno spumeo et ponti globo,
Caerulas inter catervas, inter et bipedes equos,
Fecit undantem Dionem de maritis imbribus.

Cras amet qui nunquam amavit quique amavit cras amet.

Emicant lacrimae trementes de caduco pondere,
Gutta praeceps orbe parvo sustinet casus suos:
Umor ille quem serenis astra rorant noctibus
Mane virgines papillas solvit umenti peplo.

Cras amet qui nunquam amavit quique amavit cras amet.

En pudorem florulentae prodiderunt purpurae
Et rosarum flamma nodis emicat tepentibus.
Ipsa iussit diva vestem de papillis solvere,
Ut recenti mane nudae virgines nubant rosae.

Cras amet qui nunquam amavit quique amavit cras amet.

Facta Cypridis de cruore deque Amoris osculo,
Deque gemmis deque flammis deque solis purpuris,
Cras ruborem qui latebat veste tectus ignea
Uvido marita nodo non pudebit solvere.

Cras amet qui nunquam amavit quique amavit cras amet.

. . . .
—*Incerti.*

(5) THE OLD MAN OF VERONA WHO NEVER LEFT HIS HOME

Felix, qui propriis aevum transegit in arvis,
    Ipsa domus puerum quem videt, ipsa senem;
Qui baculo nitens in qua reptavit harena
    Unius numerat saecula longa casae.
Illum non vario traxit fortuna tumultu,
    Nec bibit ignotas mobilis hospes aquas.
Non freta mercator tremuit, non classica miles,
    Non rauci lites pertulit ille fori.
Indocilis rerum, vicinae nescius urbis
    Adspectu fruitur liberiore poli.
Frugibus alternis, non consule computat annum:
    Autumnum pomis, ver sibi flore notat.
Idem condit ager soles idemque reducit,
    Metiturque suo rusticus orbe diem,
Ingentem meminit parvo qui germine quercum
    Aequavumque videt consenuisse nemus,
Proxima cui nigris Verona remotior Indis
    Benacumque putat litora Rubra lacum.
Sed tamen indomitae vires firmisque lacertis
    Aetas robustum tertia cernit avum.
Erret et extremos alter scrutetur Hiberos:
    Plus habet hic vitae, plus habet ille viae.
—*Claudian.*

(6) THE LONELY ISLE

Est procul ingenti regio summota recessu,
Insula qua resides fluctus mitescere cogit
In longum producta latus, fractasque per undas
Ardua tranquillo curvantur brachia portu.
—*Claudian.*

(7) EPITAPH

Pulchris stare diu Parcarum lege negatur.
    Magna repente ruunt; summa cadunt subito.
Hic formosa iacet: Veneris sortita figuram
    Egregiumque decus invidiam meruit.
—*Claudian.*

(8) FAREWELL TO ROME

. . . .
Exaudi, regina tui pulcerrima mundi,
    Inter sidereos Roma recepta polos,
Exaudi, nutrix hominum genetrixque deorum
    (Non procul a caelo per tua templa sumus):
Te canimus semperque, sinent dum fata, canemus:
    Hospes nemo potest immemor esse tui.
Obruerint citius scelerata obliva solem,
    Quam tuus ex nostro corde recedat honos.
Nam solis radiis aequalia munera pendis,
    Qua circumfusus fluctuat oceanus.
Volitur ipse tibi qui continent omnia Phoebus
    Eque tuis ortos in tua condit equos.
Te non flammigeris Libye tardavit harenis,
    Non armata quo reppulit Ursa gelu:
Quantum vitalis natura tetendit in axes,
    Tantum virtuti pervia terra tuae.
Fecisti patriam diversis gentibus unam:
    Profuit invitis te dominante capi.
Dumque offers victis proprii consortia iuris,
    Urbem fecisti quod prius orbis erat.
Auctores generis Venerem Martemque fatemur,
    Aeneadum matrem Romulidumque patrem:
Mitigat armatas victrix clementia viris,
    Convenit in mores numen utrumque tuos:
Hinc tibi certandi bona parcendique voluptas
    Quos timuit superat, quos superavit amat.
Inventrix oleae colitur vinique repertor
    Et qui primus humo pressit aratra puer,

Aras Paeoniam meruit medicina per artem,
    Fretus et Alcides nobilitate deus:
Tu quoque, legiferis mundum complexa triumphis,
    Foedere communi vivere cuncta facis.
Te, dea, te celebrat Romanus ubique recessus
    Pacificumque gerunt libera colla iugum.
Omnia perpetuo quae servant sidera motu,
    Nullum viderunt pulcrius imperium.
Quid simile Assyriis conectere contigit armis?
    Medi finitimos condomuere suos.
Magni Parthorum reges Macetumque tyranni
    Mutua per varias iura dedere vices.
Nec tibi nascenti plures animaeque manusque,
    Sed plus consilii iudiciique fuit.
Iustis bellorum causis nec pace superba
    Nobilis ad summas gloria venit opes.
Quod regnas minus est quam quod regnare mereris:
    Excedis factis grandia fata tuis.
. . . .
           —*Rutilius Namatianus.*

(9) TO HIS DEAD WIFE

Hactenus ut caros, ita iusto funere fletos
    Functa piis cecinit nenia nostra modis.
Nunc dolor atque cruces nec contrectabile vulnus,
    Coniugis ereptae mors memoranda mihi.
Nobilis a proavis et origine clara senatus,
    Moribus atque bonis clara Sabina magis.
Te iuvenis primis luxi deceptus in annis
    Perque novem cælebs te fleo Olympiadas.
Nec licet obductum senio sopire dolorem;
    Semper crudescit nam mihi paene recens.
Admittunt alii solacia temporis aegri:
    Haec graviora facit vulnera longa dies.
Torqueo deceptos ego vita caelibe canos,
    Quoque magis solus, hoc mage maestus ago.
Vulnus alit, quod muta domus silet et torus alget,
    Quod mala non cuiquam, non bona participo.
Maereo, si coniunx alii bona; maereo contra,
    Si mala: ad exemplum tu mihi semper ades.
Tu mihi crux ab utraque venis: sive est mala, quod tu
    Dissimilis fueris; seu bona, quod similis.
Non ego opes cassas et inania gaudia plango,
    Sed iuvenis iuveni quod mihi rapta viro.
Laeta, pudica, gravis, genus inclita et inclita forma,
    Et dolor atque decus coniugis Ausonii.

Quae modo septenos quater impletura Decembres
  Liquisti natos, pignera nostra, duos.
Illa favore dei, sicut tua vota fuerunt,
  Florent, optatis adcumulata bonis.
Et precor, ut vigeant tandemque superstite utroque
  Nuntiet hoc cineri nostra favilla tuo.
                                    —*Ausonius.*

(10) CUPID CRUCIFIED

Aeris in campis, memorat quos musa Maronis,
Myrteus amentes ubi locus opacat amantes,
Orgia ducebant heroides et sua quaeque,
Ut quondam occiderant, leti argumenta gerebant,
Errantes silva in magna et sub luce maligna
Inter harundineasque comas gravidumque papaver
Et tacitos sine labe lacus, sine murmure rivos:
Quorum per ripas nebuloso lumine marcent
Fleti, olim regnum et puerorum nomina, flores
Mirator Narcissus et Oebalides Hyacinthus
Et Crocus auricomans et murice pictus Adonis
Et tragico scriptus gemitu Salaminius Aeas;
Omnia quae lacrimis et amoribus anxia maestis
Exercent memores obita iam morte dolores:
Rursus in amissum revocant heroidas aevum.
. . . .
                                    —*Ausonius.*

(11) POETRY AND TIME

O vetustatis veneranda custos,
Regios actus simul et fugacis
Temporum cursus docilis referre,
    Aurea Clio,
Tu nihil magnum sinis interire,
Nil mori clarum pateris, reservans
Posteris prisci monumenta saecli
    Condita libris.
Sola fucatis variare dictis
Paginas nescis, sed aperta quicquid
Veritas prodit, recinis per aevum
    Simplice lingua.
Tu senescentis titulos avorum
Flore durantis reparas iuventae;
Militat virtus tibi: te notante
    Crimina pallent.
Tu fori turbas strepitusque litis
Effugis dulci moderata cantu,

Nec retardari pateris loquellas
   Compede metri.
His fave dictis: retegenda vita est
Vatis Etrusci, modo qui perenne
Romulae voci decus adrogavit
   Carmine sacro.
                              —*Phocas.*

(12) PAINTED PASSION

Pinge, precor, pictor, tali candore puellam,
Qualem pinxit Amor, qualem meus ignis anhelat.
Nil pingendo neges; tegat omnia Serica vestis,
Quae totum prodat tenui velamine corpus.
Te quoque pulset amor, crucient pigmenta medullas:
Si bonus es pictor, miseri suspiria pinge.
                              —(?) *Octavianus.*

(13) PRAYER TO VENUS

Dic quid agis, formosa Venus, si nescis amanti
Ferre vicem. Perit omne decus, dum deperit aetas.
Marcent post rorem violae, rosa perdit odorem,
Lilia post vernum posito candore nigrescunt.
Haec metuas exempla precor et semper amanti
Redde vicem, quia semper amat, qui semper amatur.
                              —(?) *Octavianus.*

(14) REPLIQUE

Non redit in florem, sed munus perdit amantis,
Quidquid vile jacet: dulce est, quodcumque negatur.
Nam si formosam facilem penetravit amator,
Fallit adulterio et munus perdit amantis.
                              —(?) *Octavianus.*

(15) THE EUNUCH'S DELIGHT

Amare liceat, si potiri non licet.
Fruantur alii: non moror, non sum invidus;
Nam sese excruciat, qui beatis invidet.
Quos Venus amavit, facit amoris compotes:
Nobis Cupido velle dat, posse abnegat.
Olli purpurea delibantes oscula
Demente morsu rosea labia vellicent,
Candentes dentes effigient suavio,
Malas adorent ore et ingenuas genas
Et pupilarum nitidas geminas gemmulas.

Quin et cum tenera membra molli lectulo
Consertiora adhaerent Veneris glutino,
Libido cum lasciva instinctos suscitat
Sinuare ad Veneris cursum femina feminae:
Inter gannitus et subantis voculas
Carpant papillas atque amplexus intiment
Reserentque sulcos molles arvo Venerio
Thyrsumque pangant hortulo Cupidinis,
Dent crebros ictus conivente lumine,
Trepidante e cursu vena et anima fessula
Eiaculent tepidum rorem niveis laticibus.
Haec illi faciant, queis Venus non invidet;
At nobis casso saltem delectamine
Amare liceat, si potiri non licet.
—*L. Apuleius, ex Menandro.*

(16) OLD AGE

Aemula quid cessas finem properare senectus?
   Cur et in hoc fesso corpore tarda venis?
Solve precor miseram tali de carcere vitam:
   Mors est iam requies, vivere poena mihi.
Non sum qui fueram: perit pars maxima nostri;
   Hoc quoque quod superest languor et horror habent.
Lux gravis in luctu, rebus gratissima laetis,
   Estque omni peius funere, velle mori.
. . . .
Me vero heu tantis defunctum in partibus olim
   Tartareas vivum constat inire vias.
Iam minor auditus, gustus minor, ipsa caligant
   Lumina, vix tactu noscere certa queo.
Nullus dulcis odor, nulla est iam grata voluptas:
   Sensibus expertem quis superesse putet?
En Lethaea meam subeunt oblivia mentem,
   Nec confusa sui iam meminisse potest:
Ad nullum consurgit opus, cum corpore languet
   Atque intenta suis a! stupet illa malis.
Carmina nulla cano: cantandi summa voluptas
   Effugit et vocis gratia vera perit.
Non fora sollicito, non blanda poemata fingo;
   Litibus haut rabidis commoda dura sequor.
Ipsaque me species quondam dilecta reliquit,
   Et videor formae mortuus esse meae.
Pro niveo rutiloque prius nunc inficit ora
   Pallor et exsanguis funereusque color.
Aret sicca cutis, rigidi stant undique nervi,
   Et lacerant uncae scabrida membra manus.

Quondam ridentes oculi nunc fonte perenni
    Deplangunt poenas nocte dieque suas;
Et quos grata prius ciliorum serta tegebant,
    Desuper incumbens hispida silva premit,
Ac velut inclusi caeco conduntur in antro:
    Torvum nescio quid ceu furiale vident.
Iam pavor est videsse senem, nec credere possis
    Hunc hominem, humana qui ratione caret.
. . . .
Hae sunt primitiae mortis, his partibus aetas
    Defluit et pigris gressibus ima petit.
Non habitus, non ipse color, non gressus euntis,
    Non species eadem quae fuit ante manet.
Labitur ex umeris demisso corpore vestis,
    Quaeque brevis fuerat iam modo longa mihi est.
Contrahimur miroque modo decrescimus: ipsa
    Diminui nostri corporis ossa putes,
Nec caelum spectare licet, sed prona senectus
    Terram, qua genita est et reditura, videt
Fitque tripes, prorsus quadrupes, ut parvulus infans,
    Et per sordentem (flebile) repit humum.
Ortus cuncta suos repetunt matremque requirunt,
    Et redit ad nihilum, quod fuit ante nihil.
Hinc est quod baculo incumbens ruitura senectus
    Assiduo pigram verbere pulsat humum
Et numerosa movens curto vestigia passu
    Talia rugato creditur ore loqui:
"Suscipe me genetrix, nati miserere laborum:
    Membra peto gremio fessa fovere tuo:
Horrent me pueri, nequeo velut ante videri:
    Horrendos partus cur sinis esse tuos?
Nil mihi cum superis: explevi munera vitae:
    Redde, precor, patrio mortua membra solo.
Quid miseros variis prodest suspendere poenis?
    Non est materni pectoris ista pati."
His dictis trunco titubantes sustinet artus,
    Neglecti repetens stramina dura tori.
Quo postquam iacuit, misero quid funere differt?
    Heu tantum adtracti corporis ossa vides.
. . . .
Vincimur infirmi defectu corporus, et qua
    Noluero, infelix hac ego parte trahor.
Omnia naturae solvuntur viscera nostrae.
    Et tam praeclarum quam male nutat opus!
His veniens onerata malis incurva senectus
    Cedere ponderibus se docet ipsa suis.
Ergo quis has cupiat per longum ducere poenas
    Paulatimque anima deficiente mori?

Morte mori melius, quam vitam ducere mortis
Et sensus membris consepelire suis.
. . . .
—*Maximian.*

(17) LYCORIS

En dilecta mihi nimium formosa Lycoris,
  Cum qua mens eadem, res fuit una mihi,
Post multos quibus indivisi viximus annos
  Respuit amplexus, heu, labefacta meos;
Iamque alios iuvenes aliosque requirit amores:
  Me vocat inbellem decrepitumque senem;
Nec meminisse solet transactae dulcia vitae
  Nec quod me potius reddidit ipsa senem;
Immo etiam causas ingrata ac perfida fingit,
  Ut spretum vitio me indicet esse meo.
Haec me praeteriens cum ductum forte videret,
  Expuet obductis vestibus ora tegens.
"Hunc" inquit "dilexi? Hic me complexus amavit?
  Huic ego saepe, nefas, oscula blanda dedi?"
Nauseat et priscum vomitu ceu fundit amorem,
  Imponit capiti plurima dira meo.
En, quid longa dies nunc affert! ut sibi quisquam
  Quondam dilectum prodere turpe putet!
Nonne fuit melius tali me tempore fungi,
  Quo nulli merito despiciendus eram,
Quam, postquam periit quicquid fuit ante decoris,
  Extinctum meritis vivere criminibus?
Iam nihil est totum quod viximus: omnia secum
  Tempus praeteriens horaque summa trahit.
Dumque tamen nivei circumdant tempora cani
  Et iam caeruleus inficit ora color,
Perstat adhuc nimiumque sibi speciosa videtur
  Atque annos secum despicit illa suos.
Et, fateor, primae retinet monumenta figurae,
  Atque inter cineres condita flamma manet.
Ut video, pulcris etiam vos parcitis, anni,
  Nec veteris formae gratia tota perit.
Reliquiis veterum iuvenes pascuntur amorum,
  Et, si quid non est, quod fuit ante placet:
Ante oculos statuunt primaevi temporis artus
  Atque in praeteritum luxuriantur opus.
At quia nos totus membrorum deserit usus,
  Notos amplexus quod remoretur abest,
Sed solus miseris superest post omnia luctus:
  Quot bona tunc habui, tot modo damna fleo.

Omni nympha pati, non omni tempore coniunx
  Quit facere: hoc vincit femina victa virum.
Ergo velut pecudum praesentia sola valebunt?
  Nil de transactis quod memoretur erit?
At fugiunt et bruta novos animalia campos
  Ac repetunt celeres pascua nota greges,
Sub qua consuevit requiescere diligit umbram
  Taurus et amissum quaerit ovile pecus,
Dulcius in solitis cantat philomela rubetis
  Fitque suum rabidis dulce cubile feris.
Tu tantum bene nota tibi atque experta relinquis,
  Hospitia et potius non manifesta petis.
Nonne placet melius certis confidere rebus?
  Eventus varios res nova semper habet.
Sum grandaevus ego, nec tu minus alba capillis:
  Par aetas animos conciliare solet.
Si modo non possum, quondam potuisse memento:
  Sit satis ut placeam me placuisse prius.
Permanet invalidis reverentia prisca colonis,
  Quod fuit in vetulo milite miles amat,
Rusticus expertum deflet cessasse iuvencum,
  Cum quo consenuit victor honorat equum.
Non me adeo primis spoliavit floribus aetas:
  En facio versus et mea fata cano.
Sit gravitas sitque ipsa tibi veneranda senectus,
  Sit quod te nosti vivere velle diu.
Quis suam in alterius condemnet crimine vitam
  Et quo pertendit claudere certet iter?
Dicere si fratrem seu dedignaris amicum,
  Dic patrem: affectum nomen utrumque tenet.
Vincat honor luxum, pietas succedat amori:
  Plus ratio quam vis caeca valere solet.
His lacrimis longos, quantum fas, flevimus annos:
  Est grave quod doleat commemorare diu.
                              —*Maximian.*

Chapter VII

(1) OF ROSES

Ver erat et blando mordenti a frigore sensu
  Spirabat croceo mane revecta dies.
Strictior Eoos praecesserat aura iugales
  Aestiferum suadens anticipare diem.

Errabam riguis per quadrua compita in hortis
    Maturo cupiens me vegetare die.
Vidi concretas per gramina flexa pruinas
    Pendere aut holerum stare cacuminibus,
Caulibus et teretes patulis conludere guttas.

. . . .

Vidi Paestano gaudere rosaria cultu
    Exorietne novo roscida lucifero.
Rara pruinosis canebat gemma frutectis
    Ad primi radios interitura die.
Ambigeres, raperetne rosis Aurora ruborem
    An daret et flores tingueret orta dies.
Ros unus, color unus et unum mane duorum;
    Sideris et floris nam domina una Venus.
Forsan et unus odor: sed celsior ille per auras
    Diffluit: expirat proximus iste magis.
Communis Paphie dea sideris et dea floris
    Praecipit unius muricis esse habitum.
Momentum intererat, quo se nascentia florum
    Germina conparibus dividerent spatiis.
Haec viret angusto foliorum tecta galero,
    Hanc tenui folio purpura rubra notat.
Haec aperit primi fastigia celsa obelisci
    Mucronem absolvens purpurei capitis.
Vertice collectos illa exsinuabat amictus,
    Iam meditans foliis se numerare suis:
Nec mora: ridentis calathi patefecit honorem
    Prodens inclusi semina densa croci.
Haec modo, quae toto rutilaverat igne comarum
    Pallida conlapsis deseritur follis.
Mirabar celerem fugitiva aetate rapinam
    Et, dum nascuntur, consenuisse rosas.
Ecce et defluxit rutili coma punica floris,
    Dum loquor, et tellus tecta rubore micat.
Tot species tantosque ortus variosque novatus
    Una dies aperit, conficit ipsa dies.
Conquerimur, Natura, brevis quod gratia talis:
    Ostenta oculis illico dona rapis.
Quam longa una dies aetas tam longa rosarum:
    Cum pubescenti iuncta senecta brevis.
Quam modo nascentem rutilus conspexit Eous,
    Hanc rediens sero vespero vidit anum.
Sed bene, quod paucis licet interitura diebus
    Succedens aevum prorogat ipsa suum.
Collige, virgo, rosas, dum flos novus et nova pubes,
    Et memor esto aevum sic properare tuum.
                          —*Ausonius.*

Ultra marina agmina tristitia
Tetigit ingens cum merore nimio
  Heu mihi misero!

Franci, Romani atque cuncti creduli
Luctu punguntur et magna molestia.
  Heu mihi misero!

Infantes, senes, gloriosi praesules,
Matronae plangunt detrimentum Caesaris.
  Heu mihi misero!

Iamiam non cessant lacrimarum flumina,
Nam plangit orbis interitum Karoli.
  Heu mihi misero!

Pater communis orfanorum omnium,
Peregrinorum, viduarum, virginum.
  Heu mihi misero!

Christe, caelorum qui gubernas agmina,
Tuo in regno da requiem Karolo.
  Heu mihi misero!

Hoc poscunt omnes fideles et creduli,
Hoc sancti senes, viduae et virgines.
  Heu mihi misero!

Imperatorem iam serenum Karolum
Telluris tegit titulatus tumulu.
  Heu mihi misero!

Spiritus sanctus, qui gubernat omnia,
Animam suam exaltet in requiem.
  Heu mihi misero!

Vae tibi Roma Romanoque populo
Amisso summo glorioso Karolo.
  Heu mihi misero!

Vae tibi sola formosa Italia,
Cunctisque tuis tam honestis urbibus,
  Heu mihi misero!

Francia diras perpessa iniurias
Nullum iam talem dolorem sustinuit,
  Heu mihi misero!

Quando augustum facundumque Karolum
In Aquisgrani glebia terrae tradidit.
  Heu mihi misero!

Nox mihi dira iam retulit somnia,
Diesque clara non adduxit lumina.
  Heu mihi misero!

Quae cuncti orbis christiano populo
Vexit ad mortem venerandum principem.
  Heu mihi misero!

O Columbane, stringe tuas lacrimas,
Precesque funde pro illo ad dominum.
  Heu mihi misero!

Pater cunctorum, misericors dominus,
Ut illi donet locum splendidissimum.
  Heu mihi misero!

O deus cunctae humanae militiae
Atque caelorum, infernorum domine,
  Heu mihi misero!

In sancta sede cum tuis apostolis
Suscipe pium, o tu Christe, Karolum.
  Heu mihi misero!
                —*Incerti.*

(2) A LOVE MESSAGE FOR BROTHER ZACHARY

Hausimus altifluo perfusas rore salivas
Ore fluenta tuo labio stillant iocundo,
Quae maduere meas multa dulcedinie fibras,
Fonte quasi flavo liquantia mella redundant.
Zacharias frater, domini venerande sacerdos,
Accola Brittaniae, Latti telluris alumne,
Hibernique decus mundi, gratissiam salpix,
Undisoni oceani famosus litoris hospes,
Ventilabrum paleas a fulvis cernis aristis,
Mittis ad astra poli splendentis farrea grana,
Flammigeras stipulas Vulcani mergis at ollas.
              —*Paulinus of Aquileja.*

(3) THE BATTLE OF FONTENOY

Aurora cum primo mane tetram noctem dividet,
Sabbatum non illud fuit, sed Saturni dolium,
De fraterna rupta pace gaudet demon impius.

Bella clamat, hinc et inde pugna gravis oritur,
Frater fratri mortem parat, nepoti avunculus;
Filius nec patri suo exhibet quod meruit.

Caedes nulla peior fuit campo nec in Marcio;
Fracta est lex christianorum sanguinis proluvio,
Unde manus inferorum, gaudet gula Cerberi.

Dextera prepotens dei protexit Hlotharium,
Victor ille manu sua pugnavitque fortiter:
Ceteri si sic pugnassent, mox foret concordia.

Ecce olim veluit Iudas salvatorum tradidit,
Sic te, rex, tuique duces tradiderunt gladio:
Esto cautus, ne frauderis agnus lupo previo.

Fontaneto fontem dicunt, villam quoque rustici,
Ubi strages et ruina Francorum de sanguine:
Orrent campi, orrent silvae, orrent ipsi plaudes.

Gramen illud ros et ymber nec humectat pluvia,
In quo fortes ceciderunt, proelio doctissimi,
Pater, mater, soror, frater, quos amici fleverant.

Hoc autem scelus peractum, quod descripsi ritmice,
Angelbertus ego vidi pugnansque cum aliis,
Solus de multia remansi prima frontis acie.

Ima vallis retrospexi, verticemque iuieri,
Ubi suos inimicos rex fortis Hlotharius
Expugnabat fugientes usque forum rivuli.

Karoli de parte vero, Hludovici pariter
Albent campi vestimentis mortuorum lineis,
Velut solent in autumno albescere avibus.

Laude pugna non est dignus, nec canatur melode,
Oriens, meridianus, occidens et aquilo
Plangant illos qui fuerunt illic casu mortui.

Maledicta dies illa, nec in anni circulo
Numeretur, sed radatus ab omni memoria,
Iubar solis illi desit, aurora crepusculo.

Noxque illa, nox amara, noxque dura nimium,
In qua fortes ceciderunt, proelio doctissimi,
Pater, mater, soror, frater, quos amici fleverant.

O luctum atque lamentum! nudati sunt mortui,
Horum carnes vultur, corvus, lupus vorant acriter:
Orrent, carent sepulturis, vanum iacet cadaver.

Ploratum et ululatum nec describo amplius:
Unusquisque quantum potest restringatque lacrimas,
Pro illorum animabus deprecemur dominum.
—*Incerti.*

(4) ALCUIN'S EXPOSITION OF THE SONG OF SONGS

Hunc cecinit Salomon mira dulcedine librum,
Qui tenet egregias sponsi sponsaeque camenas,
Ecclesiae et Christi laudes hinc inde canentes,
Et thalami memorat socios sociasque fideles.
Has, rogo, menti tuae, iuvenis, mandare memento:
Cantica sunt nimium falsi haec meliora Maronis.
Haec tibi vera canunt vitae precepta perennis,
Auribus ille tuis male frivola falsa sonabit.
—*Alcuin.*

(5) PENANCE

Deus orbis reparator, lux aeternae gloriae,
Mihi, quaeso, penitenti praebe pius veniam.

Ut admissi delitescant facinoris cumuli,
Quorum gravi mole cogor anxiari spiritu.

En ad rutila polorum non sum dignus sidera
Infelices pro delictis sublevare oculos.

Nisi tu, clemens, mearum lacrimarum rivulos
Ope tuae pietatis digneris respicere.

Ut ablata viciorum sorde puro pectore
Tibi regi sempiterno grates queam solvere.

Ergo, pius, obstinati duriciam corculix
Emollesce et medere sacro medicamine.

Qui cum patre sempiterno regni tenes solium
Unitate in perenni atque sancto spiritu.
—*Incerti.*

(6) TO LOTHAIR THE EMPEROR

Tuque favendo,
Caesar adesto,
Sceptra parentum
Qui pietate,
Quique benigna
Lege gubernas.
Te moderator
Nam deus orbis
Iussit habenas
Flectere avitas,
Imperiique
Sceptra paterni
Teque periclis
Ipse paratis
Exuit olim,
Deque cruenta
Caede furentum
Saepe reduxit,
Aurea celso
Vertice Roma
Te decorando
Nomine sanxit
Caesaris orbi
Mox fore regem.
Itala primum
Te duce tellus
Eminuit, post
Francica temet
Sceptra regentem
Mundus adorat.
Lustra per orbem
Quinque recurrunt,
Nomine postquam
Clarus et armis
Caesariana
Iura retentas.
Tempora Christus
Longa videntem
Te regat omnis,
Te veneretur
Teque tremescat
Purpura regem.
—*Wandalbert.*

(7) THE MONK'S TALE OF THE VICTORY OF PIPPIN THE KING OVER THE AVARIAN RACE

Omnes gentes qui fecisti, tu Christe, dei sobules,
Terras, fontes, rivos, montes et formasti hominem,
Avaresque convertisti ultimis temporibus.

Multa mala iam fecerunt ab antico tempore,
Fane dei destruxerunt atque monasteria,
Vasa aurea sacrata, argentes, fictilia.

Vestem sanctam polluerunt de ara sacratissima,
Linteamina levitae et sanctaemonialium
Muliebribus detrada suadente demone.

Misit deus Petrum sanctum, principem apostolum,
In auxilium Pippini magni regis filium,
Ut viam eius comitaret et Francorum aciem.

Rex accinctus dei virtute Pippin, rex catholicus,
Castra figit super flumen albidum Danubium,
Hostibus accigens totum undique presidia.

Unguimeri satis pavens Avarorum genere,
Regi dicens satis forte: 'Tu Cacane perdite!'
Atque Catunae mulieri, maledictae coniugi:

'Regna vestra consumata, ultra non regnabitis,
Regna vestra diu longe cristinis tradita,
A Pippino demollita, principe catholico.

Adpropinquat rex Pippinus forti cum exercitu,
Fines tuos occupare, depopulare populum,
Montes, silvas atque colles ponere presidia.

Tolle cito, porta tecum copiosa munera;
Sceptrum regis adorare, ut paullum possis vivere,
Aurum, gemmas illi offer, ne te tradat funeri.'

Audiens Cacanus rex, undique perterritus,
Protinus ascendens mulam cum Tarcan primatibus,
Regem venit adorare et plagare munere.

Regi dicens: 'Salve princeps, esto noster dominus,
Regnum meum tibi trado cum festucis et foliis,
Silvas, montes atque colles cum omnibus nascentiis.

Tolle tecum proles nostras, parent tibi obsequia,
De primatibus nec parcas, terga verte acie,
Colla nostra, proles nostras dicioni tradimus.'

Nos fideles cristini deo agamus gratiam,
Qui regnum regis confirmavit super regnum Uniae,
Et victoriam donavit de paganis gentibus.

Vivat, vivat rex Pippinus in timore domini,
Avus regnet et senescat et procreet filios,
Qui palatia conservent in vita et post obitum.
. . . .
Glorio aeterna patri, gloria sit filio.
—*Incerti.*

(8) BONIFACE TO HIS SISTER IN CHRIST

Aurea nam decem transmisi poma sorori,
Quae in ligno vitae crescebant floribus almis,
Illius et sacris pendebant dulcia ramis,

Cum lignum vitae pendebat in arbore mortis.
Cum quibus et ludens conprendas gaudia mentis
Et tibi venturae conplearis dulcedine vitae,
Manducans mulso inspireris nectaris haustu.
Spirantes replet nardi flagrantia nares.
Cum quibus et malis conpares regna futura:
Dulcia sic quondam celebrabis gaudia caeli.
Sunt alia alterius ligni acerbissima mala,
Pestifero vernant quae in ligno mortis amarae,
Quae Adam manducans dira est cum morte peremptus,
Antiqui infecta et flatu et felleque draconis,
Vipereo ut dudum saeve perlita veneno.
Nitatur palmis haec numquam tangere virgo,
Mandere quae nefas est et gustare profanum,
Ne dentes strideant fuscati peste maligna,
Talibus aut malis frangantur foedera sancta,
Vel superi incassum perdantur premia regni.
—*Boniface.*

(9) A BALLAD OF KING HEROD

Cum natus esset dominus,
Turbatur rex incredulus;
Magi tulerunt munera
Quos stella duxit pręvia.
Herodes rex interrogat,
Quo Christus nasci debeat,
Locumque dici flagitat,
Ut hunc necare valeat.
Adorant magi dominum,
Viamque carpunt aliam,
Nec sęvi regis impiam
Ultra vident presęntiam.
Tunc rex Herodes fervida
Succenditur insania
Mandatque sterni milia
Lactantium innumera.
Completur sęva iussio:
Mactatur omnis pusio;
Aetatis bimę parvuli,
Vel infra, subduntur neci.

Mas omnis infans occidit,
Quem novus partus protulit;
Scrutatur, ah! cunabula
Ac ipsa matrum ubera.
Quid furis, crudelissime
O carnifex et pessime?
Hic solus, qui requiritur,
Impune Christus tollitur.
Pectus tenellum rumpitur,
Matrum sinus perfunditur;
Sed lactis plus quam sanguinis
De loco stillat vulneris.
Salve, laetans exercitus,
Flores sanctorum martyrum,
Ad aram summi nominis
Qui lęti semper luditis.
Nos vos laudantes pueros
Semper iuvate precibus,
Vobiscum uti iugiter
Possimus lęti psallere.
—*Hartmann of St. Gall.*

(10) ELEGY FOR LOTHAIR THE FIRST

Cęsar, tantus eras, quantus et orbis,
At nunc in modico clauderis antro.

Post te quisque sciat se ruiturum
Et quod nulla mori gloria tollat.

Florens imperii gloria quondam
Desolata suo Cęsare marcet,
Hanc ultra speciem non habitura,
Quam tecum moriens occuluisit.

O quanto premitur Roma dolore
Pręclaris subito patribus orba!
Infirmata prius morte Leonis
Nunc, Auguste, tuo funere languet.

Leges a senibus patribus actas,
Quas elapsa diu raserat ętas,
Omnes ut fuerant ipse reformans
Romanis studuit reddere causis.

Tu longinqua satis regna locosque,
Quos nullus potuit flectere, Cęsar,
Romanos onerans viribus arcus
Ad civile decus excoluisti.

Que te non doluit, Cęsar, obisse,
Vel quę non timuit patria vivum?
Sed quę te timuit patria vivum,
Hęc te nunc doluit, Cęsar, obisse.

Nam sic lenis eras iam superatis
Et sic indomitis gentibus asper,
Ut, qui non doluit, iure timeret,
Et, qui non timuit, iure doleret.

Luge, Roma, tuum nomen in umbris
Et defecta duo lumina luge.
Arcus frange tuos sicque triumphum
De te, Roma, tuis hostibus offer.
              —*Incerti.*

(11) ANTICHRIST

Quique cupitis audire   ex meo ore carmina,
Dei summo deo nunc audite   gloriosa famina
Et de adventum Antichristi   in extremo tempore.

Antichristus est venturus   permitente domino,
In Babilionia nascitus   conceptus de diabolo,
Dan de tribu erit ortus   ex Ebreorum populo.

Triginta annos tunc latebit   incognitus a populo,
Duos annos tunc regnabit   et uno et dimidio,
Fortis potestas ei datur   in presenti seculo.

Modo cuncti abscultate   precepta apostolica:
Nemo vobis iam seducat   per suam epistolam
Nec per sermonem nec per signa nec per vana gloria.

Enoc namque missus dei   cum Helia pariter
In illo tempore tunc mortem   venient suscipere;
Antichristus hos occidet   permitente domino.

Tribus diebus tunc iacebunt   corum sancta corpora,
Die tercia resurgent   domini imperio,
Sicque gentes predicabunt   ne credant diabolo.

Et in celum sic ascendunt   reclamant ante dominum,
Ut eorum fuso sangui   divia fiat ultio,
Et vindicta facta erit   de maligno spiritu.

Ihesus Christus deus noster   qui redemit seculum
Ipse mitet ex ore suo   gladium fortissimum,
Ipse occidet Antichristum   perdicionis filium.

Tunc reddetur pax in terra   quadraginta diebus,
Tunc erit dominus venturus   vident omnes occuli,
Tunc omnis genus, tribus, lingua venit ad iudicium.
. . . .
              —*Incerti.*

(12) THE DESTRUCTION OF JERUSALEM

Arve, poli conditorem,   ponti, mundi, fluminum
Iudeorum gens adfixit   per crucis patibulum,
Quem tandem Vespasianus   ulciscitur per filium.
Ad delendam sevam gentem   convenerunt principes.

Belli Titus curam sumit   pergens Hierusolimam,
Ulcionem exercere   de Iudeis properat;
Velut leo frendens sevit   contra gentem inprobam.
Ad delendam sevam gentem   convenerunt principes.

Castra ponit erga muros,   clangor urbem concutit,
Die pasche sic conclusit   cunctis Hierusolimam
Dispersis per Palestinam   ad depredendum cuneis.
Ad delendam sevam gentem   convenerunt principes.

Dena quater iam peracta (Sunt) annorum circula,
Quod Iesus ad cęlos vectus angelorum umeris
Se dextra patris conlocavit regebat cęlestia.
Ad delendam sęvam gentem convenerunt principes.
. . . .
Gladiis se offerebant, cursim cuncti properant,
Nemo dignus impunitus absque pena corporis:
Velut quedam simulacra apparebant pallida.
Ad delendam sęvam gentem convenerunt principes.

Hibant namque tabescentes velut canes rabidi,
Lora, frenum comedentes vel plantarum coria.
Huc illucque circumvolventes efflabant passim animas.
Ad delendam sęvam gentem convenerunt principes.

Inter fratres erant bella, parentes ac liberos,
Dum de manibus non solum, sed de ipsis faucibus
Rapere cibus certabant alter ab alterutrum.
Ad delendam sęvam gentem convenerunt principes.
—*Incerti.*

(13) THE MONK OF ANGERS

Andecavis abas esse dicitur,
Ille nomen primi tenet hominum;
Hunc fatentur vinum vellet bibere
Super omnes Andecavis homines.
   Eia eia eia laudes,
   Eia laudes dicamus Libero.

Iste malet vinum omni tempore;
Quem nec dies nox nec ulla preterit,
Quod non vino saturatus titubet
Velut arbor agitata flatibus.
   Eia eia eia laudes,
   Eia laudes dicamus Libero.

Iste gerit corpus inputribile
Vinum totum conditum ut aluoe,
Et ut mire corium conficitur,
Cutis eius nunc con vino tinguitur.
   Eia eia eia laudes,
   Eia laudes dicamus Libero.

Iste cupa non curat de calicem
Vinum bonum bibere suaviter,

Sed patellis atque magnis cacabis
Et in eis ultra modum grandibus.
    Eia eia eia laudes,
    Eia laudes dicamus Libero.

Hunc perperdet Andecavis civitas,
Nullum talem ultra sibi sociat,
Qui sic semper vinum possit sorbere;
Cuius facta, cives, vobis pingite!
    Eia eia eia laudes,
    Eia laudes dicamus Libero.
              —*Incerti.*

(14) FAREWELL TO HIS CELL

O mea cella, mihi habitatio dulcis, amata,
    Semper in aeternum, o mea cella, vale.
Undique te cingit ramis resonantibus arbos,
    Silvula, florigeris semper onusta comis.
Prata salutiferis florebunt omnia et herbis,
    Quas medici quaerit dextra salutis ope.
Flumina te cingunt florentibus undique ripis,
    Retia piscator qua sua tendit ovans.
Pomiferis redolent ramis tua claustra per hortos,
    Lilia cum rosulis candida mixta rubris.
Omne genus volucrum matutinas personat odas,
    Atque creatorem laudat in ore deum.
              —*Alcuin.*

(15) ADELEID

Hoc tumulata iacet pusilla puellula busto,
    Adeleid amne sacro quae vocitata fuit.
Huic sator est Karolus, gemino diademate pollens,
    Nobilis ingenio, fortis ad arma satis.
Sumpserat haec ortum prope moenia celsa Papiae,
    Cum caperet genitor Itala regna potens;
Sed Rhodanum properans rapta est de limine vitae,
    Ictaque sunt matris corda dolore procul.
Excessit, patrios non conspectura triumphos,
    Hunc patris aeterni regna beata tenet.
              —*Songs of Peter and Paul.*

Chapter XIII

(1) TERENCE AND THE BUFFOON

(Persona Delusoris)
Mitte recordari monimenta vetusta, Terenti:
Cesses ulterius: vade, poeta vetus.
Vade, poeta, vetus, quia non tua carmina curo;
Iam retice fabulas, dico, vetus veteres.
Dico, vetus veteres iamiam depone Camenas,
Quae nil, credo, iuvant, pedere ni doceant.
Tale decens carmen, quod sic volet ut valet istud;
Qui cupit exemplum, captet hic egregium.
Huc ego cum recubo, me taedia multa capescunt:
An sit prosaicum, nescio, an metricum.
Dic mihi, dic, quid hoc est? An latras corde sinistro?
Dic, vetus auctor, in hoc quae iacet utilitas?

Nunc Terentius exit foras audiens haec et ait:
Quis fuit, hercle, pudens rogo, qui mihi tela lacescens
Turbida contorsit? quis talia verba sonavit?
Hic quibus externis scelerosus venit ab oris,
Qui mihi tam durum iecit ridendo cachinnum?
Quam graviter iaculo mea viscera laesit acuto!
Hunc ubi repperiam, contemplor, et hunc ubi quaeram.
Si mihi cum tantis nunc se offerat obvius iris,
Debita iudicio persolvam dona librato.

Ecce persona delusoris praesentatur et hoc audiens inquit:
Quam rogitas, ego sum: quid vis persolvere? cedo;
Huc praesens adero, non dona probare recuso.

Terentius:
Tune, sceleste, meas conrodis dente Camenas?
Tu quis est? unde venis, temerarie latro? quid istis
Vocibus et dictis procerum me, a! perdite, caedis?
Tene, superbe, meas decuit corrumpere Musas?

Persona delusoris:
Si rogitas, quis sum, respondeo: te melior sum:
Tu vetus atque senex, ego tyro valens adulescans;
Tu sterilis truncus, ego fertilis arbor, opimus.
Si taceas, vetule, lucrum tibi quaeris enorme.

Terentius:
Quis tibi sensus inest (quaeso), numquid melior me es?
Nunc vetus atque senex quae fecero, fac adolescens.

Si bonus arbor ades, qua fertilitate redundas?
Cum sim truncus inere, fructu meliore redundo.

Persona secum:
Nunc mihi vera sonat; sed huic contraria dicam.—
Quid magis instigas? quid talia dicere certas?
Haec sunt verba senum, qui sum post multa senescunt
Tempora, tunc mentes in se capiunt pueriles.
. . . .

Terentius:
O iuvenis, tumidae nimium ne crede iuventae:
Saepe superba cadunt, et humilliam saepe resurgunt.
O, mihi si veteres essent in pectore vires,
De te supplicium caperem quam grande nefandum.
Si mihi plura iacis et tali voce lacessis.
. . . .
—*Incerti.*

(2) EPISCOPAL COURTESIES (i)

Beatificando domno et fratre Frodeberto pape:
    Domine Frodoberto, audivimus
    Quod noster fromentus vobis non fuit acceptus.
    De vestra gesta volumus intimare,
    Ut de vestros pares numquam delectet iogo tale referre.
Quod egisti in Segeberto regnum
De Grimaldo maiorem domus,
Quem ei sustulisti sua unica ove, sua uxore,
Unde, postea in regno numquam habuit honor.
Et cum gentes venientes in Toronica regione
Misisti ipsa in sancta congregatione,
[In] monasterio puellarum,
Qui est constructus in honor(e). . . . .
Non ibidem lectiones divinis legistis,
Sed . . . . . . nis inter vos habuistis.
Oportet satis obse . . . .
    . . . . . conluctione,
Qume nec est a Deo apta
    . . . . . . ta
Sic est ab hominibus vestra sapientia
    . . . . [pru]dentiae
Sed qualem faciebatis in . . monasterio puellarum
pro pane . . . . . [in]monasterio
fuisti generatus domn . . . . . . perdidisti.
Indulge ista pauca verba . . . . Importunus de Parisi-
age terra.
—*Incerti.*

(3) EPISCOPAL COURTESIES (ii)

Domno meo Frodeberto, sine Deo,
    Nec sancto nec episcopo
    Nec saeculare clerico,
    Ubi regnat antiquus
    Hominum inimicus.
    Qui mihi minime credit,
    Facta tua vidit.
    Illum tibi necesse desidero,
    Quare non amas Deo nec credis Dei Filio.
    Semper fecisti malum.
    Contra adversarium
    Consilio satis te putas sapiente,
    Sed credimus, quod mentis.
    Vere non times Christo, nec tibi consentit.
    Cui amas, per omnia
    Eius facis opera.
    Nec genetoris tui diligebant Christum,
    Quando in monasterio fecerunt temetipsum.
    Tuos pater cum domino
    Non fecit sancta opera.
    Propter domnus digido
    Relaxavit te vivo,
    Docuit et nutri [vit],
    Unde se postea penetivit.
    Non sequis scriptura
    Nec rendis (nisi in) liqua.
    Memores, Grimaldo
    Qualem fecisti damnum.
    . . . . . um et Deo non oblituit
    De bona, que tibi fecit.
Quid inde . . . . . ? (M)uliere sua habuisti, conscientia nua nec . . . . . norum peracta, sed contra canonica . . . . . ea de sancta congregatione aput . . . . . non ex devotione, sed cum gran . . . . . cur nos scimus damnas nimis . . . . . tollis eis aurum et argentum et honoris . . . . . liberat per has regiones.
    Cur te presumis tantum
    Dampnare suum thesaurum?
    Quod, ut alibi, ubi eum rogas.
    Per tua malafacta,
    Quod non sunt apta.
    Amas puella bella
    De qualibet terra
    Pro nulla bonitate
    Nec sancta caritate.

           Bonus numquam eris,
           Dum tale via tenes.
Per tua cauta longa — satis est, vel non est? Per omnia iube te castrare, ut non pereas per talis, quia fornicatoris Deus iudicabit.
           De culpas tuas alias te posso contristare,
           Sed tu iubis mihi exinde aliquid remandare.
           Ut in quale nobis retenit in tua caritate,
           Exeant istas exemplarias
           Per multas patrias.
           Ipso Domino hoc reliquo,
           Se vidis amico,
qui te hoc nuntiat et donet consilium verum. Sed te placit, lege et pliga, in pecto repone; sin autem non vis, in butte include.

(4) VARIABILITY OF FORTUNE

    Cum polo Phoebus roseis quadrigis
        Lucem spargere caeperit,
    Pallet albentes hebetata vultus
        Flammis stella prementibus.
    Cum nemus flatu zephyri tepentis
        Vernis inrubuit rosis,
    Spiret insanum nebulosus auster:
        Iam spinis abeat decus.
    Saepe tranquillo radiat sereno
        Immotis mare fluctibus,
    Saepe ferventes aquilo procellas
        Verso concilat aequore.
    Rara si constat sua forma mundo,
        Si tantas variat vices,
    Crede fortunis hominum caducis,
        Bonis crede fugacibus.
    Constat aeterna positumque lege est
        Ut constet genitum nihil.
                          —*Boethius.*

Chapter XIV

(1) THE SNOW CHILD

Modus Liebinc.
Advertite. omnes populi. ridiculum:
  Et audite quomodo: Suevum mulier. et ipse illa. defraudaret:
    Constaniae. civis Suevulus. trans aequora:
Gazam portans navibus: domi coniugem. lascivam nimis. relinquebat:

Vix remige. triste secat mare: ecce subito. orta tempestate:
Furit pelagus. certant fulmina. tolluntur fluctus:
Post multaque exulem: vagum litore. longinquo notus: exponebat:
Nec interim. domi vacat coniunx: mimi aderant. iuvenes se-
quuntur:
Quos et immemor. viri exulis. excepta gaudens:
Atque nocte proxima: pregnans filium. iniustum fudit. iusto die:

Duobus. volutis annis: exul dictus. revertitur:
Occurrit. infida coniunx: secum trahens. puerulum:
Datis osculis. maritus illi:
'De quo' inquit '*puerum: istum habeas. dic aut extrema. patieris.*'
At illa. maritum timens: dolos versat. in omnia:
'Mi tandem. mi coniunx inquit: 'una vice. in Alpibus:
Nive sitiens. extinxi sitim:
Inde ergo gravida: istum puerum. damnoso foetu. heu gignebam:'

Anni post haec quinque. transierunt aut plus:
Et mercator vagus. instauravit remos:
Ratim quassam reficit: vela alligat. et nivis notum. duxit secum:
Transfretato mari. producebat natum:
Et pro arrabone. mercatori tradens:
Centum libras accipit: atque vendito. infanti dives. revertitur:
Ingressusque domum. ad uxorem ait:
'Consolara coniunx. consolara cara:
Natum tuum perdidi: quem non ipsa tu. me magis quidem. dilexisti:
Tempestata orta. nos ventosus furor:
In vadosas syrtes. nimis fessos egit:
Et nos omnes graviter: torret sol at il—le nivis natus. liquescebat':

Sic perfidam. Suevus coniugem. deluserat:
Sic fraus fraudem vicerat: namquem genuit. nix recte hunc sol. liquefecit.
—*Cambridge Songs.*

(2) THE SWABIAN AND THE HARE

Mendosam quam cantilenam ago
Puerulis commentatum dabo,
Quo modulos per mendaces risum
Auditoribus ingentem ferant.

Liberalis et decora
Cuidam regi erat nata,
Quam sub lege huius modi
Procis obponit querendam:
'Si quis mentiendi gnarus
Usque adeo instet fallendo,

Dum Caesaris ore fallax
Predicitur, is ducat filiam.'

Quo audito Suevus
Nil moratus inquit:
'Raptis armis ego
Cum venatum solus irem,
Lepusculus inter feras
Telo tactus occumbebat.
Mox, effusis intestinis,
Caput avulsum cum cute cędo.

Cumque cesum manu
Levaretur caput,
Aure leva effunduntur
Mellis modii centeni,
Sotiaque auris tactis
Totidem pisarum fudit.
Quibus intra pellem strictis,
Lepus ipse dum secatur,
Crepidine summe caude
Kartam regiam latentem cepi,
Que servum te firmat esse meum.'

'Mentitur,' rex clamat, 'karte et tu!'

Sic rege deluso Suevus
Arte regius est gener factus.
—*Cambridge Songs.*

(3) HERIGER

Heriger, urbis
Maguntiensis
Antistes, quendam
Vidit prophetam
Qui ad infernum
Se dixit raptum.

Inde cum multas
Referret causas
Subiunxit totum
Esse infernum
Accinctum densis
Undique silvis.

Heriger illi
Ridens respondit:

Heriger ait:
'Prudenter egit
Christus Iohannem
Ponens pincernam,
Quoniam vinum
Non bibit unquam.

Mendax probaris
Cum Petrum dicis
Illic magistrum
Esse cocorum,
Est quia summi
Ianitor cęli.

"Honore quali
Te deus cęli

'Meum subulcum
Illuc ad pastum
Volo cum macris
Mittere procis.'

Vir ait falsus:
'Fui translatus
In templu cęli
Christumque vidi
Letum sedentem
Et comedentem.

Ioannes baptista
Erat pincerna
Atque preclari
Pocula vini
Porrexit cunctis
Vocatis sanctis.

. . . . . .

Habuit ibi?
Ubi sedisti?
Volo ut narres
Quid manducasses."

Respondit homo:
"Angulo uno
Partem pulmonis
Furabar cocis;
Hoc manducavi
Atque recessi."

Herigêr illum
Iussit ad palum
Ioris ligari
Scopisque cędi,
Sermone duro
Hunc arguendo:

"Si te ad suum
Invitet pastum
Christus, ut secum
Capias cibum,
Cave ne furtum
Facias (spurcum)."
—*Cambridge Songs.*

(4) ELFRIDA

Est unus locus
In quo pascebat
Viribus fortem

Que dum in amplum
Vidit currentem
Caput abscondit,

Lupus accurrit,
Asina bina
Fecitque longum

Cum defecisse
Protulit grandem
Vocansque suam

Audiens grandem
Alfrad cucurrit:
'Cito venite,

Homburh dictus,
Asinam Alfrad,
Atque fidelem.

Exiret campum,
Lupum voracem,
Caudam ostendit.

Caudam momordit;
Levavit crura
Cum lupo bellum.

Vires sensisset,
Plangendo vocem
Moritur domnam.

Asine vocem
'Sorores,' dixit
Me adiuvate!

Asinam caram
Illius magnum
Spero, cum sevo

Clamor sororum
Turbe virorum
Assunt, cruentum

Adela namque,
Rikilam querit,
Ibant, ut fortem

At ille ruptis
Sanguinis undam
Simul voravit,

Illud videntes
Crines scindebant,
Flentes insontem

Denique parvum
Illum plorabat
Sperans exinde

Adela mitis,
Venerunt ambe,
Cor confirmarent

'Delinque mestas,
Lupus amarum
Dominus aliam

Misi ad erbam;
Audio planctum;
Uo pugnet lupo.'

Venit in claustrum,
Ac mulierum
Ut captent lupum.

Soror Alfrade,
Agatham invenit,
Sternerent hostem.

Asine costis
Carnemque totam
Silvam intravit.

Cuncte sorores
Pectus tundebant,
Asine mortem.

Portabat pullum;
Maxime Alfrad,
Prolem crevisse.

Fritherun dulcis
Ut Alverade
Atque sanarent:

Soror, querelas!
Non curat fletum:
Dabit tibi asinam.'
—*Cambridge Songs.*

(5) KAISER OTTO

Magnus Cęsar Otto,
Quem hic modus refert in nomine,
Ottinc dictus, quadam nocte
Membra sua dum collocat,
Palatium casu subito inflammatur.
Stant ministri, tremunt,
Timent dormientem attingere,
Et chordarum pulsu facto
Excitatum salvifant,
Et domini nomen carmini inponebant.

Excitatus spes suis surrexit,
Timor magnus adversis mox venturus;

Nam tum fama volitat
Ungarios signa in eum extulisse.
Iuxta litus sedebant armati,
Urbes, agros, villas vastant late;
Matres plorant filios
Et filii matres undique exulari.

'Ecquis ego,' dixerat
Otto 'videor Parthis?
Diu diu milites
Tardos moneo frustra.
Dum ego demoror, crescit clades semper;
Ergo moras rumpite
Et Parthicis mecum hostibus obviate.'
Dux Cuonrât intrepidus,
Quo non fortior alter,
'Miles,' inquit 'pereat
Quem hoc terreat bellum.
Arma induite; armis instant hostes.
Ipse ego signifer
Effudero primus sanguinem inimicum.'

His incensi bella fremunt,
Arma poscunt, hostes vocant,
Signa secuntur, tubis canunt;
Clamor passim oritur,
Et milibus centum Teutones inmiscentur.
Pauci cedunt, plures cadunt;
Francus instat, Parthus fugit;
Vulgus exangue undis obstat;
Licus rubens sanguine
Danubio cladem Parthicam ostendebat.

. . . .
Finem modo demus,
Ne forte notemur
Ingenii culpa
Tantorum virtutes
Ultra quicquam deterere,
Quas denique Maro inclitus vix equaret.
—*Cambridge Songs.*

(6) O ROMA NOBILIS!

O Roma nobilis,   Orbis et domina,
Cunctarum urbium   Excellentissima,

Roseo martyrum   Sanguine rubea,
Albis et virginum   Liliis candida;
Salutem dicimus   Tibi per omnia,
Te benedicimus: Salve per saecula.

Petre, tu praepotens   Caelorum claviger
Vota precantium   Exaudi iugiter.
Cum bis sex tribuum   Sederis arbiter
Factus placabilis   Iudica lenite.
Teque petentibus   Nunc temporaliter
Ferto suffragia   Misericorditer.

O Paule, suscipe   Nostra precamina,
Cuius philosophos   Vici industria.
Factus economus   In domo regia
Divini muneris   Appone fercula,
Ut, quae repleverit   Te sapientia,
Ipsa nos repleat   Tua per dogmata.
—*Cambridge Songs.*

(7) TO THE FLEEING BOY

O admirabile Veneris ydolum,
Cuius materiae nichil est frivolum:
Archos te pretegat, qui stellas et polum
Fecit et maria condidit et solum.
Furis ingenio non sentias dolum:
Cloto te diligat, quae baiulat colum.

Saluto puerum non per ypothesim,
Sed firmo pectore deprecor Lachesim,
Sororem Atropos, ne curet heresim.
Neptunum comitem habeas et Thetim,
Cum vectus fueris per fluvium Athesim.
Quo fugis amabo, cum te dilexerim?
Miser quid faciam, cum te non viderim?

Dura materies ex matris ossibus
Creavit homines iactis lapidibus.
Ex quibus unus est iste puerulus,
Qui lacrimabiles non curat gemitus.
Cum tristis fuero, gaudebit emulus:
Ut cerva rugio, cum fugit hinnulus.
—*Cambridge Songs.*

(8) LITTLE JOHN THE MONK

In vitis patrum veterum
Quiddem legi ridiculum,
Examploe tamen habile;
Quod vois dico rithmice.

Iohannes abba, parvulus
Statura, non virtutibus,
Ita maiori socio,
Quicum erat in heremo:

'Volo,' dicebat, 'vivere
Secure sicut angelus,
Nec veste nec cibo frui,
Qui laboretur manibus.'

Respondit frater: 'Moneo
Ne sis inceptis properus,
Frater, quod tibi post modum
Sit non cepisse satius.'

At ille: 'qui non dimicat,
Non cadit neque superat.'
Ait, et nudus heremum
Inferiorem penetrat.

Septem dies gramineo
Vix ibi durat pabulo;
Octava fames imperat,
Ut ad sodalem redeat.

Qui sero, clausa ianua,
Tutus sedet in cellula,

Cum minor voce debili
Appellat: 'frater, aperi;

Iohannes opis indigus
Notis assistit foribus;
Nec spernat tua pietas,
Quem redigit necessitas.'

Respondit ille deintus:
'Iohannes, factus angelus,
Miratur cęli cardines;
Ultra non curat homines.'

Foris Iohannes excubat
Malamque noctem tolerat,
Et pręter voluntariam
Hanc agit penitentiam.

Facto mane recipitur
Satisque verbis uritur;
Sed intentus at crustula
Fert patienter omnia.

Refocillatus domino
Grates agit et socio;
Dehinc rastellum brachiis
Temptat movere languidis.

Castigatus angustia
De levitate nimia,
Cum angelus non potui
Vir bonus esse didicit.
—*Fulbert of Chartres.*

(9) THE NIGHTINGALE

Cum telluris vere nova producuntur germina
Nemorosa circumcirca frondescunt et brachia,
Flagrat odor quam suavis florida per gramina,
Hilarescit philomela, dulcis vocis conscia;
Et extendens modulando gutturis spiramina,
Reddit voces, ac estivi temporis ad otio
Instat nocti et diei voce sub dulcisona;
Soporatis dans quitem cantus per discrimina,
Nec non pulchra viatori laboris solatia.

Vocis eius pulchritudo, clarior quam cithara,
Vincit omnes cantitando volucrum catervulas,
Implens silvas atque cunctis modulis arbustula.
Volitando scandit alta arborum cacumina,
Gloriosa valde facta—veris pro letitia—
Ac festiva satis gliscit sibilara carmina.
—*Fulbert of Chartres.*

(10) COME, SWEET FRIEND

Iam, dulcis amica, venito,
Quam sicut cor meum diligo;
Intra in cubiculum meum,
Ornamentis cunctis onustum.

Ibi sunt sedilia strata,
Et domus velis ornata,
Floresque in domo sparguntur
Herbaeque fragrantes miscentur.

Est ibi mensa apposita,
Universis cibis onusta;
Ibi clarum vinum abundat
Et quicquid te, cara, delectat.

Ibi sonant dulces symphoniae,
Inflantur et altius tibiae;
Ibi puer et docta puella
Pangunt tibi carmina bella.

Hic cum plectro citharam tangit,
Illa melos cum lyra pangit;
Portantque ministri pateras
Pigmentatis poculis plenas.

Non me iuvat tantum convivium
Quantum post dulce colloquium,
Nec rerum tantarum ubertas
Ut dilecta familiaritas.

Iam nunc veni, soror electa
Et prae cunctis mihi dilecta,
Lux meae clara pupillae
Parsque maior animae meae.

Ego fui sola in silva
Et dilexi loca secreta;

Frequenter effugi tumultum
Et vitavi popul multum.

Karissima, noli tardare;
Studeamus nos nunc amare,
Sine te non potero vivere;
Iam decet amorem perficere.

Quid iuvat deferre, electa,
Quae sunt tamen post facienda?
Fac cita quod eris factura,
In me non est aliqua mora.
—*Cambridge Songs.*

(11) LIGHTLY BLOWS THE WIND OF SUMMER

Levis exsurgit Zephirus
Et sol procedit tepidus;
Iam terra sinus aperit,
Dulcore suo diffluit.

Ver purpuratum exiit,
Ornatus suos induit;
Aspergit terram floribus,
Ligna silvarum frondibus.

Struunt lustra quadrupedes
Et dulces nidos volucres;
Inter ligna florentia
Sua decantant gaudia.

Quod oculis dum video
Et auribus dum audio,
Heu, pro tantis gaudiis
Tantis inflor suspiriis.

Cum mihi sola sedeo
Et haec revolvens palleo,
Sic forte caput sublevo,
Nec audio nec video.

Tu saltim, Veris gratia,
Exaudi et considera
Frondes, flores et gramina;
Nam mea languet anima.
—*Cambridge Songs.*

INDEX OF FIRST LINES

	PAGE
A folk rejoicing in labor, husbandmen busy and nimble...	120
Amid the Ionian Sea doth Cyprus lie....................	xvi
Among the church biographies...........................	285
Ancient of Days, Creator High, Unending, Unbeginning God.	162
Angers, one hears, has a monk of mighty thirst...........	239
At the cross the Jews disgraced him and their land, the Eternal One..	237
A third of night must pass ere dawn should bring the morn..	228
At the cry of the first bird............................	188
A wound I cannot close, long pain and sorrow............	101
Bold across high borders leaping, storms convulse the Plain of Ler......................................	183
Brigit had a snowy soul................................	184
Buthaina, if the flower of youth could raise its head anew..	137
But while God with golden glory filled the hoary caves of night	123
But I that have been easily moved to love................	120
Canst thou not make me immortal, thou that blamest me so.	195
Come, Holy Ghost, to us descending....................	145
Come, sweet friend, and be with me.....................	288
Deep in a distant bay, and deeply hidden................	99
Dreams that delude with flying shade men's minds.........	75
Ebb-tide is flowing to the sea..........................	180
Eternal author of the world............................	93
Fair fields and meadows, how I envy you.................	81
Fate to beauty still must give..........................	100
From the day's beginning to the sunset west..............	224
From your jocund lip and fluent mouth we drew...........	227
Get off the stage with those old tricks of yours...........	245
Happy is he who on his own estate.....................	99
Hear me, fair queen of the wide universe.................	100
Heavy with God, my friend, your mind you turn..........	142

INDEX OF FIRST LINES

	PAGE
Heia, fellows! Echo, resounding, sends back our heia!.......	166
Heriger, bishop...	278
He that loved not shall love on the morrow, he that has loved shall love again......................................	95
I am ashamed of thoughts that idly go astray............	188
I have sent to you, Sister, the ten golden fruits............	233
I know a spot beyond the edge of the ocean...............	159
I'll tell you a tuneful tale of lies........................	277
Importunus to Chrodebert, Greeting.....................	247
In fields of shadow (such the Maronian muse).............	102
In Hohenburg Convent.................................	280
In the valley coolly flowing o'er the pebbles laughing light..	94
I prefer a tent where the wind blows round me............	196
It was the mighty Kaiser Otto..........................	281
I wish, O eternal and ancient King, thou Son of the living God	182
I would that all the earth might know no dawn............	198
Leave thine own home, O Youth, seek distant shores!.....	74
Let him who will, now hear the song that cometh from my tongue...	236
Liadin, since I left you, days............................	187
Lightly blows the wind of summer.......................	290
Listen, my people, and be attentive and hear..............	275
Live out, my wife, the life that we have had..............	120
Lovely Lycoris that was my delight......................	112
My Lord Chrodebert..................................	247
My words for you: stags bellow on......................	183
Nealce, forever..	75
Night's first sweet silence fell, and on my bed.............	74
Now all the people Christ hath made are children of the living Lord...	231
Now from the topmost boughs resounds the song of the cuckoo...	149
Now while the moonlight down pure air is shining.........	150
Old age is jealous and delays my end....................	110
O many the tents that gave their riches to me of old!.......	194
O nightingale, what cunning stole you from...............	148
O sweeter to me than life may be is the sea and the sand where I...	76
O thou eidolon of Venus, adorable.......................	285
Our eyes deceive us, and our sense......................	74

INDEX OF FIRST LINES

	PAGE
O young, my lad, you would have me sing	150
Paint a whitelimbed girl for me	108
Pangur is proof that arts of cats	184
Pride of birth or degree proves no man to be upright	74
Prince, thou wert once so great as earth is wide	235
Rome, thou imperial queen of the universe	284
She that finds in sin a pleasure	109
Spread the board with linen snow	118
Spring, and the faint first dawn to skies less cold	117
Still let me love though I may not possess	109
Sweet little bell, struck on a windy night	185
Tell me, Venus, what's to do?	108
The banners of the king advance	146
The bitter wind tosses tonight with wailing	188
The crying Babe is prophecy	124
The land of Europe nourishes	153
Thee, O my cell, beloved spot, that to me	240
These are arrows that murder sleep	179
The trees like a hedge surround me	186
The woodland meadow encloses me	274
Thou ancient guardian over time's treasures	103
Thou, our emperor	230
Thou splendid giver of our light	92
To Bran around his coracle the billows crawl the crystal sea	161
To wife and daughter	194
Waste is the land where once the people of Mina alighted to dwell and remain	195
We have forgiven the sons of Hind	193
We were two who loved and chose each other	64
What face comes here, so glorious with light	143
What have I done, O Sleep, gentlest of heaven's sons	77
When from the Pole the roseate steeds of Apollo	249
When our Lord was born to us	234
When spring leads out new buds across the wold	287
White shields they carry in white hands	186
Within this book sang Solomon with his admired sweetness	239
Within this sepulcher	240
Youth and I together ran headlong after pleasure	197

INDEX

Abelard, 69, 208.
Abu Nuwas, 197.
Adeleid. See Songs of Peter and Paul.
Adelphus adelpha, 72, 202.
Aeterne rerum conditor. See Ambrose.
Albarus, 202, 224.
Alcuin, 33, 84, 136, 148, 203, 224, 269, 290; *Alcuin's Exposition of the Song of Songs,* 229, 346; *Farewell to His Cell,* 240, 353; *Song to A Nightingale,* 148-149, 338-339; *To the Cuckoo,* 149, 339.
Aldhelm, 167, 202, 244.
Altus prosator. See Columba.
Ambrose, 59, 92, 105, 145; *Aeterne rerum conditor,* 93-94, 323.
Antichrist, 236, 350-351.
Apostrophe to Sleep. See Statius.
Appendix Vergiliana, xiv, 303.
Appolonius, 59, 213.
Apuleius, 88, 89, 90, 305; *The Eunuch's Delight,* 108, 329-330.
Argonautica, 104.
Assignation, The. See Irma al Kais.
Athanasius, 27, 105.
Ausonius, xiv, 12, 33, 49, 72, 97, 100, 105, 106, 116, 122, 302, 305; *Cupid Crucified,* 102, 328; *Darby and Joan,* 120, 335-336; *Of Roses,* 117-118, 333-334; *Singing on the Moselle,* 120, 335; *To His Dead Wife,* 100-101, 327-328.
Augustus, 7, 21, 65, 71.
Augustine, 105, 132, 135, 208.
Autun, 35, 89, 216.
Avienus, Rufus Festus, 341. See also Himilco.

Ballad of King Herod, A. See Hartmann of St. Gall.
Bangor, 163ff., 167.
Banquet, 141, 311.
Battle of Fontenoy, The, 228-229, 345-346.
Bede, 129, 244, 249-250, 269.
Bendictbeurn, 69.
Benedict of Nursia, 107.
Bernard, 69.
Boethius, 68, 106, 107, 109, 144, 250, 304; *Variability of Fortune,* 249, 357.
Boniface, 244; *Boniface to His Sister in Christ,* 233-234, 348-349.

Book of Kings, 198.
Book of the Planet Venus. See Ibn Dawoud.
Buthaina. See Ibn Dawoud.

Cæsarius of Arles, 132.
Capella, Martianus, 67, 250.
Carmen Apologeticum, 91. See also Commodian.
Cassiodorus, 34, 39, 68, 106, 107, 207, 255, 304.
Cato, Valerius, 81, 96-97, 303.
Catullus, 11, 13, 61, 62, 63, 67, 78, 79, 83, 97, 125, 175, 218, 294, 302, 303, 308.
Charlemagne, 208-209, 227.
Charles the Great, xi, 29, 34, 41, 173, 201, 203, 211, 217, 227, 241, 251, 256, 274.
Chrodebert, 170, 250, 274; *Episcopal Courtesies,* 247-249, 355-357.
Church Bell at Night, The, 185.
Claudian, xv, xvii, 12, 86, 94, 98, 116, 117, 122, 123, 302; *Epitaph,* 100, 326; *The Lonely Isle,* 99, 326; *The Old Man of Verona,* 99, 325.
Columba, 97, 162; *Altus prosator,* 162-163, 341-342. See also Colum Cille.
Columban, xiv, 13, 68, 106, 155, 162, 163, 166 ff., 170, 244; *Ply the Oar,* 166, 342.
Colum Cille, 68, 97, 170, 171. See also Columba.
Come, Sweet Friend, 288-289, 365-366.
Commodian, 91. See also *Carmen Apologeticum.*
Constantine, 24, 27, 45, 92.
Cry of Liadin after Curither, The, 187, 315.
Crucifixion, The, 188.
Cupid Crucified. See Ausonius.
Cyprian, 89, 132.

Darby and Joan. See Ausonius.
De Heinrico, 268, 283.
Desolation. See Labid.
Destruction of Jerusalem, The, 237, 351-352.
Dialogues, 106, 306-307.

INDEX

E*legy for Lothair the First*, 235-236, 349-350.
Elfrida, 280-281, 360-361.
Encouragement to Exile. See Petronius.
Ennius, 13, 79.
Ennodius, 107, 316.
Episcopal Courtesies, xiv. See also Chrodebert; Importunus.
Epitaph. See Claudian.
Eunuch's Delight, The. See Apuleius.
Eusebius, 105.

F*arewell to His Cell.* See Alcuin.
Farewell to Rome. See Rutilius.
Faustus of Riez, 132.
Feud, The. See Shahl.
Firdusi, 198.
Flaccus, Argonautica. See *Argonautica*.
Flamenca, 258, 260.
Flightiness of Thought, 188.
Fortunatus, 66, 68, 106, 126, 131, 145; chap. VIII; 190, 218, 246, 295, 309, 338; *To Queen Radegunde on Her Retreat*, 142-143, 337; *To Queen Radegunde on Her Return*, 143, 337. See also Venantius.
Fronto, 66, 88-89, 90-91, 305.
Fulbert, 14, 69, 266; *Little John the Monk*, 285-287, 364; *The Nightingale*, 287, 364-365.

G*all*, 170, 205, 244.
Gerbert, 69, 266.
Gesta Karoli, 274.
Gildas, 157, 160, 202.
Golden Ass, 251.
Goliards, 69.
Goths, 25 ff., 38 ff., 203, 205 ff.
Gottschalk, 150, 226, 266; *Song in Exile*, 150-151, 340.
Governance of God, 48.
Gregory the Great, 21, 106, 155, 190, 269; *Veni creator spiritus*, 145-146, 337-338.
Gregory of Tours, 20, 26, 33, 68, 106, 144, 168, 218, 269, 274.

H*adrian*, 66, 87.
Hartmann of St. Gall, See *A Ballad of King Herod*, 234-235, 349.
Henry of Huntingdon, 69.
Heriger, 278-279, 359-360.
Hermit's Song, The, 182.

Hilarius of Poitiers, 92; *Morning Hymn of Hilarius*, 92-93, 322.
Hilary, 69.
Hildebert, 69.
Himilco, 152; *The Land of Europe Nourishes*, 152-153, 340-341. See also Avienus.
Hisperica famina, 72, 133, 201, 202, 218.
Honorius, 46.
Horace, 11, 16, 67, 71, 72-73, 78, 79, 83, 86, 87, 97, 104, 124, 156, 218, 241, 246, 294, 302, 308.
Hosts of Faery, The, 186.
Hymn Against the Last Judgment. See Prudentius.
Hymn for Christmas Day. See Prudentius.

I*bn Dawoud*, 136 ff., 141, 312; *Book of the Planet Venus*, 136 ff; *Buthaina*, 137.
Ibn Qozman, 140.
Ilias Latina, 72.
Illusion. See Petronius.
Importunus. See Chrodebert.
Imra al Kais, 194-195.
Invitation to the Dance. See Sidonius.
Isidore of Seville, 107, 157, 244, 304.

J*ahdar*, 194.
Jerome, 22, 35, 49, 105, 157, 206.
Jews, 11, 27, 57, 211-212.
Judith, 211-212.
Julian the Apostate, 36, 106.
Juvenal, 9, 11, 50, 72, 89, 104, 105, 208, 302.

K*aiser Otto*, 282-283, 361-362.

L*abid*, 195-196.
Lactantius, 89, 92.
Lament of the Old Woman of Beare, 180-182.
Land of Europe Nourishes, The. See Himilco; Avienus.
Latin Anthology, 78, 107, 109, 307, 309.
Lightly Blows the Wind of Summer, 290, 366.
Little John the Monk. See Fulbert.
Lonely Isle, The. See Claudian.
Lorica, 72, 202.
Love Message for Brother Zachary, A. See Paulinus.

INDEX

Love's Litany. See *Book of Kings.*
Lucan, 72, 75, 87, 89, 99, 104, 302, 304.
Lucian, 32-33, 90, 208, 305.
Lucretius, 123, 125, 303, 308.
Lycoris. See Maximian.
Lydia, xiv, 80-82, 303, 321-322. See *Appendix Vergiliana.*

Macrobius, 49.
Maisun, 196-197.
Malady of Love, The. See Petronius.
Mapes, 69.
Marcus Aurelius, 45, 89.
Mariolatry, 136, 147-148.
Martial, 9, 76, 86, 302.
Maximian, 109-110; *Lycoris,* 112-114, 332-333; *Old Age,* 110-112, 330-332.
Meleager, 104, 141, 142.
Mœsia, 105, 206.
Monasteries, 163 ff., 167 ff., 170.
Monk of Angers, The, 239, 352-353.
Monk's Tale of the Victory of Pippin, The, 231-233, 347-348.
Moonlight. See Walahfrid.
Morning Hymn. See Hilarius.
Mosella, 122.
Music, 221-222, 223, 241, 255, 258, 281; Gregorian, 218, 262.

Nealce. See Petronius.
Nemesianus, 92.
Nennius, 157.
Neo-Platonism, xii, 36, 298, 311.
Nightingale, The. See Fulbert.
Night Watch of Venus, The, 116. See also *Pervigilium;* Tiberianus.
Noblesse Oblige. See Petronius.
Notker, 124, 266, 269.

Octavianus, 307, 309; *Painted Passion,* 108, 329; *Prayer to Venus,* 108, 329; *Replique,* 109, 329.
Of Roses. See Ausonius.
Old Age. See Maximian.
Old Man of Verona, The. See Claudian.
O Roma nobilis, 284-285, 362-363.
Orosius, 157, 207.
Ovid, 11, 16, 28, 97, 155, 156, 294, 295, 300, 303.

Painted Passion. See Octavianus.
Paulinus, 126; *A Love Message for Brother Zachary,* 227-228, 344.

Penance, 229, 346-347.
Pervigilium Veneris. See Tiberianus.
Petronius, xiv, 72-91, 104, 125, 132, 141, 142, 302, 307; *Encouragement to Exile,* 74, 319; *Illusion,* 74-75, 319-320; *The Malady of Love Is Nerves,* 74, 319; *Nealce,* 75-76, 320; *Noblesse Oblige,* 74, 319; *Remembered Shores,* 76, 320-321; *We are Such Stuff as Dreams,* 75, 320.
Persius, 72, 99, 104, 303, 304.
Peter of Blois, 69.
Phædrus, 75, 312.
Philologian and His Cat, The, 184.
Phocas, xiv, 103, 116; *Poetry and Time,* 103, 328-329.
Phoenix, 92.
Planctus de Obitu Karoli, xiv, 224-226, 342-344.
Plato, 36, 131, 312.
Platonism, 36; chap. VII.
Plautus, 59, 302.
Ply the Oar. See Columban.
Poetae aevi Karolini, 214, 215.
Poetry and Time. See Phocas.
Prayer to Venus. See Octavianus.
Primas, 69.
Propertius, 73, 78, 81-82, 104, 302, 303.
Prudentius, 92, 105, 122, 127, 128, 145, 295; *Hymn Against the Last Judgment,* 123, 366; *Hymn for Christmas Day,* 124, 336.

Quintilian, 83, 104, 303.

Radegunde. See Fortunatus.
Rape of Proserpine, 122.
Ratpert, 124.
Reginald of Canterbury, 59.
Reichenau, 124.
Remembered Shores. See Petronius.
Replique. See Octavianus.
Romanesque, qualities of, 67 ff., 73.
Roswitha, 251, 265, 269, 291, 318.
Rubisca, 72, 202.
Ruin, 177.
Ruodlieb, 251, 266, 289.
Rutilius, 12, 86, 94, 98, 116; *Farewell to Rome,* 101-102, 326-327.

St. Broccan's Hymn in Praise of St. Brigit, 184-185.
St. Gall, 124, 204, 265.
Sallust, 156.

INDEX

Salvianus of Marseilles, 48, 49.
Scoffer, The. See Tarafa.
Scribe, The, 186.
Sedulius, 131.
Seneca, 76, 87, 98-99, 104, 105, 302.
Shahl, the Mountain Crag, 193.
Sidonius, 12, 33, 46, 48, 72, 97, 116, 120, 126, 255, 309; *Invitation to the Dance,* 118-119, 335.
Singing on the Moselle. See Ausonius.
Snow Child, The, 275-276, 357-358.
Song in Exile. See Gottschalk.
Song of Crede, 179-180.
Song of the Dwarf. See Jahdar.
Song of the Sea, 183.
Song to a Nightingale. See Alcuin.
Songs of Peter and Paul, *Adeleid,* 240, 353.
Statius, 72, 76-77, 86, 104, 302; *Apostrophe to Sleep,* 77, 321.
Strabo, Walahfrid. See Walahfrid.
Summer Has Gone, 183.
Swabian and the Hare, The, 277-278, 358-359.
Symmachus, 35, 49, 97.

Tacitus, 41, 44, 89, 104, 155, 156.
Tale of the Iron Charles, 237-239.
Tarafa, 195.
Terence and the Buffoon, 244-246, 354-355.
Tertullian, 66, 85, 89.
Theocritus, 104.
Tiberianus, 12, 14, 63, 91, 94, 97, 101, 105; *(Pervigilium Veneris) The Night Watch of Venus,* 95-96, 324-325; *Woodland Scene, A,* 94-95, 323-324.
Tibullus, 104, 119, 335.
To His Dead Wife. See Ausonius.
To Lothair The Emperor. See Wandalbert.
To Queen Radegunde on Her Retreat. See Fortunatus.
To Queen Radegunde on Her Return. See Fortunatus.
To the Cuckoo. See Alcuin.
To the Fleeing Boy, 285-286, 363.

Ulfilas, 26, 27, 39, 105, 206.

Variability of Fortune. See Boethius.
Venantius, 26, 72, 110; See also Fortunatus.
Veni creator spiritus. See Gregory the Great.
Vergil, 13, 59, 67, 78, 79, 81, 83, 86, 90, 92, 97, 104, 125, 155, 156, 246, 294, 295, 302, 303, 309.
Vergil the Grammarian (Vergilius Maro), 202, 218, 316-317.
Verse, accentual, 12, 13, 14, 90, 91, 206.
Vexilla regis prodeunt, 145, 338. See also Fortunatus.
Vigils of Venus, 14, 63.
Viking Terror, The, 188.
Victorinus, 157.
Vita Columbani, 72.

Walahfrid, 124, 136, 149, 266; *Moonlight,* 150, 339.
Wandalbert, *To Lothair the Emperor,* 230-231, 347.
Wanderer, 177.
We Are Such Stuff as Dreams. See Petronius.
Widsith, 176, 177, 207.
Wife's Complaint, 177.
William of Poitou, 15, 61, 62, 140, 218, 295.
Wipo, 69, 290.
Woodland Scene, 116. See also Tiberianus.